# TESTING
# STRUCTURAL
# EQUATION
# MODELS

# OTHER RECENT VOLUMES IN THE
# SAGE FOCUS EDITIONS

# TESTING STRUCTURAL EQUATION MODELS

**Kenneth A. Bollen**
**J. Scott Long**

**editors**

**SAGE** Publications
*International Educational and Professional Publisher*
Newbury Park    London    New Delhi

*For information address*:

SAGE Publications, Inc.
2455 Teller Road
Newbury Park, California 91320
E-mail: order@sagepub.com

SAGE Publications Ltd.
6 Bonhill Street
London EC2A 4PU
United Kingdom

SAGE Publications India Pvt. Ltd.
M-32 Market
Greater Kailash I
New Delhi 110 048 India

Printed in the United States of America

**Library of Congress Cataloging-in-Publication Data**

Main entry under title:

Testing structural equation models / edited by Kenneth A. Bollen,
J. Scott Long.
    p.    cm.—(Sage focus editions; v. 154)
    Includes bibliographical references.
    ISBN 0-8039-4506-X (cloth)—ISBN 0-8039-4507-8 (pbk.)
    1. Social sciences—Mathematical models.  2. Social sciences—
Methodology.  I. Bollen, Kenneth A.  II. Long, J. Scott.
H61.25.T47   1993                          92-37324
300'.1'5118—dc20                            CIP


98  99  00  01  10  9  8  7  6  5

Sage Production Editor:  Judith L. Hunter

# Contents

To Jeff Tanaka

# 1

# Introduction

KENNETH A. BOLLEN
J. SCOTT LONG

The three golden rules . . . are test, test and test.*
*(David F. Hendry, 1980)*

Structural equation models (SEMs) are a well-known component of the methodological arsenal of the social sciences.[1] Much of their attractiveness stems from their generality. Like econometric methods, SEMs allow consideration of simultaneous equations with many endogenous variables. Unlike most econometric methods, SEMs allow measurement error in the exogenous and endogenous variables. As with factor analysis developed in psychometrics and related procedures in sociometrics, SEMs permit multiple indicators of latent constructs and estimation of reliability and validity. In addition, SEMs allow more general measurement models than traditional factor-analytic structures and enable the researcher to specify structural relationships among the latent variables. Thus structural equation models are a synthesis of procedures developed in econometrics, sociometrics, and psychometrics.

Five steps characterize most applications of SEMs:

(1) model specification

---

*Notwithstanding the difficulties involved in calculating and controlling Type I and II errors.

(2) identification
(3) estimation
(4) testing fit
(5) respecification

The first step, model specification, refers to the initial model that a researcher formulates prior to estimation. This model is formulated on the basis of one's theory or past research in the area. Identification determines whether it is possible to find unique values for the parameters of the specified model. Once a model is identified, there are several estimation methods available. Selection of estimation techniques is often determined by the distributional properties of the variables being analyzed. After the estimates are obtained, the researcher can test whether the model is consistent with the data. If so, the process can stop after the fourth step. More typically, the fit of the model could be improved through respecification. Once respecified, Steps 2 through 5 may be repeated, often multiple times.

Although each step in applying SEMs has been the subject of considerable discussion, the most heated controversies surround the last two steps—testing model fit and respecification. The chapters in this book concentrate on these two steps in the process of building an adequate SEM.

### Overall Fit Controversy

Early in the literature on structural equation models, researchers saw a key feature of SEMs to be a test statistic for the null hypothesis of

$$\Sigma = \Sigma(\theta) ,$$

where $\Sigma$ is the population covariance matrix of the observed variables, $\Sigma(\theta)$ is the covariance matrix implied by a specific model, and $\theta$ is a vector containing the free parameters of the model. If the model was specified correctly and the distributional assumptions for the data were satisfied, analysts could use a test statistic with an asymptotic chi-square distribution to test the null hypothesis that the specified model leads to an exact reproduction of the population covariance matrix of the observed variables. A significant test statistic would cast doubt on the model specification.

Jöreskog (1969) sounded an early warning about overinterpreting the chi-square test statistic. He noted that in large samples even trivial deviations of a model from the actual structure could be detected and could lead to a rejection of the null hypothesis. He encouraged researchers to make more subjective assessments of fit using the test statistic for guidance: "If a value of $\chi^2$ is obtained, which is large compared to the number of degrees of freedom, this is an indication that more information can be extracted from the data. One may then try to relax the model somewhat by introducing more parameters" (p. 201). This quote foreshadows a practice of dividing the chi-square test statistic by its degrees of freedom as an early, alternative measure of overall model fit (Wheaton, Muthén, Alwin, & Summers, 1977). Unfortunately, the recommended criterion for a good fit using this chi-square divided by degrees of freedom ratio varied widely, from as high as five to as low as two or three. Furthermore, this measure did not lessen the fact that for a given degree of specification error, the chi-square ratio will increase as the sample size gets larger (Hoelter, 1983, p. 330).

Bentler and Bonett (1980), building on the work of Tucker and Lewis (1973), took a different tack in developing overall fit measures. The key idea was to generate a baseline model and its test statistic to which the hypothesized model and its test statistic could be compared. Typically, the baseline model assumed that all variables were uncorrelated. A series of related measures followed a similar strategy (Bentler, 1990; Bollen, 1989; McDonald & Marsh, 1990).

We can trace the origin of another family of measures to Jöreskog and Sörbom's (1981) goodness-of-fit index (GFI) and adjusted GFI (AGFI), which were introduced in LISREL V. These fit statistics estimated the extent to which the sample variances and covariances were reproduced by the hypothesized model. Jöreskog and Sörbom's GFI and AGFI spawned related measures and theoretical developments (Maiti & Mukherjee, 1990; Tanaka & Huba, 1985). Since the work of Tucker and Lewis (1973), Bentler and Bonett (1980), and Jöreskog and Sörbom (1981), many others have proposed measures of overall fit for SEMs. Some are closely related to these earlier works. Others are based on ideas of cross-validation and information theory (e.g., Cudeck & Browne, 1983).

Several issues repeatedly emerge in the discussion of these fit statistics. These include the following:

(1) Should the means of the sampling distributions of a fit index be unrelated to the size of the sample?

(2) What are the cutoff values of a fit index to distinguish a good from a fair or poor fit?

(3) Is it best to use measures that are normed to fall between 0 and 1, or are nonnormed measures preferable?

(4) Must we use a fit index that has a penalty for using additional parameters? If so, what should the penalty be?

(5) Is it better to estimate the statistical power of the chi-square test than to turn to fit indices?

(6) What is the role of fit measures when one is respecifying a model?

Collectively, the authors in this volume address these and related questions. They do not always give the same answers, but they do reflect current viewpoints in the field. Indeed, contributors to this volume have played major roles in shaping the debate over fit indices and respecifications.

In Chapter 2, Tanaka gives an orientation to understanding fit indices. He proposes six dimensions along which the major fit indices can be classified and presents a case for which properties of a fit index are most important. Gerbing and Anderson in Chapter 3 summarize the results from major Monte Carlo simulation studies of fit indices. They provide a useful guide to what we know about some of the finite sample results for fit indices and give their judgments of the fit indices with the best properties.

In Chapter 4, Long and Trivedi present a new simulation study. They examine the widely touted "specification tests" developed by Hausman (1978), White (1980), and others. They find that many of these tests have very poor finite sample properties. Long and Trivedi focus on single-equation regression models, but their results have implications for similar specification tests proposed for SEMs (see Arminger & Schoenberg, 1989).

In Chapter 5, Bollen and Stine apply bootstrapping methods to test statistics and fit indices in SEMs. One important result of their study is their finding that the standard bootstrapping procedures are not appropriate for hypothesis testing of overall fit. Bollen and Stine provide a corrective procedure that enables the application of the bootstrap in this context and that would be easy to implement in SEM software.

Browne and Cudeck, in Chapter 6, continue the important work they have initiated on cross-validation and information theory measures of fit for SEMs. They recommend that measures such as those developed by Steiger and Lind (1980) be more widely applied, and they illustrate how confidence intervals can be developed for such measures.

In Chapter 7, Raftery advocates that a BIC measure, similar to that used in contingency table analysis, be applied to SEM fit assessments. He explains the basic concepts behind BIC and illustrates its application to an empirical example.

Statistical modelers recognize that the power of a significance test is an important consideration in evaluating that test. In 1985, Satorra and Saris published a key article proposing methods to evaluate the power of the chi-square test of model fit in SEMs. In Chapter 8, these authors summarize their current thinking on statistical power and provide a new technique of estimating statistical power that is less demanding of information than their earlier procedure.

In recent years, researchers have devoted considerable attention to the extension of SEM techniques to categorical observed variables. However, the special conditions of assessing fit in these models have received less study. Muthén corrects this neglect in Chapter 9. He distinguishes two levels of testing when estimating SEMs with categorical observed variables. The first level concerns tests of the distributional assumptions for the continuous variables that are hypothesized to underlie the categorical variables. The second level of testing involves the structural equation model's validity. Researchers most often ignore the first level, so Muthén devotes most of his attention to simple tests.

After initial estimation of a structural equation model, it is not unusual to conclude that the fit of the model is inadequate. A common reaction is to respecify the model in an attempt to improve its fit. Bentler and Chou discuss model respecification in Chapter 10. They propose new statistics that can help locate modifications to the initial specification so as to improve its fit. Their new procedures are generalizations of the earlier ones and allow the researcher not only to test the change in chi-squares with respecification, but also to estimate the change in multiple parameter estimates without rerunning the model.

Most analysts who have experience with estimating and testing SEMs have encountered the issue of having one or more matrices "not positive definite." In our experience, one of the most frequent questions that students and practitioners ask is the meaning of a warning about a nonpositive definite matrix. Wothke has written Chapter 11 to provide a comprehensive answer to this question. He defines positive and nonpositive definite matrices, illustrates them, and explains what might cause them, their consequences, and corrective procedures that can be tried.

Karl Jöreskog was one of the earliest writers discussing model fit in SEMs. It seems appropriate that we give him the last word in this volume. In Chapter 12, he summarizes his current perspective on the best procedures for testing SEMs and the use of fit measures.

## Consensus

The contributors to this volume do not always agree on the best ways to assess model fit. As one reads the detailed arguments presented in each chapter, it is easy to lose sight of areas where consensus is emerging. In this section, we take the opportunity to highlight what we see as major points of consensus.

A first principle of agreement is that the best guide to assessing model fit is strong substantive theory. If the model makes little substantive sense, it is difficult to justify it even if its statistical fit is excellent. Similarly, structural equation modeling without the benefit of substantive expertise is a hazardous business.

A second point of consensus is that the chi-square test statistic should not be the sole basis for determining model fit. Several reasons support this belief. First, the null hypothesis underlying the test statistic is overly rigid in most cases. It assumes that the hypothesized model leads to an implied covariance matrix that exactly reproduces the covariance matrix of the observed variables in the population. There is no allowance made for the approximate nature of virtually all social science models. A second reason is that the chi-square test statistic as usually applied ignores the statistical power of the test. Tests with excessive statistical power can lead to the rejection of good models, or low statistical power can mislead us into retaining poor models. Third, failure of the variables to satisfy the distributional assumptions of the test statistic can lead to the rejection of correct models or the failure to reject incorrect models. Thus we should be skeptical of any work that draws conclusions about model fit using only the chi-square test statistic.

A third point of consensus is that no single measure of overall fit should be relied on exclusively. Given the controversy about measures of overall fit, it is imprudent to judge model fit by using one fit index rather than several. In other words, there is little benefit to turning from a reliance on the chi-square test statistic to a reliance on any other single fit index.

Fourth, most researchers also would agree that we should not ignore the fit of the components of a model. By *components of the model* we refer to specific aspects, such as the $R$-squares of equations, the magnitudes of coefficient estimates, whether the estimates are of the correct sign, and the presence of improper solutions or other unusual results. It is important to remember that even a model with excellent overall fit indices can be unacceptable because of the components of the model. Though the chapters in this volume do not focus on this issue, we nonetheless want to emphasize that researchers should always examine the components of fit along with the overall fit measures.

A final point of consensus is that it is better to consider several alternative models than to examine only a single model. Often knowledge in an area is not detailed enough to provide a single specification of a model. Estimating several models permits researchers to explore plausible structures. This basis of comparison also allows us to determine the model with the best fit, rather than attempt to assess a single model's fit in some absolute sense.

### Conclusions and Recommendations

The history of the coefficient of determination, $R^2$, in regression analysis can provide insight into the current controversy regarding overall fit measures in SEMs. The $R^2$ has a far longer history than the fit indices in SEMs, yet even today there is considerable controversy surrounding its use as a means to assess the fit of an equation or to compare the fit of different equations. Saris and Stronkhorst (1984), for instance, argue that "for good quality data an $R^2$ of approximately .90 should be required" (p. 271). In contrast, Goldberger (1991) states: "Nothing in the CR (Classical Regression) model requires that $R^2$ be high. Hence a high $R^2$ is not evidence in favor of the model, and a low $R^2$ is not evidence against it" (p. 177).

From this perspective we can view the fit index controversy in SEMs as part of a bigger controversy of how best to measure the fit of statistical models. The chapters in this book summarize what we know about SEM fit measures, provide some new methods of evaluating model fit and respecification, and give new insights into the issues.

We close with advice for the researcher who is applying SEMs and seeks guidance on methods to assess model fit. Although the chapters presented here do not discuss these issues directly, we emphasize that diagnostic checks on the data and model should be done prior to assessing model fit. For instance, outliers and influential cases should be screened for (Bollen, 1989; Bollen & Arminger, 1991) and the researcher should check to see if the distributional assumptions of an estimator are satisfied. Either of these problems can affect the fit assessment. Assuming that such checks have been completed, we offer the following advice.

We agree with the points of consensus identified above: Know your substantive area before assessing fit; do not rely only on the chi-square test statistic; report multiple fit indices; examine the components of fit as well as the overall model fit; and estimate several plausible model structures as a means of determining the best fit. But aside from these points, we want to make several others. First, when reporting multiple fit indices, choose ones that represent different families of measures. For instance, we would not advise reporting incremental fit indices only along the lines of the Tucker-Lewis coefficient or reporting only GFI-type measures. A mixture of these and other types of fit indices would be best. Second, we prefer fit indices whose means of their sampling distributions are not or are only weakly related to the sample size. Gerbing and Anderson provide a useful summary of such indices in Chapter 3. Third, we prefer fit indices that take account of the degrees of freedom of a model. Some fit indices (e.g., Bentler & Bonett's normed fit index or Jöreskog & Sörbom's GFI) do not take account of how many parameters are used in a model, so that model fit as measured with these indices can be increased just by adding a free parameter to a model. Fourth, in judging the adequacy of a model, the use of prior studies of the same or similar models is desirable whenever possible. Whether a model's fit looks good or not depends on the basis of comparison. In some areas where little prior work exists, less demanding standards may be acceptable than in other areas with extensive experience. Fifth, the objective of fitting SEMs is to understand a substantive area, not simply to obtain an adequate fit. While persistent, data-driven respecifications may produce measures of fit that are adequate by conventional standards, it is unlikely that the resulting model will add to our substantive understanding.

In the final analysis, assessing model fit in SEMs is like other areas of assessing goodness of fit. The test statistics and fit indices are very beneficial, but they are no replacement for sound judgment and substantive expertise.

## Note

1. In some fields the term *structural equation models* is restricted to the classic simultaneous equation models of econometrics. In this book we use the term to include these models as well as models that allow latent variables, multiple indicators, and errors

in the variables. General models such as these are sometimes referred to as *covariance structure models* or *LISREL models*.

## References

Arminger, G., & Schoenberg, R. J. (1989). Pseudo maximum likelihood estimation and a test for misspecification in mean and covariance structure models. *Psychometrika, 54,* 409-425.
Bentler, P. M. (1990). Comparative fit indexes in structural models. *Psychological Bulletin, 107,* 238-246.
Bentler, P. M., & Bonett, D. G. (1980). Significance tests and goodness-of-fit in the analysis of covariance structures. *Psychological Bulletin, 88,* 588-606.
Bollen, K. A. (1989). *Structural equations with latent variables.* New York: John Wiley.
Bollen, K. A., & Arminger, G. (1991). Observational residuals in factor analysis and structural equation models. In P. Marsden (Ed.), *Sociological methodology 1991* (pp. 235-262). Oxford: Basil Blackwell.
Cudeck, R., & Browne, M. W. (1983). Cross-validation of covariance structures. *Multivariate Behavioral Research, 18,* 147-167.
Goldberger, A. S. (1991). *A course in econometrics.* Cambridge, MA: Harvard University Press.
Hausman, J. A. (1978). Specification tests in econometrics. *Econometrica, 46,* 1251-1272.
Hendry, D. F. (1980). Econometrics: Alchemy or science. *Economica, 47,* 387-406.
Hoelter, J. W. (1983). The analysis of covariance structures: Goodness-of-fit indices. *Sociological Methods and Research, 11,* 325-344.
Jöreskog, K. G. (1969). A general approach to confirmatory maximum likelihood factor analysis. *Psychometrika, 34,* 183-202.
Jöreskog, K. G., & Sörbom, D. (1981). *LISREL V.* Mooresville, IN: Scientific Software.
Maiti, S. S., & Mukherjee, B. N. (1990). A note on distributional properties of the Jöreskog-Sörbom fit indices. *Psychometrika, 55,* 721-726.
McDonald, R. P., & Marsh, H. W. (1990). Choosing a multivariate model: Noncentrality and goodness of fit. *Psychological Bulletin, 107,* 247-255.
Saris, W. E., & Stronkhorst, L. H. (1984). *Causal modelling in nonexperimental research: An introduction to the LISREL approach.* Amsterdam: Sociometric Research Foundation.
Satorra, A., & Saris, W. E. (1985). The power of the likelihood ratio test in covariance structure analysis. *Psychometrika, 50,* 83-90.
Steiger, J. H., & Lind, J. C. (1980, May). *Statistically based tests for the number of common factors.* Paper presented at the annual meeting of the Psychometric Society, Iowa City, IA.
Tanaka, J. S., & Huba, G. J. (1985). A fit index for covariance structure models under arbitrary GLS estimation. *British Journal of Mathematical and Statistical Psychology, 38,* 233-239.
Tucker, L. R., & Lewis, C. (1973). A reliability coefficient for maximum likelihood factor analysis. *Psychometrika, 38,* 1-10.
Wheaton, B., Muthén, B., Alwin, D., & Summers, G. (1977). Assessing reliability and stability in panel models. In D. R. Heise (Ed.), *Sociological methodology 1977* (pp. 84-136). San Francisco: Jossey-Bass.
White, H. (1980). A heteroskedasticity-consistent covariance matrix estimator and a direct test for heteroskedasticity. *Econometrica, 48,* 817-838.

## 2

# Multifaceted Conceptions of Fit
# in Structural Equation Models

## J. S. TANAKA

The issue of fit assessment in structural equation models has been the subject of both theoretical and empirical papers (e.g., Bentler, 1990; Bentler & Bonett, 1980; Bollen, 1990; Jöreskog & Sörbom, 1988; Marsh, Balla, & McDonald, 1988; McDonald, 1989; McDonald & Marsh, 1990; Mulaik et al., 1989; Tanaka & Huba, 1985, 1989). These multiple perspectives on the fit of observed data to structural equation models attest to the methodological interest in this problem, as well its relevance for substantive researchers who wish to determine the consistency of their data with a hypothetical structural equation model of interest. Given the large number of alternative fit indices available, investigators may have difficulty choosing among them. This is particularly difficult because the seminal articles on this topic reach no consensus about what constitutes "good fit."

Before additional measures are introduced to this literature, the similarities and differences among existing measures need to be evaluated systematically. Some of the evaluation can proceed empirically. La Du and Tanaka (1989, 1992) considered whether substantively meaningful

AUTHOR'S NOTE: Portions of this chapter were presented at the 1990 meeting of the Society of Multivariate Experimental Psychology, Newport, Rhode Island. This research is supported, in part, by the University of Illinois University Scholars Program. I would like to acknowledge the thoughtful comments of the editors, William Chaplin, Robert Cudeck, Terence La Du, Herbert Marsh, and several anonymous reviewers on previous drafts.

differences are detected when comparing results of different fit indices calculated from the same model and data. As an alternative to examining empirical relations among fit measures, this chapter considers the conceptual relations among fit measures. The goal here is to address the issue of fit index similarity by providing a categorization scheme for existing fit indices along the major conceptual dimensions on which they differ.

The proposed conceptual structure is sufficiently broad so that its major dimensions will capture the key components of both existing and yet-to-be-developed fit indices. The proposed structure emphasizes the interconnections among the different measures available, thus highlighting the different perspectives of those proposing alternative measures of fit. Although such a general framework is desirable, it is likely that a proposed general framework is not unique. Other simple conceptual structures might also account for the interrelations among structural equation model fit indices, but it is not my aim in this chapter to suggest a unique structure.

First, I will introduce some standard notation to facilitate the development of the points presented. Next, I will review major contributions to the assessment of fit in structural equation models. For each of these developments, I will discuss how they can be evaluated along different dimensions of data-model congruence. These dimensions include whether (a) the indices are sample based versus population based, (b) models are penalized for their relative complexity, (c) the indices are "normed" versus "nonnormed," (d) the fit described by these indices is "absolute" versus "relative," (e) there are consistent estimator-level effects (i.e., are fit indices "estimation method free" or "estimation method specific"), and (f) the fit indices demonstrate a dependence on sample size. The implications of choice of fit assessments will be described for each discussed index.

## Notation

Let $S$ be a sample covariance matrix with typical element $\{s_{ij}\}$ obtained on $p$ observed variables from a sample of $N$ individuals. In some developments, it is helpful to assume that the multivariate distribution is of a particular form, but that assumption will be highlighted only when it is necessary. Let $p^* = p(p + 1)/2$ be the number of nonredundant elements in $S$. Standard sources in matrix algebra (e.g., Graybill,

1983) introduce the notation $s = \text{vecs}(S)$ where the vecs operator maps the $p \times p$ matrix $S$ into the $p^* \times 1$ vector $s$. Specifically, $s$ contains the $p^*$ nonredundant lower triangular elements of the matrix $S$.

Let $\Sigma(\theta)$ define a matrix-valued function $\Sigma$ mapping an $r$-dimensional vector of estimated parameters $\theta$ into a $p$-dimensional space where $r \leq p^*$. Let $\sigma(\theta) = \text{vecs}[\Sigma(\theta)]$. As given by, for example, Browne (1982), one important aspect of covariance structure modeling is in estimating parameters of the structure so as to minimize the discrepancy between $s$ and $\sigma(\theta)$. In any sample of data, this discrepancy can be formalized as $e = s - \sigma(\theta)$. As elements of $e$ will, in general, demonstrate heteroscedasticity, the minimized discrepancy is usually formulated in terms of a weighted sum of squares (e.g., Shapiro, 1985). Let $f$ represent a discrepancy function in the sense of Shapiro (1985), where a general discrepancy function might be weighted least squares and its variants (including maximum likelihood). From this framework, one goal of fitting any covariance structure model is to summarize the $p^*$ elements of $S$ in terms of a smaller number of parameters, $r$.

There are two major traditions in classifying fit assessment in covariance structure models. Initial developments in this area emphasized classic null hypothesis testing approaches. Given this perspective and some background assumptions (e.g., independently and identically distributed units of analysis, typically from a multivariate normal distribution, although see Amemiya & Anderson, 1990), statements can be made about the (asymptotic) behavior of some function of $f$. In this framework, one can evaluate the null hypothesis that the hypothesized model is consistent with data observations. A statistic $v(f)$ can be calculated that, under certain regularity conditions, is asymptotically chi-square distributed and can be compared with critical reference values of a chi-square distribution with $q$ degrees of freedom for a test at a prespecified Type I error level $\alpha$. Here, $q$ is simply $p^* - r$, where $r$ is the number of freely estimated parameters in $\theta$. Thus, in this first strategy, fit can be defined in terms of the dichotomous decision of whether or not $v$ is less than the $(1 - \alpha)\%$ critical value for a $q$ degrees of freedom central chi-square distribution.

Many authors have been dissatisfied with this strategy of model testing. In this goodness-of-fit, "accept-support" strategy, it is easy to see that one can reject the null hypothesis simply by increasing the sample size. With the increased statistical power of such a test, ignorable differences between the hypothesized model and the observed data may be detected. Conversely, in small samples, insufficient statistical power may lead an investigator to commit a Type II error. As expressed by Steiger (1989), the literature on structural equation models has tended to emphasize Type I as opposed to Type II errors. While this discussion focuses primarily on sample size, investigators have pointed out other factors that can influence the statistical power in structural equation models (Matsueda & Bielby, 1986; Satorra & Saris, 1985).

A second criticism has centered on the plausibility of any model for an observed sample of data. As pointed out by, for example, Cudeck and Henly (1991) and McDonald (1989), models are, by definition, simplifications of an underlying process. Given this, the validity of the standard structural equation modeling null hypothesis may be uninteresting. Even the standard statistical underpinnings of these models are incorrect unless one can believe that $\Sigma = \Sigma(\theta)$ in the population as opposed to $\Sigma(\theta)$, representing a simplification of $\Sigma$ (Cudeck & Henly, 1991).

Thus some investigators (e.g., Tanaka, Panter, Winborne, & Huba, 1990) have suggested a deemphasis in classical hypothesis testing approaches in covariance structure modeling and a greater emphasis on comparative model fit (e.g., Steiger, Shapiro, & Browne, 1985). The notion of employing relative versus absolute standards in model assessments has long been emphasized in this literature (see, e.g., Jöreskog, 1974).

## The Role of Adjunctive Fit Assessment

A second strategy of fit assessment differs from these null hypothesis-based tests of model fit by avoiding the dichotomous decision strategy implied by a statistical decision rule. In a seminal paper, Bentler and Bonett (1980) extended the logic of Tucker and Lewis (1973) by considering the relative fit of competing models. They argued that the utility of fit assessment would be enhanced by an expression emphasizing a normed zero-one metric with values approaching one indicative of increasing levels of fit. The formula for their widely used fit measure, $\Delta$, as well as the formulas for other fit indices that are not defined in the text, are given in the appendix to this chapter.

In discussing the philosophical underpinnings of the problem of fit assessment, Bentler and Bonett (1980) make a number of critical points. First, they emphasize the difference between statistical significance and practical significance in tests of structural equation models. This represents an early expression of concern in structural equation models with notions related to power and Type II error, echoing well-known concerns from general linear models (e.g., Cohen, 1988). Although criticisms of the specifics of Bentler and Bonett's paper have been made by a number of authors (e.g., Sobel & Bohrnstedt, 1985; Tanaka, 1987), it remains influential (Bentler & Bonett, 1987), if only for the reason that many applications of structural equation modeling have employed this method of fit assessment.

The Bentler and Bonett logic of fit is based on comparisons to some baseline model. Fit assessments in this framework can be thought of as *relative* in that $\Delta$ is defined only in terms of choice of a specific baseline model. Thus $\Delta$ can be made arbitrarily large (or small) depending upon which model is chosen as a comparison standard. In other work, I have also shown how $\Delta$ can be influenced by choice of estimation method (Tanaka, 1987).

This relativism has been championed as both a strength (Bentler & Bonett, 1980) and a weakness (Sobel & Bohrnstedt, 1985) of $\Delta$. If a common metric for defining $\Delta$ could be established, such as the joint uncorrelatedness assumption in most applications of "null model" logic, then the index would provide a convenient assessment of the proportion of fit accounted for by a particular model relative to this baseline. Note, however, that this proportion of fit accounted for is not isomorphic to a proportion of variance accounted for measure that is standard in general linear model applications, such as regression ($R^2$) or analysis of variance applications (e.g., $\eta^2$). If adoption of such a standard is not common, or if it is inappropriate given a particular research question, then the fit index baseline becomes more arbitrary. Recent fit indices continue null model logic (Bentler, 1990). While it is true that most applications have used the uncorrelated variables null model, I am aware of investigators who have used alternative, more substantively based null models with the result that corresponding models appear poorer. It is also likely that use of a null model other than the typical standard of uncorrelated variables is more relevant to addressing the incremental validity of tested models. This conceptual point is addressed in a general framework by Meehl (1991, p. 39) in his discussions of the "reasonable range" of an incremental effect and its value in providing more specific knowledge about an investigated phenomenon. Within a substantive domain, Humphreys (1990) has discussed the problems of using the uncorrelated variables null model in the domain of human abilities.

At approximately the same time the Bentler-Bonett index appeared, Jöreskog and Sörbom (1981) released the computer program LISREL V and introduced the goodness-of-fit index (GFI) and the adjusted goodness-of-fit index (AGFI) for the estimation methods then available in the program. Although different indices were defined for maximum likelihood and unweighted least squares estimators, no rationale was developed for the presentation of these statistics. Due to the ubiquity of the LISREL program, the GFI and AGFI indices, generally in their maximum likelihood forms, were reported as frequently as the Bentler-Bonett index in modeling applications. However, the absence of any rationale for the GFI and AGFI made interpretations difficult.

These developments led to an awakened interest in alternative approaches that provided omnibus assessments of the fit of latent variable structural equation models. James, Mulaik, and Brett (1982), for example, criticized many of the available fit assessments because these measures favored complex over simple models. Specifically, highly parameterized models would typically be selected over more parsimonious models, because of the positive relation between improved model fit and the addition of parameters. Alternatively, Mulaik (1990) has presented this argument in terms of the number of parameters that are not estimated or, inversely, the number of degrees of freedom available to conduct model tests. James et al. (1982) thus introduced the parsimonious fit index, using the Bentler-Bonett normed fit index as a basis and then adding an adjustment for model complexity. It should also be noted that a similar development was suggested by Steiger and Lind (1980; Steiger, 1989), who felt that fit assessments should be scaled in two dimensions: fit and simplicity.

Subsequently, a large number of different indices were introduced (see Marsh et al., 1988, for an encyclopedic account of possible alternatives). The proliferation of fit indices made the choice of an index difficult for investigators. This, in turn, resulted in empirical applications of structural equation modeling methods presenting multiple fit indices. Although, for the most part, these indices led to the same substantive conclusion about the fit of any specific model because of moderate to high intercorrelations among the indices (Marsh et al., 1988), it was, in principle, possible to obtain divergent indications of model fit (e.g., La Du & Tanaka, 1989; Tanaka, 1987).

Given the ambiguity that can arise from multiple fit measures, it is essential to develop some unifying set of principles for comparing fit indices. It is clear from a review of the literature on fit indices that different indices emphasize different aspects of model fit.

Table 2.1 presents and defines the six dimensions along which fit indices in structural equation models might differ. Although it is possible

**Table 2.1** Definitions of Dimensions Along Which Fit Indices Can Vary

| Dimension | Definition |
|---|---|
| (1) Population based versus sample based | Population-based fit indices estimate a known population parameter; sample-based fit indices described the data-model fit in the observed sample at hand. |
| (2) Simplicity versus complexity | Fit indices that favor simple models penalize models in which many parameters are estimated; fit indices that do not employ such a correction do not penalize for model complexity. |
| (3) Normed versus nonnormed | Fit indices that are normed are constructed to lie within an approximate (0, 1) range; nonnormed fit indices do not necessarily lie in this range. |
| (4) Absolute versus relative | Relative fit indices are defined with respect to a specific model that serves as an anchor for subsequent model comparisons; absolute fit indices do not employ such a comparison anchor. |
| (5) Estimation method free versus estimation method specific | Estimation method-free fit indices provide characterizations of model fit that are unaffected by the choice of a specific estimation method; estimation method-specific fit indices provide different fit summaries across different methods of estimation. |
| (6) Sample size independent versus sample size dependent | Sample-size-independent fit indices are not affected by sample size, either directly or indirectly; sample-size-dependent fit indices vary as a function of observed sample size. |

that other potential dimensions of difference could be identified, these dimensions characterize many of the decisions that have been invoked in justifying the use of structural equation model fit indices and thus reflect major ideas along which important discriminations can be made. Interestingly, many of these concerns parallel results in general (e.g., Graybill, 1976) and generalized (e.g., McCullagh & Nelder, 1984) linear models. Whenever appropriate, analogues will be developed between fit assessments in these related literatures and the structural equation modeling literature. In many respects, the proposed structure is an extension of the early work by Steiger and Lind (1980).

In addition to providing an organizational structure for the various fit indices that have been proposed, this taxonomy will help investigators to identify which particular fit indices they wish to use to evaluate models in particular applications. By making explicit that alternative fit indices emphasize different dimensions, this system of classification makes it possible for investigators to select indices on the basis of their own particular concerns. Further, researchers who need to evaluate models across different research studies will be able to determine clearly those fit dimensions emphasized by other investigators. The conceptual framework presented here should clarify the specific set of criteria an investigator wishes to optimize in the evaluation of competing models within a particular data set.

## Sample-Based Versus Population-Based Indices: The Roles of Description and Inference

The primary impetus for the development of these fit indices was to provide a description of model-data congruence so that model evaluation did not rest on a single dichotomous decision adjudicated by the chi-square statistic. Fit indices were originally used to assess the overall congruence between a specific model and observed data. Although such logic still predominates, a more recent emphasis in fit indices has been on the comparative fit of competing models. It is ironic that a focus on comparative model fit is wholly consistent with Jöreskog's original writings in this area (e.g., Jöreskog, 1974). In this early work, the role of omnibus model fit was deemphasized and considered subordinate to identifying the best model from among prespecified alternatives.

Because a simple dichotomous decision rule is inadequate for summarizing model fit, some investigators have chosen to view sample fit indices as estimates of population quantities (Bentler, 1990; Bollen, 1989a; McDonald, 1989; Steiger, 1989). Among these authors, Steiger (1989), in particular, has emphasized the availability of standard errors and confidence intervals for fit indices that provide a stronger inferential focus for these measures.

The desire for a firmly based statistical framework for fit indices in structural equation modeling has existed for some time (see, e.g., Steiger & Lind, 1980). The recent crystallization of this desire has led to the development of a class of indices that estimate population parameters. Bentler (1990), Bollen (1989a), and McDonald (1989; McDonald & Marsh, 1990) have developed such indices, all of which employ information from the noncentral chi-square distribution. A related concern (Browne & Cudeck, 1989; Cudeck & Browne, 1983) involves the cross-validity of models in either the multiple-sample (Cudeck & Browne, 1983) or single-sample (Browne & Cudeck, 1989) case. In all of the above cases and in all of the indices proposed by these investigators, concerns are being expressed about the adequacy of data from a single sample to characterize an underlying population structure.

The evolution of fit indices based on logic that is predominantly descriptive to a logic that has an inferential framework is justified by a number of concerns. The expression of a fit index as an estimator of a population parameter increases the likelihood of developing possible sampling theory and inferential tests for an index (Steiger, 1989). Issues of consistency and bias of a sample estimate can also be addressed (e.g., Maiti & Mukherjee, 1990). However, the notion of a descriptive and inferential basis for the same index is hardly novel. For example, in general linear models, Cohen's (1988) notion of effect size, a descriptive measure of the magnitude of the relation between predictors and an outcome variable, is tied to the noncentrality parameter of the referent noncentral $F$ distribution when the general linear model null hypothesis is false. Thus it may not be necessary to dichotomize this issue of fit indices into categories of descriptive versus inferential measures, but rather to couch this question in terms of how the resulting quantities are interpreted.

The choice between whether an index is employed descriptively or inferentially may depend on the situation faced by an investigator. Investigators may simply want to know whether their hypothesized theoretical models are consistent with the data they observe. In this initial exploratory phase of an investigation, the future cross-validity of results may become more important after the consistency of a finding within a particular observed sample can be established. The idea of using structural equation models in such an exploratory fashion is discussed by Kroonenberg and Lewis (1982) and by Tanaka et al. (1990). A second condition is endemic to any circumstance under which an estimated sample quantity is thought to be estimating a population parameter: The relevant parent population must be identified. Identification of the parent population is particularly important when samples are small, perhaps because of the unique features of a group being studied (Tanaka, 1987). As Cudeck and Henly (1991) point out, too often developments in the structural equation modeling literature on fit determination seem to assume that sample size is a variable subject to manipulation by an experimenter. Because the conditions under which samples become sufficiently large for the asymptotic statistical theory of structural equation modeling to apply have yet to be ascertained (Tanaka, 1987), there are no guidelines for deciding if samples are sufficiently large to move confidently from description to inference.

This result is analogous to multiple correlation results in the general linear model. The sample multiple correlation is a biased estimator of the population multiple correlation (e.g., Cohen & Cohen, 1983). Specifically, a "shrunken" or adjusted $R^2$ is given by

$$R_S^2 = 1 - (1 - R^2)[(N - 1)/(N - k - 1)] , \qquad [1]$$

where $N$ is the sample size in a model with $k$ predictors. Browne (1975) has discussed a small sample (i.e., small $N$, small $N - k$) correction given as

$$R_{S_B}^2 = [(N - k - 3)R_S^4 + R_S^2]/(N - 2k - 2)R_S^2 + k . \qquad [2]$$

$R_S^2$ can be rewritten in terms of the degrees of freedom associated with two different models for the data. Let $df_1 = N - 1$ be the degrees of freedom associated with a "null model," where predictors are hypothesized to have a null effect on the outcome (i.e., $R^2 = 0$). Let $df_2 = N - k - 1$ be the degrees of freedom associated with an alternative model, where the $k$ predictors have a joint influence on the outcome (i.e., $R^2 \neq 0$). Alternatively, $df_1$ and $df_2$ can be thought of as the degrees of freedom associated with estimates of $\hat{\sigma}^2$ under the different model restrictions.

We can rewrite $R_S^2$ in terms of $df_1$ and $df_2$:

$$R_S^2 = 1 - (1 - R^2)(df_1/df_2) . \qquad [3]$$

Under this formulation, it becomes clear how Jöreskog and Sörbom's GFI and AGFI are related to the $R^2$ and $R_S^2$ of the univariate general linear model. Further, this develops the theme (Tanaka & Huba, 1989) that the Jöreskog and Sörbom GFI (labeled $\gamma$ in their paper) is a general coefficient of determination for structural equation models under arbitrary generalized least squares estimation. To develop this point explicitly, consider the GFI as presented by Tanaka and Huba (1989). Their $\hat{\gamma}$ coefficient is defined as

$$\hat{\gamma} = tr(\hat{\sigma}^T W \hat{\sigma})/tr(s^T W s) , \qquad [4]$$

where $W$ is a $p^* \times p^*$ weight matrix (e.g., Browne, 1982).

The Jöreskog and Sörbom (1981) definition of AGFI can be expressed as a function of $\gamma$.

$$\text{AGFI} = 1 - (1 - \hat{\gamma})[p(p+1)/2\text{df}] , \qquad [5]$$

where df is the degrees of freedom associated with the specific model being tested. Because we have previously defined $p(p+1)/2 = p^*$, we can rewrite Equation 5 as a function of $p^*$:

$$\text{AGFI} = 1 - (1 - \hat{\gamma})(p^*/\text{df}) . \qquad [6]$$

Expressed in this form, it becomes clear that, like the $R_S^2$, the AGFI employs a shrinkage correction under two competing models for covariances: a model consisting of the data observations with $p^*$ degrees of freedom and an alternative structural model with df degrees of freedom.

A further simplification can be obtained because df is also a function of $p^*$ with df $= p^* - r$, where $r$ is the number of estimated model parameters. Employing this identity, Equation 6 can be rewritten as follows:

$$\text{AGFI} = 1 - (1 - \hat{\gamma})[1 - (r/p^*)]^{-1} . \qquad [7]$$

From Equation 7, it is clear that AGFI $\rightarrow \hat{\gamma}$ as $r/p^* \rightarrow 0$. In other words, AGFI and $\gamma$ will become approximately equal as relatively few parameters are estimated relative to the total number of observed variances and covariances in $S$. Given the similarity between the sets $\{R^2, R_S^2\}$ and $\{\hat{\gamma}, \text{AGFI}\}$, it may be appropriate to denote AGFI as $\hat{\gamma}_S$ to reinforce the idea that AGFI is the shrunken version of $\hat{\gamma}$.

Recently, Maiti and Mukherjee (1990) described the distributional properties of the GFI indices and demonstrated that $\hat{\gamma}$ was a biased estimator of $\gamma$, where the population $\gamma$ is defined as

$$\gamma = \frac{p}{p + 2f_0} , \qquad [8]$$

where $f_0 = -\frac{1}{2}\text{tr}[V(\hat{\Sigma}_0 - \Sigma_0)]$, $V = \hat{\Sigma}_0^{-1}\Sigma_0\hat{\Sigma}_0^{-1}$, $\Sigma_0$ is the true population covariance matrix, and $\hat{\Sigma}_0$ is the reproduced covariance obtained fitting the model to $\Sigma_0$ by maximum likelihood. Maiti and Mukherjee introduced a bias-correction factor of $2\text{df}/N$. Ignoring the component attributable to sample size, the shrinkage implied by this correction includes the term $1 - (r/p^*)$ (demonstrating the logic of the AGFI proposed by Jöreskog & Sörbom, 1981).

It is also useful to compare this perspective on model parsimony with that proposed by Mulaik et al. (1989), who discuss a parsimonious goodness-of-fit index (PGFI) defined as

$$PGFI = [2df/p(p + 1)]\hat{\gamma}.$$  [9]

Again, PGFI can be expressed as a function of $p^*$ and $r$:

$$PGFI = [1 - (r/p^*)]\hat{\gamma}.$$  [10]

Comparing Equations 7 and 9, it is clear that different types of parsimony-based adjustments are being made to $\hat{\gamma}$ in $\hat{\gamma}_S$ and the PGFI. If we let $k = 1 - (r/p^*)$, then we can rewrite Equations 7 and 9 as

$$\gamma_S = 1 - (1 - \hat{\gamma})(1/k)$$  [11]

and

$$PGFI = k\hat{\gamma}.$$  [12]

For any model that is not underidentified, $k$ will take on values between 0 and 1. Further, for any model invariant under constant scaling factor (Browne, 1982), $1 - \hat{\gamma} \geq 0$ (Dijkstra, 1990). Therefore, it follows that an inequality chain holds among $\hat{\gamma}$, $\hat{\gamma}_S$, and PGFI:

$$PGFI \leq \hat{\gamma}_S \leq \hat{\gamma}.$$  [13]

Although the $\hat{\gamma}_S$ appears to be a natural extension of the logic of $R_S^2$ in the univariate general linear model, there is no natural interpretation of PGFI. Because PGFI makes its parsimony correction directly to $\hat{\gamma}$, it must be the case that PGFI is less than $\hat{\gamma}$, except in those rare instances where no parameters are estimated. Bollen (1989a) extends a variant of this logic to $\Delta$ and to his incremental fit index.

These results are presented to demonstrate that simple analogies can be drawn between structural equation modeling fit indices and parallel results from general linear modeling. Thus, in the same way that an investigator can choose between reporting $R^2$ and $R_S^2$ for regression results, an investigator can choose among $\hat{\gamma}$, $\hat{\gamma}_S$, and PGFI in summarizing model fit. The first column of Table 2.2 highlights those fit measures that estimate a population parameter.

## Simple Versus Complex Models

Another basis for categorizing fit indices is the extent to which they penalize heavily parameterized models. James et al. (1982), extending work by Tucker and Lewis (1973) and Jöreskog and Sörbom (1981), discuss penalties for complex, highly parameterized models that will typically fit better than simpler models. This point has also been discussed in unpublished work by Steiger and Lind (1980), who suggest that model simplicity and model fit be the two dimensions along which fit should be summarized. The penalty notion is also developed in the Akaike information criterion (AIC) (e.g., Akaike, 1987; Browne & Cudeck, 1989; Cudeck & Browne, 1983; McArdle, 1988) for model selection, where, all other things being equal, more heavily parameterized models will be penalized relative to simpler models with fewer parameters.

A comparison of Equations 4 and 7 for $\hat{\gamma}$ and $\hat{\gamma}_S$, respectively, demonstrate a way of including complexity in model evaluation. Some other proposals do not demonstrate as clear an analogy to general linear model results (e.g., the PGFI results given above). The AIC clearly represents the penalty logic and encourages investigators to select the simplest from a range of alternative models. Further, simple models are generally more replicable (e.g., Browne & Cudeck, 1989; Cudeck & Browne, 1983).

Previously presented results illustrate analogies that can be developed between sample- and population-based estimators of the squared multiple correlation coefficient in multiple regression and adjusted versions of the $\gamma$ coefficient in structural equation models. Specifically, these results demonstrate how fit indices that penalize for complex models (e.g., $\hat{\gamma}_S$) can be linked to logic based on sample estimators of population quantities. Given this, a selection from among $\hat{\gamma}$, $\hat{\gamma}_S$, and PGFI in expressing the omnibus fit of a covariance structure model might reflect an interest in sample-based versus population-based measures of fit. Further, as extended to the AIC indices, fit index selection might be guided by optimizing information about the observed sample versus optimizing information about future samples drawn from the same population. Although this theme will be echoed in a later section, other fit indices that have been proposed (e.g., the Bentler-Bonett $\Delta$ or the Tucker-Lewis/Bentler-Bonett $\rho$) do not seem to have properties that can be related to the general linear model. The second column of Table 2.2 identifies fit measures that make adjustments for the number of estimated parameters when assessing model fit.

### Normed Versus Nonnormed Indices

Another basis for comparing fit indices is if they are expressed in a standard metric, typically ranging from 0 to 1. From the perspective of mapping structural equation fit indices into the knowledge structure of researchers, this would fit conveniently into the ideas individuals have about $R^2$ measures and the corresponding notion of proportion of variance accounted for. This ease of interpretation formed one of the key dimensions for fit indices defined by La Du (1986). Early precedents in this area were set by Bentler and Bonett (1980), who provided both normed and nonnormed versions of fit indices for structural equation models under the assumption that individuals might be more readily able to understand the former as proportion-of-fit measures.

Other indices currently in use in latent variable structural equation modeling are only approximately normed to a 0-1 metric (e.g., the Tucker-Lewis coefficient) or have relatively arbitrarily defined metrics (e.g., the AIC). Of course, any nonnormed measure has the potential for being normed to a 0-1 metric; some appropriate baseline for the norming can be defined. For example, if the AIC were to be used in conjunction with the "null model logic" of Bentler and Bonett (1980), one could define a normed AIC measure that would have associated with it the same interpretational problems associated with $\Delta$ (see Sobel & Bohrnstedt, 1985). Similarly, the comparative fit indices of Bentler (1990) rely on an arbitrary baseline model. Dijkstra (1990) has shown that, for models that are invariant under a constant scaling factor, $\hat{\gamma}$ will always range between 0 and 1. Given the inequality chain in Equation 12, it is clear that, in general, PGFI and $\hat{\gamma}_s$ will rarely attain a (0, 1) range.

In the literature, two different normative standards have been suggested. The "null model" logic presented by Bentler and Bonett (1980) employs observed variables that are mutually uncorrelated (i.e., is a diagonal matrix by the null hypothesis). The second standard employs the observed data $s$, as in the $\gamma$ measures. Thus models are compared with the observed data in terms of the total observed variance that is accounted for by a hypothesized model.

Bentler and Bonett (1980), using results of Tucker and Lewis (1973), introduced the null model to provide a second anchor point for model comparisons. Their argument is that if the number of estimated model parameters $r$ approaches $p*$, an investigator approaches a saturated model with as many estimated parameters as observed data points (i.e., variances and covariances). Because a saturated model would leave no discrepancies between the hypothesized model and the data, Bentler and Bonett argue that any model that is a restriction of the saturated model (i.e., where $r < p*$) involves an implicit comparison to the saturated model. One could conceptualize the chi-square goodness-of-fit statistic as the distance between the hypothesized (restricted) model of interest and a saturated model.

The anchor point introduced by Bentler and Bonett is a reference at the other end of this distance continuum. Rather than asking about the distance to a saturated model, null model logic introduced the concept of distance from some comparison model that was more restricted than the model of interest. Thus null model logic set up a dimension of parametric restrictions such that models could be compared with both highly restricted and highly unrestricted (saturated) models. Other indices also provide these dual anchors for comparison (see, e.g., Bentler, 1990; Tucker & Lewis, 1973).

The $\gamma$-based comparison to observed data can be rationalized from another perspective. When observed data are used as the standard, one can think of this standard as representing a "premodel" state. The observed data represent information in the absence of a model. If a model is subsequently hypothesized for these data, the $\gamma$-based indices provide information regarding the extent to which the model explains observed data. In this sense, the $\gamma$-based indices capture information about how well a hypothesized model recaptures the observed data. Again, it can be noted that this is the same as the general linear model perspective in calculating $R^2$ where $R^2$ is expressed as a ratio of model-explained data variation to total observed data variation.

In general, most investigators in the behavioral sciences would prefer measures of fit that are normed in an appropriate range (e.g., Cohen, 1988; Humphreys, 1990). Expressed as either a proportion of total fit (e.g., $\hat{\Delta}$) or a proportion of total variance (e.g., $\hat{\gamma}$), these normed indices provide a clear indication of the incremental fit of a model. However, the different types of indices reflect the state of information available about alternative model representations. Null model logic implicitly places a model to be tested along a continuum from highly restricted to highly unrestricted models. Investigators must choose the restricted baseline models to which models of substantive interest will be compared. As Sobel and Bohrnstedt (1985) have shown, selection of such restricted models may not always be straightforward.

On the other hand, the use of the $\gamma$ family of indices can be thought of as comparing some substantive model of interest to the observed data before any simplification provided by a model is hypothesized. Thus these indices calibrate the representativeness of the model relative to a situation where no model is proposed to account for the data. Fit index interpretations that result are conditional on the anchor points chosen to define the metrics for comparison. However, not all measures share this feature. For example, similar claims cannot be made for the AIC index. While the model selection rule for the AIC is simple (i.e., choose the model with the smallest AIC value among a set of competing models), researchers may reluctantly choose among several models that have closely competing AIC values. Recent research by La Du and Tanaka (1992) addresses the sensitivity of AIC and other fit indices to known correct and incorrect model change. Innovative uses of AIC-based logic have relied on some heuristic simplification in the presentation of AIC values (e.g., McArdle, 1988). Although interpretational rules exist for nonnormed fit indices in latent variable structural equation models, users will probably prefer normed measures. The third column of Table 2.2 presents those fit measures normed to an (approximate) (0, 1) metric.

## Absolute Versus Relative Fit Indices

Many fit indices (e.g., the null model baseline of Bentler & Bonett, 1980) rely on a baseline for comparison. In some cases, this null model posits zero correlations among observed variables, but this may not always be appropriate (Sobel & Bohrnstedt, 1985). More recently, Bentler's (1990) development of fit indices based on noncentrality parameters has also employed a baseline for comparison based on the degree of model misspecification. Interestingly, in this work, Bentler again develops a comparative baseline using uncorrelated variables mode, despite the reservations that have been voiced previously about this standard. Such fit indices are described as being relative in that they rely on three sources of information for their computation: the sample covariance matrix, the reproduced covariance matrix from the hypothesized model, and a reference point (e.g., a null model) that serves as an anchor for describing fit.

McDonald and Marsh (1990) develop the notion of an absolute goodness-of-fit index that is estimated from sample quantities by

$$m_k = \exp\{-\tfrac{1}{2}[f_k - (q_k/n)]\}, \qquad [14]$$

where $\exp(x)$ is the exponential function applied to $x$; $f_k$ is the minimum of a discrepancy function for model $k$, which, under appropriate assumptions, can be multiplied by $n$ to yield an asymptotic chi-square variate with $q_k$ $(= p^* - r)$ degrees of freedom; $p^*$ is as previously defined; and $n$ is $N$, the total sample size, minus 1. According to McDonald and Marsh, this index can be considered to be "absolute" because it does not depend on a relative comparison to another model.

An alternative interpretation of the McDonald and Marsh index is that an implicit comparison is being made to the saturated model; that is, $m_k$ takes on the value of 1 at the saturated model where $v_k = q_k = 0$. In this case, where there is a one-to-one correspondence between a (saturated) model and the observed data, the McDonald and Marsh index $m_k$ is a relative index in the same way Tanaka and Huba (1989) have conceptualized $\gamma$ to be a relative fit index. In the case of $\gamma$, comparisons are made relative to a weighted function of the observed variances and covariances.

Because there are nonsaturated models for which $q_k$ equals $f_k$, more generally $m_k \to 1$ as $nf_k + r \to p^*$. If $f_k$ is rewritten as $\hat{e}W\hat{e}$, with these quantities as previously defined, then it becomes clear that $m_k$ approaches 1 as an additive function of residuals, $\hat{e}$, and the number of parameters estimated, $r$, approaches the total number of observed data points.

An alternative way of thinking about the issue of "absolute" and "relative" fit indices is to focus on the anchor point for establishing model fit. Comparative fit indices such as those presented by Bentler and Bonett (1980) and Bentler (1990) define some arbitrarily selected comparison point such as the model of mutually uncorrelated observed variables. The logic of these indices implies that no more complicated model can be hypothesized for data if the data support the mutual uncorrelatedness model.

The $\hat{\gamma}$ fit index employs the observed data as its comparison point. Values of $\hat{\gamma}$ approach 1 with increased data-model congruence. The McDonald and

Marsh $m_k$ measure uses models for which $q_k = f_k$ as its baseline for comparison. Thus the $\hat{\gamma}$ index (and indices based on $\hat{\gamma}$) explicitly, and the $m_k$ index implicitly, employs the observed data as a baseline for comparison. Thus these indices mimic familiar fit measures such as $R^2$ by including a comparison to an analogous "total sum of squares" component that, in the case of $\hat{\gamma}$, is exactly a weighted total sum of squares.

Other indices such as the AIC do not have any simple comparison point unless the AIC for some substantively uninteresting model such as mutual uncorrelatedness is employed as the baseline. This lack of dependence on the observations from the current sample of data may be what makes the AIC useful in the cross-validation measures of Browne and Cudeck (1989) and Cudeck and Browne (1983), although, as McDonald (1989) has shown, these will depend on the size of the sample observed. The fourth column of Table 2.2 identifies relative fit measures.

### Estimation Method-Free Versus Estimation Method-Specific Indices

Estimation method has been largely overlooked in the structural equation modeling literature. Given the historical predominance of maximum likelihood methods, maximum likelihood procedures have been used most often. However, many other estimators exist, including noniterative estimators (e.g., Bentler, 1982; Hägglund, 1982), estimators asymptotically equivalent to maximum likelihood estimators (e.g., Browne, 1974), and estimators based on elliptical (e.g., Bentler, 1983; Browne, 1982) or more general (e.g., Bentler, 1983; Browne, 1982; Ihara, Berkane, & Bentler, 1990) distributions. Thus it is likely that investigators may be selecting from a broader range of alternatives in the future.

Given the same data set, summaries of fit based on different estimation procedures should yield approximately the same results. La Du (1986) suggests that an additional criterion for fit indices should be that they are relatively insensitive to deviations from multivariate normality. Here, the La Du notion of invariance will be modified to a criterion of conditional invariance for fit indices. This condition is defined using the general form of $\hat{\gamma}$, from Tanaka and Huba (1985, 1989):

*Definition:* A fit index with the form of $\hat{\gamma}$ will be said to be conditionally invariant if $\hat{\gamma}_i$, based on a weight matrix $W_i$, cannot be distinguished from $\hat{\gamma}_j$, based on a weight matrix $W_j$, for $W_i \neq W_j$.

This definition can be altered. For example, indistinguishability can be indexed through use of the asymptotic distribution theory associated with $\hat{\gamma}$ or functions of $\hat{\gamma}$ (Steiger, 1989). In this form, the conditional invariance definition could be expressed as the failure to reject the null hypothesis $\hat{\gamma}_i = \hat{\gamma}_j$. However, for some estimators, different sets of regularity conditions would hold. For example, one could not test this hypothesis using maximum likelihood and asymptotically distribution-free estimators, but could, in principle, test it for the asymptotically equivalent maximum likelihood and normal theory generalized least squares estimator of Browne (1974). Such an alteration would formally restrict conditional invariance to asymptotically equivalent estimators. As an example of when one might not want conditional invariance to hold, consider a parallel definition applied to the chi-square statistic in which it is clear that a test statistic $v_i$ based on the $W_i$ from maximum likelihood should not be conditionally invariant with respect to a test statistic $v_j$ based on an asymptotically distribution-free weight matrix $W_j$.

In the domain of fit indices, investigators often behave as if the conditional invariance definition holds. For example, the AIC is strictly justified only when maximum likelihood estimators are used (e.g., Browne & Cudeck, 1989; Cudeck & Browne, 1983), yet this index may be applicable to a broader class of estimators. Further, there has been some speculation (e.g., Bentler & Bonett, 1980) but relatively little empirical work suggesting that conditional invariance should hold across different estimators for summary fit indices.

Based on an observation made in Tanaka (1987), recent theoretical (Tanaka & Huba, 1989) and empirical (La Du & Tanaka, 1989, 1992) work has begun to address the issue of estimator effects on summary measures of fit. These effects can be seen most clearly with respect to the $\gamma$ index, because of dependence on the weight matrix $W$ used in the minimized quadratic form (see Equation 4). Tanaka and Huba (1989) show that special case forms of $\gamma$ exist under three popular forms of estimation. Under unweighted least squares, where $W$ has as part of its structure $I \otimes I$, where $I$ is the $p \times p$ identity matrix and $\otimes$ denotes the Kronecker product, $\hat{\gamma}_{ULS}$ is given as

$$\hat{\gamma}_{ULS} = tr(\hat{\Sigma})/tr(S) .\qquad [15]$$

Under normal theory, generalized least squares where the structure of $W$ contains $S \otimes S$, $\hat{\gamma}_{NGLS}$ is given as

$$\hat{\gamma}_{\text{NGLS}} = \text{tr}(S^{-1}\hat{\Sigma})^2/p \ . \tag{16}$$

Finally, under maximum likelihood, where $W$ contains $\hat{\Sigma} \otimes \hat{\Sigma}$, $\hat{\gamma}_{\text{ML}}$ is given as

$$\hat{\gamma}_{\text{ML}} = p/\text{tr}(\hat{\Sigma}^{-1}S)^2 \ . \tag{17}$$

From Equations 15 and 16, it is clear that $\hat{\gamma}_{\text{GLS}}$ and $\hat{\gamma}_{\text{ML}}$ will tend to conditional invariance to the extent that $\text{tr}(S^{-1}\hat{\Sigma})^2 \rightarrow \text{tr}(\hat{\Sigma}^{-1}S)^2$. In an empirical demonstration, La Du and Tanaka (1989) have shown that such convergence is not assured in small samples. Further, their results address the case of either known population models or models that represent trivial misspecifications from a known population model. The introduction of specification error (MacCallum, 1986) would hinder the convergence and conditional invariance of $\hat{\gamma}_{\text{GLS}}$ and $\hat{\gamma}_{\text{ML}}$ to a greater extent. Some research has extended this behavior to the broader class of indices based on noncentrality parameters as discussed by Bentler (1990) and McDonald and Marsh (1990) (see La Du & Tanaka, 1992). The fifth column of Table 2.2 identifies those fit measures that explicitly vary as a function of estimation method.

### Sample Size-Independent Versus Sample Size-Dependent Indices

The role of sample size and its influence in the determination of overall model fit has been an important concern in structural equation modeling (e.g., Cudeck & Henly, 1991). Researchers are conscious of the incompatibilities between asymptotic statistical theory requiring samples that increase in size toward infinity and data that are available from finite samples. Some guidance and understanding of the role that sample size plays in the determination of model fit is important in study design analysis. Sufficiently large samples are necessary if we are to evaluate reliably a particular model of interest. Often, this is couched in terms of asking when samples are "big enough" (Tanaka, 1987) to balance the trade-off between sufficient statistical power to test a model and excessive statistical power so that substantively uninteresting model-data deviations are nevertheless statistically significant.

Within the domain of fit measures that have been proposed for structural equation models, Bollen (1989b, 1990) has articulated the need to address different components of sample size ($N$) influences that can influence model fit. More specifically, Bollen (personal communication, March 1992) has identified numerous ways that $N$ influences fit in structural equation models. In this discussion, two central sample size influences will be addressed. The first is when sample size directly enters into the computation of the fit measure, and the second is when the sampling distribution of the fit measure is affected by sample size.

An obvious way in which sample size can affect a fit measure is when it is employed directly in the computation of the statistics. The chi-square goodness-of-fit statistic for ML estimators, for example, is given by ($N - 1$) times the minimum of the ML discrepancy function. It is clear that, for a fixed value of the ML discrepancy function, the chi-square goodness-of-fit statistic will become larger with increasing sample size. This sample size effect can also be thought of in terms of increasing statistical power to detect model-data discrepancies of the same magnitude. In other words, a model-data discrepancy of the same magnitude will reject the null hypothesis of model fit in a large sample size as opposed to a small sample size. The AIC is another example of a fit measure that is directly influenced by $N$.

This type of sample size dependence, where $N$ enters directly into the computation of a statistic, has been confused in the structural equation modeling literature with other sample size effects. Bollen (1989b, 1990) has discussed ways in which $N$ might affect the moments of the sampling distributions of fit measures with a specific interest in the behavior of first-order moments (means). This discussion will follow the treatment given in Bollen (1989b, 1990), focusing on sample size influences on the mean of the sampling distribution of fit measures.

As one example, Bollen (1989b, 1990) employs the Bentler-Bonett normed fit index ($\hat{\Delta}$), which was introduced as a way of addressing sample size dependencies in model fit. The sample value of $\hat{\Delta}$ depends on the difference between the discrepancy function for some model of interest and the discrepancy function of some baseline, comparison model (see the appendix to this chapter for a complete presentation of the formula for $\Delta$). As Bollen (1989b, p. 271) points out, if ($N - 1$)$f_1$ is chi-square distributed, then the mean of the $f_1$ should approximate $df_1/(N - 1)$, where $df_1$ are the degrees of freedom associated with the model with discrepancy function $f_1$. While the same should be true of the baseline model $f_0$ from which $\hat{\Delta}$ is calculated, Bollen suggests that there are difference in the rate at which $f_0$ and $f_1$ decline with $N$ (p. 271). From this, Bollen concludes that the mean of the sampling distribution of $\Delta$ is greater in larger samples than it is in smaller samples. Similar sample size effects on the mean of the sampling distribution of fit indices have been reported in simulation work by Marsh et al. (1988) and by La Du and Tanaka (1989), among others.

As a result of the work that has been conducted examining sample size effects on fit index measures, some preliminary recommendations can be offered for how researchers might choose statistics to evaluate model fit. Of the two kinds of sample size influences reviewed here, it is clear that there are trade-offs in determining fit index preference. For example, if one were to choose a fit measure such as the IFI, whose sampling distribution mean is relatively unaltered by sample size (Bentler, 1990; Bollen, 1989b), it is clear that sample size does play a role in the calculation of this statistic. An alternative strategy for being better able to select among different fit measures would be for researchers to develop sensitivities to fit index sampling distribution means in the interpretation of model fit (La Du & Tanaka, 1992). This idea is implicit in Steiger's (1989) focus on confidence intervals for some fit index measures. In either case, a decision rule based on a point estimate value of a particular fit index and particularly one whose sampling distribution moments vary as a function of $N$ is unlikely to provide much systematic guidance about fit. In the sixth column of Table 2.2, fit indices are identified whose sampling distribution means have been demonstrated either theoretically or empirically to depend on sample size. Fit measures that are calculated using sample size as a factor such as the AIC are not marked in this column.

## Some Guidelines for Selecting Among Fit Indices

Given that the six dimensions of fit can be identified, it is worthwhile to provide guidelines that help investigators select among them. Table 2.2 summarizes some popular indices along these six dimensions. Below, I present recommendations for the use of these indices in terms of how "controversial" I believe these recommendations will be.

I do not believe that there can be much dispute about the goal of having fit index measures reflect the consistent results about model fit across different estimation methods or at least among those estimators that are conditionally invariant. Since estimation method-specific

**Table 2.2** Category Membership for Some Popular Fit Indices Along the Six Dimensions

| Fit Index | Population Based? | Favor Simple Models? | Normed to Approximate (0, 1) Interval | Relative? | Estimation Method Specific? | Sample Size Dependent? |
|---|---|---|---|---|---|---|
| $\hat{\Delta}$ | | | X | | X | X |
| $\hat{\rho}$ | | X | X | X | | |
| $\hat{\gamma}$ | X | | X | | X | X |
| $\hat{\gamma}_S$ | | X | X | | X | X |
| AIC | | X | | | X | X |
| PGFI | | X | X | | X | X |
| IFI | X | X | X | X | | |
| $m_k$ | X | X | X | X | | |
| CFI | X | | X | X | | X |

NOTE: An X indicates that the index possesses the column attribute. $\hat{\Delta}$ = Bentler-Bonett normed fit index; $\hat{\rho}$ = Tucker-Lewis reliability coefficient; $\hat{\gamma}$ = Tanaka-Huba estimator of $\gamma$; $\hat{\gamma}_S$ = Tanaka-Huba shrunken estimator of $\gamma$; AIC = Akaike information criterion; PGFI = Mulaik et al. parsimonious goodness-of-fit index; IFI = Bollen incremental fit index; $m_k$ = McDonald-Marsh absolute index; CFI = Bentler comparative fit index.

measures have outperformed estimation method-free measures along this dimension (La Du & Tanaka, 1989), a strong recommendation can be made for estimation method-specific fit assessments. Similarly, the influence of sample size in statistical decision making (Cohen, 1988; Cudeck & Henly, 1991) would recommend that sample size-dependent rather than sample size-independent measures of fit should be employed. To gauge sample size influences, the bias-corrected version of $\hat{\gamma}$ can be used. It might be noted in passing that the last column of Table 2.2, describing sample size effects, is somewhat limited in definition, considering only those fit measures where sample size influences the mean of the sampling distribution of the fit statistics. It could be argued (as has been done by Cudeck & Henly, 1991) that any sample-data comparison will have some sample size effects associated with it, given the relation between sample size and the sampling variability of sample covariances. It may be interesting to explore interrelations among sample size, its impact on the variability of sample covariances, and the joint impact of these factors on model fit. An early attempt to explore this complex issue can be found in my own work (Tanaka, 1987).

For many reasons, investigators prefer simple methods for communicating the results of model fit. One method of communicating this simplicity is through the use of normed fit measures. Measures that are not normed in a simple metric such as the AIC are often expressed in such a metric to obtain this simplicity of communication. For example, a normed AIC measure might compare the AIC for a target model to a null model AIC.

I believe there is some diversity of opinion with respect to the final three dimensions. All fit indices must employ some standard of comparison to answer questions about the degree to which a target model's fit is improved. While it has been argued that the specification of mutually uncorrelated observed variables has become the consensus null model, this does not reflect the best accumulation of knowledge regarding modeled phenomena. As Lloyd Humphreys (1990) has pointed out, a null model of mutually uncorrelated variables may represent an unrealistic standard in the domain of human abilities, where models are evaluated relative to a simple one-factor model. I do not believe the null model specification issue to be a closed book, and would thus argue in favor of fit indices such as $\hat{\gamma}$ that use a more reasonable anchor point, the observed data.

Finally, if one can develop analogies between general linear models and structural equation modeling, choice of a fit index along simplicity/complexity and sample-based/population-based dimensions is straightforward. As in univariate general linear models, this should represent the investigator's choice of presenting $R^2$ or adjusted $R^2$ measures. While different disciplines have adopted varying opinions on this issue, I believe that it is typically the case that investigators are most interested in describing the sample at hand before making population generalizations. If this is true, it is clear that sample-based fit measures will be preferred. Of course, this would most certainly be the case when populations are not well specified or when samples are small and limited in their generalizability.

## Conclusions

Six dimensions have been identified along which structural equation model fit indices can be compared. As Marsh et al. (1988) have implied, variations on these dimensions (and others) can generate any number of alternative indices. But given the wide variety of indices already available to investigators, there would appear to be little to be gained from the development of additional indices of fit. The preceding results demonstrate how selection among the variety of fit indices that are available can be made on the basis of the different dimensions of emphasis an investigator is interested in optimizing. However, there is a more fundamental issue that is typically of interest to investigators who fit structural equation models to their data: the certainty one can have in terms of selecting a representative model for observed data.

As Cudeck and Henly (1991) have recently pointed out, this is a problem of statistical decision making. They correctly note that in any model selection process, the issue of deciding on an appropriate model is multidimensional and is guided by aspects of scientific judgment that are not necessarily directly translatable from any set of numbers. As structural equation modeling moves into its next generation (Tanaka, 1990), selection from among different models, all of which provide adequate levels of fit to a given data set, might recognize this complexity. As long as the "rules" that guided a particular investigator to select a given model representation for data are clearly stated, the replicability in model selection steps is assured, even if other investigators choose to use another set of "rules" or criteria in the model selection process.

The direct implication of this suggestion is that model evaluation cannot be mechanistically guided by any single number or set of numbers summarizing data-model congruence. The application of structural equation modeling, when guided from this perspective, will focus less on the absolute fit of any single model than on the demonstration of the process leading an investigator to choose the best model for representation of data. Of course, this is not radically different from the statistical underpinnings of structural equation modeling given by Jöreskog (1974), who suggested that the absolute fit of a model is less important than the comparative fit of multiple alternative models for data. This also represents satisfactory treatment of model fit as well; after all, it is not the case that any covariance structure model can be assumed to represent the definitive explanation of a phenomenon under investigation. Models represent "best guesses" that are subject to further verification or refutation.

Issues in the assessment of omnibus fit in structural equation modeling have occupied a central place in the scientific literature on these models. However, as is the case in the general linear model, ascertainment of omnibus fit, either in well-fitting or poorly fitting models, is not sufficient. Often, more interesting model diagnostics are relevant in determining less global aspects of misfit. Given the wide variety of omnibus fit assessments that specifically address the issue of global fit, it is worthwhile for the structural equation modeling literature to turn next to the question of how more locally directed model diagnostics might determine the components of fit.

## APPENDIX

This appendix presents formulas for the computation of the various fit indices that are discussed in this chapter. Formulas that have been presented in the text are not repeated here.

### Normed Fit Index (Bentler & Bonett, 1980)

Let $f_0$ be the value of a discrepancy function (e.g., ML, GLS) for some baseline model and $f$ be the value of the discrepancy function for some model of interest. Then, the normed fit index $\hat{\Delta}$ is defined as

$$\hat{\Delta} = \frac{f_0 - f_1}{f_0} .$$

Given the relation between the discrepancy function and the chi-square goodness-of-fit statistic, this formula is sometimes given as

$$\hat{\Delta} = \frac{T_0 - T_1}{T_0} ,$$

where $T_0$ is the value of the test statistic for the baseline model and $T_1$ is the value of the test statistic for the model of interest.

### Nonnormed Fit Index
### (Bentler & Bonett, 1980; Tucker & Lewis, 1973)

Introduced by Tucker and Lewis (1973) in the context of factor analysis models, the nonnormed fit index $\hat{\rho}$ was subsequently discussed in the context of structural equation models by Bentler and Bonett (1980). With $f_0$ and $f_1$ defined as above, the nonnormed fit index is given as

$$\hat{\rho} = \frac{(f_0/\mathrm{df}_0) - (f_1/\mathrm{df}_1)}{\left[ (f_0/\mathrm{df}_0) - \dfrac{1}{N-1} \right]} ,$$

where $df_0$ and $df_1$ are the degrees of freedom associated with $f_0$ and $f_1$, respectively.

## Incremental Fit Index (Bollen, 1989b, 1990)

Bollen (1989b, 1990) proposed a modification of the Bentler-Bonett $\Delta$ that was intended to decrease the dependence of $\hat{\Delta}$ on sample size while simultaneously controlling for the degrees of freedom available to evaluate the target model of interest. Referred to as $\Delta_2$ in Bollen (1989b, 1990), this incremental fit index (IFI) is given as

$$\text{IFI} = \frac{f_0 - f_1}{f_0 - \dfrac{df_1}{N-1}}.$$

## Akaike Information Criterion (Akaike, 1987)

Cudeck and Browne (1983; Browne & Cudeck, 1989) have advanced the use of fit measures based on the logic of the Akaike information criterion. Strictly applicable only for maximum likelihood estimation, the AIC is defined as

$$\text{AIC} = T_1 + 2r,$$

where, as in the text, $r$ refers to the number of free parameters in the model being evaluated and $T$ is the value of the test statistic for the model being evaluated.

## Comparative Fit Index (Bentler, 1990)

The comparative fit index, like the measure of centrality proposed by McDonald (1989; McDonald & Marsh, 1990), is based on the noncentrality parameter of the chi-square of the goodness-of-fit test statistic. To present a formula for the calculation of the CFI in an observed sample, it will be helpful to develop some notation. As before, let a baseline model have a test statistic $T_0$ with $df_0$ degrees of freedom. Let the model being evaluated have associated test statistic $T$, with df, degrees of freedom. Let $l_0 = T_0 - df_0$ and let $l_1 = T_1 - df_1$. Then the CFI can be computed in a sample as

$$\text{CFI} = 1 - \frac{l_i}{l_j},$$

where $l_i = \max(l_1, 0)$ and $l_j = \max(l_0, l_1, 0)$. This definition of CFI constrains observed values in the range (0, 1).

# References

Akaike, H. (1987). Factor analysis and AIC. *Psychometrika, 52,* 317-332.

Amemiya, Y., & Anderson, T. W. (1990). Asymptotic chi-square tests for a large class of factor analysis models. *Annals of Statistics, 18,* 1453-1463.

Bentler, P. M. (1982). Confirmatory factor analysis via noniterative estimation: A fast, inexpensive method. *Journal of Marketing Research, 19,* 417-424.

Bentler, P. M. (1983). Some contributions to efficient statistics in structural models: Specifications and estimation of moment structures. *Psychometrika, 48,* 493-517.

Bentler, P. M. (1990). Comparative fix indexes in structural models. *Psychological Bulletin, 107,* 238-246.

Bentler, P. M., & Bonett, D. G. (1980). Significance tests and goodness of fit in the analysis of covariance structures. *Psychological Bulletin, 88,* 588-606.

Bentler, P. M., & Bonett, D. G. (1987). This week's citation classic (comments on Bentler & Bonett, 1980). *Current Contents A & H, 9,* 16.

Bollen, K. A. (1989a). A new incremental fit index for general structural equation models. *Sociological Methods & Research, 17,* 303-316.

Bollen, K. A. (1989b). *Structural equations with latent variables.* New York: John Wiley.

Bollen, K. A. (1990). Overall fit in covariance structure models: Two types of sample size effects. *Psychological Bulletin, 107,* 256-259.

Browne, M. W. (1974). Generalised least squares estimators in the analysis of covariance structures. *South African Statistical Journal, 8,* 1-24.

Browne, M. W. (1975). Predictive validity of a linear regression equation. *British Journal of Mathematical and Statistical Psychology, 28,* 79-87.

Browne, M. W. (1982). Covariance structures. In D. M. Hawkins (Ed.), *Topics in applied multivariate analysis* (pp. 72-141). Cambridge: Cambridge University Press.

Browne, M. W., & Cudeck, R. (1989). Single sample cross-validation indices for covariance structures. *Multivariate Behavioral Research, 24,* 445-455.

Cohen, J. (1988). *Statistical power analysis for the behavioral sciences* (2nd ed.). Hillsdale, NJ: Lawrence Erlbaum.

Cohen, J., & Cohen, P. (1983). *Applied multiple regression/correlation analysis for the behavioral sciences* (2nd ed.). Hillsdale, NJ: Lawrence Erlbaum.

Cudeck, R., & Browne, M. W. (1983). Cross-validation of covariance structures. *Multivariate Behavioral Research, 18,* 147-167.

Cudeck, R., & Henly, S. J. (1991). Model selection in covariance structures analysis and the "problem" of sample size: A clarification. *Psychological Bulletin, 109,* 512-519.

Dijkstra, T. K. (1990). Some properties of estimated scale invariant covariance structures. *Psychometrika, 55,* 327-336.

Graybill, F. A. (1976). *Theory and application of the linear model.* North Scituate, MA: Duxbury.

Graybill, F. A. (1983). *Matrices with applications in statistics* (2nd ed.). Belmont, CA: Wadsworth.

Hägglund, G. (1982). Factor analysis by instrumental variables methods. *Psychometrika, 47,* 209-221.

Humphreys, L. G. (1990). View of a supportive empiricist. *Psychological Inquiry, 1,* 153-155.

38     Multifaceted Conceptions of Fit

Ihara, Y., Berkane, M., & Bentler, P. M. (1990). Covariance structure analysis with heterogeneous kurtosis parameters. *Biometrika, 77,* 575-585.

James, L. R., Mulaik, S. A., & Brett, J. M. (1982). *Causal analysis: Assumptions, models, and data.* Beverly Hills, CA: Sage.

Jöreskog, K. G. (1974). Analyzing psychological data by structural analysis of covariance matrices. In D. H. Krantz, R. C. Atkinson, R. D. Luce, & P. Suppes (Eds.), *Contemporary developments in mathematical psychology* (Vol. 2, pp. 1-56). San Francisco: Freeman.

Jöreskog, K. G., & Sörbom, D. (1981). *Analysis of linear structural relationships by maximum likelihood and least squares methods* (Research Report 81-8). Uppsala, Sweden: University of Uppsala.

Jöreskog, K. G., & Sörbom, D. (1988). *LISREL 7: A guide to the program and applications.* Chicago: SPSS.

Kroonenberg, P. M., & Lewis, C. (1982). Methodological issues in the search for a factor model: Exploration through confirmation. *Journal of Educational Statistics, 7,* 69-89.

La Du, T. J. (1986). *Assessing the goodness of fit of linear structural equation models: The influence of sample size, estimation method, and model specification.* Unpublished doctoral dissertation, New York University, Department of Psychology.

La Du, T. J., & Tanaka, J. S. (1989). The influence of sample size, estimation method, and model specification on goodness-of-fit assessments in structural equation models. *Journal of Applied Psychology, 74,* 625-636.

La Du, T. J., & Tanaka, J. S. (1992). *Incremental fit index changes for nested structural equation models.* Manuscript submitted for publication.

MacCallum, R. C. (1986). Specification searches in covariance structure models. *Psychological Bulletin, 100,* 107-120.

Maiti, S. S., & Mukherjee, B. N. (1990). A note on the distributional properties of the Jöreskog-Sörbom fit indices. *Psychometrika, 55,* 721-726.

Marsh, H. W., Balla, J. W., & McDonald, R. P. (1988). Goodness-of-fit indices in confirmatory factor analysis: Effects of sample size. *Psychological Bulletin, 103,* 391-411.

Matsueda, R. L., & Bielby, W. T. (1986). Statistical power in covariance structure models. In N. B. Tuma (Ed.), *Sociological methodology 1986* (pp. 120-158). San Francisco: Jossey-Bass.

McArdle, J. J. (1988). Dynamic and structural equation modeling with repeated measures data. In J. R. Nesselroade & R. B. Cattell (Eds.), *Handbook of multivariate experimental psychology* (Vol. 2, pp. 561-614). New York: Plenum.

McCullagh, P., & Nelder, J. A. (1984). *Generalized linear models.* London: Chapman & Hall.

McDonald, R. P. (1989). An index of goodness-of-fit based on noncentrality. *Journal of Classification, 6,* 97-103.

McDonald, R. P., & Marsh, H. W. (1990). Choosing a multivariate model: Noncentrality and goodness of fit. *Psychological Bulletin, 107,* 247-255.

Meehl, P. E. (1991). Why summaries of research on psychological theories are often uninterpretable. In R. E. Snow & D. E. Wiley (Eds.), *Improving inquiry in social science: A volume in honor of Lee J. Cronbach* (pp. 13-59). Hillsdale, NJ: Lawrence Erlbaum.

Mulaik, S. A. (1990). *An analysis of the conditions under which the estimation of parameters inflates goodness-of-fit indices as measures of model validity.* Paper presented at the annual meeting of the Psychometric Society, Princeton, NJ.

Mulaik, S. A., James, L. R., Van ·Alstine, J., Bennett, N., Lind, S., & Stillwell, C. D. (1989). An evaluation of goodness of fit indices for structural equation models. *Psychological Bulletin, 105,* 430-445.

Satorra, A., & Saris, W. E. (1985). The power of the likelihood ratio test in covariance structure analysis. *Psychometrika, 50,* 83-90.

Shapiro, A. (1985). Asymptotic equivalence of minimum discrepancy function estimators to G.L.S. estimators. *South African Statistical Journal, 19,* 73-81.

Sobel, M. E., & Bohrnstedt, G. W. (1985). Use of null models in evaluating the fit of covariance structure models. In N. B. Tuma (Ed.), *Sociological methodology 1985* (pp. 152-178). San Francisco: Jossey-Bass.

Steiger, J. H. (1989). *EzPATH: A supplementary module for SYSTAT and SYGRAPH.* Evanston, IL: SYSTAT.

Steiger, J. H., & Lind, J. M. (1980). *Statistically based tests for the number of common factors.* Paper presented at the annual meeting of the Psychometric Society, Iowa City, IA.

Steiger, J. H., Shapiro, A., & Browne, M. W. (1985). On the multivariate asymptotic distribution of sequential chi-square statistics. *Psychometrika, 50,* 253-263.

Tanaka, J. S. (1987). "How big is big enough?" Sample size and goodness of fit in structural equation models with latent variables. *Child Development, 58,* 134-146.

Tanaka, J. S. (1990). Towards a second generation of structural modeling. *Multivariate Behavioral Research, 25,* 187-191.

Tanaka, J. S., & Huba, G. J. (1985). A fit index for covariance structure models under arbitrary GLS estimation. *British Journal of Mathematical and Statistical Psychology, 38,* 197-201.

Tanaka, J. S., & Huba, G. J. (1989). A general coefficient of determination for covariance structure models under arbitrary GLS estimation. *British Journal of Mathematical and Statistical Psychology, 42,* 233-239.

Tanaka, J. S., Panter, A. T., Winborne, W. C., & Huba, G. J. (1990). Theory testing in personality and social psychology with structural equation models: A primer in twenty questions. In C. Hendrick & M. S. Clark (Eds.), *Review of personality and social psychology* (Vol. 11, pp. 217-242). Newbury Park, CA: Sage.

Tucker, L. R., & Lewis, C. (1973). A reliability coefficient for maximum likelihood factor analysis. *Psychometrika, 38,* 1-10.

*3*

# Monte Carlo Evaluations of Goodness-of-Fit Indices for Structural Equation Models

DAVID W. GERBING
JAMES C. ANDERSON

The empirical assessment of proposed models is a vital aspect of the theory development process, and central to this assessment are the values of goodness-of-fit indices obtained from the analysis of a specified model. In this chapter our primary goal is to provide the substantive researcher with guidance regarding the choice of indices to use in evaluating the fit of a structural equation model. A principal source of evaluation of the fit indices is Monte Carlo research, which investigates the distributional properties of statistics by repeated sampling from simulated distributions, usually with the underlying population model known a priori. However, the inherent limitations of Monte Carlo research necessitate a consideration of the definitional and conceptual properties of the indices as well. A related goal of this chapter, then, is to provide some guidelines and suggestions for future Monte Carlo research regarding the evaluation of these proposed fit indices.

In the next section, we briefly review the different types of fit indices that have been proposed and the general role of Monte Carlo research in their evaluation. The ways in which Monte Carlo studies of structural equation models differ from each other, and some of the compromises that each specific design entails, are presented next. We then discuss some of the contributions these studies have made regarding our understanding of fit indices, as well as some recent theoretical advances regarding our understanding of the nature of these indices. The chapter ends with some recommendations for specific fit indices and suggestions for future research.

## Types of Fit Indices

Initially, only the $p$ value associated with the likelihood ratio $\chi^2$ statistic was used to evaluate fit, under the null hypothesis that the population covariances are identical with those predicted from the model estimates. However, researchers soon realized that the interpretation of this $p$ value was confounded by sample size: In large samples, good-fitting models were rejected on the basis of trivial misspecification, and in small samples the test lacked power, as it was too forgiving of important misspecifications.[1] Researchers discovered that nearly all models they tested with reasonable sample sizes failed to fit the data according to the $p$ value of the $\chi^2$ statistic. Another problem with this statistic is that a test of statistical significance does not provide information regarding the *degree* of fit. Primarily for these reasons, researchers began to search for alternate fit indices during the early 1980s (Bentler & Bonett, 1980; Hoelter, 1983; James, Mulaik, & Brett, 1982; Jöreskog & Sörbom, 1981).

The problem is that this search has yielded many indices, none of which has been endorsed as the "best index" by the majority of researchers. As an illustration of the resulting proliferation of indices, the structural equation modeling program introduced in Version 6 of SAS (SAS Institute, 1989), PROC CALIS, prints the values of almost 20 such fit indices—a rather dramatic increase from the earlier process of using only the formal hypothesis test based on the $\chi^2$ associated $p$ value. To decide on the appropriateness of the model, the substantive researcher must now sort through and understand the meaning of the values for these various indices.

For many researchers, the ideal fit index would

(1) indicate degree of fit along a continuum bounded by values such as 0 and 1, where 0 reflects a complete lack of fit and 1 reflects perfect fit;

(2) be independent of sample size (higher or lower values would not be obtained simply because the sample size is large or small); and

(3) have known distributional characteristics to assist interpretation and allow the construction of a confidence interval.

Unfortunately, no one index has been shown to satisfy these conditions acceptably; further, not all researchers would even agree with all of these criteria. Cudeck and Henly (1991), for example, argue that the influence of sample size is not necessarily undesirable. So there may never be a single index that should always be used to the exclusion of the others. In Steiger's (1990) words, "There can never be a best coefficient for assessing fit . . . any more than there is a single best automobile" (p. 179). So—how to choose?

One way to categorize fit indices is in terms of the criteria they are defined to assess. Not surprisingly, different fit indices have been proposed to assess different criteria. Is the goal to account for the observed covariances? To maximize the fit of a cross-validated model? Should the number of overidentifying restrictions, the df, be considered with a penalty function that diminishes fit for fewer df? Should the measurement model be separated from the structural model?

Perhaps the most widely used criterion of fit is the degree to which the model accounts for the sample covariances. Two families of indices exist for assessing the discrepancy between predicted and observed covariances. One type of index directly assesses how well the covariances predicted from the parameter estimates reproduce the sample covariances. The widely used goodness-of-fit index (GFI) from the LISREL program (Jöreskog & Sörbom, 1981, 1989) is an example of such an index (Mulaik et al., 1989; Tanaka & Huba, 1985). Tanaka and Huba (1989) have shown how this family of indices represents variations of a general coefficient of determination, expressed within a multivariate framework.

A related set of indices assesses fit by the degree to which the model accounts for the sample covariances relative to a more restricted, nested model—usually the null model in which all indicators are specified as uncorrelated, as with Bentler and Bonett's (1980) normed fit index (NFI). The null model serves as a statistical baseline of comparison for the evaluation of fit, thus providing a basis for assessing the incremental fit of the substantive model of interest relative to the substantively uninteresting baseline model. From a philosophy of science perspective, structural equation models can be effectively conceptualized as a comparative technique in which a posited model is evaluated against rival theoretical alternatives (Anderson & Gerbing, 1988). So, even if one prefers stand-alone indices such as GFI, explicit comparisons of incremental fit indices from the substantive model of interest with those indices obtained from a null or other model should also be reported.

However, the fit indices for directly assessing how well a model accounts for the observed covariances, or those that assess the fit of the model relative to a null model, do not address the problem that high fit can be obtained simply because a very large number of parameters relative to df are estimated—regardless of the specifics of the proposed model. In the extreme case in which df = 0, these indices indicate perfect fit even though the causal processes summarized by the model may be false. Accordingly, some researchers have proposed modifying this type of index to reflect the available df (James et al., 1982; Mulaik et al., 1989) so that, in general, the fewer available df, the smaller the obtained value of the fit index. Also, these indices do not address the problem that occurs when a good-fitting measurement submodel covers up a poor-fitting structural submodel. The measurement submodel is usually associated with many more df than is the structural submodel, with the result that indices such as GFI and NFI applied to the entire model may be reasonably high even when the structural submodel is misspecified (see Mulaik et al., 1989).

Two types of corresponding incremental fit indices can be defined for most of the stand-alone indices (Marsh, Balla, & McDonald, 1988). The general form of the first class of these indices, called "Type 1 incremental indices" by Marsh et al. (1988), is

$$\frac{|I_0 - I_t|}{I_0},$$

where $I_t$ and $I_0$ represent the values of the stand-alone index for the target model and null models, respectively. For example, the Bentler-Bonett (1980) normed fit index is an incremental fit index that is defined in terms of the minimal values of the respective fit functions. To facilitate comparison with other fit indices described throughout this chapter, NFI can be equivalently expressed in terms of the $\chi^2$ values as

$$NFI = \frac{\chi_0^2 - \chi_t^2}{\chi_0^2},$$

where 0 refers to the null model and t refers to the target model.

A Type 1 index involves only the values of the corresponding stand-alone index for the target and null models. A Type 2 index has the same form in the numerator as does a Type 1 index, but its denominator is defined by

$$| I_0 - E(I_t) |,$$

where $E(I_t)$ is the expected value of the target model for the stand-alone index if the target model is true, and $I_0$ is the value of the stand-alone index for the null model. For example, the Tucker-Lewis (1973) index (TLI) is a Type 2 incremental fit index based on the stand-alone value of $\chi^2/df$. Because the expected value of $\chi_t^2$ is equal to the df of a correctly specified target model $(df_t)$, the expected value of $\chi_t^2/df_t$ is 1.0, so,

$$\mathrm{TLI} = \frac{\dfrac{\chi_0^2}{df_0} - \dfrac{\chi_t^2}{df_t}}{\dfrac{\chi_0^2}{df_0} - 1}.$$

Further, at least for the more useful Type 2 indices, such as TLI, each Type 2 index asymptotically equals the value of the Type 1 index that is defined with the same stand-alone index (Mulaik et al., 1989).

As mentioned previously, a problem with any fit index such as NFI, GFI, or TLI that indicates the degree to which the model accounts for the sample covariances is that improved fit can be obtained simply by freeing more parameters until $df = 0$ and "perfect fit" is obtained. Yet, the more parsimonious models are desired over their overfitted counterparts, as the goal is to explain as much as possible with as few parameters as possible. Accordingly, James et al. (1982) have proposed a new class of indices that assess a different criterion, adjusting for the gain of df in the specification of parsimonious models, that is, those models with a relatively large df. This adjustment of fit index $I_t$ is accomplished by

$$\frac{df_t}{df_0} I_t,$$

although $df_0$ may be defined differently depending on the specific index that is modified, sometimes including the diagonal elements of the observed covariance matrix as with GFI, and sometimes including only the off-diagonal elements as with NFI (Mulaik et al., 1989). The resulting modified index is called a *parsimony index*.

Monte Carlo analysis cannot help choose a criterion of fit, but it does provide a primary means for evaluating the efficacy of various fit indices to assess a given criterion. Unfortunately, the sampling distributions of most indices under perfect fit, as well as under varying degrees of model misspecification and violations of underlying assumptions, have not been derived mathematically. As summarized by Bentler (1990), "Essentially nothing is known about the theoretical sampling distribution of the various estimators" (p. 245). The mathematical derivation of these distributions is particularly difficult given the circumstances under which the fit indices are typically used: relatively small samples (yet the estimation theory is asymptotic), misspecification of the underlying model, and violations of assumptions such as multivariate normality.

The purpose of a Monte Carlo analysis is to generate a series of specific empirical sampling distributions for each index studied. Each sampling distribution shows the overall performance of the index under specified conditions, such as for the evaluation of any possible relation between the mean of an index over repeated samples and sample size. Sampling distributions also provide the norms for interpreting a given index value as indicating either acceptable or unacceptable fit. Without the guidance provided by the generation of specific sampling distributions, the substantive researcher is unable to judge whether the indexed value obtained for a proposed model indicates acceptable fit.

Ideally, Monte Carlo analysis would not be necessary, as the distributional characteristics of an index would be obtained through mathematical derivation, and, indeed, a formal derivation is always preferred to the relatively small number of empirically derived distributions that can be studied by the Monte Carlo method. As we see in the next section, the chief limitation of Monte Carlo research is that there are too many possibilities to be considered effectively in any one study, so the results necessarily represent a compromise. Another limitation is that statistics such as the mean and standard deviation computed from the empirically generated sampling distributions are themselves sample statistics that only approximate the actual population values, although if the number of replications is large the accuracy of this approximation should be sufficient. These limitations notwithstanding, in the absence of a general, mathematically derived distribution, Monte Carlo research provides the only means for obtaining information on the specific sampling distributions for specified models and selected sample sizes.

## Adequacy Versus Manageability of Design in Monte Carlo Analyses

The Monte Carlo researcher must address several issues before choosing a design to study the behavior of selected fit indices. These issues include the number and kind of models, properties of the data, potential misspecifications, the sample sizes used to compute each sample covariance matrix, and the precision of the resulting estimates in terms of the number of replications of each condition. Once the design is selected and a series of covariance matrices generated for each cell in the design, a structural equation program such as LISREL, EQS, or PROC CALIS computes the fit index for each generated sample covariance matrix for a correctly specified or deliberately misspecified model.

The result of this procedure is a set of fit indices organized by a traditional factorial design. An analytic method such as ANOVA or regression analysis should be used to compare the performance of indices systematically across the various levels of the design. An ANOVA provides tests of significance between the levels of the independent variables in the design such as the different levels of sample size, as well as the interactions of the levels of different independent variables. A regression analysis allows the estimation of the values of the fit indices for levels not included in the original design, particularly for those values that fall between levels explicitly included in the design. Because a relatively large number of replications for each cell, such as 100 or 200, is desired so that the sample statistics computed from the resulting sampling distributions closely approximate their population counterparts, a concern endemic to Monte Carlo work is the difference between *practical* and *statistical* significance. Indices that reflect the size of an effect should replace or at least complement traditional significance tests in these situations because the large sample sizes may lead to virtually all effects being statistically significant.

### Range of Models

Perhaps the most obvious decision facing the Monte Carlo researcher is the choice of representative models. Most substantive applications involve from two to about six factors, with about two to six indicators per factor. Accordingly, the models analyzed in most Monte Carlo studies span this range, although the details across models can vary dramatically. The factor loadings can vary from low to medium to high, and they can be the same for all factors or loadings, or their values can be mixed within the same model. The structural model can represent many different forms, or the structural relations can be unanalyzed, and instead represented as correlations between the factors, as in a confirmatory factor analysis model.

Some Monte Carlo studies of fit indices have considered only a few or several different models. Perhaps the most ambitious effort in terms of the number of models tested was by Anderson and Gerbing (1984), who employed 54 different confirmatory factor models and five levels of sample size varying from 50 to 300 in their factorial design. Together, these models represented a systematic variation of their salient characteristics.

Finally, we note that some researchers use one, or a few, "well-known" models from the substantive literature instead of specifying their models free of content. One model that has been used as a basis for several such Monte Carlo studies is the alienation and stability model (Wheaton, Muthén, Alwin, & Summers, 1977).

## True Versus False Models

The technique used exclusively in the early Monte Carlo studies by Bearden, Sharma, and Teel (1982), Boomsma (1983, 1985), and Anderson and Gerbing (1984) was to generate data with pseudorandom numbers according to the population covariance matrix that is implied by the correct specification of a model, and then use that specification to test against the generated sample data. These analyses demonstrate how well the indices indicate correct specification, but they do not show how sensitive the indices are to misspecification. Yet, at least as important as correctly indicating true fit is the ability of the index to distinguish between the lack of fit due to sampling variability and that due to misspecification. More recent Monte Carlo studies such as those by Marsh et al. (1988), La Du and Tanaka (1989), and Bentler (1990) have also included misspecified models.

## Normal Versus Nonnormal Data

The most common technique is to sample data from a multivariate normal distribution, but other types of data can also be analyzed. These nonnormal data can be used to evaluate the robustness of an estimation procedure such as maximum likelihood (ML) that assumes multivariate normality, or they can be used to evaluate procedures that do not make this assumption. Evaluating the fit indices with nonnormal data is important because probably more often than is realized, data are not collected with simple random sampling.

### Interval Versus Polychotomous Data

Some estimation procedures, such as ML, assume interval data and corresponding covariances. Other techniques assume only that the data are polychotomous and that the corresponding correlations are polyserial. The majority of studies have assumed interval data, but some recent work has explored the analysis of polychotomous data (Babakus, Ferguson, & Jöreskog, 1987).

### Proper Versus Improper Solutions

An improper solution is one with at least one indicator error variance less than an arbitrarily small positive number such as .005. Some Monte Carlo analyses include both proper and improper solutions. Other authors delete improper solutions from the analysis, usually then generating new data to retain equal replication sizes across the cells in the design. Another possibility is to constrain the solutions to be proper, since improper solutions that are attributable only to sampling error can be constrained without adversely affecting the performance of the fit indices (Gerbing & Anderson, 1987).

### Estimation Method

For structural equation models the traditional method of estimation has been ML, but several other possibilities exist. These alternate estimation procedures include generalized least squares (GLS), methods that assume an elliptical distribution, and asymptotically distribution-free estimation (ADF) (Browne, 1984). Work by Tanaka in particular has focused on the effect of estimation method on fit indices (La Du & Tanaka, 1989; Tanaka & Huba, 1985, 1989).

## Review of Monte Carlo Studies

The first Monte Carlo study of fit indices for structural equation models was reported by Boomsma (1982, 1983). However, the only fit statistic studied in these early studies was the $\chi^2$ test. For the 12 confirmatory factor analysis models studied, Boomsma showed that, especially for small samples of size 25 or 50, the $\chi^2$ value tended to be too large. This result means that the corresponding $p$ value would tend to be too small, so that the correct underlying model would be rejected more often than the error rate specified by the significance test. For example, for a two-factor model with four indicators per factor and loadings of .6, .6, .8, and .8 on each of the factors, 17% of the $\chi^2$ values were larger than the .05 critical value of $\chi^2 = 30.15$ for a sample size of only 25. This value dropped to 7% for a sample size of 50, and decreased to 6% for a sample size of 400. This result was of interest because it showed that the $\chi^2$ value tended to reject the null hypothesis of acceptable fit more than it should, even for models that were perfectly specified, a finding that only exacerbated the oversensitivity of this test for models with some, although perhaps minor, misspecification.

The first Monte Carlo study of a fit index other than $\chi^2$ was done by Bearden et al. (1982), who also studied the Bentler and Bonett (1980) NFI. Unfortunately, this study examined only two correctly specified models, although at nine samples sizes each, ranging from 25 to 10,000. The mean $\chi^2$ value was again too large for small sample sizes, but the new result was that NFI was also found to be too small for small sample sizes. For large samples, those of size 500 or larger, the mean NFI was .99 or above, as it should be. However, for the four-factor model the mean NFI varied from .80 to .95 for samples of size 25 to 100, considerably less than the predicted value of 1.0. For the substantive researcher working with a small sample size, this means that the indication of even perfect fit as indicated by NFI is less than its theoretical value of 1.00.

A comprehensive Monte Carlo study by Anderson and Gerbing (1984) generated empirical sampling distributions for the $\chi^2$ associated $p$ value, GFI and AGFI, and TLI under correctly specified models and multivariate normality. This study—the first to investigate GFI, AGFI, and TLI—systematically investigated the effect on these indices of three different numbers of indicators (2-4), three different levels of loadings (all .6, all .9, or mixed), three different numbers of factors (2-4), and two levels of factor correlations (.3 or .5). With 100 replications for each of the 270 cells in the design, 43,410 LISREL solutions were computed to obtain 27,000 proper and converged solutions, which served as the data for subsequent analyses.

Unlike previous researchers, Anderson and Gerbing (1984) analyzed the resulting sampling distributions within the context of a formal balanced factorial design. Given the large sample sizes, virtually all effects were statistically significant, so a criterion of practical significance was adopted in which at least 3% of the variance was accounted for by the effect. A primary finding of this study was that the distributions of

GFI and AGFI were also influenced by sample size, accounting for 28.3% and 41.7% of the variance of their respective distributions. As with NFI, the bias was downward; the overall respective means were .949 and .903. Mean values of GFI varied from .909 for $n = 50$ up to .983 for $n = 300$. As Anderson and Gerbing (1984) conclude, "Whereas GFI (and hence AGFI) is independent of sample size in that sample size is not an explicit part of the equation that defines GFI, the distribution of GFI values is strongly affected by sample size" (p. 172), a finding later illustrated in additional contexts by Bollen (1990).

Another interesting finding of this study is that TLI was not affected by sample size. In support of this finding, less than 3% of the variance of TLI was attributable to sample size, and the means for different levels of sample size were all approximately equal to 1.0, demonstrating no pattern of monotonic increase or decrease across the five levels. Of course, sample size had an enormous effect on the variability of the estimates of TLI (as well as the other fit indices) so that even with 11 outliers removed from the 27,000 computed values of TLI, the standard deviation of TLI for a sample of size 50 was 1.690, a value that decreased to .056 for a sample of size 300. TLI also had considerably larger standard errors than GFI and AGFI. For example, the mean standard deviation of GFI for $n = 75$ is .045, whereas the corresponding values for TLI were 2.579 computed over all 27,000 values and 1.026 with the 11 outliers removed. Although the value of TLI is not biased even in these small samples, unfortunately it is less precisely estimated than competing indices such as GFI.

Another pattern of results briefly noted by Anderson and Gerbing (1984), but not discussed or explained in that paper, was that the fit indices indicated less fit as the number of factors in the model, or the number of indicators per factor, increased. For example, the mean value of GFI varied from .939 to .805 as the respective number of indicators per factor increased from two to three to four. Or the mean and fifth percentile values of four indicators per factor models analyzed with a sample size of 50 were only .851 and .771, respectively—particularly low values given that the models were correctly specified. The reason for this dramatic decrease is probably related to the issue of parsimony. Models with few indicators per factor or a small number of factors have fewer df, leaving more "room to maneuver" the parameter estimates so as to minimize the fit function, which in turn is a function of the residuals. The more available df, the more difficult for the algorithm to minimize the discrepancy between the observed and predicted covariances, with the result that GFI (and AGFI) tended to decrease. The values of TLI, on the other hand, were relatively impervious to this effect.

Finally, regarding the Anderson and Gerbing (1984) study, we note that the values of the obtained mean fit indices indicate the potential existence of bias, but these means are not useful to the substantive researcher in terms of setting a minimum value of acceptable fit. To facilitate this decision making, Anderson and Gerbing included values not only of the means and standard deviations of the fit indices, but also of the corresponding fifth (or ninety-fifth) percentiles. The substantive researcher could know, for example, that for a sample of size 100 the mean GFI was .952, but the fifth percentile was .887. That is, even with a perfectly specified model, 5% of the obtained values were below .887, which would be a value the researcher could use to judge the acceptability of his or her model, given approximately equal sample sizes and other similar model characteristics.

Although comprehensive, Anderson and Gerbing's (1984) study did not address misspecifications, nor did they include NFI in their analyses. Marsh et al. (1988) undertook work on these issues in a Monte Carlo study of fit indices that analyzed four models with 10 replications per cell. Three of these four models also were misspecified to different degrees, so that the ability of the indices to detect misfit could be studied. Marsh et al. also introduced a variety of new fit indices into the literature; indeed, they introduced algorithms for defining new Type 1 and Type 2 incremental fit indices. These researchers analyzed the distributions of 29 different indices, including traditional indices such as GFI, NFI, and TLI as well as many of the new indices introduced in their paper.

Although generalization of Marsh et al.'s results is limited to some extent by having only 10 replications per cell, a primary finding was that the mean values of all of the stand-alone and Type 1 indices were related to sample size, and this effect becomes more pronounced for smaller sample sizes. This conclusion replicates the previous findings of Bearden et al. (1982) regarding NFI and Anderson and Gerbing (1984) regarding GFI. Further, Marsh et al. demonstrated the generality of this sample size effect to entire classes of fit indices. Thus from this research it appears that the development of fit indices based on a different set of considerations than those of the stand-alone Type 1 indices is desired.

Another finding by Marsh et al. (1988) regarding the Type 1 indices is related to the desire of many researchers to define minimally acceptable values of a fit index, such as .90, that are intended to apply to all models and situations. Using the same three-factor model applied to the four data sets, Marsh et al. compared the models misspecified to varying degrees with the correctly specified model. Of course, for the misspecified models the reason for lack of fit in terms of nonzero residuals is caused by misspecification and sampling error, whereas for the correctly specified model only sampling error leads to nonzero residuals. A desirable—although not mathematically necessary—property of a fit index is that it attain a higher value if only sampling error prevents perfect fit in one data set and sampling error and misspecification of the same model contribute to nonzero residuals in another data set. Indeed, the fit index should have a mean value of 1.00 in the presence of sampling error if there is no misspecification. Some of the Type 2 indices, such as TLI, do indeed exhibit these properties. For example, at a sample size of 100, the mean value of TLI for the perfectly specified model is .99, a value that decreases to .96 and .87 for increasingly misspecified models analyzed on different data from the perfectly specified model.

The Type 1 indices, however, exhibit a different pattern. For example, at sample size 100, the mean NFI value for the perfectly specified model was .83, but the mean NFI values for two misspecified models on other data sets were .93 and .89. Thus Marsh et al. (1988) conclude that these fit indices "may not be comparable across data sets" (p. 406). The reason for this is that for the data generated by a correctly specified model, the null model produces a bad fit, as expected. However, for a misspecified model on a different data set the null model can produce a considerably worse fit. The incremental fit of the misspecified model over the extremely poor-fitting null model can actually be better than the incremental fit of a correctly specified model over its corresponding null model. That is, "the problem with the Type 1 incremental indexes is that they are substantially influenced by the badness of fit of the null model, as well as the goodness of fit of the target model" (Marsh et al., 1988, p. 399). This lack of comparability mitigates the interpretability of the size of the index in regard to a judgment of the acceptability of fit.

Replicating Anderson and Gerbing (1984), Marsh et al. (1988) also found a lack of relationship to sample size for TLI across all models and sample sizes. Further, Marsh et al. found four other Type 2 indices, each of which is also based on the $\chi^2$ statistic, to be independent of sample size. Moreover, because the mean values of these five indices for the perfectly specified model were close to 1.00, these values tended to be higher for the correctly specified models than for the misspecified models. So, unlike the Type 1 indices, the values of these five Type 2 indices were comparable across data sets.

Bollen (1989) notes the unwelcome relation of the widely used NFI with sample size and, building upon previous work (Bollen, 1986), defines a new incremental fit index called DELTA2 that is designed to correct this problem. Bollen defines DELTA2 as

$$DELTA2 = \frac{\chi_0^2 - \chi_t^2}{\chi_0^2 - df_t},$$

where, as before, $\chi_0^2$ and $\chi_t^2$ represent the computed values of the test statistics for the null and target models, respectively.

The rationale underlying DELTA2 is that if the model is correctly specified, then the denominator of DELTA2 is the expected value of its numerator. The reason for this is that, given a correct model, and multivariate normality for maximum likelihood estimation, the obtained $\chi_t^2$ is in fact distributed as $\chi^2$, which means that its expected value is $df_t$. The expected value of $\chi_0^2$ can only be given as its mean, and the best single estimate of this mean is the obtained $\chi_0^2$. In essence, the denominator of DELTA2 provides a baseline by which to evaluate the numerator, the difference in the $\chi^2$ values of the null and target models. One resultant advantage of this modification of NFI is that this rationale provides a basis for obtaining a mean value of 1.00 across repeated sampling of a correctly specified model. A second advantage is that for given values of $\chi_0^2$ and $\chi_t^2$, an adjustment for the available df is provided in that a model with fewer parameters to estimate will provide a higher DELTA2 value than a model with more parameters to estimate.

To provide empirical support for DELTA2, Bollen (1989) conducted a small Monte Carlo analysis of DELTA2, NFI, TLI, and a previously proposed index (Bollen, 1986). On the basis of the evaluation of a single correctly specified model at three sample sizes, 75, 150, and 300, Bollen (1989) obtained mean values of DELTA2 of 1.008, 1.005, and 1.001. These results were free of the bias exhibited by NFI, and the standard errors of DELTA2 were considerably less than those of the similarly unbiased TLI. Accordingly, on this evidence DELTA2 appears to represent an improvement over both NFI and TLI.

For completeness, before discussing more recent developments regarding the development of fit indices, we examine three additional Monte Carlo studies. In the first study, Babakus et al. (1987) assessed the sensitivity of maximum likelihood confirmatory factor analysis to violations of measurement scale and distribution assumptions. The $\chi^2$

associated $p$ value, GFI, AGFI, and the root mean squared residual (RMR) indices were analyzed. Of interest here, a single-factor model with four indicators was investigated under two levels of sample size (100 and 500) and five levels of categorization, where random samples of continuous data were transformed into five-point scales that had one of the following sample distributions: a normal frequency distribution, a U-shaped frequency distribution, or three frequency distributions of varying skewness. Babakus et al. found that for the nonnormal categorizations, there was an upward bias in the $\chi^2$ values, leading to more frequent rejection of the null hypothesis than would be expected. The effects of sample size were mixed, depending on the particular nonnormal categorization. Nonnormal categorization had a slight effect on GFI and AGFI values, although the decreases were not of practical significance; in contrast, RMR values were noticeably greater under nonnormal categorizations. Finally, considering the results for the goodness-of-fit indices, the Pearson product-moment correlation performed better than the polychoric correlation, which has been recommended for multivariate analysis of ordinal data (Jöreskog & Sörbom, 1989) (although the polychoric correlation performed better in terms of parameter estimates and standard errors).

La Du and Tanaka (1989) conducted a Monte Carlo study that examined the behavior of GFI and NFI under two types of estimation methods: ML and GLS. They also analyzed simulated multivariate data under a known population model, as well as samples drawn from a data base of self-report and behavioral data that was known to be not multivariate normal, and for which the correct model was only approximately known. In addition, La Du and Tanaka also studied misspecifications of the correct model. One result was that the sample size effect was demonstrated for samples as small as 35 in size, although this effect was moderated for NFI computed with the GLS fit function. The respective marginal means (collapsing across correctly and incorrectly specified models) for GFI and NFI from the ML solutions of the simulated data dropped from .989 and .969 for a sample size of 300 to .922 and .809 for a sample size of 35. However, NFI computed with the GLS fit function for both the simulated and data-base data was only slightly influenced by sample size, decreasing to respective mean values as relatively high as .915 and .944 for a sample size of 35.

In terms of estimation procedures, La Du and Tanaka (1989) found that the obtained value of a fit index is dependent on the estimation method. For example, they compared the usual Jöreskog and Sörbom

(1981) GFI appropriate for ML estimation, $GFI_{ML}$, with a version of GFI developed specifically for GLS estimation, $GFI_{GLS}$ (Tanaka & Huba, 1985). The marginal mean from the simulated data for $GFI_{ML}$ was .032 larger when applied to ML estimation as opposed to GLS estimation, whereas $GFI_{GLS}$ was .034 larger when applied to GLS estimation as opposed to ML. However, this estimation procedure was moderated by an interaction with sample size; the discrepancy between estimation-appropriate and estimation-inappropriate fit values decreased as sample size increased. This result is not unexpected, given that ML and GLS are asymptotically equivalent assuming multivariate normality.

In terms of misspecification, the fit indices generally behaved as desired. A trivial misspecification of a model, such as adding a path where there is none in the correct model, had little influence on the fit indices. A more substantive misspecification, such as deleting an important path, led to a substantial decrement in the values of the fit indices. The exception to this pattern was the GLS version of NFI, which was relatively insensitive to this more substantive misspecification. La Du and Tanaka (1989) conclude that the general bias of the fit indices in small samples and the effects of a specific estimation procedure imply that both sample size and estimation procedure should be considered when one is trying to compare fit indices across different studies.

Building upon the idea of examining fit indices for different estimation methods, Maiti and Mukherjee (1991) proposed a fit index called the index of structural closeness (ISC), which is defined as the ratio of a function of the residuals and observed covariances computed with ML and GLS, respectively. Maiti and Mukherjee evaluated the performance of ISC in a Monte Carlo study along with $GFI_{ML}$ and $GFI_{GLS}$ for both correctly specified and misspecified models. This study included the smallest sample size for any Monte Carlo study of fit indices, 20. The generalization of results may be somewhat limited, however, because the researchers studied a model of intraclass structure instead of the usual multiple-indicator measurement models found in most substantive applications and Monte Carlo studies of structural equation models.

One finding of this study is that the sample size effect was demonstrated further at this unrealistically low sample size of 20, with the corresponding mean respective values of $GFI_{ML}$ and $GFI_{GLS}$ for a correctly specified model at .70 and .59. These values increase to .96 for both indices at a sample size of 200. Unfortunately, the proposed ISC demonstrated this effect even more severely, varying from a mean value of .34 to .92 for correctly specified models at sample sizes of 20 and 200, respectively. Maiti and Mukherjee (1991) also found that $GFI_{GLS}$ was the least sensitive to model misspecification, particularly for small sample sizes. For example, for the most severely misspecified model at a sample size of 40, $GFI_{ML} = .15$, ISC $= .06$, and $GFI_{GLS} = .70$.

### Recent Developments: Indices Based on Noncentrality

As we have seen, one of the primary findings of the Monte Carlo studies of fit indices during the 1980s was that the values of many of the widely used indices, such as Jöreskog and Sörbom's (1981) GFI and Bentler and Bonett's (1980) NFI, depended on sample size. The obtained values of these indices were noticeably biased downward in the relatively small sample sizes characteristic of much substantive research. Other indices, such as TLI and DELTA2, were impervious to sample size, although the standard errors of TLI tended to be larger than other fit indices such as GFI (Anderson & Gerbing, 1984; Marsh et al., 1988) and DELTA2 and NFI (Bollen, 1989).

Based upon the initial work of Steiger and Lind (1980), a recent advance in our theoretical understanding of the fit indices explains this relation of obtained value to sample size. The key insight—applied by McDonald (1989), McDonald and Marsh (1990), and Bentler (1990)— is the use of the noncentrality parameter $\delta$ from the noncentral $\chi^2$ distribution. This parameter not only provides a theoretical basis for many widely used indices, it also contributes to the development of a promising new class of indices.

The equations for most proposed fit indices can be expressed in terms of the noncentrality parameter by taking expected values of the sample-based formulas so as to derive their population versions. Understanding what is being estimated in the population by a statistical fit index is itself a theoretical advance. The interesting result shown by Bentler (1990) and McDonald and Marsh (1990) is that the population versions of most of the widely used indices can be expressed solely or primarily as a function of $\delta$, df, and sometimes sample size, represented as $n$. For example, the population version of TLI can be written as

$$\text{population TLI} = \frac{\dfrac{\delta_0}{df_0} - \dfrac{\delta_t}{df_t}}{\dfrac{\delta_0}{df_0}}.$$

In particular, the population version of TLI is not expressed as a function of sample size. Unlike TLI, the population versions of NFI are functions of sample size (Bentler, 1990; McDonald & Marsh, 1990), as is also true of GFI (Maiti & Mukherjee, 1990; McDonald & Marsh, 1990). For example, the population version of NFI can be written as

$$\text{population NFI} = \frac{(\delta_0 - \delta_t) + \dfrac{df_0 - df_t}{n}}{\delta_0 + \dfrac{df_0}{n}}.$$

This result explains the robustness of TLI to sample size, as well as the sensitivity of the Type 1 indices to sample size—the corresponding population value of indices such as NFI and GFI are a different value for each different sample size.

Extending this logic further, McDonald (1989) and Bentler (1990) note that $\delta$ can be defined as a stand-alone index in its own right, where small values indicate good fit. To do so, $d$, a sample estimate of $\delta$, is needed. According to an asymptotic result from Wald (1943), it follows that

$$d = \frac{\chi^2 - df}{n},$$

so $d$ can be readily computed from the output of any structural equation modeling solution that provides a likelihood ratio test statistic.[2] Noting that small values of $d$ indicate good fit, McDonald (1989) defines the following index of centrality:

$$\text{centrality index} = \exp(-\tfrac{1}{2}d),$$

which is bounded by 0 and 1, where 1 indicates perfect fit.

Incremental fit indices based on $\delta$ alone can be defined, following the same logic used to define other incremental fit indices in which the fit of the target model is compared with the fit of the null model. That is, this index shows the reduction in noncentrality of the target model relative to the null model. Under the mild assumption that the sample sizes are equal for the target and null models, the corresponding relative fit index is called the relative noncentrality index (RNI) by McDonald and Marsh (1990, p. 250) and the fit index (FI) by Bentler (1990, p. 241):

$$\text{RNI} = \text{FI} = \frac{d_0 - d_t}{d_0} = 1 - \frac{d_t}{d_0}.$$

Because of the more descriptive nature of the term, we will refer to this index as RNI. For comparability with the expression of the fit indices previously defined in this chapter, RNI can also be expressed in terms of $\chi^2$ and df. In this form,

$$\text{RNI} = \frac{(\chi_0^2 - \text{df}_0) - (\chi_t^2 - \text{df}_t)}{\chi_0^2 - \text{df}_0}.$$

Moreover, if a structural equation computer program does not calculate RNI directly, this is the equation that would be used for its calculation.

Similar to TLI, RNI incorporates $d$ in the defining equation of its population counterpart. Both TLI and RNI also provide unbiased estimates of their corresponding population counterparts, so their mean values over repeated sampling should not be influenced by sample size. However, as noted by McDonald and Marsh (1990), the population form of TLI contains the James et al. (1982) parsimony ratio $\text{df}_t / \text{df}_0$. Bentler (1990) points out that because of the incorporation of this ratio in TLI, RNI is a better estimator of TLI when judged solely by its statistical properties. First, although neither RNI nor TLI is necessarily bounded by 0 and 1, RNI will be negative less often than TLI, and it will also be larger than 1.0 less often, and when it is, RNI will exceed 1.0 by a smaller value. Second, the standard error of RNI is less than the standard error of TLI, yielding a more precise measure of fit. Unless the substantive researcher explicitly wishes to have the parsimony ratio embedded within the fit index, RNI is generally preferred over TLI.

Also, Bentler (1990) shows that asymptotically both NFI and DELTA2 converge to the same population value underlying RNI. That is, both NFI and DELTA2 asymptotically index the reduction in noncentrality of the target model relative to the null model. Thus both indices are also representative of this new type of fit index based on noncentrality, although, as previously discussed, DELTA2 is free of the sample size bias exhibited by NFI.

Although RNI is normed in the population in that its values are bounded by 0 and 1, particularly in small samples its values can range beyond 0 and 1 (Bentler, 1990). Asymptotically, $\text{df}_t = E(\chi_t^2)$, but consider a model that is "overfitted" in the sense that $\text{df}_t > \chi_t^2$. Then $d_t < 0$, so as long as the null model indicates relatively poorer fit such that $df_0$ > $\chi_0^2$, RNI > 1. Given that the population value of RNI is normed, obtaining a sample value of RNI > 1 simply indicates excellent fit, and the researcher would know that this obtained value larger than 1.0 is due to sampling error, and that the true underlying value is 1.0 or a value close to 1.0. This obtained sample value of RNI > 1 is no more anomalous than the situation in which a model is misspecified and the population value of RNI for that model is accordingly reduced to a value such as .75. In this case the obtained sample values of RNI would freely range on either side of .75, just as the obtained sample values of RNI freely range on either side of 1.00 under repeated sampling for a perfectly specified model in the presence of sampling error.

However, for intended interpretational ease rather than necessity, some researchers might prefer that the sample index also be normed. Accordingly, Bentler (1990, p. 241) defines the comparative fit index (CFI) as

$$CFI = 1 - \frac{\tilde{d}_t}{\tilde{d}_0},$$

where $\tilde{d}_t = \max(d_t, 0)$ and $\tilde{d}_0 = \max(d_0, d_t, 0)$. Thus, by definition, both $\tilde{d}_t$ and $\tilde{d}_0$ are nonnegative. Because of this, and because $\tilde{d}_0 \geq \tilde{d}_t$, CFI must lie between 0 and 1 inclusive. Also, note that whenever the value of RNI is between 0 and 1 inclusive, then CFI = RNI. However, when RNI < 0, then CFI > RNI, and similarly, when RNI > 1, then CFI < RNI. So the sole purpose of CFI is to truncate the distribution of RNI such that values of RNI smaller than 0 or larger than 1 are brought into the 0-1 range, inclusive. The result of this transformation is that the standard error of CFI will be less than that of RNI for some models and sample sizes, but that for relatively good-fitting models, in which RNI > 0 for any reasonable sample size, CFI will provide some downward bias in the estimate of the corresponding population value of RNI. Moreover, because this bias will increase as sample size decreases, CFI will exhibit a slight relation to sample size.

Bentler (1990) conducted a small Monte Carlo study based on a perfectly specified model as well as a misspecified version of this model so as to provide a preliminary evaluation of RNI and CFI, as well as to compare their performance with TLI and Bollen's (1989) incremental fit index DELTA2 (which Bentler refers to as IFI). Bentler included sample sizes of 50, 100, 200, 400, 800, and 1,600, and computed 200 replications per model-sample size combination so as to obtain relatively precise estimates of the corresponding population means and standard deviations. With sample sizes of 400 or larger for the correctly specified model, the obtained mean values of RNI and DELTA2 were equal to 1.000, and were within ±.001 of 1.000 for sample sizes down to 50. The mean values of CFI, however, varied from .980 from a sample size of 50 to .999 to a sample size of 1,600, indicating that the downward bias of CFI is present at all levels of sample size studied, but that it is not severe.

In terms of variability for the correctly specified model, DELTA2 and RNI had the same standard error for samples of size 200 and larger, but DELTA2 was slightly less variable for the smaller sample sizes: .045 compared with .053 for $n = 50$, and .025 compared with .027 for $n = 100$. Because of the forced norming, CFI has the smallest sampling variability, although the largest values of RNI and DELTA2 observed for samples of 100 or larger were only 1.053 and 1.048, respectively. And the larger variance of TLI shown for the general case by Bentler (1990) is of practical consequence. By contrast, for all sample sizes, the standard error of TLI was at least twice as large as the standard errors for RNI, DELTA2, and CFI.

For the misspecified model (Bentler, 1990), RNI, DELTA2, and CFI all indicate approximately the same reduction of their respective values from 1.00, a reduction of approximately .05. For the smaller sample sizes, RNI and DELTA2 yield values slightly larger than .950; for example, at $n = 100$, mean RNI = .952 and mean DELTA2 = .955, whereas mean CFI = .950. And again, for the smaller sample sizes, DELTA2 has slightly less variability than RNI, and CFI has the lowest sampling variability and TLI the largest variability of all four of these indices.

### Recommendations and Suggestions for Future Research

By itself, Monte Carlo research of arbitrarily developed fit indices will not provide the "ideal" index, or a set of complementary indices. As follows from the theoretical developments of McDonald and Marsh (1990) and Bentler (1990), some indices provide inherently more information regarding fit than others, even if the corresponding sampling distributions are unknown. Although Monte Carlo analysis can give some indications of usefulness, the inherent properties of an index also dictate usefulness. The meaning of indices developed without theoretical underpinnings cannot be fully developed with Monte Carlo techniques because not all possible combinations of types of models, sample sizes, and misspecifications can be empirically explored.

The theoretical developments of the new indices based on noncentrality and the limitations of Monte Carlo research notwithstanding, comprehensive Monte Carlo research continues to serve as the primary vehicle for providing the normative interpretations of the fit indices. Although recent theoretical developments enhance our understanding of the meaning of the indices and have led to the development of potentially more useful indices that avoid downward bias, a primary problem now is to establish the behavior under misspecification of the recently developed indices. Are some of these indices more sensitive to misspecification than others? Are some not sufficiently sensitive, so that the "reverse" problem of downward bias occurs, with the values of the indices too close to 1.00 even in the presence of misspecification? Without such normative information, interpreting the size of the value of a fit index as indicating reasonable fit for specific types of models cannot be accomplished.

However, Monte Carlo study of misspecified models is not as straightforward as with correctly specified models because of the difficulty in characterizing the degree of misspecification. What constitutes a severe misspecification? Structural models are commonly misspecified when "true" paths are omitted or "false" paths are included. Yet the severity of each of these structural misspecifications depends on the pattern of specified paths in the structural model as a whole, not simply on these misspecified paths. That is, the severity of misspecification will depend on both the presence or disruption of direct and indirect paths relating the factors to one another (Heise, 1975). Further, although past research has focused on misspecification of structural paths, fundamentally, misspecification can occur in either or both the structural and measurement submodels. A common measurement model misspecification is the assignment of one or more measures to the factors other than their true factors. The severity of this misspecification would depend not only on the correlation of a measure with its "true" factor and the correlation of the "true" factor with the factor to which the measure was falsely assigned, but rather on the entire set of parameters and their values for the true measurement model. Even from this brief discussion it is apparent that it will be a challenging task for Monte Carlo researchers to devise a characterization that adequately captures the complexity of misspecification.

A further difficulty in the Monte Carlo study of misspecification is the absence of a priori expected values for the fit indices that can serve as baselines from which to study the effects of sampling error, misspecification, and their potential interaction. Thus, for example, the expected value of RNI for a correctly specified model is 1.0; unfortunately, there is no corresponding value for any misspecified model. So, to provide some baseline for understanding the effects of misspecification, each sample of generated data would be need to be fit to the correctly specified model, as well as each misspecification of that model that is studied. With this procedure, a researcher would obtain an estimate of the decrement of the fit index value owing to misspecification above and beyond that caused by sampling error. The practice of analyzing misspecified models and correctly specified models on different data sets confounds sampling error with misspecification error.

Another limitation of most Monte Carlo studies that have been conducted regarding goodness of fit is their lack of scope in terms of the number of models considered. The results of small Monte Carlo studies that consider only a few models and sample sizes are only suggestive. What is needed is analysis of a wide range of models that are studied under a variety of systematic degrees of misspecification so that reasonable minimum values that indicate acceptable fit under different circumstances can be established. Modern computer technology makes possible much more systematic and comprehensive studies than have typically been conducted. General system control languages such as IBM's REXX and Digital's DCL for VAXes eliminate the tedious and time-consuming repetition that can accompany the generation of thousands of samples, so that Monte Carlo researchers should include tens of models under various levels of misspecification in each study. Moreover, these models chosen for analysis should be based on a formal classification of published substantive research. Defining the models studied by Monte Carlo methods according to the characteristics of published models would result in greater generality of results for substantive researchers, as well as contribute to the comparability of knowledge accumulated across multiple studies. Although Monte Carlo research will never supplant theoretical derivations of sampling distributions, large-scale systematic research programs that incorporate contemporary advances in hardware and system software would be better able to provide useful interpretative guidelines for the substantive researcher.

In the end, the focus of the entire enterprise should be to give the substantive researcher this type of guidance regarding acceptable fit of the model, relying primarily on theoretical developments that are augmented with Monte Carlo evidence. The traditional $\chi^2$ and associated $p$ value will continue to be relied upon and reported. The values of the standardized residuals (the number of values greater than two in magnitude, and the magnitude of the largest values) will continue to assist in locating misspecification, and provide an informal index of fit. Other techniques for identifying misspecification, such as the Hausman test (Arminger & Schoenberg, 1989) for assessing whether or not the disturbance terms in the structural equations are independent of the explanatory variables, may also begin to be used by substantive researchers.

In terms of the overall assessment of fit, at the present time the recommended stand-alone index is the McDonald (1989) noncentrality index. The recommended incremental fit indices are the Bentler (1990) and McDonald and Marsh (1990) RNI (or the bounded counterpart CFI) and Bollen's (1989) DELTA2. These indices show promise as the best candidates yet for satisfying the criterion of a suitable fit index, although more complete understanding of their properties and suitability awaits further research.

## Notes

1. In addition, the distribution of the test statistic for maximum likelihood estimation depends on the assumption of multivariate normality. More recently developed estimation procedures such as elliptical estimators (Bentler, 1983) and asymptotically distribution-free estimators (Browne, 1984) do not require this assumption.

2. McDonald and Marsh (1990) work with a rescaled noncentrality parameter that is divided by $n$, from which the previous equation is derived. Bentler (1990) works with the original parameter.

## References

Anderson, J. C., & Gerbing, D. W. (1984). The effect of sampling error on convergence, improper solutions, and goodness-of-fit indices for maximum likelihood confirmatory factor analysis. *Psychometrika, 49,* 155-173.

Anderson, J. C., & Gerbing, D. W. (1988). Structural equation modeling in practice: A review and recommended two-step approach. *Psychological Bulletin, 103,* 411-423.

Arminger, G., & Schoenberg, R. J. (1989). Pseudo maximum likelihood estimation and a test for misspecification in mean and covariance structure models. *Psychometrika, 54,* 409-425.

Babakus, E., Ferguson, C. E., Jr., & Jöreskog, K. (1987). The sensitivity of confirmatory maximum likelihood factor analysis to violations of measurement scale and distributional assumptions. *Journal of Marketing Research, 24,* 222-228.

Bearden, W. O., Sharma, S., & Teel, J. R. (1982). Sample size effects on chi-square and other statistics used in evaluating causal models. *Journal of Marketing Research, 19,* 425-530.

Bentler, P. M. (1983). Some contributions to efficient statistics in structural models: Specification and estimation of moment structures. *Psychometrika, 48,* 493-517.

Bentler, P. M. (1990). Comparative fit indexes in structural models. *Psychological Bulletin, 107,* 238-246.

Bentler, P. M., & Bonett, D. G. (1980). Significance tests and goodness of fit in the analysis of covariance structures. *Psychological Bulletin, 88,* 588-606.

Bollen, K. A. (1986). Sample size and Bentler and Bonett's nonnormed fit index. *Psychometrika, 51,* 375-377.

Bollen, K. A. (1989). A new incremental fit index for general structural equation models. *Sociological Methods & Research, 17,* 303-316.

Bollen, K. A. (1990). Overall fit in covariance structure models: Two types of sample size effects. *Psychological Bulletin, 107,* 256-259.

Boomsma, A. (1982). The robustness of LISREL against small sample sizes in factor analysis models. In K. G. Jöreskog & H. Wold (Eds.), *Systems under indirect observation: Causality, structure, prediction (Part I).* Amsterdam: North-Holland.

Boomsma, A. (1983). *On the robustness of LISREL (maximum likelihood estimation) against small sample size and non-normality.* Unpublished doctoral dissertation, University of Groningen, Groningen, The Netherlands.

Boomsma, A. (1985). Nonconvergence, improper solutions, and starting values in LISREL maximum likelihood estimation. *Psychometrika, 50,* 229-242.

Browne, M. W. (1984). Asymptotically distribution-free methods in the analysis of covariance structures. *British Journal of Mathematical and Statistical Psychology, 37,* 62-83.

Cudeck, R., & Henly, S. J. (1991). Model selection in covariance structure analysis and the "problem" of sample size: A clarification. *Psychological Bulletin, 109,* 512-519.

Gerbing, D. W., & Anderson, J. C. (1987). Improper solutions in the analysis of covariance structures: Their interpretability and a comparison of alternative specifications. *Psychometrika, 52,* 99-111.

Heise, D. R. (1975). *Causal analysis.* New York: John Wiley.

Hoelter, J. (1983). The analysis of covariance structures: Goodness-of-fit indices. *Sociological Methods & Research, 11,* 325-344.

James, L. R., Mulaik, S. A., & Brett, J. M. (1982). *Causal analysis: Models, assumptions, and data.* Beverly Hills, CA: Sage.

Jöreskog, K. G., & Sörbom, D. (1981). *LISREL V: Analysis of linear structural relationships by the method of maximum likelihood.* Chicago: National Educational Resources.

Jöreskog, K. G., & Sörbom, D. (1989). *SPSS LISREL VII and PRELIS user's guide and reference.* Chicago: SPSS.

La Du, T. J., & Tanaka, J. S. (1989). The influence of sample size, estimation method, and model specification on goodness-of-fit assessment in structural equation models. *Journal of Applied Psychology, 74,* 625-635.

Maiti, S. S., & Mukherjee, B. N. (1990). A note on distributional properties of the Jöreskog-Sörbom fit indices. *Psychometrika, 55,* 721-726.

Maiti, S. S., & Mukherjee, B. N. (1991). Two new goodness-of-fit indices for covariance matrices with linear structures. *British Journal of Mathematical and Statistical Psychology, 44,* 153-180.

Marsh, H. W., Balla, J. R., & McDonald, R. P. (1988). Goodness-of-fit indexes in confirmatory factor analysis: The effect of sample size. *Psychological Bulletin, 103,* 391-410.

McDonald, R. P. (1989). An index of goodness-of-fit based on noncentrality. *Journal of Classification, 6,* 97-103.

McDonald, R. P., & Marsh, H. W. (1990). Choosing a multivariate model: Noncentrality and goodness of fit. *Psychological Bulletin, 107,* 247-255.

Mulaik, S. A., James, L. R., Van Alstine, J., Bennett, N., Lind, S., & Stillwell, C. D. (1989). An evaluation of goodness of fit indices for structural equation models. *Psychological Bulletin, 105,* 430-445.

SAS Institute Inc. (1989). *SAS/STAT user's guide, version 6* (4th ed., Vol. 1). Cary, NC: Author.

Steiger, J. H. (1990). Structural model evaluation and modification: An internal estimation approach. *Multivariate Behavioral Research, 25,* 173-180.

Steiger, J. H., & Lind, J. C. (1980, May). *Statistically based tests for the number of common factors.* Paper presented at the annual meeting of the Psychometric Society, Iowa City, IA.

Tanaka, J. S., & Huba, G. J. (1985). A fit index for covariance structure models under arbitrary GLS estimation. *British Journal of Mathematical and Statistical Psychology, 38,* 197-201.

Tanaka, J. S., & Huba, G. J. (1989). A general coefficient of determination for covariance structure models under arbitrary GLS estimation. *British Journal of Mathematical and Statistical Psychology, 42,* 233-239.

Tucker, L. R., & Lewis, C. (1973). The reliability coefficient for maximum likelihood factor analysis. *Psychometrika, 38,* 1-10.

Wald, A. (1943). Tests of statistical hypotheses concerning several parameters when the number of observations is large. *Transactions of the American Mathematical Society, 54,* 426-482.

Wheaton, B., Muthén, B., Alwin, D., & Summers, G. (1977). Assessing reliability and stability in panel models. In D. R. Heise (Ed.), *Sociological methodology 1977* (pp. 84-136). San Francisco: Jossey-Bass.

*4*

# Some Specification Tests
# for the Linear Regression Model

J. SCOTT LONG
PRAVIN K. TRIVEDI

If the assumptions of the regression model are correct, ordinary least squares (OLS) is an efficient and unbiased estimator of the model's parameters. If the assumptions of the model are incorrect, bias or inefficiency may result. Given the costs of applying OLS when the assumptions are violated, a great deal of recent work in econometrics has focused on the development of tests to detect violations of the assumptions (see Godfrey, 1988, for a review of this literature). These tests are referred to collectively as *specification tests*. If these tests are passed, interpretation of the OLS estimates and application of standard statistical tests are justified. If one or more of the tests fail, modification of the model or alternative methods of estimation and testing may be required. Despite their potential, substantive researchers have been slow to apply specification tests, in part because of the absence of these tests from statistical packages. The development of simple computational formulas is overcoming this obstacle. A second problem is uncertainty regarding the small-sample performance of these tests and consequently of an appropriate strategy for applying specification tests.

The objective of this chapter is to evaluate some important and computationally convenient specification tests for the normal regression

AUTHORS' NOTE: We would like to thank Ken Bollen, Ronald Schoenberg, and Karl Schuessler for their comments on this chapter.

model as applied to cross-sectional data, and in the process to propose a strategy for applying specification tests. Because these tests achieve their optimal properties in large samples, their size and power in finite samples are of great interest and will be evaluated with Monte Carlo simulations. Our strategy for applying specification tests is to start with tests of the mean or first moment of the regression function. These include White's test of functional form and Ramsey's RESET test. If tests of the first moment are passed, tests of homoscedasticity, skewness, and kurtosis of the errors (i.e., second, third, and fourth moments) should be performed. Such tests are based on a decomposition of White's information matrix test.

A specification test for the full covariance structure model has recently been developed by Arminger and Schoenberg (1989). This test is designed to detect misspecifications caused by errors that are correlated with the independent variables, such as is the case with omitted variable bias. Standard test statistics used in covariance structure models, such as LR tests and modification indices, will not detect such misspecifications. While our focus in this chapter is on specification tests dealing with the simpler case where there is no measurement model, in the conclusion we consider the implications of our results for the development of specification tests for the full model.

We begin with an overview of specification testing. This is followed by formal presentation of the normal regression model and each test of specification. The last part of the chapter presents Monte Carlo results.

## Overview

In 1978, J. A. Hausman published the influential paper "Specification Tests in Econometrics," which presented a general method of testing for specification error. The idea behind this test is simple. Consider a model with a set of parameters $\theta$. Let the null hypothesis $H_0$ be that the model is correctly specified, with the alternative hypothesis $H_1$ that the model is misspecified. Consider two estimators, $\hat{\theta}$ and $\tilde{\theta}$. $\hat{\theta}$ is consistent, asymptotically normal, and efficient under $H_0$. $\tilde{\theta}$ is consistent under both $H_0$ and $H_1$, but is inefficient under $H_0$. If the model is correctly specified, then $\hat{\theta}$ and $\tilde{\theta}$ should have similar values. If the model is misspecified, then $\hat{\theta}$ and $\tilde{\theta}$ should differ. In effect, a Hausman test assesses whether the difference between $\hat{\theta}$ and $\tilde{\theta}$ is likely to have occurred by chance if the model were correctly specified.

Halbert White (1980a, 1980b, 1981, 1982) has developed a pair of specification tests that are based on the Hausman principle. The first is called the *information matrix test,* or simply the *IM test.* Rather than comparing two estimates of the structural coefficients $\theta$, the IM test compares two estimates of the information matrix $I(\hat{\theta})$. With maximum likelihood estimation $I(\hat{\theta})$ can be estimated with either minus the expected value of the Hessian of the likelihood function or the expected value of the outer product of the gradients (OPG) of the likelihood function. If the model is correctly specified, then minus the expected value of the Hessian and the expected value of the OPG will be equal (see Judge, Griffiths, Hill, Lütkepohl, & Lee, 1985, p. 179). The IM test is based on the idea that if two estimates of $I(\hat{\theta})$ are far apart, then misspecification is indicated. Significant values of this test indicate heteroscedasticity or nonnormality of the errors. A second test is White's *test for functional misspecification.* This test compares the OLS estimates of the structural coefficients to weighted least squares (WLS) estimates. If the OLS and WLS estimates are far apart, then functional misspecification is indicated.

Ramsey's (1969) RESET (*regression specification error test*) is similar in purpose to White's test for functional form.[1] The RESET test is based on the notion that if the functional form of the model is incorrect, then the correct specification might be approximated by the inclusion of powers of the variables in the original model. The original set of independent variables is augmented by powers of these variables. If the coefficients associated with the added variables are statistically significant, misspecification from sources such as incorrect functional form or the exclusion of relevant variables is suggested.

On the basis of the IM and functional form test, White (1981) suggests "a natural procedure for the validation of any regression model" (p. 423). First, the IM test is applied. If the test is passed, the estimates of the structural coefficients and the standard errors should be consistent and the usual methods of hypothesis testing are justified. If the model fails the IM test, then White's test for functional misspecification should be performed. If the functional form test fails, the hypothesis of correct functional form is rejected and OLS is inconsistent. If the test is passed, the functional form can be accepted as provisionally correct and OLS will be an unbiased estimator of the structural coefficients. Since the IM test failed, the standard OLS estimator of the variances and covariances of the estimates is biased. Consequently, standard statistical tests must be replaced by those based on a heteroscedasticity consistent estimator (discussed below).

Given that misspecification of the first moment is more fundamental and its consequences are more serious than misspecification of higher moments, this sequence of testing is reversed. If the functional form is incorrect, estimates from the incorrect model are at best approximations to those from the correct model, and interpretation of the estimates should be avoided. Heuristically, if the conditional mean estimate is inconsistent, tests of the conditional variance cannot be interpreted. Since it is possible to pass the IM tests and fail a test of functional form, the implicit assumption that passing the IM test eliminates the need for testing functional misspecification should be reconsidered. A sounder strategy is to begin with a test of functional misspecification. If it is passed, the IM test should be performed. If it fails, the OLS estimator of the structural coefficients is still consistent, but the estimator of the covariance matrix is inconsistent. This inconsistency can be corrected by calculating a heteroscedasticity consistent covariance matrix.

In evaluating specification tests, the related issues of orthogonality and robustness are of concern. Specification tests evaluate the null hypothesis of no misspecification against some alternative. Such tests may be joint or unidimensional. *Joint tests* simultaneously test for departures from the null in several directions. For example, the information matrix test is a joint test of the normality and homoscedasticity of the errors. A statistically significant joint test indicates the presence of either several or just one misspecification. Such a test is difficult to interpret because the specific cause of the violation is undetermined. *Unidimensional tests* evaluate departures in a single direction (e.g., homoscedasticity only). Ideally, the test will have high power against departures from the null in one direction, but be insensitive or orthogonal to departures in another direction. If two tests have this property, the tests are asymptotically *orthogonal*. Given two variants of the same test, one would prefer the variant that has the orthogonality property. Note that tests may be asymptotically orthogonal but correlated in finite samples. Tests that are strongly correlated provide little guidance regarding which assumption has been violated or what the appropriate remedy is. Orthogonality is related to the notion of robustness. A particular specification test may require that an auxiliary assumption is maintained. For example, a test of linearity may assume that the errors are homoscedastic. If a test is sensitive to the auxiliary assumptions, the test lacks robustness. A robustified version of a test attempts to prevent this, usually with the loss of some power if the robustification was not necessary.

A modern and attractive interpretation of a specification test is a conditional moment (CM) test. Every specification test may be thought of as a restriction on some conditional moment. For example, a functional form test is a test of a restriction on the conditional mean function, a heteroscedasticity test is a test of a restriction on the conditional variance function, a test of symmetry of the distribution is a test of a restriction on the third moment of the distribution, and so forth. An excellent exposition of this viewpoint is provided by Pagan and Vella (1989). Every CM test can be interpreted as a test of $E[m(y, X, \Theta | X)] = 0$, where $\Theta$ is an unknown parameter and $(y, X)$ are data; $m(.)$ is called the moment function. To implement the test, $\Theta$ must be replaced by a consistent estimator. Specification tests have two aspects: the choice of the suitable moment function and implementation of the test. Implementation requires the estimator $\hat{\Theta}$, the asymptotic variance of $m(y, X, \hat{\Theta})$, and a method of computing the test statistic $T$. $T$ is usually of the form $T = [m(y, X, \hat{\Theta})]^2 / \text{var}[m(y, X, \hat{\Theta})]$. Competing variants of a CM test may therefore differ in terms of (a) the choice of the CM function, (b) the asymptotic variance of the CM function, and (c) the auxiliary regression used to compute $T$. These differences in the construction of tests will be referred to below and used to interpret some of the results of the Monte Carlo simulations.

### The Regression Model

The multiple regression model may be written as

$$y = X\beta + u ,$$

where $y$ is a $(n \times 1)$ vector of values for the dependent variable, $\beta$ is a $(K \times 1)$ vector of unknown parameters, $X$ is a $(n \times K)$ matrix of rank $K$ containing nonstochastic independent variables, and $u$ is a $(n \times 1)$ vector of stochastic disturbances. The first column of $X$ may contain ones to allow for an intercept. For purposes of describing the specification tests, it is useful to consider the assumptions of the model in terms of conditional expectations of the error vector $u$.

*Assumption 1.* $E(u|X) = 0$: The expected value of the error is zero for a given value of $X$. The simplest violation of this assumption occurs if the conditional expectation is a nonzero constant, which affects only estimates of the intercept. More serious violations occur when the value of the conditional expectation depends upon the values of $X$ for a given observation. This can occur when the correct functional form is nonlinear and a linear model is estimated, or when an independent variable is incorrectly excluded from $X$. Such misspecifications are referred to as misspecifications of the first order, because they concern the first moment of the error. In general, violations of the first order render the OLS estimator biased and inconsistent.

*Assumption 2.* $\text{var}(u|X) = E(u^2|X) = \sigma^2 I$: Errors have a constant variance and are uncorrelated across observations. When the variances of the errors are uniform the errors are homoscedastic; if the variances are not uniform, the errors are heteroscedastic. In the presence of heteroscedasticity, the OLS estimator $\hat{\beta}_{OLS}$ is unbiased, but inefficient. The estimator of the variances and covariances of $\hat{\beta}_{OLS}$ is biased and the usual tests of significance are inappropriate. Because this assumption concerns expectations of the second moment of the errors, violations can be thought of as misspecification of the second order.

*Assumption 3.* $u \sim N$: The errors are normally distributed with a bounded variance. If the errors are *not* normal, the OLS estimator of $\beta$ is still a best linear unbiased estimator and the usual tests of significance have asymptotic justification. However, the OLS estimator is no longer the maximum likelihood estimator and the small sample behavior of significance tests is uncertain. Since the normal distribution is symmetric and mesokurtic, the normality assumption implies that $E(u^3|X) = 0$ and $E(u^4|X) = 3(\sigma^2)^2$. Thus violations of the normality assumption can be thought of as misspecifications of the third and fourth order conditional moments.

The specification tests detailed below are designed to detect violations of these assumptions.

## White's Test of Functional Misspecification

White's (1980b, 1981) test of functional misspecification is a test of misspecification of the first order. Assume that the correct functional form is

$$y = g(X, \beta) + e .$$

A test of functional form involves testing the hypothesis that $y = X\beta + u$ is correct against the alternative that $y = g(X,\beta) + e$, where $g(X,\beta) \neq$

$X\beta$. To develop this test, White considers the regression model $y = X\beta + u$ as an approximation to $y = g(X,\beta) + e$. $\beta^*$ is defined as the vector of parameters that minimize the weighted distance between the expected values of $y$ from the two model specifications $y = g(X,\beta) + e$ and $y = X\beta + u$. That is, $\beta^*$ makes the linear approximation as close as possible to the nonlinear specification, where "close as possible" involves minimizing the squared, weighted distance between the predicted $y$s from the two specifications. Specifically, $\beta^*$ minimizes the function

$$\int [g(x, \beta) - x\beta]^2 f(x)dx ,$$

where $f(x)$ is a weighting function. If $\hat{\beta}_{OLS}$ is the OLS estimator from the equation $y = X\beta + u$, $\hat{\beta}_{OLS}$ will approximate $\beta^*$ in the sense that $g(X,\beta)$ is linearized using a Taylor expansion and all higher-order terms are dropped. Under regularity conditions discussed by White (1980b, pp. 152-155),

$$\sqrt{n}(\hat{\beta}_{OLS} - \beta^*)$$

is distributed normally with mean zero and a covariance matrix $\hat{V}_{HC}$ defined as follows. Let

$$\hat{V}_{OLS} = n^{-1} \sum_{i=1}^{n} (y_i - X_i\hat{\beta}_{OLS})^2 X_i' X_i ,$$

where $X_i$ is a $(1 \times K)$ vector of the values of $X$ for observation $i$. Then,

$$\hat{V}_{HC} = (X'X/n)^{-1} \hat{V}_{OLS}(X'X/n)^{-1} .$$

This estimator is called the heteroscedasticity consistent covariance matrix, or simply the HC covariance matrix.

When $g(X,\beta) = X\beta$, $\beta^* = \beta_{OLS}$ regardless of the weighting function $f(x)$. When $g(X,\beta) \neq X\beta$ the least squares approximation $\beta^*$ depends on the weighting function $f(x)$. White's test of functional misspecification involves obtaining an OLS estimate $\hat{\beta}_{OLS}$ and a weighted least squares estimate $\hat{\beta}_{WLS}$ based on an *arbitrary* weighting function $w(x)$. Functional misspecification is indicated by $\hat{\beta}_{OLS}$ and $\hat{\beta}_{WLS}$ being significantly apart. The test statistic (White, 1980b, p. 157) is defined as

$$\lambda_{FF} = n(\hat{\beta}_{OLS} - \hat{\beta}_{WLS})' \hat{\Psi}^{-1}(\hat{\beta}_{OLS} - \hat{\beta}_{WLS}) , \qquad [1]$$

where

$$\hat{\Psi} = (X'X/n)^{-1}\hat{V}_{OLS}(X'X/n)^{-1} + (X'\Omega^{-1}X/n)^{-1}\hat{V}_{WLS}(X'\Omega^{-1}X/n)^{-1}$$

$$- (X'X/n)^{-1}\hat{U}(X'\Omega^{-1}X/n)^{-1} - (X'\Omega^{-1}X/n)^{-1}\hat{U}(X'X/n)^{-1}$$

with

$$\hat{V}_{WLS} = n^{-1} \sum_{i=1}^{n} w(X_i)^2(y_i - X_i\hat{\beta}_{WLS})^2 X_i'X_i$$

and

$$\hat{U} = n^{-1} \sum_{i=1}^{n} w(X_i)(y_i - X_i\hat{\beta}_{OLS})(y_i - X_i\hat{\beta}_{WLS})X_i'X_i .$$

$\lambda_{FF}$ is asymptotically distributed $\chi^2$ with $K$ degrees of freedom. If $\lambda_{FF}$ is larger than the critical value at the given significance level, the null hypothesis that $g(X,\beta) = X\beta$ is rejected.

It is essential to realize that the size and power of this test depend on the choice of the weight function $w(x)$. Statistical theory provides little guidance for selecting optimal weights, a problem that will be shown below to limit greatly the application of this test.

### The RESET Test

Ramsey's (1969) RESET test is another test for misspecification of the first order, including incorrect functional form and the exclusion of relevant variables. If

$$y = X\beta + u \qquad [2]$$

is the null model being considered, a possible alternative model can be written as

$$y = X\beta + Z\alpha + u^* .$$    [3]

If the correct variables $X$ are in the model but the linear equation, Equation 2, is the incorrect functional form, a polynomial approximation to the correct form $y = g(X) + e$ can be made by defining the $Z$s in Equation 3 as powers of $\hat{y} = X\hat{\beta}$. Since $\hat{y}$ is a linear combination of the $X$s, this adds powers of the $X$s to the equation, albeit in a constrained manner. With this definition of the $Z$s, Equation 3 can be written as

$$y = X\beta + \sum_{j=1}^{P} \hat{y}^{j+1}\alpha_j + u^* .$$    [4]

A RESET test of order $P$ involves testing whether the addition of $\hat{y}^2$ through $\hat{y}^{P+1}$ to the right-hand side of $y = X\beta + u$ results in a significant improvement in fit. The test statistic is the standard $F$ test of the hypothesis $H_0$: $\alpha = 0$. To define this test, partition the covariance matrix of $\begin{pmatrix} \hat{\beta} \\ \hat{\alpha} \end{pmatrix}$ as

$$V = \begin{bmatrix} V_{\beta\beta} & V_{\beta\alpha} \\ V_{\alpha\beta} & V_{\alpha\alpha} \end{bmatrix} .$$

Then let $V^{\alpha\alpha}$ be the partition in $V^{-1}$ corresponding to $V_{\alpha\alpha}$. The $F$ test is defined as

$$\lambda_R = \frac{1}{P}\hat{\alpha}'\hat{V}^{\alpha\alpha}\hat{\alpha} ,$$    [5]

which is distributed as $F$ with $P$ and $n - K - P$ degrees of freedom if the model is correctly specified.

The RESET test assumes that the errors are distributed normally with a constant variance. Thus it tests the null hypothesis $H_0$: $u \sim N(0,\sigma^2 I)$ against the alternative $H_1$: $u \sim N(\mu,\sigma^2 I)$, where $\mu$ is not zero. When used as part of a sequence of specification tests, the sensitivity of the test to misspecifications of the second and higher orders is problematic, because a decision to reject the hypothesis of correct functional form may be a consequence of heteroscedasticity or nonnormality. This indicates a need for a version of the RESET test that is robust to these violations.

### Robust RESET Tests

Several authors have suggested that the RESET test can be robustified for heteroscedasticity by replacing the standard OLS covariances matrix for $\hat{\alpha}$ with the robust or HC version (see, e.g., Godfrey, 1988, p. 107). The resulting Wald test is defined as

$$\lambda_{RW} = \frac{1}{P}\hat{\alpha}'\hat{V}_{HC}(\hat{\alpha})^{-1}\hat{\alpha} , \qquad [6]$$

where $\hat{V}_{HC}(\hat{\alpha})$ contains that HC covariance matrix for the $\hat{\alpha}$s from Equation 4. This test statistic is distributed as $F$ with $P$ and $n - K - P$ degrees of freedom if the model is correctly specified (Milliken & Graybill, 1970). While this adjustment is appealing because of its computational simplicity, simulations presented below suggest that it has poor size and power properties. This poor performance is consistent with results of Chesher and Austin (1991).

A second robust test was constructed as a Lagrange multiplier test, following Davidson and MacKinnon (1985). This test examines whether the residuals from the null model $y = X\beta + u$ are correlated with the excluded $Z$s after removing the linear influence of the $X$s from the $Z$s. To robustify the test for heteroscedasticity, the HC covariance matrix from the null model 2 is used as the weight matrix in the quadratic form of the test statistic. Specifically, the test statistic is defined as

$$\lambda_{RLM} = \hat{u}'Z_v\left(\frac{n-K}{n-K-P}Z_v'\hat{\Omega}Z_v\right)^{-1} Z_v'\hat{u} , \qquad [7]$$

where $(n - K)/(n - K - P)$ is a degrees of freedom correction. $\hat{\Omega}$ is a diagonal matrix with diagonal elements equal to the squares of the residuals from Equation 2. $Z_v$ is a $(n \times P)$ matrix where the $i$th column contains $\hat{v}_i$ from the regression

$$z_i = \delta_0 + X\delta + v_i , \qquad i = 1, \ldots, P .$$

Thus the $i$th column of $Z_v$ contains the $Z$s after removing the linear influence of the $X$s. $\lambda_{RLM}$ tests whether the $u$s from Equation 2 are correlated with that part of the $Z$s that is uncorrelated with the $X$s. By using an HC covariance matrix from Equation 2, the resulting test should be robust to heteroscedasticity. The test statistics are asymptotically distributed as $\chi^2$ with $P$ degrees of freedom (Davidson & MacKinnon, 1985).[2]

### The Information Matrix Test

If a test of functional form fails, there is no justification for proceeding to test for second- and higher-order misspecifications or to interpret the estimated parameters. If the functional form appears adequate, it is reasonable to proceed to test for violations of Assumptions 2 and 3 involving higher moments of the error terms. White's information matrix test, originally designed as an omnibus misspecification test without specific alternatives, has this feature.

Under the assumptions of the regression model given above, the $y$s are distributed $N(X\beta, \sigma^2 I)$. If the parameters $\beta$ and $\sigma^2$ are stacked in the vector $\theta' = (\beta'\ \sigma^2)$, the resulting log-likelihood equation is

$$l(\theta) = -\frac{n}{2}\ln \sigma^2 - \frac{1}{2\sigma^2}(y - X\beta)'(y - X\beta) .$$

The maximum likelihood estimator $\tilde{\theta}$ is the value that maximizes the likelihood function. The score or gradient vector of the log-likelihood can be written as

$$d(\theta) = \frac{\partial l(\theta)}{\partial \theta} .$$

If $\theta°$ is the true value of $\theta$, the expected value of $d(\theta)$ will be zero when evaluated at $\theta°$.

The asymptotic theory of maximum likelihood estimation shows that the covariance matrix of $\tilde{\theta}$ approaches $[I(\theta)/n]^{-1}$. If the regularity conditions for maximum likelihood estimation hold, the information matrix can be expressed in either of two ways. First,

$$I(\theta) = E\left[\left(\frac{\partial l(\theta)}{\partial \theta}\right)\left(\frac{\partial l(\theta)}{\partial \theta}\right)'\right].$$

This is the outer product of the gradient or OPG version. Second, the information matrix can be written as a function of the Hessian of the log-likelihood function. Let the Hessian be written as

$$D(\theta) = \frac{\partial^2 l(\theta)}{\partial\theta\,\partial\theta'}.$$

The information matrix then equals

$$I(\theta) = -E[D(\theta)],$$

where the right-hand side is the Hessian version of the information matrix. If the assumptions of the model are correct and certain regularity conditions hold, then

$$E\left[\left(\frac{\partial l(\theta)}{\partial\theta}\right)\left(\frac{\partial l(\theta)}{\partial\theta}\right)'\right] = -E\left[\frac{\partial^2 l(\theta)}{\partial\theta\,\partial\theta'}\right]$$

or, in our earlier notation, $E[d(\theta)d(\theta)'] = -E[D(\theta)]$.

The equality of the Hessian and OPG versions of the information matrix when the model is correctly specified is the basis for the IM test. If we define $l_i(\theta)$ as the value of the log-likelihood function for observation $i$, we may define

$$\Delta(\theta) = \sum_{i=1}^{n}\left[\frac{\partial^2 l_i(\theta)}{\partial\theta\,\partial\theta'} + \frac{\partial l_i(\theta)}{\partial\theta}\,\frac{\partial l_i(\theta)}{\partial\theta'}\right]. \tag{8}$$

$\Delta(\theta)$ is a $(q \times q)$ symmetric matrix, where $q$ is the number of $\beta$s plus one for $\sigma^2$. Since $E[\Delta(\theta)]$ should equal $0$ if the model is correctly specified, White proposes $\Delta(\tilde{\theta})$ as a measure of misspecification. He demonstrates that $\sqrt{n}\,\Delta(\tilde{\theta})$ is normally distributed with mean zero when the model is correctly specified. A $\chi^2$ statistic is constructed based on the lower triangle of $\Delta(\tilde{\theta})$ (since the matrix is symmetric). For simplicity, we will refer to this test statistic as $\Delta(\theta)$.

To understand how this test statistic depends on the assumptions of the regression model, it is useful to consider the results of Hall (1987), who demonstrates that $\Delta(\theta)$ can be decomposed as

$$\Delta(\mathbf{\theta}) = \delta_1 + \delta_2 + \delta_3, \qquad\qquad [9]$$

where the $\delta$s are asymptotically uncorrelated. $\delta_1$ is a test of the second moments of the error distribution that closely resembles White's (1980a) earlier test of heteroscedasticity and Breusch and Pagan's (1979) test for heteroscedasticity. $\delta_2$ is a test of the skewness or third moment of the error terms that resembles the $\sqrt{b_1}$ test of skewness. $\delta_3$ is a test of kurtosis or the fourth moment that is similar to the $b_2$ test of kurtosis. This decomposition is accomplished by partitioning Equation 8 according to the components $\mathbf{\beta}$ and $\sigma^2$ of $\mathbf{\theta}$. Thus $\delta_1$ is based on

$$E\left[\left(\frac{\partial l(\mathbf{\theta})}{\partial \mathbf{\beta}}\right)\left(\frac{\partial l(\mathbf{\theta})}{\partial \mathbf{\beta}}\right)'\right] = -E\left[\frac{\partial^2 l(\mathbf{\theta})}{\partial \mathbf{\beta} \, \partial \mathbf{\beta}'}\right],$$

which is a function of $u^2$. $\delta_2$ is based on

$$E\left[\left(\frac{\partial l(\mathbf{\theta})}{\partial \mathbf{\beta}}\right)\left(\frac{\partial l(\mathbf{\theta})}{\partial \sigma^2}\right)'\right] = -E\left[\frac{\partial^2 l(\mathbf{\theta})}{\partial \mathbf{\beta} \, \partial \sigma^2}\right],$$

which is a function of $u^3$. And $\delta_3$ is based on

$$E\left[\left(\frac{\partial l(\mathbf{\theta})}{\partial \sigma^2}\right)\left(\frac{\partial l(\mathbf{\theta})}{\partial \sigma^2}\right)'\right] = -E\left[\frac{\partial^2 l(\mathbf{\theta})}{\partial \sigma^2 \, \partial \sigma^2}\right],$$

which is a function of $u^4$.

The computation of the $\hat{\delta}$s is relatively simple. First, estimate the regression

$$y = X\mathbf{\beta} + u . \qquad\qquad [10]$$

Let $\hat{u}^2$, $\hat{u}^3$, and $\hat{u}^4$ contain the second, third, and fourth powers of the residuals from Equation 10. Let $\hat{\sigma}^2$ be the maximum likelihood estimate

$$\hat{\sigma}^2 = \frac{1}{n} \sum_{i=1}^{n} \hat{u}_i^2 .$$

Second, create $Z$ to contain all of the unique products and bivariate cross-products of the $X$s. Specifically, $Z$ contains $x_1 x_1, x_1 x_2, \ldots, x_1 x_K$, $x_2 x_3, \ldots, x_2 x_K, \ldots, x_K x_K$. If $x_1$ is the constant 1, then $x_1 x_1 = 1$, $x_1 x_2 =$

$x_2$, and so on. Using these as a starting point, the components of the IM test can be easily computed. In the following expression the superscript H indicates that the formulas are based on Hall's construction of the test. To compute $\hat{\delta}_1^H$ estimate the regression

$$\frac{\hat{u}^2}{\hat{\sigma}^2} = Z\tau + v .$$  [11]

Then,

$$\hat{\delta}_1^H = \frac{SS_{EXP}}{2} ,$$  [12]

where $SS_{EXP}$ is the explained sum of squares from the regression. To compute $\hat{\delta}_2^H$ , estimate the regression

$$\hat{u}^3 = Z\tau + v .$$  [13]

Let $SS_{UNTOT}$ be the total uncentered sum of squares $\frac{1}{n}\sum_{i=1}^n y_i^2$ and $SS_{RES}$ be the residual sum of squares $\frac{1}{n}\sum_{i=1}^n \hat{v}_i^2$. Then

$$\hat{\delta}_2^H = \frac{SS_{UNTOT} - SS_{RES}}{6(\hat{\sigma}^2)^3} .$$  [14]

$\hat{\delta}_3^H$ is computed as

$$\hat{\delta}_3^H = \frac{n}{24}\left(\frac{\sum_{i=1}^n \frac{\hat{u}_i^4}{n}}{(\hat{\sigma}^2)^2} - 3\right)^2 .$$  [15]

The joint test is then computed as

$$\hat{\delta}^H = \hat{\delta}_1^H + \hat{\delta}_2^H + \hat{\delta}_3^H .$$  [16]

$\hat{\delta}^H, \hat{\delta}_1^H, \hat{\delta}_2^H$ and $\hat{\delta}_3^H$ are asymptotically distributed as $\chi^2$ with $K(K+3)/2$, $[K(K+1)/2] - 1$, $K$, and 1 degrees of freedom. Recall that $K$ is the number of columns of $X$, possibly including a column of ones for the intercept.

A major advantage of Hall's formulation of the IM test is that it may suggest which aspects of the assumption $y \sim N(X\beta, \sigma^2 I)$ are being violated. To the extent that asymptotic property of the $\delta$s being uncorrelated is approximated in small samples, $\hat{\delta}_1^H$ should be robust to violations of skewness and kurtosis, $\hat{\delta}_2^H$ should be robust to violations of heteroscedasticity and kurtosis, and $\hat{\delta}_3^H$ should be robust to violations of heteroscedasticity and skewness. While Hall's $\delta$s are asymptotically uncorrelated, our simulations suggest that in small samples they are substantially correlated. Consequently, $\hat{\delta}_1^H$ can be statistically significant as a result of skewness, rather than heteroscedasticity, and similarly for $\hat{\delta}_2^H$ and $\hat{\delta}_3^H$.

Cameron and Trivedi (1990a, 1990b) demonstrate that the IM test can be viewed as a test with explicit alternatives. In the process, they provide an *orthogonal decomposition* of the IM test. Let $X$, $Z$, and $\hat{\sigma}^2$ be defined as above. In addition, let $R_{UN}^2$ be the uncentered coefficient of determination, defined as

$$R_{UN}^2 = 1 - \frac{\sum\limits_{i=1}^{n} \hat{v}_i^2}{\sum\limits_{i=1}^{n} \hat{y}_i^2},$$

where the $\hat{v}_i$ are the residuals from a given regression. Note that most regression packages do *not* provide the uncentered coefficient of determination.

To estimate $\delta_1^{CT}$, run the regression

$$(\hat{u}^2 - \hat{\sigma}^2) = Z\tau + v. \qquad [17]$$

Then,

$$\hat{\delta}_1^{CT} = nR_{UN}^2. \qquad [18]$$

To estimate $\delta_2^{CT}$, run the regression

$$(\hat{u}^3 - 3\hat{\sigma}^2\hat{u}) = X\tau + v. \qquad [19]$$

Then,

$$\hat{\delta}_2^{CT} = nR_{UN}^2 . \tag{20}$$

To estimate $\delta_3^{CT}$ , run the regression

$$(\hat{u}^4 - 6\hat{\sigma}^2\hat{u}^2 - 3\hat{\sigma}^4) = \iota\tau + \nu , \tag{21}$$

where $\iota$ is a vector of ones. Then,

$$\hat{\delta}_3^{CT} = nR_{UN}^2 . \tag{22}$$

The joint test is then computed as

$$\hat{\delta}^{CT} = \hat{\delta}_1^{CT} + \hat{\delta}_2^{CT} + \hat{\delta}_3^{CT} . \tag{23}$$

As with the Hall version of the test, $\hat{\delta}^{CT}$, $\hat{\delta}_1^{CT}$ , $\hat{\delta}_2^{CT}$ , and $\hat{\delta}_3^{CT}$ are asymptotically distributed as $\chi^2$ with $K(K + 3)/2$, $[K(K + 1)/2] - 1$, $K$, and 1 degrees of freedom. The Monte Carlo experiments presented below indicate that their estimates for the δs are substantially less correlated in small samples than are those based on Hall's formulas.

Components of Hall's version of the IM test may be compared to Cameron and Trivedi's (CT's) version in terms the choice of the conditional moment function and the implementation of the test. The comparison is between Hall's expressions, given by Equations 11, 13, and 15, and CT's expressions, given by Equations 17, 18, and 21. For testing heteroscedasticity, both use essentially the same conditional moment function based on $\hat{u}$ and $\hat{\sigma}^2$, so there should be little difference between the performance of the two on this account. For tests of symmetry and excess kurtosis, there is a slight difference, because CT use conditional moment functions that are orthogonal to each other, but Hall does not. The key difference between the two lies in the treatment of the variance term in the test. Hall's expressions for the tests use the variance of the conditional moment function that would be obtained if the null hypothesis were to hold. In this case the variance of the second, third, and fourth moment restrictions would be indeed $2\hat{\sigma}^4$, $6\hat{\sigma}^6$, and $24\hat{\sigma}^8$, respectively. CT's versions of the corresponding tests does not use this assumption. Therefore, it is to be expected that Hall's variants would have better size properties, but would be less robust and powerful than CT's variants, which do not impose the variance assumption on the test statistic. We may also expect that the use of the same (inconsistent) estimate of residual variance in the components of the IM test will cause these components to be mutually correlated.

A further point concerns the implementation of the test using $nR^2$ from an auxiliary regression. Observe that when the alternative hypothesis is valid, the auxiliary regressions given in Equations 17, 19, and 21 have heteroscedastic residuals, which will induce a bias in the estimate of the residual variance and the uncentered $R^2$ from these auxiliary regressions, thereby affecting the properties of the tests. An alternative to the $nR^2$-based test is a heteroscedasticity consistent Wald test of the hypothesis that the slope parameters in the auxiliary regressions in equations 17 and 19, and the intercept in 21, are all zero. As little is known about the merits of the heteroscedasticity consistent Wald test relative to the $nR^2$-based test, Monte Carlo simulations were undertaken to compare them. Although a more detailed discussion is given later, we anticipate the major conclusion of these experiments: The heteroscedasticity consistent Wald test has unsatisfactory size properties, especially with regard to tests of heteroscedasticity in small samples.

### Heteroscedasticity Consistent Covariance Matrices

If specification tests of the first order are passed, but those for higher order (and particularly heteroscedasticity) are not, standard tests of statistical significance are inappropriate. In such cases heteroscedasticity consistent tests should be considered. These tests are based on results of White (1980a), who extended earlier work of Eicker (1967) and Fuller (1975).

In the presence of heteroscedasticity, the OLS estimator $\hat{\beta}_{OLS}$ is unbiased, but inefficient. The usual OLS estimator of $V(\hat{\beta}_{OLS})$ is biased and the usual tests of significance are inconsistent. If the exact form of heteroscedasticity is known to be $V(u) = \sigma^2\Omega$, the covariance matrix of $\hat{\beta}_{OLS}$ is

$$V(\hat{\beta}_{OLS}) = \sigma^2(X'X)^{-1}X'\Omega X(X'X)^{-1}.$$

In general, the specific values of $\sigma^2\Omega$ are not known. White's HC estimator of $V(\hat{\beta})$ involves substituting for $\Omega$ the matrix $D$ that contains $\hat{u}_i^2$ on the diagonal and 0s on the off-diagonal. The resulting HC estimator is

$$\hat{V}_{HC}(\hat{\beta}_{OLS}) = \sigma^2(X'X)^{-1}X'DX(X'X)^{-1} . \qquad [24]$$

White recommends that if specification tests for the first order are passed but test of higher-order misspecification fail, tests based on the HC covariance matrix should be used.

## Monte Carlo Studies

Each of the tests discussed above is justified on the basis of asymptotic considerations. Since exact results for small-sample behavior are unavailable, Monte Carlo simulations provide a means for examining the small-sample behavior of these tests. These simulations involve a series of experiments in which (a) a population is generated with a known data structure, (b) a large number of random samples are drawn from the population, (c) test statistics are computed for each sample, and (d) the test results across all samples are used to assess the size and power of the tests. Details of our simulations are now given.

### Data Structures

Eight data structures were used (see Table 4.1 for a summary). For each data structure, one population was generated with an $R^2$ of approximately 0.4 and another with an $R^2$ of approximately 0.8. Three independent variables were used. $X_1$ was generated with a uniform distribution ranging from 1 to 2, except for data structures 6 and 7, in which the range is 0 to 100; $X_2$ with a normal distribution with means zero and variance one; and $X_3$ with a $\chi^2$ distribution with one degree of freedom with values ranging from 0 to about 15.[3] The correlations among the $X$s are approximately equal to

|       | $X_1$ | $X_2$ | $X_3$ |
|-------|-------|-------|-------|
| $X_1$ | 1.00  | 0.82  | 0.57  |
| $X_2$ | 0.82  | 1.00  | 0.46  |
| $X_3$ | 0.57  | 0.46  | 1.00  |

Structure 1 was generated to conform to the null hypothesis of no misspecification. The remaining seven structures represented various types of misspecification. Structure 2 has errors that are distributed as $t$ with 5 degrees of freedom, which corresponds to a case with moderately

**Table 4.1 Description of Data Structures for Monte Carlo Simulations**

| Data Structure | Description | Systematic Component | Errors | Error Variance | $R^2$ | Estimated Model |
|---|---|---|---|---|---|---|
| 1 | correct specification | $y = 1 + x_1 + x_2 + x_3$ | normal | $\sigma_i^2 = \sigma^2$ | 0.4 | $y = 1 + x_1 + x_2 + x_3$ |
|   |   |   |   |   | 0.8 |   |
| 2 | $t$-distributed errors | $y = 1 + x_1 + x_2 + x_3$ | $t$ (5 df) | $\sigma_i^2 = \sigma^2$ | 0.4 | $y = 1 + x_1 + x_2 + x_3$ |
|   |   |   |   |   | 0.8 |   |
| 3 | $\chi^2$-distributed errors | $y = 1 + x_1 + x_2 + x_3$ | $\chi^2$ (5 df) | $\sigma_i^2 = \sigma^2$ | 0.4 | $y = 1 + x_1 + x_2 + x_3$ |
|   |   |   |   |   | 0.8 |   |
| 4 | heteroscedasticity on $X_1$ | $y = 1 + x_1 + x_2 + x_3$ | normal | $\sigma_i^2 = \sigma^2 \sqrt{x_{1i}}$ | 0.4 | $y = 1 + x_1 + x_2 + x_3$ |
|   |   |   |   |   | 0.8 |   |
| 5 | heteroscedasticity on $X_3$ | $y = 1 + x_1 + x_2 + x_3$ | normal | $\sigma_i^2 = \sigma^2 \sqrt{x_{3i} + 0.25}$ | 0.4 | $y = 1 + x_1 + x_2 + x_3$ |
|   |   |   |   |   | 0.8 |   |
| 6 | nonlinearity in $X_1$ | $y = 1 + \sqrt{x_1} + x_2 + x_3$ | normal | $\sigma_i^2 = \sigma^2$ | 0.4 | $y = 1 + x_1 + x_2 + x_3$ |
|   |   |   |   |   | 0.8 |   |
| 7 | nonlinearity in $X_3$ | $y = 1 + x_1 + x_2 + \sqrt{x_3}$ | normal | $\sigma_i^2 = \sigma^2$ | 0.4 | $y = 1 + x_1 + x_2 + x_3$ |
|   |   |   |   |   | 0.8 |   |
| 8 | excluding $X_1$ | $y = 1 + x_1 + x_2 + x_3$ | normal | $\sigma_i^2 = \sigma^2$ | 0.4 | $y = 1 + x_2 + x_3$ |
|   |   |   |   |   | 0.8 |   |

thick tails. Structure 3 has errors that are distributed as $\chi^2$ with 5 degrees of freedom, which corresponds to a moderate amount of skewness in the errors. Structure 4 incorporates heteroscedasticity of the form $\sigma_i^2 = \sigma^2\sqrt{X_{1i}}$, where the value $\sigma^2$ is determined by the $R^2$ required. Given the uniform [1,2] distribution of $X_1$, this represents a moderate amount of heteroscedasticity. Structure 5 incorporates heteroscedasticity of the form $\sigma_i^2 = \sigma^2\sqrt{X_{3i}} + 0.25$, where the value $\sigma^2$ is determined by the $R^2$ required and 0.25 is added to avoid extremely small variances in those cases were $X_3$ is close to zero. Given the uniform distribution of $X_3$, this represents a substantial amount of heteroscedasticity. Structure 6 was generated with the nonlinear equation $Y = 1 + \sqrt{X_1} + X_2 + X_3$. Given the range of $X_1$ from 1 to 2, only a slight departure from linearity is involved. Structure 7 was generated with the nonlinear equation $Y = 1 + X_1 + X_2 + \sqrt{X_3}$. Given the range of $X_3$ from 0 to 15, a substantial departure from linearity is involved. For each of these structures the model estimated was $Y = \beta_0 + \beta_1 X_1 + \beta_2 X_2 + \beta_3 X_3$. Structure 8 was generated in the same way as Structure 1, that is, without specification errors. However, in this case the model estimated was $Y = \beta_0^* + \beta_2^* X_2 + \beta_3^* X_3$.

## The Experiment

For each data structure the following experiment was run twice, once for an $R^2$ of .4 and once for an $R^2$ of .8. Each experiment consisted of the following:

(1) A total of 150,000 observations with a known structure were generated and saved to disk. These observations were thought of as the *population*. A regression was run on the population to determine the exact values of the population parameters.

(2) From each population a random *sample* with replacement was drawn. This was repeated 1,000 times for each of the sample sizes: 25, 50, 100, 250, 500, and 1,000.

(3) Test statistics and parameter estimates were computed for each sample.

## Summary of Experiments

Our simulations were used to assess the small sample size and power of each test. The tests that were evaluated are summarized in Table 4.2. If a data structure did not violate the assumptions being evaluated, the size of the test was assessed by comparing the nominal significance level

**Table 4.2** Description of Tests Evaluated With Monte Carlo Simulations

| Test | Equation | Description |
|------|----------|-------------|
| White's test for functional misspecification, Version 1 | 1 | weight function: $w_i = 1/X_i\hat{\beta}$ |
| White's test for functional misspecification, Version 2 | 1 | weight function: $w_i = \hat{e}_i^2$ |
| RESET Test | 5 | standard $F$ test of added variables |
| Robust Wald RESET Test | 6 | Wald test using robust covariance matrix |
| Robust LM RESET Test | 7 | LM test using robust covariance matrix |
| IM Test—total | 15 | Hall version |
| IM Test—heteroscedasticity component | 11 | Hall version |
| IM Test—skewness component | 13 | Hall version |
| IM Test—kurtosis component | 14 | Hall version |
| IM Test—total | 22 | Cameron and Trivedi version |
| IM Test—heteroscedasticity component | 17 | Cameron and Trivedi version |
| IM Test—skewness component | 19 | Cameron and Trivedi version |
| IM Test—kurtosis component | 21 | Cameron and Trivedi version |

of the test to the empirical significance level. The empirical significance level was defined as the proportion of times that the correct null hypothesis was rejected over the 1,000 replications. Results are presented for nominal significance levels of 0.05, 0.10, and 0.20. In results not shown, tests were evaluated at significance levels from 0.01 to 0.99 in increments of .01. If a data structure violated the assumptions evaluated by the test, the power of the tests is indicated by the proportion of times the null hypothesis is rejected at the 0.05, 0.10, and 0.20 levels.

Results are presented in the order corresponding to the strategy for testing that has been advocated. We begin with tests for specification of the first order, namely, the White test and the RESET test. Tests for specification errors of the second and higher order are then considered with the IM test and its components.

Before presenting the results for the White test, we offer discussion of how information on the power and size of a test is being plotted. Figure 4.1 is an example of the plots. The horizontal axis represents the size of the sample. Values of 25, 50, 100, 250, 500, and 1,000 are plotted. The vertical axis indicates the percentage of time that the null hypothesis of no misspecification was rejected. This is referred to as

PANEL 1: Size Properties

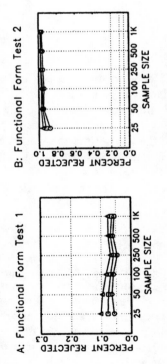

PANEL 2: Power Properties for Detecting Nonlinearity

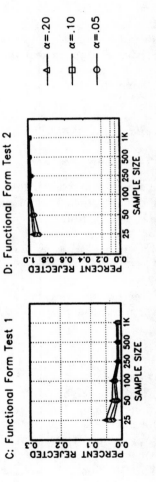

**Figure 4.1.** Size and power of White's test for functional misspecification. Test 1 uses $w_i = 1/X_i\hat{\beta}$. Test 2 uses $w_i = \hat{e}_i^2$. $R^2 = 0.40$. Panel 2 examines nonlinearity of the form $y = \beta_0 + \beta_1 x_1 + \beta_2 x_2 + \beta_3\sqrt{x_3}$.

the *empirical alpha.* The range of the vertical axis will vary with the particular set of results being presented. For each test, results are given for three *nominal alphas,* with $\alpha = 0.05$ represented by circles, $\alpha = 0.10$ by squares, and $\alpha = 0.20$ by triangles. Horizontal dotted lines are plotted at 0.05, 0.10, and 0.20. While the range of the vertical axis varies with the particular set of results being presented, the dotted lines are always at the same locations. If data were generated without any specification error and a test had perfect small sample size properties, the empirical alphas should fall directly on these dotted lines. If data were generated with specification errors that the test should detect, the higher the location of the empirical alphas, the greater the power of the test to detect the specification error.

### Specification Tests of the First Order

#### White's Test of Functional Form

White's test of functional form is designed to detect specification errors of the first order. To implement this test an "arbitrary" weighting function is chosen. Since theory provides little guidance in choosing a weighting function, three sets of weights were considered based on suggestions in the literature. Version 1 of the test defines the weight as $w_i = (X_i\hat{\beta})^{-2} = \hat{y}_i^{-2}$; the weights are inversely proportional to the expected value of $y$ for the null model (White, 1980b, pp. 158-159). Version 2 defines the weight as follows. Let $\hat{u}_i^2$ be the squared residuals from Equation 2. Run the regression

$$w_i = \hat{u}_i^2 = \alpha_0 + Q_i\alpha + v_i,\qquad [25]$$

where $Q$ consists of $X$ plus all cross-products of the $X$s (e.g., $X_1X_2$, $X_1X_3$). Then the weights are defined as $\hat{w}_i$ from Equation 25. Those observations with the largest residuals (i.e., those that conform least well to the model) are given the greatest weight, which should make the test more powerful (White, 1981). For both Versions 1 and 2, extremely small values were set equal to 0.00000001 and large values were set equal to 50. Version 3 defines the weights as 1 for large values of the dependent variable and .001 for small values of the dependent variable (White, 1980b, p. 159). Several variations on these weighting schemes were also tried.

Figure 4.1 demonstrates the practical problems involved in applying White's test of functional form. Panel 1 presents the size properties of Versions 1 and 2 of the test. For Version 1, the empirical alphas for the 0.05 significance level are close to 0.05, those for the 0.10 level begin at about .075 for $n = 25$ and decrease to 0.05 for $n = 1,000$, those for the 0.20 level begin at 0.10 and also decrease. Version 1 rejects $H_0$ slightly less frequently than it theoretically should. Version 2 of the test almost always rejects $H_0$, regardless of the significance level, and thus would not be useful in practice. These results hold for other significance levels. For example, with a sample size of 25, Version 1 rejects the correct null hypothesis only 28% of the time using $\alpha = 0.90$, whereas Version 2 rejects the correct null 98% of the time using $\alpha = 0.01$. Panel 2 presents the power of the test to detect nonlinearity based on Structure 7. Version 1 of the test rejects the $H_0$ less often than it did with the correct specification, whereas Version 2 rejects $H_0$ nearly every time.

The results presented in Figure 4.1 are typical of those obtained with other weighting functions and other data structures. For all weights considered, either the size properties are unacceptable or the test had too little power to be useful. Although it is possible that better weighting functions would improve the test, our experimentation suggests that these may be elusive. On the basis of our simulations we conclude that without operational procedures for choosing weights, White's test for functional misspecification is not practical for detecting misspecification in the regression model.

**RESET Test**

The RESET test is also a test for misspecification of the first order. Since the standard form of the RESET test assumes homoscedasticity, robust Wald and Lagrange multiplier versions of the test were constructed using White's HC covariance matrix. In all versions we included the second through fourth powers of $\hat{y}$, so $P = 3$.

Figure 4.2 shows the size properties of the RESET test using Data Structure 1 with $R^2 = 0.4$. Results are nearly identical for $R^2 = 0.8$. The size properties of the standard RESET test (plot A) are quite good. Size properties of the robust Wald RESET test (plot B) are very poor for small sample sizes, but improve steadily as the sample increases. However, even by $n = 1,000$ the robust Wald test rejects the true $H_0$ substantially more often than the nominal alpha. The robust LM RESET test rejects the $H_0$ too seldom, although by $n = 100$ the size properties

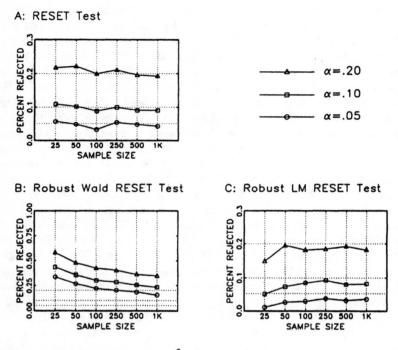

**Figure 4.2.** Size of RESET test. $R^2 = 0.40$.

approximate those of the standard RESET test. Given the substantially better size properties of the LM version compared with the Wald version, only the LM version is considered hereafter.

Figure 4.3 examines the properties of the RESET and LM RESET tests in the presence of heteroscedasticity. Panel 1 presents the results for a slight amount of heteroscedasticity (Data Structure 4) with $R^2 = 0.4$. Panel 2 presents the results for a moderate amount of heteroscedasticity (Data Structure 5) with $R^2 = 0.4$. Results are very similar for $R^2 = 0.8$. In Panel 1, with a slight amount of heteroscedasticity, the size properties of both versions of the RESET test remain similar to those obtained in the absence of heteroscedasticity, with the standard RESET test being superior to the LM version. Panel 2, with more extreme heteroscedasticity, demonstrates the sensitivity of the standard RESET test to heteroscedasticity. As sample size increases, the percentage rejected increases sharply. The robust LM version of the test is not affected by heteroscedasticity and has reasonable size properties beginning with $n = 50$.

Figure 4.4 shows the behavior of the RESET test in the presence of nonnormal errors (Data Structures 2 and 3). The standard RESET test has similar properties as when no misspecification was present, although there is a tendency to reject $H_0$ too frequently when the errors have a $\chi^2$ distribution. For $t$-distributed errors the empirical alphas for the LM test are too small at $n = 25$, but improve as $n$ increases. By $n = 1,000$, the empirical alphas are almost exactly equal to the nominal alphas. It is unclear whether the empirical alphas will stay at this level for higher $n$s or continue to increase. For $\chi^2$ errors the empirical alphas are too small, but become reasonably close by $n = 100$.

Figures 4.5, 4.6, and 4.7 examine the power of the RESET test to detect misspecifications of the first order. Figure 4.5 is based on Data Structure 7, which contains some nonlinearity. Panel 1 is based on $R^2 = 0.4$. Neither test detects the nonlinearity, with empirical alphas being similar to those for data without misspecification. Panel 2 is based on $R^2 = 0.8$. For all sample sizes, the standard RESET has larger empirical alphas than the LM RESET test, but by $n = 100$ the differences are small. Figure 4.6 is based on Data Structure 6, which contains greater nonlinearity. Panel 1 is based on $R^2 = 0.4$. The tests behave similarly, with the ability of the test to detect nonlinearity increasing steadily with sample size. Panel 2 is based on $R^2 = 0.8$. For all sample sizes the standard RESET test has larger empirical alphas, but by $n = 100$ the percentage difference is small. As before, the power to detect nonlinearity increases substantially with the larger $R^2$. Figure 4.7 considers the cases of an excluded variable. Both tests are extremely powerful by $n = 250$, with the LM version again being somewhat less powerful for all samples. Unlike the cases for nonlinearity, the power of the test decreases with the larger $R^2$.

**Summary**

White's test of functional form is not useful for detecting misspecifications of the first order. The standard RESET and the robust LM RESET tests are very effective for detecting first-order specification error. In the absence of heteroscedasticity the standard RESET test has slightly better size properties and is slightly more powerful. However, it is affected by heteroscedasticity, whereas the LM version of the test is not. Given the likelihood of heteroscedasticity in real-world data and the relatively slight disadvantages of the LM test, the robust LM RESET

*(text continues on p. 97)*

92

PANEL 1: SLIGHT HETEROSCEDASTICITY

A: RESET Test          B: Robust LM RESET Test

PANEL 2: MODERATE HETEROSCEDASTICITY

C: RESET Test          D: Robust LM RESET Test

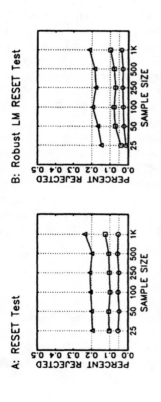

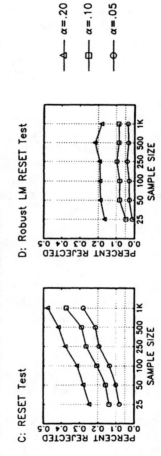

**Figure 4.3.** Properties of RESET and LM REST tests in the presence of heteroscedasticity. $R_2 = 0.40$.

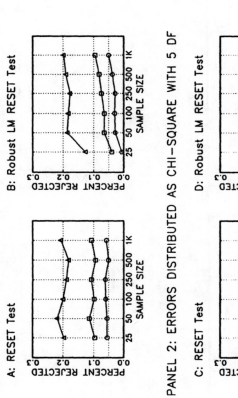
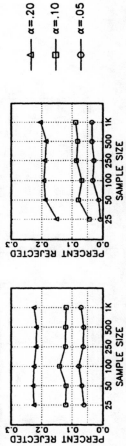

Figure 4.4. Properties of RESET and LM RESET tests in the presence of nonormal errors. $R_2 = 0.40$.

93

94

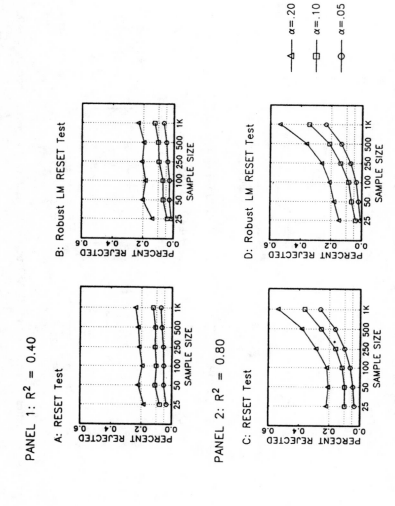

**Figure 4.5.** Power of RESET and LM RESET tests to detect slight nonlinearity of the form $y = \beta_0 + \beta_1 x_1 + \beta_2 x_2 + \beta_3 \sqrt{x_3}$.

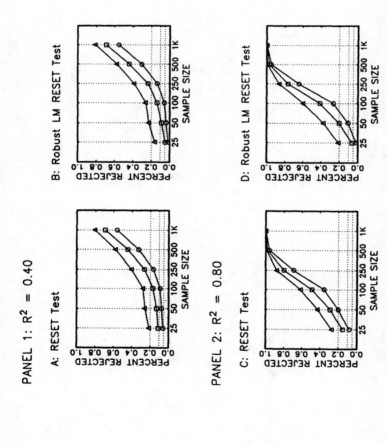

**Figure 4.6.** Power of RESET and LM RESET tests to detect moderate nonlinearity of the form $y = \beta_0 + \beta_1\sqrt{x_1} + \beta_2 x_2 + \beta_3 x_3$.

95

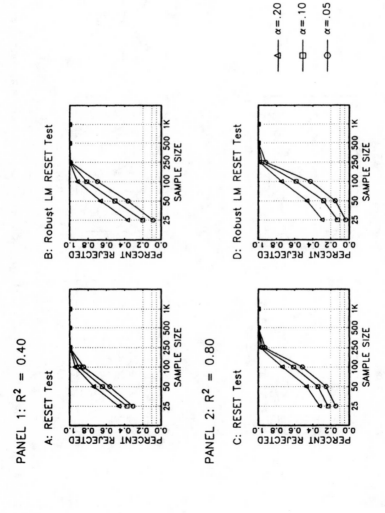

**Figure 4.7.** Power of RESET and LM RESET tests to detect excluded variable.

96

test appears to be the preferred test. The robust Wald test has poor size properties for samples up to 1,000 and is not recommended.

## Specification Tests of Higher Order

### Size Properties

White's IM test is designed to detect misspecification of the second and higher orders. As shown by Hall, the test can be decomposed into components detecting heteroscedasticity, skewness, and kurtosis. Figure 4.8 examines the size properties of the test for each component plus the combined test score for both the Hall method of computation and the method of Cameron and Trivedi (CT).

For the overall test, both versions have empirical size close to the nominal size at the 0.05 level. One exception is the too small size of the CT version for $n = 25$ and the too large size of the Hall version for $n = 100$. At the 0.10 level, both the empirical size of the overall tests are very close to 0.10 by $n = 100$. Below that, the sizes are too small. At the 0.20 level, both versions have sizes that are too small but improve with sample size, with the Hall version being less well behaved. In results not shown here, the size properties of the Hall version continue to deteriorate as the significance level increases.

The components of the IM test reveal the following. Consider first the Hall version. At the 0.20 level, the empirical size is substantially too small at $n = 25$, with increasingly better size as $n$ increases. By $n = 500$ the empirical size is quite close to the nominal size. At the 0.10 level, the trend is similar, although the overall behavior of the test is better. The size properties at the 0.05 level are extremely good for all sample sizes. Consider now the CT version of the test. At the 0.20 and 0.10 levels of the test the heteroscedasticity and skewness portions of the test have somewhat better size properties than the Hall version. At the 0.05 level the two versions are similar, except at $n = 25$, where the Hall version behaves better. The size of the kurtosis portion of the CT version of the test becomes too large after $n = 25$ but improves somewhat above 250.

### Power for Nonnormal Errors

Figures 4.9 and 4.10 examine the power of the IM test for violations of the assumption that the errors are normally distributed. Figure 4.9

98

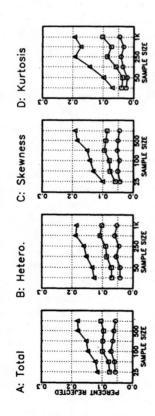

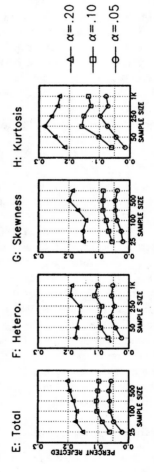

**Figure 4.8.** Size of information matrix test. $R^2 = 0.40$.

PANEL 1: HALL VERSION OF IM TEST

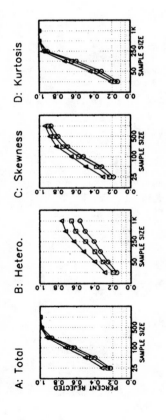

PANEL 2: CAMERON AND TRIVEDI VERSION OF IM TEST

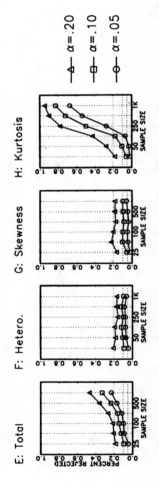

**Figure 4.9.** Power of information matrix test to detect errors distributed as $t$ with 5 df.

99

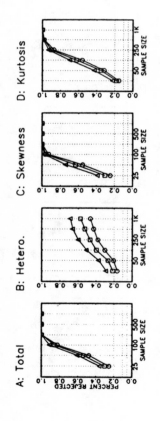

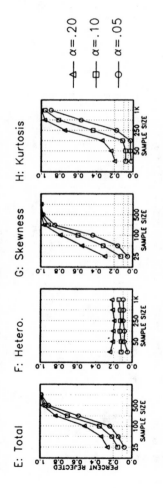

**Figure 4.10.** Power of information matrix test to detect errors distributed as $\chi^2$ with 5 df.

100

considers errors that are $t$ distributed with 5 df for the cases with $R^2 =$ 0.4; results are similar for $R^2 = 0.8$. Having errors that are $t$ as opposed to normal should introduce kurtosis but not heteroscedasticity or skewness. Herein lies the major difference between the Hall and CT versions of the test. In the Hall version, the computation of a specific component of the test assumes that there are no violations of the other components being tested. For example, the computation of the skewness component assumes there is no heteroscedasticity or kurtosis. In the CT version, the tests are robustified for violations of other assumptions. Thus in Panel 1 of Figure 4.9 we see that the Hall version of the tests rejects the hypothesis of no heteroscedasticity and of no skewness quite frequently, even though there is neither heteroscedasticity nor skewness in the data. In Panel 2 we see that the CT version rejects these hypotheses at approximately the significance level of the test. In the kurtosis portion of the test, the Hall version is more powerful than the CT version, particularly when used at lower significance levels.

The greater sensitivity of the Hall version of the tests to violations that are not being tested is reflected in the correlations among the test statistics. Tests of heteroscedasticity and skewness have a correlation of 0.71 for the Hall versions, compared with 0.27 for the CT versions; tests of heteroscedasticity and kurtosis have a correlation of 0.49 for the Hall versions, compared with −0.02 for the CT versions; and tests of skewness and kurtosis have a correlation of 0.83 for the Hall versions, compared with −0.18 for the CT versions.

Figure 4.10 presents the results for errors from a $\chi^2$ distribution with 5 df. Such errors introduce skewness and kurtosis, but not heteroscedasticity. The Hall version detects heteroscedasticity; the CT version does not. On the other hand, the Hall version is more powerful at detecting violations of skewness and kurtosis. Once again, the Hall tests are more highly correlated than the CT versions.

### Power for Heteroscedasticity

Figures 4.11 and 4.12 examine the ability of the IM test to detect heteroscedasticity. In Figure 4.11 the variance of the errors is proportional to the square root of $X_1$; in Figure 4.12 it is proportional to the square root of $X_3 + 0.25$ and is much stronger. Results are for $R^2 = 0.4$; results are very similar for $R^2 = 0.8$ (not shown).

With slight heteroscedasticity, both the Hall and CT versions of the test behave similarly, with the Hall version being just slightly more

102

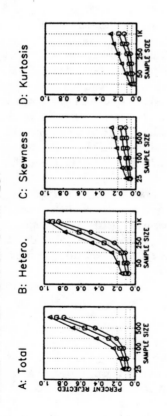

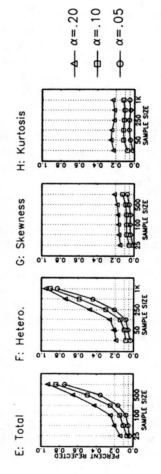

PANEL 1: HALL VERSION OF IM TEST

A: Total    B: Hetero.    C: Skewness    D: Kurtosis

PANEL 2: CAMERON AND TRIVEDI VERSION OF IM TEST

E: Total    F: Hetero.    G: Skewness    H: Kurtosis

Figure 4.11. Power of information matrix test to detect slight heteroscedasticity. $R^2 = 0.40$.

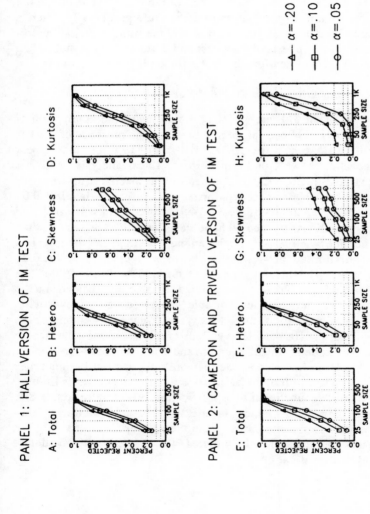

**Figure 4.12.** Power of information matrix test to detect moderate heteroscedasticity. $R^2 = 0.40$.

103

powerful. Given the modest amount of heteroscedasticity, the tests require 1,000 cases before the null hypothesis is rejected 75% of the time using a 0.05 significance level. The skewness and kurtosis portions of the test behave quite similarly to how they did in our tests of size.

In the case of a modest amount of heteroscedasticity, shown in Figure 4.12, several differences are seen. First, as would be expected, the power of the test increases. With a sample size of 250 the null of no misspecification is rejected nearly 100% of the time. The Hall version of the test remains somewhat more powerful, particularly when a significance level of 0.05 is used. Finally, the more extreme heteroscedasticity results in tests of skewness and kurtosis that are more often significant. This is more often the case with the Hall version of the test.

### Power for Nonlinearity and an Excluded Variable

The power of the IM test to detect violations of the assumption of linearity will depend upon the degree to which the presence of nonlinearity in the data generating process will result in errors that appear heteroscedastic, skewed, or kurtotic in the linear analysis. With the nonlinear Data Structure 7, the hypothesis of no specification error was rejected less than 10% of the time using a significance level of 0.05 when $n = 1,000$, regardless of the $R^2$. With Data Structure 6, which had more severe nonlinearity, the null hypothesis was still rejected less than 10% of the time when $R^2 = 0.4$. With an increase in the $R^2$ the tests had some, but still limited, power. This is shown in Figure 4.13. At the 0.20 level, $H_0$ was rejected less than 40% of the time with $n = 1,000$. The power of the IM test to detect an excluded variable also depends on the degree to which the excluded variable generated heteroscedasticity, skewness, or kurtosis in the model analyzed. Figure 4.14 compares the performance of the Hall and CT versions of the test in the cases where $X_1$ has been excluded from the equation and $R^2 = 0.4$. Results are similar for $R^2 = 0.8$. Overall, we conclude that while the IM test is sometimes referred to as a test of functional misspecification, its power is limited. To the extent that functional misspecification results in residuals that are heteroscedastic, skewed, or kurtotic, the IM test will indicate functional misspecification. In cases where the assumptions regarding the higher-order moments are not violated, the IM test will not detect functional misspecification.

PANEL 1: HALL VERSION OF IM TEST

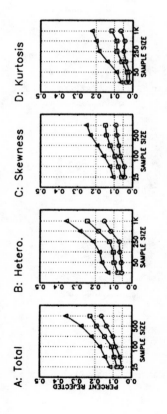

PANEL 2: CAMERON AND TRIVEDI VERSION OF IM TEST

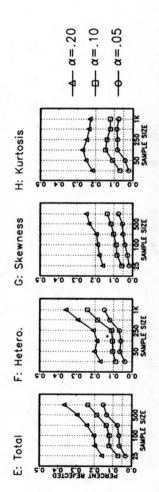

**Figure 4.13.** Properties of information matrix test in the presence of moderate nonlinearity of the form $y = \beta_0 + \beta_1\sqrt{x_1} + \beta_2 x_2 + \beta_3 x_3$. $R^2 = 0.80$.

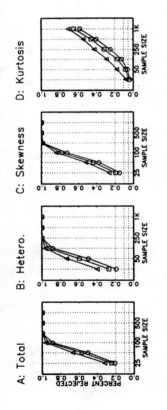

PANEL 1: HALL VERSION OF IM TEST

A: Total    B: Hetero.    C: Skewness    D: Kurtosis

PANEL 2: CAMERON AND TRIVEDI VERSION OF IM TEST

E: Total    F: Hetero.    G: Skewness    H: Kurtosis

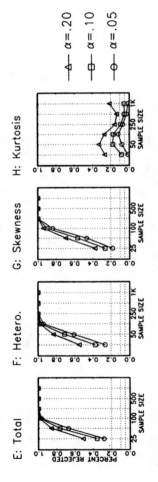

$\alpha = .20$
$\alpha = .10$
$\alpha = .05$

**Figure 4.14.** Properties of information matrix test in the presence of an excluded variable. $R^2 = 0.40$.

**Table 4.3** Empirical Size of the Heteroscedasticity Consistent Wald Versions of the IM Test

| Sample Size | Empirical Size | | |
| | Heteroscedasticity | Skewness | Excess Kurtosis |
|---|---|---|---|
| 25 | 0.969 | 0.148 | 0.026 |
| 50 | 0.867 | 0.060 | 0.052 |
| 100 | 0.694 | 0.046 | 0.081 |
| 250 | 0.461 | 0.039 | 0.097 |
| 500 | 0.338 | 0.038 | 0.071 |

## The Heteroscedasticity Consistent Wald Version of the IM Test

Finally, consider the properties of heteroscedasticity consistent Wald tests of heteroscedasticity, skewness, and excess kurtosis based on CT's auxiliary regression equations, Equations 17, 19, and 21. As previously explained, one tests the hypothesis that the slope parameters in regressions 17 and 19 and the intercept parameter in 21 are zero. Monte Carlo experiments were carried out to compare the size and power of the original variants of CT tests and the corresponding heteroscedasticity consistent variants. To conserve space we report only a small selection of the output.

Table 4.3 gives the empirical size of heteroscedasticity consistent variants of the three IM tests at the 5% nominal level. In this case the rejection rate for all tests should be 5%, because the data were generated without misspecification. However, the rejection rate for the heteroscedasticity test is 96.9% for $n = 25$. While the rejection rate decreases as $n$ increases, it is still as high as 33.8% for $n = 500$. Thus the heteroscedasticity consistent variant of the test overrejects and is unsatisfactory, whereas the $nR^2$ variant of the same test shows far less size distortion. By contrast, once sample size exceeds 50, skewness and excess kurtosis tests show little size distortion.

Table 4.4 shows the rejection rates for the three tests when the data are generated by a model with moderate heteroscedasticity. Although the heteroscedasticity test appears to have high power, the reported rejection frequency overstates the power of the test because the appropriate concept here is size-corrected power. Given that the test overrejects when

**Table 4.4** Empirical Rejection Rates in the Presence of Heteroscedasticity for the Heteroscedasticity Consistent Wald Versions of the IM Test

| | Percentage Rejected | | |
| Sample Size | Heteroscedasticity | Skewness | Excess Kurtosis |
|---|---|---|---|
| 25 | 0.967 | 0.467 | 0.037 |
| 50 | 0.888 | 0.050 | 0.052 |
| 100 | 0.793 | 0.035 | 0.063 |
| 250 | 0.809 | 0.035 | 0.041 |
| 500 | 0.941 | 0.052 | 0.050 |

the null hypothesis is true, the nominal rejection frequency overstates the power of the test. For $n$ larger than 50, the size distortion was not a serious problem for either the skewness or the heteroscedasticity tests. It is seen that size and power are roughly equal for these tests. We conclude that heteroscedasticity consistent tests produce very mixed results.

## Conclusions

The tests considered in this chapter provide a potentially useful set of tools for assessing regression models. To be useful for applied work, a test must have reasonable size properties and enough power to detect departures from the null that may be expected in applied work. Our Monte Carlo experiments show a tendency toward overrejection in some tests. Tests with severe size distortion cannot be recommended unless they are corrected for this distortion. There are at least two ways of adjusting a test to achieve lower size distortion. First, using asymptotic expansions of the test statistic, one may calculate an adjustment factor for the test statistic. Alternatively, one might calculate adjusted critical values for tests at conventional significance levels. Both these approaches typically involve nonstandard calculations that applied researchers will find burdensome. Obviously, computationally simple tests with desirable size and power properties are preferable. Our Monte Carlo results suggest that specific variations of the RESET and IM tests have these characteristics.

The following strategy for testing should provide a useful assessment of one's model. First, the RESET test and the robust LM RESET test (rather than the heteroscedasticity robust Wald version of RESET) should be applied. If both tests pass, suggesting an adequate conditional mean specification, the IM test of higher-order moment misspecification should be used. If the standard RESET test fails, but the robust version passes, correct functional form is indicated but higher-order moment misspecification seems likely. Again the IM test should be considered. In applying the IM test, the decomposition suggested by Hall is useful for determining the specific violation that may cause the IM test to fail. While Hall's decomposition is useful, components of Hall's version of the test are not robust to departures from the null. For example, when the null is false, Hall's components of the test will be correlated, which limits its ability to specify violations. The alternative variant of the IM test based on an orthogonal decomposition has proven to be more robust when implemented along the lines of Cameron and Trivedi (1990b).

While specification tests have significant potential for the applied researcher, our results suggest the importance of carefully evaluating their properties with Monte Carlo methods. In addition, evaluation is needed to determine the behavior of these tests under additional violations of assumptions (e.g., the presence of outliers in the data) and with multiple violations of assumptions (e.g., nonlinearity and heteroscedasticity). Given the sometimes surprising behavior of specification tests for the simple case of regression, it is essential that as specification tests for the covariance structure model (Arminger & Schoenberg, 1989) are developed, their properties are thoroughly examined with Monte Carlo methods before they are routinely applied.

## Notes

1. White's test for functional form can be viewed as a variable augmentation test, as can the RESET test. For details, see Godfrey (1988, pp. 152-155).

2. $\lambda_{RLM}$ is awkward to compute because it requires combining the residuals $\hat{v}_i$ from $P$ regressions with the residuals $\hat{u}$ from the original regression. There does not appear to be a single auxiliary regression that will simplify the computations.

3. Random numbers were generated using the procedures RNDUS and RNDNS in GAUSS Version 2.1 (Aptech Systems, 1991). The functions are based on a multiplicative congruential method for generating random numbers.

## References

Aptech Systems. (1991). *GAUSS version 2.1.* Kent, WA: Author.

Arminger, G., & Schoenberg, R. J. (1989). Pseudo maximum likelihood estimation and a test for misspecification in mean and covariance structure models. *Psychometrika, 54,* 409-425.

Breusch, T. S., & Pagan, A. R. (1979). A simple test for heteroscedasticity and random coefficient variation. *Econometrica, 47,* 1287-1294.

Cameron, A. C., & Trivedi, P. K. (1990a). *Conditional moment tests and orthogonal polynomials.* Working paper.

Cameron, A. C., & Trivedi, P. K. (1990b). *The information matrix test and its implied alternative hypotheses.* Working paper.

Chesher, A., & Austin, G. (1991). The finite-sample distributions of heteroskedasticity-robust Wald statistics. *Journal of Econometrics, 47,* 153-173.

Davidson, R., & MacKinnon, J. (1985). Heteroskedasticity-robust tests in regression directions. *Annales de l'INSEE, 59/60,* 183-218.

Eicker, F. (1967). Limit theorems for regressions with unequal and dependent errors. In *Proceedings of the Fifth Berkeley Symposium on Mathematical Statistics and Probability* (Vol. 1, pp. 59-82). Berkeley: University of California Press.

Fuller, W. A. (1975). Regression analysis for sample survey. *Sankhya, Series C, 37,* 117-132.

Godfrey, L. G. (1988). *Misspecification tests in econometrics: The Lagrange multiplier principle and other approaches.* New York: Cambridge University Press.

Hall, A. (1987). The information matrix test for the linear model. *Review of Economic Studies, 54,* 257-263.

Hausman, J. A. (1978). Specification tests in econometrics. *Econometrica, 46,* 1251-1272.

Judge, G. G., Griffiths, W. E., Hill, R. C., Lütkepohl, & Lee, T. C. (1985). *The theory and practice of econometrics* (2nd ed.). New York: John Wiley.

Milliken, G. A., & Graybill, F. A. (1970). Extensions of the general linear hypothesis model. *Journal of the American Statistical Association, 65,* 797-807.

Pagan, A. R., & Vella, F. (1989). Diagnostic tests for models based on individual data. *Journal of Applied Econometrics* (Suppl. S4), S29-S60.

Ramsey, J. B. (1969). Tests for specification errors in classical linear least-squares regression analysis. *Journal of the Royal Statistical Society, Series B, 31,* 350-371.

White, H. (1980a). A heteroskedasticity-consistent covariance matrix estimator and a direct test for heteroskedasticity. *Econometrica, 48,* 817-838.

White, H. (1980b). Using least squares to approximate unknown regression functions. *International Economic Review, 21,* 149-170.

White, H. (1981). Consequences and detection of misspecified nonlinear regression models. *Journal of the American Statistical Association, 76,* 419-433.

White, H. (1982). Maximum likelihood estimation of misspecified models. *Econometrica, 50,* 1-24.

*5*

# Bootstrapping
# Goodness-of-Fit Measures
# in Structural Equation Models

### KENNETH A. BOLLEN
### ROBERT A. STINE

Assessing overall fit is a topic of keen interest to structural equation modelers, yet measuring goodness of fit has been hampered by several factors. First, the assumptions that underlie the chi-square tests of model fit often are violated by the approximate nature of the model, excessive kurtosis of the observed random variables, or a small to moderate sample size. Second, many fit measures (e.g., Bentler & Bonett's [1980] normed fit index) have unknown statistical distributions, so that hypothesis testing, confidence intervals, or comparisons of significant differences in these fit indices are not possible.[1] Finally, we have little knowledge about the distribution and behavior of the fit measures for misspecified models or for nonnested models.

Given this situation, bootstrapping techniques would appear to be an ideal means for tackling these problems. Indeed, Bentler's (1989) EQS 3.0 and Jöreskog and Sörbom's (in press) LISREL 8 have bootstrap resampling options to bootstrap fit indices. The purposes of this chapter

AUTHORS' NOTE: We wish to thank Kwok-fai Ting for RA work done for this project and the anonymous referees for their comments. This work was presented at the Department of Economics, Universitat Pompeu Fabra, Barcelona, Spain, and at the 1992 Social Science Methodology Conference in Trento, Italy. Partial support for Bollen's research on this project is from NSF, SES-8908361 and SES-9121564.

are (a) to demonstrate that the usual bootstrapping methods will fail when applied to the original data, (b) to explain why this occurs, and (c) to propose a modified bootstrap method for the chi-square test statistic for model fit.

We begin with a section that reviews the bootstrapping method. Two sections on hypothesis testing with bootstrapping procedures follow: the first on tests of means and the second on the likelihood ratio chi-square tests in structural equation models. In these two sections, we demonstrate and explain the failure of the usual bootstrapping scheme and present modified bootstrap procedures that have superior performance. The brief section that follows explains how to apply the modified bootstrap procedure to chi-square difference tests for nested models. Results of the previous two sections are then illustrated in an empirical example. Next we examine whether such modifications work for other fit indices for structural equation models. The chapter concludes with a review of the major results and description of the remaining problems facing bootstrap applications in this area.

## Naive Bootstrapping

Several introductions to the bootstrap methodology are available (e.g., Efron, 1982; Efron & Tibshirani, 1986; Stine, 1989). In brief, the usual bootstrap method is as follows. Let $\{X_1, X_2, \ldots, X_N\}$ be a random sample of size $N$ with each $X_i$ independently drawn from the same population that has a cumulative distribution function $G$ that is characterized by a parameter $\theta$. Our estimator of $\theta$ is symbolized as $\hat{\theta}$, and we wish to know its sampling distribution. For the random variables, $\{X_1, X_2, \ldots, X_N\}$, we observe a given sample $\{x_1, x_2, \ldots, x_N\}$. The bootstrap method samples from the population defined by the *empirical* distribution function $G_N$ to estimate the sampling distribution of $\hat{\theta}$. The empirical distribution function, $G_N$, is that distribution with mass $1/N$ on $x_1, x_2, \ldots, x_N$. That is, we form a bootstrap sample, $\{X_1^*, X_2^*, \ldots, X_N^*\}$, by taking $N$ independent draws *with replacement* from $\{x_1, x_2, \ldots, x_N\}$. The bootstrap estimate, $\hat{\theta}^*$, is computed using the same formula as that for $\hat{\theta}$, but it is calculated using the bootstrap sample. Repeating this process $B$ times gives $\hat{\theta}^*(1), \hat{\theta}^*(2), \ldots, \hat{\theta}^*(B)$. From these bootstrap replicates of $\hat{\theta}$ we estimate the bootstrap distribution of $\hat{\theta}$, including its mean and variance.

Although this general bootstrap procedure works well in many cases, it can fail. For example, bootstrapping gives a misleading impression of the distribution of the maximum of a sample (Bickel & Freedman, 1981). *The success of the bootstrap depends on the sampling behavior of a statistic being the same when the samples are drawn from the empirical distribution and when they are taken from the original population.* In some situations this assumption does not hold, and the resulting bootstrap estimates perform poorly.[2] Bootstrapping transformed data sometimes can correct the problem. The sections that follow illustrate these points.

### Hypothesis Tests on the Mean

Consider the distribution of the usual $Z$ statistic when testing the null hypothesis that $\mu = 0$ when $X_1, \ldots, X_N$ are a sample from a normal distribution with mean $\mu$ and known variance $\sigma$ equal to 1. Then the distribution of the test statistic

$$Z = \frac{\overline{X}}{\frac{\sigma}{\sqrt{N}}} = \sqrt{N}\,\overline{X} \qquad [1]$$

is normal with mean zero and variance 1 under $H_0$. Thus $Z^2$ is chi-square with one degree of freedom and yields a test equivalent to the usual two-sided $Z$ test. The procedure rejects the null hypothesis when $Z^2$ exceeds, say, 3.84, which is the upper 5% point in the chi-square distribution with one degree of freedom (df). More generally, the chi-square distribution with 1 df is the basis for finding the $p$ value associated with the observed test statistic.

Consider the following bootstrap approach to evaluate the $p$ value of this test. As in the "naive" bootstrap scheme, resample the data and generate $B$ copies of the observed statistic. That is, repeat the following procedure $B$ times:

(1) Resample $\{x_1, x_2, \ldots, x_N\}$ to obtain $\{x_1^*, x_2^*, \ldots, x_N^*\}$.
(2) Compute $\overline{x}^*$, the mean of the bootstrap sample.
(3) Form $z^{*2} = N\overline{x}^{*2}$.

Although one might be tempted to use the collection $\{z^{*2}(1), z^{*2}(2), \ldots, z^{*2}(B)\}$ to assess the significance of our observed test

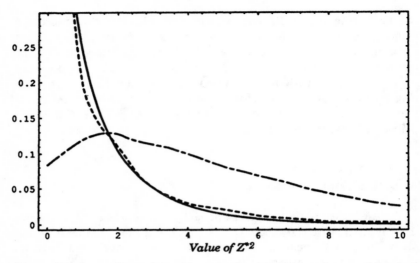

**Figure 5.1.** Comparison of the chi-square density with one degree of freedom (solid line) to the naive bootstrap density (— - —) and modified bootstrap density (- - - -) of $Z^{*2}$.

statistic, to do so would be wrong. To demonstrate this we generated 150 observations from the $N(0,1)$ distribution. Then we applied the preceding bootstrap algorithm. Figure 5.1 shows the chi-square distribution with one degree of freedom (solid line) and the bootstrap distribution of $Z^{*2}$ based on 500 bootstrap samples (— - —).[3] The difference is dramatic. The bootstrap density is shifted to the right, with a peak near 2. In contrast, the chi-square density is monotonically decreasing over the same range. The 0.05 critical value based on the bootstrap is about 13, compared with 3.84 based on a chi-square with 1 df. The bootstrap critical value of 13 is determined so that only 5% of the bootstrap replications $Z^{*2}$ exceed this value.

The bootstrap fails in this simple example because the fundamental bootstrap assumption does not hold. That is, bootstrap resampling from the observations does not resemble sampling from a population in which the null hypothesis holds. This failure manifests itself in a variety of ways, but it is perhaps most easily seen by comparing the expected value of $Z^2$ to that of the bootstrap replications. Notice that we do not need simulations; all of the calculations are exact, as though we had performed an infinite number of replications ($B = \infty$).

First, consider the expected value of $Z^2$. Suppose that $X_1, X_2, \ldots, X_N$ are a sample from a population with mean $\mu$ and variance $\sigma^2$. It follows that

$$E(Z^2) = NE(\overline{X} - \mu + \mu)^2 \tag{2}$$

$$= NE[(\overline{X} - \mu)^2] + N\mu^2$$

$$= \sigma^2 + N\mu^2 ,$$

where the second equality follows from noting that $E(\overline{X} - \mu) = 0$ and the third is a restatement of the result that $\text{VAR}(\overline{X}) = \sigma^2/N$. In the prior example, $X_1, X_2, \ldots, X_N$ are $N(0,1)$ and $E(Z^2)$ reduces to 1, which is the expected value of a chi-square random variable having one degree of freedom.

To find the expected value of $Z^{*2}$, we basically repeat the familiar steps leading to Equation 2. We must, however, compute the expected value with respect to the population associated with the bootstrap observations $X_i^*$. Since the $X_i^*$ are drawn from the empirical distribution $G_N$, we need to compute the expected values with respect to this population rather than to $G$. Let $E^*$ denote the expected value that puts weight $1/N$ on each $x_1, x_2, \ldots, x_N$. The expected value with respect to $E^*$ gives averages associated with infinite bootstrap resampling from $G_N$ without needing simulation. The two essential results we require are

$$E^*(X_i^*) = \sum_{i=1}^{N} x_i/N = \overline{x} \tag{3}$$

and

$$\text{VAR}^*(X_i^*) = E^*(X_i^* - \overline{x})^2 = v^2 , \tag{4}$$

where

$$v^2 = \sum_{i=1}^{N} (x_i - \overline{x})^2/N . \tag{5}$$

As a consequence, when computing expected values with $E^*$, one replaces the usual parameters $\mu$ and $\sigma^2$ with the sample values $\overline{x}$ and $v^2$.

Note that $v^2$ is the maximum likelihood estimator (MLE) of $\sigma^2$ under normality and it is almost the usual unbiased estimator of $\sigma^2$, differing by having the divisor of $N$ rather than $N-1$. It follows from Equations 3 and 4 that the expected value of bootstrap replications of the sample mean is

$$E^*(\overline{X}^*) = \overline{x} \qquad [6]$$

and the variance is

$$\text{VAR}^*(\overline{X}^*) = v^2/N. \qquad [7]$$

Note that the original observations $x_1, x_2, \ldots, x_N$ are treated as fixed constants when applying $E^*$, so all of these expectations are in fact conditional on the observed sample.

With these results in hand, we can compute the expected value of the bootstrap replications of $Z^{*2}$ and discover the source of the problem in this naive resampling scheme. Following the derivation of Equations 2, 6, and 7 implies that

$$E^*(Z^{*2}) = NE^*(\overline{X}^*)^2 \qquad [8]$$

$$= NE^*(\overline{X}^* - \overline{x} + \overline{x})^2$$

$$= NE^*[(\overline{X}^* - \overline{x})]^2 + N\overline{x}^2$$

$$= v^2 + N\overline{x}^2$$

$$= v^2 + z^2.$$

Thus the expected value of the bootstrap replicates $Z^{*2}$ is the observed value of the test statistic plus an additional term that approaches $\sigma^2$ as $N$ increases. Considering the specific illustration with $X_1, X_2, \ldots, X_N$ distributed $N(0,1)$, Equation 2 implies that the $E(Z^2) = 1$, whereas Equation 8 shows that the expected value of $Z^{*2}$ is

$$E(V^2 + Z^2) = \frac{N-1}{N} + 1 = 2 - \frac{1}{N}. \qquad [9]$$

As a result, $Z^2$ averages near 1 but the average of $Z^{*2}$ is about 2.

We should point out that other features of the distribution of $Z^{*2}$ are also misleading. For example, $Z^{*2}$ has greater sampling variance than $Z^2$ and its distribution is fundamentally different. One cannot correct this problem by a simple change of location with rescaling. Babu (1984) gives a thorough, technical description of these issues, and Freedman (1981) describes a related problem occurring in regression analysis without an intercept.

So where does this bootstrapping scheme go wrong? Recall that the significance of a test statistic like $Z^2$ is the probability of observing a statistic of that size or larger *when the null hypothesis is true*. Consider the test of $H_0$: $\mu = 0$ using $Z^2$. Under the naive resampling as done in the example, the mean of the bootstrap population, namely, the average of the observed sample, is almost surely not zero. Thus these bootstrap samples are drawn from a population for which the null hypothesis does not hold, regardless of whether $H_0$ holds for the unknown population from which $X_1, X_2, \ldots, X_N$ are drawn. Hence the bootstrap values of the test statistic reject $H_0$ too often. It is only natural that $Z^2$ appears in Equation 8 for the expected value of $Z^{*2}$, because it represents how poorly the null hypothesis holds in the observed sample.

In this simple case, it is relatively easy to "repair" the bootstrap scheme. To make the null hypothesis true under bootstrapping resampling, center the data around the sample mean $\bar{x}$ and draw bootstrap samples from $\{(x_1 - \bar{x}), (x_2 - \bar{x}), \ldots, (x_N - \bar{x})\}$. Resampling from these centered values forces the mean of the bootstrap population to be zero so that $H_0$ holds. The resulting bootstrap replicates provide an estimated $p$ value of the test statistic. To illustrate this we took the same simulated data as before except that we formed deviation scores before applying the bootstrapping resampling. The third curve (- - - -) in Figure 5.1 is the modified bootstrap distribution. The centered resampling scheme leads to a more accurate estimate of the distribution of $Z^2$ and is closer to the chi-square distribution (solid line). For example, the $\chi^2$ with 1 df critical value is 3.84 for a Type I error of 0.05. Centered resampling gives a mean of 1.2 and a critical value of 4.9; that is, 4.9 is greater than all but 5% of the bootstrap replicates. Recall that for the naive bootstrap distribution, the corresponding critical value is about 13.[4]

### Likelihood Ratio Test Statistic

The subject of this section is the application of the bootstrap method to the distribution of the likelihood ratio-based test statistic used in structural equation models. The maximum likelihood (ML) fitting function is

$$F_{ML}[S, \Sigma(\theta)] = \ln |\Sigma(\theta)| + \text{tr}[S \, \Sigma^{-1}(\theta)] - \ln |S| - p, \qquad [10]$$

where $\Sigma(\theta)$ is the population covariance matrix implied by a model, $\theta$ is the $t \times 1$ vector that contains the free parameters of the model, $S$ is the unbiased sample covariance matrix of the observed variables, and $p$ is the number of observed variables.[5] A vector $\hat{\theta}$ is chosen to minimize Equation 10. Then the fitting function is used to test the null hypothesis, $H_0: \Sigma = \Sigma(\theta)$. The test statistic $T = (N-1)F_{ML}[S, \Sigma(\hat{\theta})]$ is asymptotically distributed as a noncentral chi-square variate with degrees of freedom equal to $\frac{1}{2}(p+1)p - t$ and noncentrality parameter $\kappa$, provided that the observed variables have no excessive multivariate kurtosis. The noncentrality parameter $\kappa$ equals $(N-1)F_{ML}[\Sigma, \Sigma(\theta_0)]$ with $\theta_0$ chosen to minimize $F_{ML}[\Sigma, \Sigma(\theta)]$ over choices of $\theta$ (Browne, 1984, p. 70, corollary 4.1).

Naive bootstrapping of the test statistic involves repeating the following procedure $B$ times:

(1) Resample the original data and form $S^*$, the covariance matrix for the bootstrap sample.
(2) Fit the hypothesized model to $S^*$ by minimizing $F_{ML}[S^*, \Sigma(\theta^*)]$ over choices of $\theta^*$.
(3) Compute $T^* = (N-1)F_{ML}[S^*, \Sigma(\hat{\theta}^*)]$, where $\hat{\theta}^*$ is the value of $\theta^*$ that minimizes $F_{ML}[S^*, \Sigma(\theta^*)]$.

The test statistic $T$ for the original sample would then be compared to the bootstrap distribution of $T^*(1), T^*(2), \ldots, T^*(B)$ for tests of statistical significance.

Naive bootstrapping of the chi-square statistic for structural equation models is inaccurate. To understand why, consider the expected values and variances of $T$ and $T^*$. Since $T \{= (N-1)F_{ML}[S, \Sigma(\hat{\theta})]\}$ is distributed as a noncentral chi-square variable in large samples, we have

$$AE(T) = df + \kappa, \qquad [11]$$

where $AE(.)$ is the asymptotic expectation, df stands for the degrees of freedom, and $\kappa$ is the noncentrality parameter. If the model is valid and the other assumptions for the test hold, then κ is zero and $T$ follows a central chi-square distribution. The variance of $T$ is

$$AVAR\ (T) = 2df + 4\kappa\ , \qquad [12]$$

where AVAR(.) denotes the asymptotic variance. For a valid model where κ is zero, Equation 12 reduces to 2 df.

The distribution of $T^*$ approximates a noncentral chi-square distribution when resampling from the bootstrap population. In the original population, the noncentrality parameter κ equals $(N-1)F_{ML}[\Sigma, \Sigma(\theta_0)]$. In the bootstrap population, the noncentrality parameter is $(N-1)F_{ML}[S, \Sigma(\hat{\theta})]$, which equals $T$.[6] Consequently, we are led to the approximation

$$E^*(T^*) \approx df + T\ . \qquad [13]$$

Taking expectations with respect to the original population and substituting from Equation 13 gives

$$E[E^*(T^*)] \approx df + df + \kappa \qquad [14]$$

$$\approx 2df + \kappa\ .$$

Similarly, the approximate bootstrap variance of $T^*$ is

$$VAR^*(T^*) \approx 2df + 4T\ , \qquad [15]$$

where $VAR^*(.)$ represents the variance over the bootstrap samples. The expectation of Equation 15 with respect to the original population is

$$E[VAR^*(T^*)] \approx 6df + 4\kappa\ . \qquad [16]$$

Hence the mean of the bootstrap distribution of $T^*$ is larger than the mean of $T$ by approximately df, and the variance of $T^*$ exceeds that of $T$. The observed value of the test statistic $T$ is the noncentrality value in the bootstrap population. $H_0$ is violated when bootstrapping regardless of whether it holds in the actual population. As a result, the bootstrap approximation fails to match the sampling distribution associated with the original population.

These results are *approximations* for two reasons. The noncentral chi-square distribution for $T$ is an asymptotic result, and the expression for the noncentrality parameter $\kappa$ assumes that the observed variables originate from a distribution with no excess kurtosis.[7] Even if the original data are a sample from a multinormal distribution, a given sample can appear very nonnormal, leading to excessive kurtosis in the bootstrap population. Also, the bootstrap distribution is discrete, whereas the original population distribution is continuous. Despite these limitations, we have found these approximations helpful in understanding and predicting the results of naive bootstrapping of the test statistic.

As with the chi-square test of $H_0$: $\mu = 0$, it is possible to develop a bootstrap procedure that applies to this more complex model. The idea again is to resample a set of observations for which the null hypothesis is true. For a test of $H_0$: $\Sigma = \Sigma(\theta)$, the bootstrap population from which we resample must have the covariance structure specified by the null hypothesis.[8]

To generate such a population requires a little matrix algebra, including the idea of the square root of a matrix. Let $Y$ denote the $N \times p$ data matrix of the centered observed variables. Also, $S = Y'Y/(N-1)$ denotes the sample covariance matrix of $Y$ and $\hat{\Sigma}$ $[= \Sigma(\hat{\theta})]$ is the estimated implied covariance matrix. Let $M = M^{1/2\prime}M^{1/2}$ represent a square root factorization of the positive definite matrix $M$, such as that given by a Cholesky factorization (see Beran & Srivastava, 1985). Then the covariance matrix of

$$Z = YS^{-1/2}\hat{\Sigma}^{1/2} \qquad [17]$$

is indeed $\hat{\Sigma}$, since

$$Z'Z/(N-1) = \hat{\Sigma}^{1/2}S^{-1/2}Y'YS^{-1/2}\hat{\Sigma}^{1/2}/(N-1) \qquad [18]$$

$$= \hat{\Sigma}^{1/2}S^{-1/2}SS^{-1/2}\hat{\Sigma}^{1/2}$$

$$= \hat{\Sigma}^{1/2}S^{-1/2}S^{1/2}S^{1/2}S^{-1/2}\hat{\Sigma}^{1/2}$$

$$= \hat{\Sigma}^{1/2}\hat{\Sigma}^{1/2}$$

$$= \hat{\Sigma} .$$

Now perform the bootstrap by resampling the rows of $Z$ rather than the original observations in the rows of $Y$. The test statistic $T$ calculated for the covariance matrix of $Z$ will be zero, since the sample covariance matrix of $Z$ equals $\hat{\Sigma}$.

The modified bootstrapping procedure involves repeating the following procedure $B$ times:

(1) Resample the modified data, $Z$, and form $S_m^*$, the covariance matrix for the bootstrap sample of the modified data.

(2) Fit the hypothesized model to $S_m^*$ by minimizing $F_{ML}[S_m^*, \Sigma(\theta_m^*)]$ over choices of $\theta_m^*$.

(3) Compute $T_m^* = (N - 1)F_{ML}[S_m^*, \Sigma(\hat{\theta}_m^*)]$, where $\hat{\theta}_m^*$ is the value of $\theta_m^*$ that minimizes $F_{ML}[S_m^*, \Sigma(\theta_m^*)]$.

The means and variances of the modified test statistic, $T_m^*$, are

$$E^*(T_m^*) \approx df \qquad\qquad [19]$$

$$E[E^*(T_m^*)] \approx df$$

and

$$VAR^*(T_m^*) \approx 2df \qquad\qquad [20]$$

$$E[VAR^*(T_m^*)] \approx 2df .$$

The bootstrap sampling distribution of $T_m^*$, the modified test statistic, behaves as the sampling distribution of $T$ from the original population when the null hypothesis is true. As before, we note that these results are approximations, for the reasons stated previously.

We illustrate these ideas with a simulation of a single latent variable $(\xi_1)$ measured with eight indicators $(x_1$ to $x_8)$:

$$x_i = \lambda_{i1}\xi_1 + \delta_i , \qquad\qquad [21]$$

where $i = 1$ to 8, $\lambda_{i1}$ is a coefficient giving the effect of $\xi_1$ on $x_i$, $\delta_i$ represents random measurement error with $E(\delta_i) = 0$, and $\text{cov}(\delta_i, \xi_1) = 0$. The eight values of the $\lambda_{i1}$s are 1, 1.2, 1.4, 1.6, 1, 1.2, 1.4, and 1.6, respectively. The variances of the $\delta_i$s are 2, 4, 6, 8, 2, 4, 6, and 8, respectively, and the variance of the factor is 1. We generated data from normal distributions that conform to the model for an $N$ of 150. The test statistic $T$ for this sample is 23.1. The critical value for a chi-square variate with 20 df is 31.4 for a Type I error of 0.05. Thus the data are consistent with $H_0$: $\Sigma = \Sigma(\theta)$.

We then applied the naive bootstrap method to this sample; that is, we resampled with replacement the original sample, estimated the covariance matrix for the bootstrap sample, and calculated $T^*$ for each bootstrap sample. Next, we used the previously described modified bootstrap procedure, where we transformed the original $Y$ to $Z$ and then bootstrapped the data of $Z$. Figure 5.2a overlays the bootstrap distribution of $T_m^*$ from the modified procedure (- - - -) on top of the Monte Carlo simulated distribution of $T$ (— — —) and a chi-square distribution with 20 degrees of freedom (solid line). In addition, the naive bootstrap distribution of $T^*$ is plotted (— - —).

The bootstrap approximation to the density based on $T^*$ is shifted to the right and has greater variance than the chi-square density. These properties are consistent with the approximations in Equations 14 and 16. Clearly, the naive bootstrap distribution is quite inaccurate. The density for the modified bootstrap density and the simulated density are both less peaked and longer tailed than the chi-square density. Figure 5.2b magnifies the right tails of these three densities. The modified bootstrap approximation is the longest tailed, with the simulated estimate between the bootstrap and the chi-square. The longer tail for the Monte Carlo simulation than for the chi-square is consistent with other Monte Carlo simulation studies and is consistent with the finding that the usual test statistic rejects the null hypothesis too frequently in small samples (e.g., Boomsma, 1982).

### Testing Nested Models

Chi-square difference tests are commonly used for comparing the fit of nested models. It would be useful to have a method to bootstrap a test statistic that enables us to compare nested models. The preceding modified bootstrapping procedure applies to this test statistic as well. The null hypothesis for the chi-square test is that the more restrictive model is valid and the less restrictive model is not required. The key to applying the modified method is to transform the data so that the null hypothesis is true in the bootstrap population. That is, apply the transformation of $Y$ to $Z$ (see Equation 17) using the $\hat{\Sigma}$ fitted under the most

**(a)**

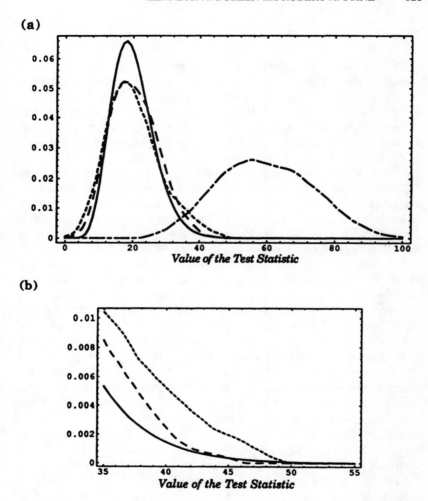

**(b)**

**Figure 5.2.** Comparison of the chi-square approximation with 20 degrees of freedom (solid line) and the simulated density of $T_m$ (— — —) to the naive bootstrap density of $T^*$ (— · —) and modified bootstrap density of $T_m^*$ (- - - -): (a) complete densities, (b) right tails, omitting the naive bootstrap density.

restrictive model. Fit both models to the same bootstrapped covariance matrix and form the difference in the test statistics. The empirical example that follows illustrates this procedure.

## Industrialization and Political Democracy Example

To illustrate our modified bootstrap procedure further, we use a model of the relationship between industrialization and political democracy in 75 developing countries (see the path diagram in Figure 5.3). It is a panel model with two latent endogenous variables, political democracy in 1960 ($\eta_1$) and 1965 ($\eta_2$), and one latent exogenous variable, industrialization in 1960 ($\xi_1$). Industrialization is measured with three indicators, and political democracy for 1960 and 1965 is measured with the same four indicators. For Model A, shown in Figure 5.3, the measurement errors for the same indicator at two points in time are allowed to correlate, as are the errors for measures that are ratings from the same judge. For Model B, we restrict all measurement error covariances to zero. Detailed descriptions of the variables, models, and the ML estimates may be found in Bollen (1989).[9]

Bootstrap methods are helpful in this situation because we do not know whether the sample is sufficiently large to rely on the asymptotic chi-square distribution for the test. Using the ML fitting function and associated test statistics, we find $T_A$ is 39.6 with 38 df for Model A and $T_B$ is 73.6 with 44 df for Model B. Comparing these to the corresponding chi-square distributions, we find that Model A has quite a good fit ($p = .40$), whereas Model B has a worse fit ($p < .01$). Performing a nested chi-square difference test, we have ($T_B - T_A$) equal to 34 with 6 df, which is highly significant ($p < .001$). Thus the usual methods would lead us to conclude that Model A fits well, but Model B without correlated measurement errors has a very poor fit.

We then formed the modified bootstrap distribution, assuming that the more restrictive, simpler Model B is correct. Figure 5.4 shows this distribution based on 250 replications. The $T_B$ of 73.6 has a bootstrap $p$ value of .055, that is, $T_B$ is larger than all but 5.5% of the bootstrap replications under $H_0$. The resulting $p$ value is considerably higher than that found with the usual methods. For this example Model B has a much better fit based on the bootstrap distribution than was found using the usual chi-square-based test. We also used the modified bootstrap procedure to analyze the change in fit of Model B versus Model A. Here again we assume Model B is correct for the modified bootstrap. Figure 5.5 plots the bootstrap density for differences in the bootstrap test statistics for Models B and A (- - - -) and a chi-square distribution with 6 df (solid). Note also the difference in the chi-square and bootstrap distributions in this case. The bootstrap $p$ value for a difference of 34

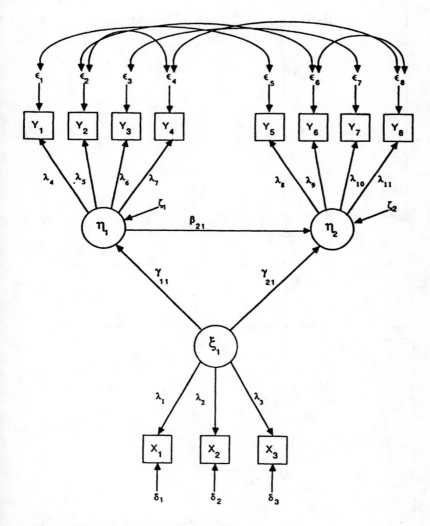

**Figure 5.3.** Path diagram, Model A.

is near zero, since none of the bootstrapped differences was this large. So, for this example, the modified bootstrapped test statistic suggests a different *p* value for Model B, but still indicates that Model A is much superior, giving a highly significant improvement in the test statistic.

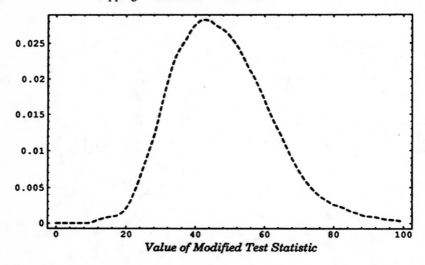

**Figure 5.4.** Modified bootstrap density of the test statistic $T_m^*$ in the industrialization and political democracy Model B.

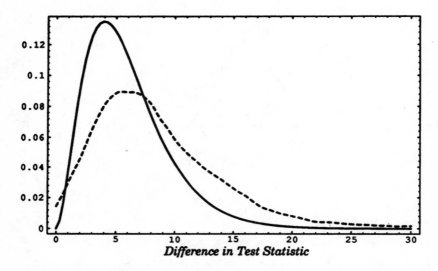

**Figure 5.5.** Comparison of the chi-square density with 6 degrees of freedom (solid line) to the modified bootstrap density (- - -) of the difference in the test statistic $T$ for Models A and B.

### Modified Bootstrap Method and Other Fit Indices

Naive bootstrapping also leads to inaccurate representations of the distribution of other overall fit indices. Table 5.1 lists some overall fit indices used in structural equation models. For instance, Bentler and Bonett's (1980) normed fit index ($\hat{\Delta}_1$) is

$$\hat{\Delta}_1 = \frac{T_b - T_h}{T_b}, \tag{22}$$

where the subscript of b stands for the baseline model, usually taken to be a model of uncorrelated variables, and h denotes the hypothesized model. The asymptotic expectation of its numerator is

$$AE(T_b - T_h) = df_b + \kappa_b - (df_h + \kappa_h). \tag{23}$$

The asymptotic expectation of the denominator is

$$AE(T_b) = df_b + \kappa_b. \tag{24}$$

In contrast, approximations for the corresponding quantities for the bootstrapped normed fit index are

$$E[E^*(T_b^* - T_h^*)] \approx 2df_b + \kappa_b - (2df_h + \kappa_h) \tag{25}$$

and

$$E[E^*(T_b^*)] \approx 2df_b + \kappa_b. \tag{26}$$

A comparison of the asymptotic expectations of the numerators and denominators from the original population and the corresponding approximations for the bootstrapped samples reveals that they do not match. Although it is not true that AE(numerator/denominator) equals AE(numerator)/AE(denominator), the bootstrap distribution of the normed fit index will differ from the distribution obtained by repeated sampling of the original population. A similar series of steps would reveal the differences in the approximations to the expected values of the numerators and denominators for the other fit indices in Table 5.1.

**Table 5.1** Overall Fit Indices in Structural Equation Models

$$\hat{\Delta}_1 = \frac{T_b - T_h}{T_b} \qquad\qquad \hat{\Delta}_2 = \frac{T_b - T_h}{T_b - df_h}$$

$$\hat{\rho}_2 = \frac{\dfrac{T_b}{df_b} - \dfrac{T_h}{df_h}}{\dfrac{T_b}{df_b} - 1} \qquad\qquad \widehat{AIC} = T_h - 2df_h$$

$$\widehat{GFI} = 1 - \frac{tr[(\hat{\Sigma}^{-1}S - I)^2]}{tr[(\hat{\Sigma}^{-1}S)^2]} \qquad \widehat{RMR} = \left[2\sum_{i=1}^{q}\sum_{j=1}^{i}\frac{(s_{ij} - \hat{\sigma}_{ij})^2}{q(q+1)}\right]^{1/2}$$

NOTE: $q$ = number of observed variables in the analysis, $s_{ij}$ = sample covariance between the $i$ and $j$ observed variables, and $\hat{\sigma}_{ij}$ = model-implied estimated covariance between the $i$ and $j$ observed variables. See Bollen (1989, pp. 269-281) and references therein for further discussion of these measures and their properties. The Akaike information criterion (AIC) is scaled slightly differently from that appearing in Bollen (1989b).

In the preceding section we showed how to modify the bootstrap procedure to allow hypothesis testing with the usual test statistic. Does this modification work with the other fit indices? The answer depends on whether the distributions of the fit indices from the modified bootstrap procedure mirror the corresponding distributions obtained if we resample from the original population. Figure 5.6 is the plot of the fit indices for the eight-indicator one-factor simulation model. We plot the bootstrap densities of the fit indices from the modified (- - - -) and naive (— - —) procedures and densities from a Monte Carlo simulation from a multinormal population (solid) having covariance matrix given by the single factor model. In Figure 5.6 the modified bootstrap densities of the fit indices are much closer to the corresponding Monte Carlo densities than are the naive bootstrap densities.

The absolute values of the indices in Table 5.1 are at their maxima when the usual null hypothesis [$H_0$: $\Sigma = \Sigma(\theta)$] is true. Thus the chi-square test statistic implicitly tests whether the fit indices are at their perfect fit values. In this sense we already have a significance test for the fit indices.[10] However, as with the usual chi-square test statistic, we may find that in a sufficiently large sample we routinely reject the null hypothesis of a perfect fit due to the approximate nature of the models.

An alternative is to apply the modified bootstrap procedure to data where a restrictive baseline model rather than the hypothesized model is taken to be the true model. For a fit index this would correspond to an implicit null hypothesis that its population value takes a value that

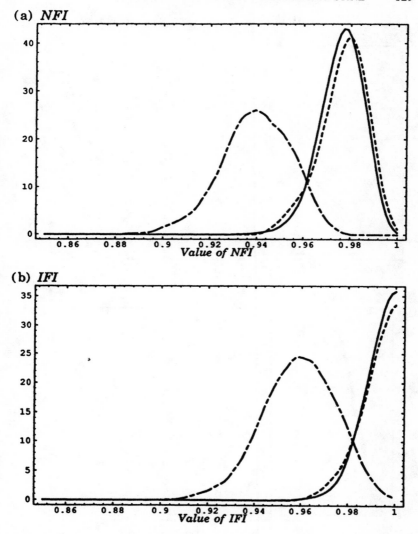

**Figure 5.6.** Comparison of simulated densities (solid line) of goodness-of-fit measures from Table 5.1 to naive (— · —) and modified (- - - -) bootstrap densities. Note that NFI, IFI, and NNFI in the figures represent $\hat{\Delta}_1$, $\hat{\Delta}_2$, and $\hat{\rho}^2$, respectively, from Table 5.1.

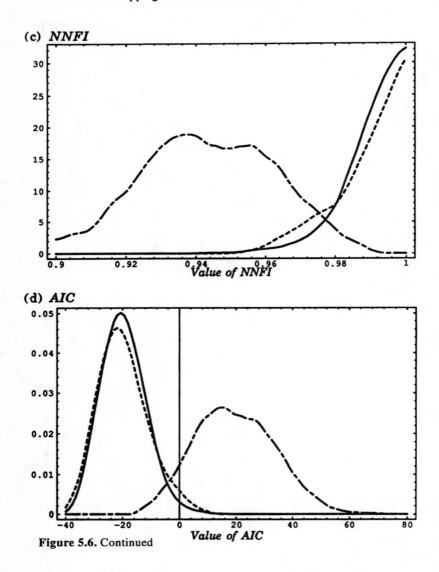

**Figure 5.6.** Continued

indicates a poor fit. With the typical baseline model of uncorrelated variables, this hypothesis would be rejected in nearly all cases. With less restrictive baseline models, this need not be true. However, the

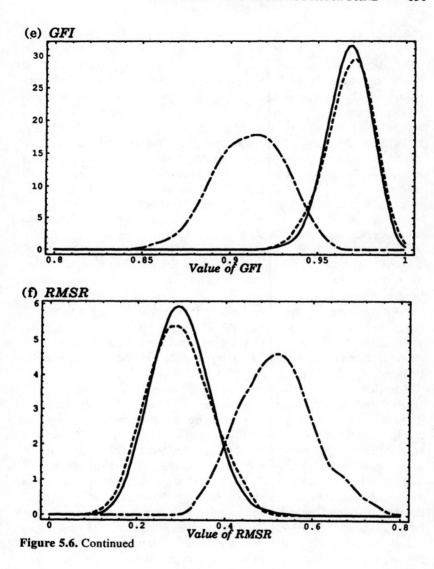

**Figure 5.6.** Continued

usual "chi-square" test statistic based on the modified bootstrap could be used in this situation as well, so that direct hypothesis testing of perfect fit or "no fit" with the fit indices may not be needed.

## Conclusions

In many areas of statistics the bootstrap has proved to be a very useful tool to approximate the distribution of parameter estimates and other statistics. The structural equation area is beginning to see more applications of the bootstrap and usage is likely to increase with the availability of bootstrapping resampling in EQS 3.0 (Bentler, 1989) and LISREL 8 (Jöreskog & Sörbom, in press). In this chapter we have sounded a warning that the naive bootstrap generally does not work with the test statistics and fit indices commonly employed to gauge overall model fit.[11] Our analytical approximations have explained why this is true, and our simulation examples have illustrated the issue.

In response to this problem we have proposed a modified bootstrap procedure that applies to hypothesis testing with the usual test statistic. With the modification, researchers can gain insight into the behavior of the test statistic with nonnormal data or in moderate sample sizes. We have also explained how to test nested hypotheses with the modified bootstrap method.

To implement the modification requires access to matrix programming software, such as APL, GAUSS, or SAS's Proc IML, and the ability to find a square root of a positive definite matrix. With this, the original data can be transformed as described in the chapter and the bootstrap applied to the transformed data.

The benefits of applying the modified bootstrap procedure to fit indices such as the normed or incremental fit index are less clear-cut. The modification described here led to bootstrap distributions of the fit indices that were more similar to the distributions that would occur in resampling a population where the hypothesized model is valid. But it may not be necessary to bootstrap the fit indices under the hypothesis of a perfect fit. We can use the chi-square test statistic from the modified bootstrap procedure to test whether the hypothesized model holds, and this hypothesis is typically equivalent to the null hypothesis that a fit index in the population equals its maximum (or sometimes minimum) value. Or, for nested models, we can test the null hypothesis that the fit indices are equal in the population by using the modified bootstrap procedure for the usual test statistic for nested hypotheses that we proposed. Another alternative for fit indices that contain baseline models is to use the modified bootstrap procedure and generate the transformation so that the baseline model is valid, but this typically creates an overly restrictive model that we will nearly always reject.

A remaining problem is to devise a test of the null hypothesis that a fit index takes some specific value other than its maximum or minimum (e.g., $H_0$: incremental fit index = .95). Cudeck and Browne (in press) recently proposed a method to generate data that leads to both a specific minimum value for a fitting function and a corresponding implied covariance matrix. With their method it may be possible to generate an implied covariance matrix that corresponds to a fit between the maximum and the minimum. Substituting such an implied covariance matrix into the modified bootstrap procedure may enable tests that a fit index takes a specific value in the population.

## Notes

1. Recent work by Maiti and Mukherjee (1990) has identified the distribution of Jöreskog and Sörbom's (1986) GFI and AGFI, but their results are based on asymptotic theory, so even in this case we do not know when a sample is sufficiently large for such theory to apply.

2. Efron and Tibshirani (1986) give sufficient conditions that permit the use of bootstrap approximations.

3. See Silberman (1986) for a description of the procedures that we use for density estimation in this and the other figures.

4. Fisher and Hall (1990) provide further discussion about the problems that might be encountered when using bootstrapping methods for hypothesis testing.

5. $F_{ML}[S, \Sigma(\theta)]$ derives from assuming either a multinormal distribution for the observed variables or a Wishart distribution for $S$ (see Bollen, 1989, pp. 131-135). Browne (1984) justifies the same fitting function by generalized least squares principles, using the less restrictive assumption that the observed variables come from a distribution with kurtosis the same as a multinormal distribution, a condition of "no excess kurtosis." No excess kurtosis is less restrictive than multinormality, so that we use it throughout the discussion as a distributional assumption for the fitting function in Equation 10. Strictly speaking, Equation 10 no longer gives the maximum likelihood fitting function for nonnormal variables, even though it is justified as long as the kurtosis is the same as that for normal variables. However, to avoid new names for the same fitting function and to proceed with the less restrictive assumption of no excess kurtosis, we continue to refer to Equation 10 as $F_{ML}[S, \Sigma(\theta)]$.

6. This is analogous to the $E^*(Z^{*2})$ result, where the observed test statistic is part of the expectation in Equation 8.

7. In some problems excessive kurtosis does not matter. See Satorra (1990) and references therein. Also see Satorra's footnote 3 for a discussion of the distributional assumptions underlying the fitting function.

8. We considered the possibility of modifying $T^*$ as a way to correct the bootstrap distribution. For example, the bootstrap distribution of $T^* - df$ has the same mean as $T$, but its variance and higher-order moments are incorrect.

9. See Bollen and Arminger (1991) for an outlier analysis for this model and data.

10. It is possible that the statistical tests based on the modified bootstrap distributions of the fit indices will have different statistical power from the usual test statistic. And this could lead to the desire to use tests based on the fit indices rather than the usual test statistic.

11. Our results do not contradict those in Bollen and Stine (1990), where we showed the usefulness of bootstrap methods in estimating the variability of direct, indirect, and total effects.

## References

Babu, G. J. (1984). Bootstrapping statistics with linear combinations of chi-squares as weak limits. *Sankhya, Series A, 46,* 85-93.

Bentler, P. M. (1989). *EQS structural equations program manual.* Los Angeles: BMDP Statistical Software.

Bentler, P. M., & Bonett, D. G. (1980). Significance tests and goodness of fit in the analysis of covariance structures. *Psychological Bulletin, 88,* 588-606.

Beran, R., & Srivastava, M. S. (1985). Bootstrap tests and confidence regions for functions of a covariance matrix. *Annals of Statistics, 13,* 95-115.

Bickel, P., & Freedman, D. (1981). Some asymptotic theory for the bootstrap. *Annals of Statistics, 9,* 1196-1217.

Bollen, K. A. (1989). *Structural equations with latent variables.* New York: John Wiley.

Bollen, K. A., & Arminger, G. (1991). Observational residuals in factor analysis and structural equation models. In P. Marsden (Ed.), *Sociological methodology 1991* (pp. 235-262). Oxford: Basil Blackwell.

Bollen, K. A., & Stine, R. (1990). Direct and indirect effects: Classical and bootstrap estimates of variability. In C. C. Clogg (Ed.), *Sociological methodology 1990* (pp. 115-140). Oxford: Basil Blackwell.

Boomsma, A. (1982). The robustness of LISREL against small sample sizes in factor analysis models. In K. G. Jöreskog & H. Wold (Eds.), *Systems under indirect observation (Part I)* (pp. 149-173). Amsterdam: North-Holland.

Browne, M. W. (1984). Asymptotically distribution-free methods in the analysis of covariance structures. *British Journal of Mathematical and Statistical Psychology, 37,* 62-83.

Cudeck, R., & Browne, M. W. (in press). Constructing a covariance matrix that yields a specified minimizer and a specified minimum discrepancy function value. *Psychometrika.*

Efron, B. (1982). *The jackknife, the bootstrap, and other resampling plans.* Philadelphia: Society for Industrial and Applied Mathematics.

Efron, B., & Tibshirani, R. (1986). Bootstrap methods for standard errors, confidence intervals and other measures of statistical accuracy. *Statistical Science, 1,* 54-74.

Fisher, N., & Hall, P. (1990). On bootstrap hypothesis testing. *Australian Journal of Statistics, 32,* 177-190.

Freedman, D. A. (1981). Bootstrapping regression models. *Annals of Statistics, 9,* 1218-1228.

Jöreskog, K. G., & Sörbom, D. (1986). *LISREL VI.* Mooresville, IN: Scientific Software.

Jöreskog, K. G., & Sörbom, D. (in press). *LISREL 8.* Mooresville, IN: Scientific Software.

Maiti, S. S., & Mukherjee, B. N. (1990). A note on distributional properties of the Jöreskog-Sörbom fit indices. *Psychometrika, 55,* 721-726.

Satorra, A. (1990). Robustness issues in structural equation modeling: A review of recent developments. *Quality and Quantity, 24,* 367-386.

Silberman, B. W. (1986). *Density estimation for statistics and data analysis.* London: Chapman & Hall.

Stine, R. (1989). An introduction to bootstrap methods: Examples and ideas. *Sociological Methods & Research, 8,* 243-291.

*6*

# Alternative Ways
# of Assessing Model Fit

### MICHAEL W. BROWNE
### ROBERT CUDECK

Models are fitted to data in an attempt to understand underlying processes that have been operating. To be useful, they should be parsimonious and clearly understood. Models with superfluous parameters that assume meaningless values are clearly to be avoided. On the other hand, models should be appropriate to the data and fit closely. The difficulty is that the fit of the model can usually be improved by increasing the number of parameters, leading to the temptation to include meaningless parameters that are employed only to give an impression of goodness of fit. There thus is a conflict between the two desirable characteristics of a model: interpretability and goodness of fit.

The interpretability of a model can be judged only subjectively and is not amenable to the application of statistical methods. This does not render this characteristic of a model any less important; it is only more difficult to investigate. The assessment of fit of a model can be done in many ways and will be the topic of this chapter. We shall, however, attempt to reduce the conflict between the desire for parsimony and the desire for close fit by examining measures of fit that take the number of parameters in the model into account and do not necessarily show an improvement as parameters are added to the model.

AUTHORS' NOTE: We would like to thank the editors and referees for helpful comments.

In applications of the analysis of covariance structures in the social sciences it is implausible that any model that we use is anything more than an approximation to reality. Since a null hypothesis that a model fits exactly in some population is known a priori to be false, it seems pointless even to try to test whether it is true. If the sample size is sufficiently large in a practical investigation, it can be expected that even models that approximate the covariance matrix closely will be rejected. Statistical goodness-of-fit tests are often more a reflection on the size of the sample than on the adequacy of the model.

Rather than trying to ask whether a model is correct, or fits the population covariance matrix exactly, it is sensible to assess the degree of lack of fit of the model. Many fit indices have been suggested; reviews may be found in Bollen (1989, pp. 256-289) and in Mulaik et al. (1989). In this chapter we shall consider the assessment of lack of fit, giving particular attention to (a) what type of lack of fit is being investigated, and (b) how precise the assessment is that we have obtained.

Simple measures of lack of fit of the model will be considered. Measures of comparative fit that incorporate a null model as well as the model under consideration in a single index (e.g., Bollen, 1989, pp. 269-276; Mulaik et al., 1989, pp. 432-435) will not be dealt with. Even approximations to their distributions are seldom available, and their values depend on the particular null model chosen. Rather than incorporate a questionable null model into the assessment of fit of a model of interest, we prefer to make use of a set of competing models, and to compare separate measures of lack of fit of individual models. This set may incorporate an oversimplified, or null, model. A comparison of the fit of a model under investigation with a null model is accomplished by comparing two separate measures of fit, not by making use of a single index whose magnitude is affected both by the null model and by the model under investigation. Furthermore, two models of interest are compared by means of measures of lack of fit whose values are not influenced by the arbitrary choice of a third, or null, model.

A framework for types of model fit has been set up by Linhart and Zucchini (1986). This is based on discrepancies between distributions of random variables. We shall employ an adaptation by Cudeck and Henly (1991) of this framework to discrepancies between covariance matrices. Two types of error involved in fitting the model will be considered: error of approximation and overall error (Cudeck & Henly, 1991; Linhart & Zucchini, 1986). Error of approximation is relevant to the question, How well would the model, with unknown, but optimally chosen, parameter values fit the population covariance matrix if it were available? It is nonstochastic and does not depend on sample size. Overall error is relevant to the question, How well can the model *with parameter values determined from the (possibly small) sample at our disposal* be expected to fit the population covariance matrix? This is stochastic, and its distribution does depend on sample size.

Measures of error of approximation are not directly observable and can be estimated only from a sample. Following suggestions first made by Steiger and Lind (1980), and applied recently by Steiger (1989), we shall supplement point estimates by interval estimates to bring the lack of precision of the estimate to the user's attention. Degrees of freedom will be incorporated into a measure of error of approximation (Mulaik et al., 1989; Steiger, 1990; Steiger & Lind, 1980) in accordance with our wish to avoid a conflict with the requirement of parsimony. We shall also suggest a test of close fit of a model in an attempt to avoid the negative influence on practice of the usual tests of exact fit.

In multiple regression, it is known that if the sample is small, overall error is generally reduced by making use of a smaller number of predictors than if the sample is large. A similar principle applies in the analysis of covariance structures. As will be seen below, if the sample is small, a more accurate representation of the population covariance matrix can be obtained from an oversimplified model than from a more complex model. We shall deal with the estimation of overall error through cross-validation (Cudeck & Browne, 1983) and through the estimation of the expected value of a cross-validation index using a single sample (Browne & Cudeck, 1989).

The application of measures of fit will be illustrated by means of some examples. Both small and large samples will be included to emphasize the differences between measures of error of approximation and measures of overall error. Proofs of some results employed are sketched in the chapter appendix.

## Fitting a Covariance Structure

Let the $p \times p$ matrix, $S$, be the usual unbiased estimator of the population covariance matrix, $\Sigma_0$, obtained from a sample of size $n + 1$. A model for a covariance matrix is represented by the matrix valued function $\Sigma(\gamma)$, where $\gamma$ is a $q \times 1$ vector of parameters of the model. We assume that all $q$ parameters are identified.

For example, consider a restricted factor analysis covariance structure,

$$\Sigma = \Lambda\Phi\Lambda' + \Psi ,$$

where $\Lambda$ is a $p \times m$ factor matrix with some elements constrained to be zero, $\Phi$ is an $m \times m$ factor correlation matrix, and $\Psi$ is a $p \times p$ diagonal matrix of unique variances. The parameter vector, $\gamma$, then consists of the free elements of $\Lambda$, the distinct off-diagonal elements of $\Phi$, and the diagonal elements of $\Psi$:

$$\gamma = (\lambda_{11}, \lambda_{12}, \ldots, \lambda_{pm}, \varphi_{12}, \varphi_{13}, \varphi_{23}, \ldots, \varphi_{m-1,m}, \psi_{11}, \psi_{22}, \ldots, \psi_{pp})' .$$

The covariance structure is fitted to the sample covariance matrix $S$ by minimizing a suitably defined discrepancy function $F[S, \Sigma(\gamma)]$ with respect to $\gamma$ to yield a vector $\hat{\gamma}$ of parameter estimates and a fitted covariance matrix $\hat{\Sigma} = \Sigma(\hat{\gamma})$.

This discrepancy function, $F(S, \Sigma)$, is a nonnegative scalar valued function of two covariance matrices, $S$ and $\Sigma$, that is equal to zero if and only if $S = \Sigma$. An indication of the fit of the model to $S$ is therefore provided by the closeness of the minimum discrepancy function value, $\hat{F} = F(S, \hat{\Sigma})$, to zero. Well-known discrepancy functions are the normal theory maximum likelihood discrepancy function

$$F_{\mathrm{ML}}(S, \Sigma) = \ln |\Sigma| - \ln |S| + \mathrm{tr}(S\Sigma^{-1}) - p \qquad [1]$$

and the normal theory generalized least squares discrepancy function

$$F_{\mathrm{GLS}}(S, \Sigma) = \frac{1}{2}\mathrm{tr}[S^{-1}(S - \Sigma)]^2 . \qquad [2]$$

A third discrepancy function is the asymptotically distribution free (ADF) discrepancy function (Browne, 1984)

$$F_{\mathrm{ADF}}(S, \Sigma) = (s - \sigma)'\hat{\Gamma}^{-1}(s - \sigma) , \qquad [3]$$

where $s$ and $\sigma$ are vectors, with

$$p^* = \frac{1}{2}p(p + 1)$$

elements, formed from the distinct elements of $S$ and $\Sigma$, respectively, and $\hat{\Gamma}$ is a consistent estimate of the covariance matrix of the elements of $s$. The discrepancy functions in Equations 1 and 2 are both correctly specified (see Browne & Shapiro, 1988, p. 198) if the data are drawn from a multivariate normal distribution and the discrepancy function in Equation 3 is correctly specified if the data are drawn from arbitrary distributions with finite moments, including the multivariate normal distribution.

If the null hypothesis that the population covariance matrix $\Sigma_0$ satisfies the model,

$$H_{0:} \text{ There exists a } \gamma_0 \text{ such that } \Sigma_0 = \Sigma(\gamma_0) , \qquad [4]$$

holds, and if the discrepancy function is correctly specified for the distribution of the data, then the asymptotic distribution of $n \times \hat{F}$ is chi-squared with

$$d = p^* - q \qquad [5]$$

degrees of freedom and the estimator $\hat{\gamma}$ is asymptotically efficient. Thus, if the data are drawn from a multivariate normal distribution, $H_0$ is true, and $n$ is large enough, all three discrepancy functions will yield test statistics with approximate chi-squared distributions. If the data are drawn from a nonnormal distribution, then the ADF discrepancy function is correctly specified and yields a test statistic with an approximate chi-squared distribution if $n$ is large enough. The sample size required for the distribution of the ADF statistic to be well approximated by the chi-squared distribution will, however, be substantial. This is because the estimates of fourth-order moments that are involved in the computation of $\hat{\Gamma}$ in Equation 3 are imprecise unless the sample size is large.

As we pointed out above, it is implausible that the null hypothesis $H_0$ will ever hold in practical applications of the analysis of covariance structures. Consider more realistic situations where the population covariance matrix, $\Sigma_0$, does not satisfy the model exactly. There then exists no vector $\gamma_0$ such that $\Sigma_0 = \Sigma(\gamma_0)$. We therefore define the population value of the parameter vector to be the value $\gamma_0$ of $\gamma$ that yields the minimum $F_0 = F(\Sigma_0, \tilde{\Sigma}_0)$ of the discrepancy between the population covariance matrix $\Sigma_0$ and the fitted matrix $\tilde{\Sigma}_0 = \Sigma(\gamma_0)$. If the discrepancy function is correctly specified for the distribution of the data, if $n$ is not too small, and if $F_0$ is not too large (see Steiger, Shapiro, & Browne, 1985, Theorem 1) the distribution of $n \times \hat{F}$ is approximately noncentral chi-squared with $d$ degrees of freedom and noncentrality parameter $n \times F_0$.

We shall assume henceforth that the discrepancy function employed is correctly specified for the distribution of the data and make use of the approximate noncentral chi-squared distribution of $n \times \hat{F}$. The results we present will be approximate, and the notation $a_n \approx b_n$ will indicate that the quantities $a_n$ and $b_n$, both dependent on $n$, are approximately equal for large enough $n$ (see the chapter appendix for more detail).

## Types of Error

We shall consider (see Cudeck & Henly, 1991, p. 514) discrepancies among three matrices: $\Sigma_0$, $\tilde{\Sigma}_0$, and $\hat{\Sigma}$. The first, $\Sigma_0$, is the population covariance matrix and generally does not satisfy the model under consideration. The second, $\tilde{\Sigma}_0 = \Sigma(\gamma_0)$, is the best fit of the model to $\Sigma_0$ in terms of the selected discrepancy function, $F$. Both $\Sigma_0$ and $\tilde{\Sigma}_0$ are unknown fixed matrices. The third, $\hat{\Sigma} = \Sigma(\hat{\gamma})$, is the best fit of the model to the sample covariance matrix $S$ and is random, varying from one sample to another.

*Error of approximation* refers to the lack of fit of the model to the population covariance matrix $\Sigma_0$. It is reflected by the differences between elements of $\Sigma_0$ and corresponding elements of the nonstochastic fitted matrix $\tilde{\Sigma}_0$. A possible measure of error of approximation is $F_0 = F(\Sigma_0, \tilde{\Sigma}_0)$, the *discrepancy due to approximation*. This measure of lack of fit is bounded below by zero, and will be zero if and only if $\Sigma_0 = \tilde{\Sigma}_0$ and the model fits the population covariance matrix exactly. It is an unknown constant and in general will be reduced if parameters are added to a model.

When presenting asymptotic approximations, indicated by the symbol $\approx$, we shall assume that the errors of approximation in $(\Sigma_0 - \tilde{\Sigma}_0)$ are not large relative to the stochastic errors in $(S - \Sigma_0)$ (see the chapter appendix for more detail).

*Error of estimation* refers to the differences between elements of $\hat{\Sigma}$, the model fitted to the sample, and $\tilde{\Sigma}_0$, the model fitted to the population. A measure of error of estimation is $F(\tilde{\Sigma}_0, \hat{\Sigma})$, the *discrepancy due to estimation*. This is a random variable and is not directly observable. Its expected value may be approximated (Proposition A1 in the chapter appendix) by

$$\mathscr{E}F(\tilde{\Sigma}_0, \hat{\Sigma}) \approx n^{-1}q \,, \qquad\qquad [6]$$

which increases as parameters are added to the model and $n$ remains unchanged.

Finally, *overall error* refers to the differences between elements of $\Sigma_0$, the population covariance matrix that need not satisfy the model, and $\hat{\Sigma}$, the model fitted to the sample. A measure of overall error is $F(\Sigma_0, \hat{\Sigma})$, the overall discrepancy. Again, this is a random variable that is not directly observable. The expected overall discrepancy is approximately the sum of the error of approximation and the expected error of estimation (Proposition A2 and Corollary A2.1 in the appendix):

$$\mathscr{E}F(\Sigma_0, \hat{\Sigma}) \approx F(\Sigma_0, \tilde{\Sigma}_0) + \mathscr{E}F(\tilde{\Sigma}_0, \hat{\Sigma}) \qquad\qquad [7]$$

$$\approx F(\Sigma_0, \tilde{\Sigma}_0) + n^{-1}q \,.$$

As parameters are added to the model and $q$ increases, the error of approximation, $F(\Sigma_0, \tilde{\Sigma}_0)$, decreases and the expected error of estimation, $\mathscr{E}F(\tilde{\Sigma}_0, \hat{\Sigma}) \approx n^{-1}q$, increases. It follows from Equation 7 that the expected overall discrepancy, $\mathscr{E}F(\Sigma_0, \hat{\Sigma})$, can increase as parameters are added to a model. This will tend to happen if $n$ is small and the expected error of estimation increases quite rapidly with $q$. When $n$ is small, an *oversimplified model* with few parameters can yield a *smaller overall error* than a realistic model with more parameters, even though the realistic models fits $\Sigma_0$ more closely in terms of error of approximation.

We shall be concerned mainly with the discrepancy due to approximation, $F(\Sigma_0, \tilde{\Sigma}_0)$, and the overall discrepancy, $F(\Sigma_0, \hat{\Sigma})$. Both measure the degree to which the population covariance matrix, $\Sigma_0$, is approximated by the model, but in different ways. The discrepancy due to estimation, $F(\tilde{\Sigma}_0, \hat{\Sigma})$, is of only secondary interest. It has been considered here because of its effect on overall error in Equation 7.

### Assessment of Error Due to Approximation

The sample discrepancy function value $\hat{F} = F(S, \hat{\Sigma})$ is an appreciably biased estimator of the discrepancy due to approximation, $F_0 = F(\Sigma_0, \tilde{\Sigma}_0)$. Since $n \times \hat{F}$ has an asymptotic noncentral chi-squared distribution with noncentrality parameter $\lambda = n \times F_0$ and $d$ degrees of freedom, the expected value of $\hat{F}$ may be approximated by

$$\mathscr{E}\hat{F} \approx F_0 + n^{-1}d. \qquad [8]$$

Consequently, a less biased point estimator of the discrepancy due to approximation, $F_0 = F(\mathbf{\Sigma}_0, \tilde{\mathbf{\Sigma}}_0)$, would be given by $\hat{F} - n^{-1}d$ (see McDonald, 1989). This can assume negative values, so that we shall employ

$$\hat{F}_0 = \text{Max}\{\hat{F} - n^{-1}d, 0\} \qquad [9]$$

as a point estimate of the discrepancy due to approximation.

The imprecision of sample values of fit indices is not conveyed to users when they are presented in isolation. These are point estimates of population values and can vary considerably from one sample to another. The precision of an interval estimate is clear from the width of the confidence interval. It is therefore good practice to provide confidence intervals on measures of lack of fit as proposed by Steiger and Lind (1980). We shall consider the 90% confidence interval on $F_0$ in particular, but similar methods may be used to provide $100(1 - \alpha)\%$ confidence intervals in general. Let $G(x|\lambda, d)$ be the cumulative distribution function of the noncentral chi-squared distribution with noncentrality parameter $\lambda$ and $d$ degrees of freedom. Given $x = n \times \hat{F}$ and $d$, the lower limit $\hat{\lambda}_L$ of the 90% confidence interval on $n \times F_0$ is the solution for $\lambda$ of the nonlinear equation

$$G(x \mid \lambda, d) = 0.95 \qquad [10]$$

if $G(x|0, d) \geq 0.95$, and $\hat{\lambda}_L = 0$ otherwise. Similarly, the upper limit $\hat{\lambda}_U$ is the solution for $\lambda$ of

$$G(x \mid \lambda, d) = 0.05 \qquad [11]$$

if $G(x|0, d) \geq 0.05$, and $\hat{\lambda}_U = 0$ otherwise. We have used an algorithm due to Farebrother (1987) to evaluate $G(x|\lambda, d)$ and the secant method to solve each of the two equations iteratively. An alternative algorithm that uses a series expansion to yield $\lambda$ directly, given $x$ and $d$, has been given by Ding (1987). In situations where $\lambda$ is very large and Farebrother's algorithm cannot be used, we have employed an approximate transformation to a normal deviate due to Moschopoulos (1983).

After $\hat{\lambda}_L$ and $\hat{\lambda}_U$ have been obtained, the 90% confidence interval on $F_0$ is given by $(n^{-1}\hat{\lambda}_L; n^{-1}\hat{\lambda}_U)$. Since $F_0$ generally decreases when parameters are added to the model, its use to measure the lack of fit of a model may entice the user to choose a model with a substantial number of parameters. This conflicts with our desire for parsimony. It is therefore preferable to use Steiger's (1990; Steiger & Lind, 1980) root mean square error of approximation (RMSEA)

$$\epsilon_a = \sqrt{\frac{F_0}{d}} \qquad [12]$$

as a measure of the *discrepancy per degree of freedom* for the model. In the cases of the normal theory GLS discrepancy function in Equation 2 and the ADF discrepancy function in Equation 3, $\epsilon_a$ is truly a root mean square. These discrepancy functions are quadratic forms and, at their minima, may be expressed as sums of squares of $d$ terms. Notice that these root mean squares are nonstochastic in the present application, as they summarize errors of approximation, not random errors. In the case of the ML discrepancy function in Equation 1, $\epsilon_a$ is a close approximation to a root mean square. At its minimum, the ML discrepancy function, $F_{ML}(\Sigma_0, \tilde{\Sigma}_0)$, may be closely approximated (see Browne, 1974, Proposition 7) by the quadratic form $\frac{1}{2}tr[\tilde{\Sigma}_0^{-1}(\Sigma_0 - \tilde{\Sigma}_0)]^2$, which may be expressed as a sum of squares of $d$ terms representing systematic errors.

Like $F_0$, the RMSEA in Equation 12 is bounded below by zero and will be zero only if the model fits exactly. It will decrease if the inclusion of additional parameters substantially reduces $F_0$, but can increase if the inclusion of additional parameters reduces $F_0$ only slightly. Consequently, it exerts less pressure on users to discard parsimonious models than do $F_0$ and those fit indices that are monotonic functions of $F_0$. Practical experience has made us feel that a value of the RMSEA of about 0.05 or less would indicate a close fit of the model in relation to the degrees of freedom. This figure is based on subjective judgment. It cannot be regarded as infallible or correct, but it is more reasonable than the requirement of exact fit with the RMSEA = 0.0. We are also of the opinion that a value of about 0.08 or less for the RMSEA would indicate a reasonable error of approximation and would not want to employ a model with a RMSEA greater than 0.1.

If a scale-invariant discrepancy function such as those in Equations 1, 2, and 3 is employed, the RMSEA is not affected by the scales of the variables. In this it differs from the mean square error used as a discrepancy measure in multiple linear regression, which is affected by the scale of the dependent variable. In the present situation there is no need to divide the discrepancy for the model under consideration by the discrepancy for a null model to obtain a scale-free fit index.

The RMSEA is a function of $\Sigma_0$ and has an unknown value. Use of Equations 9 and 12 shows that a point estimate of the RMSEA is given by

$$\hat{\epsilon}_a = \sqrt{\frac{\hat{F}_0}{d}} \qquad [13]$$

$$= \sqrt{\text{Max}\left\{\left(\frac{\hat{F}}{d} - \frac{1}{n}\right), 0\right\}}$$

and a 90% confidence interval by

$$(\hat{\epsilon}_{a_L} ; \hat{\epsilon}_{a_U}) = \left(\sqrt{\frac{\hat{\lambda}_L}{nd}} ; \sqrt{\frac{\hat{\lambda}_U}{nd}}\right). \qquad [14]$$

If the lower limit of the confidence interval is zero, the test, based on $n \times \hat{F}$, of the null hypothesis of exact fit in Equation 4 would not reject the null hypothesis at the 5% level. Thus the confidence interval contains the information provided by the corresponding goodness-of-fit test. The advantage of the confidence interval is that a nonzero upper limit is a reminder that the model cannot be regarded as correct.

Other measures of fit that take degrees of freedom into account are available (Bollen, 1989, pp. 269-281; Mulaik et al., 1989). Of these, the one most closely related to the estimated RMSEA in Equation 13 is the chi-squared test statistic divided by the degrees of freedom (e.g., Bollen, 1989, p. 278):

$$\frac{n \times \hat{F}}{d} = n \times \hat{\epsilon}_a^2 + 1, \qquad \text{whenever } \hat{\epsilon}_a > 0.$$

This fit index will rank competing models in the same order as the point estimate, $\hat{\epsilon}_a$, of the RMSEA, but the multiplication by $n$ obscures its relationship to the error of approximation.

### A Test of Close Fit

The usual test of the null hypothesis of *exact fit* in Equation 4 has a negative influence on applications of the analysis of covariance structures. Because this null hypothesis is invariably false in practical situations, it will almost certainly be rejected if $n$ is sufficiently large. This discourages the use of large samples. It also encourages the inclusion of uninterpretable additional parameters in a model to reduce the power of the test and thereby avoid the rejection of $H_0$. We therefore suggest a null hypothesis of *close fit* and a corresponding statistical test.

The null hypothesis of exact fit in Equation 4 may be expressed in the alternative form

$$H_0: \epsilon_a = 0.0 \, .$$

It then is a test of a point hypothesis concerning the RMSEA. We replace this point hypothesis by a less implausible interval hypothesis of close fit,

$$H_0: \epsilon_a \leq 0.05 \, . \qquad [15]$$

The test statistic, $n \times \hat{F}$, used for the test of exact fit is also used for the test of close fit, but the exceedance probability is given by

$$P = 1.0 - G(x \mid \lambda^*, d) \, ,$$

where $x = n \times \hat{F}$ and $\lambda^* = n \times d \times 0.05^2$. The null hypothesis is rejected in favor of the alternative

$$H_1: \epsilon_a > 0.05$$

if the exceedance probability is less than a prespecified level (e.g., $P < 0.05$ or $P < 0.01$).

The null hypothesis of close fit in Equation 15 will be not be rejected at the 5% level ($P > 0.05$) whenever the lower limit of the 90% confidence interval on the error of approximation in Equation 14 is less than 0.05.

As we mentioned earlier, the choice of 0.05, used in Equation 15 as an upper limit for a close-fitting model, is a subjective one based on a substantial amount of experience with estimates of the RMSEA. It is, however, no less subjective than the choice of 5% as a significance level. What can be said about the null hypothesis of close fit in Equation 15 is that it is far less unrealistic than the null hypothesis of exact fit.

## *Cross-Validation and the Estimation of the Overall Discrepancy*

Cross-validation has been in use for many years for investigating the predictive validity of a linear regression equation, and has more recently been suggested for use in the analysis of covariance structures (Cudeck & Browne, 1983). Two independent samples from the same population are involved: a calibration sample, $C$, of size $n_C + 1$ yielding a covariance matrix $S_C$, and a validation sample, $V$, of size $n_V + 1$ yielding a covariance matrix $S_V$. The model is fitted to the calibration sample covariance matrix $S_C$, yielding a fitted covariance matrix $\hat{\Sigma}_C$. The cross-validation index is

$$\text{CVI} = F(S_V, \hat{\Sigma}_C) \, ,$$

the discrepancy between the validation sample covariance matrix $S_V$ and the fitted model, $\hat{\Sigma}_C$, obtained from the calibration sample. It thus measures the extent to which $\hat{\Sigma}_C$, obtained from the calibration sample, fits the validation sample covariance matrix.

The *conditional* expectation of the CVI *over validation samples holding the calibration sample fixed,* is given approximately (Proposition A3) by

$$\underset{V}{\mathscr{E}} \, \text{CVI} = \underset{V}{\mathscr{E}} \left\{ F(S_V, \hat{\Sigma}_C) \mid \hat{\Sigma}_C \right\} \approx F(\Sigma_0, \hat{\Sigma}_C) + n_V^{-1} p^* \, . \tag{16}$$

Thus the CVI is a biased estimator of $F(\Sigma_0, \hat{\Sigma}_C)$, the overall discrepancy value for the particular calibration sample employed. The amount of bias depends on the validation sample size and the number of variables. It would be easy to adjust the estimate for bias by taking $F(S_V, \hat{\Sigma}_C) - n_V^{-1} p^*$. This would lead to the possibility of inadmissible negative estimates, and is hardly worth doing because the bias term, $n_V^{-1} p^*$, is the same for all competing models fitted to the calibration sample. The adjustment for bias would have no effect on the rank order of competing models.

It is possible to repeat the process using the original calibration sample as validation sample and the original validation sample as calibration sample. This yields two different (biased) estimates, not of the same quantity, but of two different quantities: the values of the overall discrepancies for the two samples under consideration (see Equation 16).

The necessity to split the available data to form two samples is a disadvantage of the cross-validation procedure, particularly when the sample size is small. This tends to increase the overall error for the calibration sample, which is the quantity being investigated. Browne and Cudeck (1989) suggest that this problem be avoided by estimating the *expected value of the cross-validation index,* for both calibration and validation samples, using the calibration sample alone.

Since a validation sample is no longer explicitly drawn, we may assume for convenience that $n_V = n_C = n$. Substitution of Equation 6 into Equation 16 shows that the expected value of the cross-validation index (ECVI) then is approximately

$$\text{ECVI} = \underset{C}{\mathscr{E}} \underset{V}{\mathscr{E}} F(S_V, \hat{\Sigma}_C) \approx F(\Sigma_0, \tilde{\Sigma}_0) + n^{-1}(p^* + q) . \qquad [17]$$

Letting $S = S_C$ and $\hat{\Sigma} = \hat{\Sigma}_C$, it follows from Equations 8 and 5 that the expected value of the function (Browne & Cudeck, 1989)

$$c = F(S, \hat{\Sigma}) + 2n^{-1}q , \qquad [18]$$

of the sample discrepancy $F(S, \hat{\Sigma})$, alone will be approximately equal to the ECVI,

$$\underset{C}{\mathscr{E}} c \approx \underset{C}{\mathscr{E}} \underset{V}{\mathscr{E}} F(S_V, \hat{\Sigma}_C) = \text{ECVI} .$$

Like the CVI, the statistic $c$ is nonnegative. In the particular case where the maximum likelihood discrepancy function $F_{ML}(S, \Sigma)$ in Equation 1 is employed, $c$ is linearly related to the Akaike information criterion (Akaike, 1973) and will yield the same rank order of competing models.

The estimator, $c$, of the ECVI is approximately unbiased but can assume inadmissible values. It can be seen from Equation 17 that (approximately)

$$\text{ECVI} \geq n^{-1}(p^* + q) .$$

This inequality need not be satisfied by the estimate $c$. It would be easy to rectify this situation by taking $\text{Max}\{c, n^{-1}(p^* + q)\}$ as the estimate of the ECVI, but the inequality is an approximation in any case and the linear relationship with the Akaike information criterion would then no longer hold.

As before, it is helpful to supplement the point estimate, $c$, of the ECVI by an interval estimate

$$(c_L; c_U) = \left( \frac{(\hat{\lambda}_L + p^* + q)}{n} ; \frac{(\hat{\lambda}_U + p^* + q)}{n} \right).$$

Since $c_L \geq n^{-1}(p^* + q)$, it is possible to have $c < c_L$ if the value of $c$ is inadmissible.

When the sample size is small it is helpful to compare the point estimates of the ECVI for competing models, bearing the interval estimates in mind to avoid paying too much attention to small differences. One possible competing model is the saturated model where $\Sigma$ is any $p \times p$ positive definite matrix so that $q = p^*$. In this case it follows from Equation 17 that

$$\text{ECVI} \approx n^{-1}p(p + 1) .$$

This approximation applies to any discrepancy function that is correctly specified for the data. In the special case of the maximum likelihood discrepancy function, $F_{ML}(S, \Sigma)$, the ECVI for the saturated model is given exactly (Browne & Cudeck, 1989) by

$$\text{ECVI} = (n - p - 1)^{-1}p(p + 1) . \qquad [19]$$

Browne and Cudeck (1989) have therefore suggested that, when $F_{ML}(S, \hat{\Sigma})$ is used as discrepancy function, the estimate $c$ of the ECVI in Equation 18 be replaced by

$$c^* = F_{ML}(S, \hat{\Sigma}) + 2(n - p - 1)^{-1}q \qquad [20]$$

so that $c^* = $ ECVI in Equation 19 when $q = p^*$. A corresponding approximate 90% confidence interval on the ECVI is given by

$$(c_L^*; c_U^*) = \left( \frac{(\hat{\lambda}_L + p^* + q)}{n - p - 1}; \frac{(\hat{\lambda}_U + p^* + q)}{n - p - 1} \right), \qquad [21]$$

where $\hat{\lambda}_L$ and $\hat{\lambda}_U$ are obtained by solving Equations 10 and 11 as before but with $x = (n - p - 1) \times F_{ML}(S, \hat{\Sigma})$.

Our main interest is in the overall discrepancy. Comparison of Equations 7 and 17 shows that the relationship between the ECVI and the expected overall discrepancy, $\mathscr{E}F(\Sigma_0, \hat{\Sigma})$, is given by

$$\text{ECVI} \approx \mathscr{E}F(\Sigma_0, \hat{\Sigma}) + n^{-1}p^* . \qquad [22]$$

Since $p^*$ is a constant, the rank order of competing models according to the ECVI is the same as the rank order according to the expected overall discrepancy.

There consequently is a difference between the CVI and the single-sample estimate, $c$, of the ECVI. Comparison of Equations 16 and 22 shows that the cross-validation procedure investigates the overall discrepancy for a particular calibration sample, whereas the single-sample procedure investigates the expected overall discrepancy over all possible calibration samples. Another difference between the two procedures is that the cross-validation procedure does not require that the discrepancy function be correctly specified for the distribution of the data while the single-sample procedure does require a correctly specified discrepancy function. As a result, the single-sample procedure is more sensitive to distributional assumptions than is the cross-validation procedure.

### Examples

We now present four examples to illustrate the use of the methods described above. The first illustrates the use of estimates of overall error to select a possibly oversimplified model when $n$ is small, the second illustrates the use of estimates of the RMSEA and of tests of close fit to select a sufficiently close-fitting model when $n$ is large, and the last two show how the test of close fit can retain a model discarded by the usual goodness-of-fit test. In all cases, the model was fitted by maximum likelihood, using $F_{ML}(S, \Sigma)$ in Equation 1. Other examples of the application of estimates of the RMSEA to assess the fit of models may be found in Browne and Du Toit (1991, 1992).

### Choice of the Number of Factors
### When the Sample Size Is Small

Naglieri and Jensen (1987) compared the factor structure of a battery of 24 intelligence tests in two samples of size 86. They interpreted three factors. We repeated their analysis on the white sample (Naglieri & Jensen, 1987, Table 2), fitting the unrestricted factor analysis model with from 0 to 10 factors. The fit measures obtained are shown in Table 6.1.

It can be seen that the point estimates, $c^*$, of the ECVI decrease at first as $m$ increases, reach a minimum at $m = 3$, and then increase again. This indicates that it would be unwise to interpret results for more than three or four factors because of the fact that the sample size is small. Notice that Naglieri and Jensen chose three factors. The width of the confidence intervals $(c_L^*; c_U^*)$ makes it clear that the ECVI estimated will not necessarily reach a minimum at $m = 3$, but this is not important. The purpose of the index is not to give the exact number of factors to be retained, but rather to give a rough indication of the number of factors that can subsequently be modified by subjective judgment. In this particular situation, the number of factors indicated by $c^*$ and the number chosen by the investigators happens to coincide.

For $m \geq 6$, $c^*$ has values that cannot be assumed by the ECVI (but can be assumed by the CVI). This can be seen from the fact that $c^* < c_L^*$. Also, for $m \geq 7$, we have $c_L^* = c_U^*$ since, in these cases, $G(x|0, d) < 0.05$, so that Equations 10 and 11 have no solutions and $\hat{\lambda}_L = \hat{\lambda}_U = 0.0$.

The ECVI for the saturated model (shown in the last row of Table 6.1) is 10.0. This differs from the estimates $c^*$ for the factor analysis models in that it is not a stochastic estimate but rather a fixed quantity (19) that would be exact if the assumption of a multivariate normal distribution for the data were correct. It is interesting that it exceeds the upper bounds of all confidence intervals on the ECVI for the competing set of factor analysis models with differing numbers of factors. It follows from Equation 21 that the expected overall discrepancy for the saturated model would be poorer than that for any of the factor analysis models. This is due (see Equation 7) to the fact that the small sample size results in substantial errors of estimation.

**Table 6.1 Fit Measures for the Naglieri and Jensen Intelligence Data ($n = 85$, $p = 24$)**

| $m$ | $q$ | $d$ | $\hat{F}$ | $\hat{\epsilon}_a$ | $(\hat{\epsilon}_{a_L}; \hat{\epsilon}_{a_U})$ | $c^*$ | $(c^*_L; c^*_U)$ | $n \times \hat{F}$ | Probability Exact[a] | Probability Close[b] |
|---|---|---|---|---|---|---|---|---|---|---|
| 0 | 24 | 276 | 14.870 | 0.205 | (0.194; 0.217) | 15.670 | (14.230; 17.240) | 1264.00 | 0.00 | 0.00 |
| 1 | 48 | 252 | 7.065 | 0.128 | (0.114; 0.141) | 8.665 | (7.784; 9.678) | 600.51 | 0.00 | 0.00 |
| 2 | 71 | 229 | 4.915 | 0.098 | (0.083; 0.113) | 7.282 | (6.612; 8.086) | 417.81 | 0.00 | 0.00 |
| 3 | 93 | 207 | 3.702 | 0.078 | (0.060; 0.095) | 6.802 | (6.550; 7.470) | 314.70 | 0.00 | 0.00 |
| 4 | 114 | 186 | 3.141 | 0.072 | (0.051; 0.090) | 6.941 | (6.900; 7.548) | 266.99 | 0.00 | 0.04 |
| 5 | 134 | 166 | 2.538 | 0.059 | (0.034; 0.081) | 7.005 | (7.233; 7.534) | 215.74 | 0.01 | 0.25 |
| 6 | 153 | 147 | 2.079 | 0.049 | (0.005; 0.073) | 7.179 | (7.550; 7.644) | 176.72 | 0.05 | 0.51 |
| 7 | 171 | 129 | 1.690 | 0.037 | (0.000; 0.066) | 7.390 | (7.850; 7.850) | 143.61 | 0.18 | 0.74 |
| 8 | 188 | 112 | 1.460 | 0.036 | (0.000; 0.068) | 7.727 | (8.133; 8.133) | 124.13 | 0.20 | 0.74 |
| 9 | 204 | 96 | 1.246 | 0.035 | (0.000; 0.069) | 8.046 | (8.400; 8.400) | 105.89 | 0.23 | 0.73 |
| 10 | 219 | 81 | 0.952 | 0.000 | (0.000; 0.060) | 8.252 | (8.650; 8.650) | 80.90 | 0.48 | 0.88 |
| Sat. | 300 | 0 | 0.000 | 0.000 | | 10.00 | | | | |

NOTE: $m$ = number of factors; $q$ = number of free parameters; $d$ = degrees of freedom; $\hat{F}$ = (minimum) sample discrepancy function value; $\hat{\epsilon}_a$ = point estimate of the RMSEA (in Equation 13); $(\hat{\epsilon}_{a_L}; \hat{\epsilon}_{a_U})$ = 90% confidence interval on the RMSEA (in Equation 14); $c^*$ = point estimate of the ECVI (in Equation 20); $(c^*_L; c^*_U)$ = 90% confidence interval on the ECVI (in Equation 21); $n \times \hat{F}$ = the value of the likelihood ratio test statistic.

a. The corresponding exceedance probability for the test of exact fit (Equation 4).
b. The corresponding exceedance probability for the test of close fit (Equation 15).

The point estimates, $\hat{\epsilon}_a$, of the RMSEA decrease steadily as $n$ increases and do not drop below 0.05 until $m = 6$. Also, the exceedance probability for the test of *close fit* does not go above 0.05 (becomes not significant at the 5% level) until $m = 5$. This suggests that if a larger sample were available it is possible that more than three factors could be extracted and interpreted. The test of *exact fit* becomes not significant at the 5% level when $m = 7$. The lower bound of the interval estimate of the RMSEA is $\hat{\epsilon}_{a_L} = 0.0$, but the nonzero upper bound $\hat{\epsilon}_{a_U} = 0.066$ is a reminder that it would not be reasonable to suppose that the factor analysis model with $m = 7$ factors would necessarily fit the population covariance matrix.

## Choice of the Number of Factors
## When the Sample Size Is Large

We now consider a factor analysis of a set of ability measures by McGaw and Jöreskog (1971) based on a correlation matrix pooled over four samples with $n = 11,743 - 4 = 11,739$ degrees of freedom. The total sample size is very large, and one can expect that there will be very little error of estimation. This is reflected in the point estimates $c^*$ of the ECVI shown in Table 6.2.

These estimates of the ECVI behave in a manner very different from those in Table 6.1. They decrease steadily as the number of factors, $m$, increases and are very close to the sample discrepancy function values $\hat{F}$. The associated confidence intervals $(c_L^*; c_U^*)$ are narrow and the lower bound $c_L^*$ exceeds the ECVI of 0.039 for the saturated model in all cases. Clearly, the saturated model will yield a smaller expected overall discrepancy than any of the factor analysis models. Also, all tests of exact fit of the factor analysis model yield exceedance probabilities essentially equal to zero and clearly reject the null hypothesis in Equation 4.

This does not mean that none of the factor analysis models should be used. The saturated model does not tell us anything about the relationships between variables and is completely unhelpful.

The test of close fit clearly rejects models with fewer than four factors and clearly accepts models with four or more factors. For $m \geq 4$, exceedance probabilities are essentially equal to 1. This does not necessarily mean that four factors must automatically be taken. Interpretability must be taken into account in addition to goodness of fit. Four factors do, however, yield a close fit of the model. It is worth noting that McGaw and Jöreskog chose to interpret four factors.

**Table 6.2** Fit Measures for the McGaw and Jöreskog Ability Data ($n = 11,739$, $p = 21$)

| $m$ | $q$ | $d$ | $\hat{F}$ | $\hat{\epsilon}_a$ | $(\hat{\epsilon}_{a_L}; \hat{\epsilon}_{a_U})$ | $c^*$ | $(c_L^*; c_U^*)$ | $n \times \hat{F}$ | Probability Exact | Probability Close |
|---|---|---|---|---|---|---|---|---|---|---|
| 0 | 21 | 210 | 4.932 | 0.153 | (0.152; 0.154) | 4.936 | (4.869; 5.003) | 57,915 | 0.00 | 0.00 |
| 1 | 42 | 189 | 1.839 | 0.098 | (0.097; 0.099) | 1.846 | (1.805; 1.888) | 21,597 | 0.00 | 0.00 |
| 2 | 62 | 169 | 1.114 | 0.081 | (0.079; 0.082) | 1.125 | (1.093; 1.157) | 13,079 | 0.00 | 0.00 |
| 3 | 81 | 150 | 0.583 | 0.062 | (0.060; 0.063) | 0.597 | (0.574; 0.620) | 6,846 | 0.00 | 0.00 |
| 4 | 99 | 132 | 0.302 | 0.047 | (0.046; 0.048) | 0.319 | (0.303; 0.336) | 3,548 | 0.00 | 1.00 |
| 5 | 116 | 115 | 0.180 | 0.039 | (0.037; 0.040) | 0.200 | (0.187; 0.213) | 2,118 | 0.00 | 1.00 |
| 6 | 132 | 99 | 0.098 | 0.030 | (0.028; 0.032) | 0.121 | (0.112; 0.130) | 1,145 | 0.00 | 1.00 |
| 7 | 147 | 84 | 0.053 | 0.023 | (0.022; 0.025) | 0.078 | (0.072; 0.085) | 627 | 0.00 | 1.00 |
| 8 | 161 | 70 | 0.034 | 0.020 | (0.018; 0.022) | 0.061 | (0.056; 0.067) | 403 | 0.00 | 1.00 |
| Sat. | 231 | 0 | 0.000 | 0.000 | | 0.039 | | | | |

NOTE: See notes to Table 6.1 for explanation of columns.

## Acceptance of Models Rejected by the Test of Exact Fit

Jöreskog (1978, pp. 473-475) fitted two different circumplex models to a correlation matrix between six abilities obtained from a sample of size 710. One, which we call Model E, was an equally spaced circumplex with no error of measurement. The other, Model U, was a circumplex with unequal spacing between tests and with allowance made for error of measurement. Fit measures are shown in Table 6.3.

Both models are clearly rejected by the test of exact fit, and Jöreskog (1978, p. 475) regarded both as fitting unsatisfactorily. However, neither model is rejected by the test of close fit. The simpler model, E, yields smaller point estimates of both the RMSEA and the ECVI than the more highly parameterized model, U.

## An Example of Structural Equation Modeling From Sociology

Hauser, Tsai, and Sewell (1983) investigated the effects of a variety of family socioeconomic factors on educational and occupational attainment. In this study, data from 2,038 observations on $p = 26$ variables were studied by means of path models that specified various combinations of regressions among 17 latent variables. Hauser et al.'s data analysis strategy was to modify an initial model by reducing the number of "direct paths in the model to those which are both theoretically plausible and empirically necessary to account for the data" (p. 22). Hauser et al. presented information on the performance of five nested models (p. 29). Each of these is successively more restricted than the others that precede it in the analysis. Summary measures of fit for these models are shown in Table 6.4.

All five models are clearly rejected by the usual likelihood ratio test of exact fit with all exceedance probabilities less than 0.005. Hauser et al. (1983) computed likelihood difference tests between each pair of adjacent models. They noted that each of these difference tests was statistically significant and attributed this to the large sample size. Conventional reasoning would require that the most highly parameterized model, Model 1, should be retained, because the deterioration in fit when parameters are discarded is statistically significant. By contrast, Hauser et al. (1983) favored the most restricted model, Model 5, for theoretical reasons, essentially ignoring the likelihood ratio difference tests. This is the model emphasized in their later discussion.

Some support for this course of action is provided by the point estimates, $\hat{\epsilon}_a$, of the RMSEA and the tests of close fit reported in Table 6.4.

**Table 6.3** Fit Measures for Jöreskog's Circumplex Analyses ($n = 709$, $p = 6$)

| Model | $q$ | $d$ | $\hat{F}$ | $\hat{\epsilon}_a$ | $(\hat{\epsilon}_{a_L}; \hat{\epsilon}_{a_U})$ | $c^*$ | $(c^*_L; c^*_U)$ | $n \times \hat{F}$ | Probability Exact | Close |
|---|---|---|---|---|---|---|---|---|---|---|
| E | 9 | 12 | 0.038 | 0.042 | (0.021; 0.063) | 0.064 | (0.048; 0.091) | 27.05 | 0.01 | 0.70 |
| U | 17 | 4 | 0.023 | 0.066 | (0.035; 0.101) | 0.071 | (0.061; 0.093) | 16.47 | 0.00 | 0.17 |
| Sat. | 21 | 0 | 0.000 | 0.000 | | 0.060 | | | | |

NOTE: See notes to Table 6.1 for explanation of columns.

**Table 6.4** Fit Measures for Path Models from Hauser, Tsai, and Sewell ($n = 2{,}037$, $p = 26$)

| Model | $q$ | $d$ | $\hat{F}$ | $\hat{\epsilon}_a$ | $(\hat{\epsilon}_{a_L}; \hat{\epsilon}_{a_U})$ | $c^*$ | $(c^*_L; c^*_U)$ | $n \times \hat{F}$ | Probability Exact | Close |
|---|---|---|---|---|---|---|---|---|---|---|
| 1 | 189 | 162 | 0.159 | 0.022 | (0.019; 0.026) | 0.347 | (0.324; 0.374) | 324.4 | 0.00 | 1.00 |
| 2 | 185 | 166 | 0.200 | 0.027 | (0.023; 0.030) | 0.384 | (0.357; 0.415) | 406.6 | 0.00 | 1.00 |
| 3 | 176 | 175 | 0.211 | 0.027 | (0.024; 0.030) | 0.386 | (0.358; 0.418) | 430.2 | 0.00 | 1.00 |
| 4 | 175 | 176 | 0.218 | 0.027 | (0.024; 0.031) | 0.392 | (0.363; 0.425) | 444.0 | 0.00 | 1.00 |
| 5 | 172 | 179 | 0.238 | 0.029 | (0.026; 0.032) | 0.409 | (0.379; 0.443) | 485.4 | 0.00 | 1.00 |
| Sat. | 351 | 0 | 0.000 | 0.000 | | 0.349 | | | | |

NOTE: See notes to Table 6.1 for explanation of columns.

Exceedance probabilities for the test of close fit are all close to 1.0, suggesting that all five models may be regarded as fitting closely. The values of $\hat{\epsilon}_a$ increase slightly as parameters are discarded. The largest is for Model 5 and is only 0.029, so that even this model may be regarded as fitting closely. It therefore appears to be reasonable to concentrate on the most parsimonious model, Model 5, even though the corresponding value of $\hat{\epsilon}_a$ is slightly inferior to (higher than) those for the other models.

Because of the large sample size, the difference between the point estimate, $c^*$, of the ECVI and the sample discrepancy function value, $\hat{F}$, is nearly constant over the five models. This illustrates that the ECVI is not helpful for choosing a parsimonious model when $n$ is very large.

## Discussion

Fit indices should not be regarded as measures of usefulness of a model. They contain some information about the lack of fit of a model, but none about plausibility. An attempt has been made to measure lack of fit in ways that allow parsimonious models to compete with highly parameterized models. This avoids too serious a conflict between the requirements of fit and parsimony. It does not guarantee that the proposed fit indices will point out a useful model. Consequently, they should not be used in a mechanical decision process for selecting a model. Model selection has to be a subjective process involving the use of judgment.

It is worth bearing in mind that we have limited our attention to discrepancy functions that are correctly specified for the distribution of the data. This was done so that we would have an approximation for the distribution of the sample discrepancy function value, $F(S, \hat{\Sigma})$. These discrepancy functions yield errors of estimation with desirable statistical properties. It is not known whether they define the errors of approximation $(\Sigma_0 - \tilde{\Sigma}_0)$ in a sensible manner or yield a helpful discrepancy due to approximation, $F(\Sigma_0, \tilde{\Sigma}_0)$. It is possible that other discrepancy functions can be found that will have advantages when errors of approximation are considered.

We have specifically considered covariance structures in this chapter. The methods for assessing model fit that have been described here are, however, applicable in other situations where models are fitted to sample moments by minimizing discrepancy functions. The only change that is necessary is to redefine $p^*$ to represent the number of distinct sample moments involved in the analysis. In Browne and Du Toit (1991), for example, the fit of structures for the mean vector and covariance matrix simultaneously is evaluated with $p^* = p(p + 3)/2$.

A PC computer program, FITMOD (Browne, 1991), is available for computing point and interval estimates of the ECVI and RMSEA and the test of close fit.

## APPENDIX

This appendix sketches proofs of some results stated in this chapter. Rigorous mathematical detail is omitted.

We assume that the elements of $(\Sigma_0 - \tilde{\Sigma}_0)$ are of $O(n^{-1/2})$ so that the errors of approximation are not large relative to the stochastic errors in $(S - \Sigma_0)$, which are of $O_p(n^{-1/2})$. (This implies a population drift process [see, e.g., Steiger et al., 1985] with a sequence of population covariance matrices $\Sigma_0 = \Sigma_{0,n}$ converging to a point where the model is satisfied, $\tilde{\Sigma}_0 = \Sigma(\gamma_0)$, as $n \to \infty$.)

A column vector with $p^* = \frac{1}{2}p(p + 1)$ elements formed from the distinct elements of a symmetric $p \times p$ matrix, represented by a boldface capital letter, will be denoted by the corresponding lowercase letter in bold. Thus $s$ and $\sigma_0$ represent $p^* \times 1$ vectors formed from the distinct elements of $S$ and $\Sigma_0$.

We assume that the asymptotic distribution of $n^{1/2}(s - \sigma_0)$ is multivariate normal with a null mean vector and a nonsingular $p^* \times p^*$ covariance matrix $\Gamma_0$. Consider a discrepancy function $F(U, V)$. This a nonnegative, twice continuously differentiable function of two $p \times p$ positive definite matrices $U$ and $V$ such that $F(U, V) = 0$ if and only if $U = V$. We assume that the discrepancy function is "correctly specified" for the distribution of the data (see Browne & Shapiro, 1988, Assumption C6), that is,

$$\Gamma_0^{-1} = (\partial^2/\partial v \partial v')F(\tilde{\Sigma}_0, \tilde{\Sigma}_0) .$$

It follows (Browne & Shapiro, 1988, Proposition A1; Shapiro, 1985) that if $U$ and $V$ are in a neighborhood of $\tilde{\Sigma}_0$, then $F(U, V)$ may be approximated by a quadratic function:

$$F(U,V) = (u - v)'\Gamma_0^{-1}(u - v) + o(\| u - \tilde{\sigma}_0 \|^2) + o(\| v - \tilde{\sigma}_0 \|^2) . \qquad [A1]$$

We have used the notation $a_n \approx b_n$ to mean that $a_n$ is approximately equal to $b_n$. More precisely, we use $a_n \approx b_n$ to stand for $a_n = b_n + o(n^{-1})$ when $a_n$ and $b_n$

are sequences of nonstochastic variables and for $a_n = b_n + o_p(n^{-1})$ when $a_n$ and $b_n$ are sequences of random variables.

It follows from Equation A1 that the discrepancy due to approximation may be approximated by the quadratic function

$$F(\Sigma_0, \tilde{\Sigma}_0) \approx (\sigma_0 - \tilde{\sigma}_0)' \, \Gamma_0^{-1}(\sigma_0 - \tilde{\sigma}_0) \,, \qquad [A2]$$

since $\|\sigma_0 - \tilde{\sigma}_0\|^2$ is $O(n^{-1})$. Also, since $\|\hat{\sigma} - \tilde{\sigma}_0\|^2$ is $O_p(n^{-1})$, the discrepancy due to estimation may be approximated by

$$F(\tilde{\Sigma}_0, \hat{\Sigma}) \approx (\tilde{\sigma}_0 - \hat{\sigma})' \, \Gamma_0^{-1}(\tilde{\sigma}_0 - \hat{\sigma}) \,, \qquad [A3]$$

and the overall discrepancy by

$$F(\Sigma_0, \hat{\Sigma}) \approx (\sigma_0 - \hat{\sigma})' \, \Gamma_0^{-1}(\sigma_0 - \hat{\sigma}) \,. \qquad [A4]$$

We use a first-order Taylor expansion to approximate $\hat{\sigma} = \sigma(\hat{\gamma})$:

$$\hat{\sigma} \approx \tilde{\sigma}_0 + \Delta_0(\hat{\gamma} - \gamma_0) \,, \qquad [A5]$$

where

$$\Delta_0 = (\partial/\partial\gamma')\sigma(\gamma_0)$$

is a $p^* \times q$ matrix.

*Proposition A1.* The expected value of the discrepancy due to estimation may be approximated by

$$\mathcal{E}F(\tilde{\Sigma}_0, \hat{\Sigma}) \approx n^{-1}q \,. \qquad [A6]$$

*Proof.* Use of Equations A3 and A5 shows that

$$\mathcal{E}F(\tilde{\Sigma}_0, \hat{\Sigma}) \approx \mathcal{E}(\tilde{\sigma}_0 - \hat{\sigma}) \, \Gamma_0^{-1}(\tilde{\sigma}_0 - \hat{\sigma})$$

$$\approx \mathcal{E}(\hat{\gamma} - \gamma_0)' \, \Delta_0' \, \Gamma_0^{-1}\Delta_0(\hat{\gamma} - \gamma_0)$$

$$= \mathrm{tr}\{\Delta_0' \, \Gamma_0^{-1}\Delta_0 \, \mathcal{E}\, [(\hat{\gamma} - \gamma_0)(\hat{\gamma} - \gamma_0)']\} \,.$$

Since (Browne, 1984, Corollary 2.1)

$$\mathscr{E}\,[(\hat{\boldsymbol{\gamma}} - \boldsymbol{\gamma}_0)(\hat{\boldsymbol{\gamma}} - \boldsymbol{\gamma}_0)'] \approx n^{-1}(\boldsymbol{\Delta}_0'\,\boldsymbol{\Gamma}_0^{-1}\boldsymbol{\Delta}_0)^{-1}\,,$$

approximation A6 follows.                                           □

*Proposition A2.* The expected value of the overall discrepancy may be approximated by the sum of the discrepancy due to approximation and the expected value of the discrepancy due to estimation:

$$\mathscr{E}F(\boldsymbol{\Sigma}_0, \hat{\boldsymbol{\Sigma}}) \approx F(\boldsymbol{\Sigma}_0, \tilde{\boldsymbol{\Sigma}}_0) + \mathscr{E}F(\tilde{\boldsymbol{\Sigma}}_0, \hat{\boldsymbol{\Sigma}})\,. \qquad [A7]$$

*Proof.* Use of Equation A4 shows that

$$\mathscr{E}F(\boldsymbol{\Sigma}_0, \hat{\boldsymbol{\Sigma}}) \approx \mathscr{E}(\boldsymbol{\sigma}_0 - \tilde{\boldsymbol{\sigma}}_0 + \tilde{\boldsymbol{\sigma}}_0 - \hat{\boldsymbol{\sigma}})'\,\boldsymbol{\Gamma}_0^{-1}(\boldsymbol{\sigma}_0 - \tilde{\boldsymbol{\sigma}}_0 + \tilde{\boldsymbol{\sigma}}_0 - \hat{\boldsymbol{\sigma}}) \qquad [A8]$$

$$= (\boldsymbol{\sigma}_0 - \tilde{\boldsymbol{\sigma}}_0)'\,\boldsymbol{\Gamma}_0^{-1}(\boldsymbol{\sigma}_0 - \tilde{\boldsymbol{\sigma}}_0) + 2(\boldsymbol{\sigma}_0 - \tilde{\boldsymbol{\sigma}}_0)'\,\boldsymbol{\Gamma}_0^{-1}\mathscr{E}(\tilde{\boldsymbol{\sigma}}_0 - \hat{\boldsymbol{\sigma}})$$

$$+ \mathscr{E}(\tilde{\boldsymbol{\sigma}}_0 - \hat{\boldsymbol{\sigma}})'\,\boldsymbol{\Gamma}_0^{-1}(\tilde{\boldsymbol{\sigma}}_0 - \hat{\boldsymbol{\sigma}})\,.$$

Since $(\boldsymbol{\sigma}_0 - \tilde{\boldsymbol{\sigma}}_0)$ is $O(n^{-1/2})$ by assumption and $\mathscr{E}(\tilde{\boldsymbol{\sigma}}_0 - \hat{\boldsymbol{\sigma}})$ is $o(n^{-1/2})$, we have

$$(\boldsymbol{\sigma}_0 - \tilde{\boldsymbol{\sigma}}_0)'\,\boldsymbol{\Gamma}_0^{-1}\mathscr{E}(\tilde{\boldsymbol{\sigma}}_0 - \hat{\boldsymbol{\sigma}}) \approx 0\,. \qquad [A9]$$

Substitution of Equations A9, A2, and A3 into A8 yields Equation A7.     □

*Corollary A2.1.*

$$\mathscr{E}F(\boldsymbol{\Sigma}_0, \hat{\boldsymbol{\Sigma}}) \approx F(\boldsymbol{\Sigma}_0, \tilde{\boldsymbol{\Sigma}}_0) + n^{-1}q$$

*Proof.* This follows immediately from substitution of Equation A6 into A7.   □

*Proposition A3.* The *conditional* expectation of the CVI *over validation samples holding the calibration sample fixed* may be approximated by

$$\mathscr{E}_V \{F(S_V, \hat{\boldsymbol{\Sigma}}_C) \mid \hat{\boldsymbol{\Sigma}}_C\} \approx F(\boldsymbol{\Sigma}_0, \hat{\boldsymbol{\Sigma}}_C) + n_V^{-1}p^*\,. \qquad [A10]$$

*Proof.* Use of Equations A1 and A4 shows that

$$\mathscr{E}_V \{F(S_V, \hat{\boldsymbol{\Sigma}}_C) \mid \hat{\boldsymbol{\Sigma}}_C\} \approx \mathscr{E}_V (s_V - \hat{\boldsymbol{\sigma}}_C)'\,\boldsymbol{\Gamma}_0^{-1}(s_V - \hat{\boldsymbol{\sigma}}_C) \qquad [A11]$$

$$= \underset{V}{\mathscr{E}} \, (s_V - \sigma_0 + \sigma_0 - \hat{\sigma}_C)' \, \Gamma_0^{-1}(s_V - \sigma_0 + \sigma_0 - \hat{\sigma}_C)$$

$$= \underset{V}{\mathscr{E}} \, (s_V - \sigma_0)' \, \Gamma_0^{-1}(s_V - \sigma_0) + 2 \, (\sigma_0 - \hat{\sigma}_C)' \, \Gamma_0^{-1}\underset{V}{\mathscr{E}} \, (s_V - \sigma_0)$$

$$+ (\sigma_0 - \hat{\sigma}_C)' \, \Gamma_0^{-1}(\sigma_0 - \hat{\sigma}_C) \, .$$

The asymptotic distribution of $n_V(s_V - \sigma_0)'\Gamma_0^{-1} \, (s_V - \sigma_0)$ is central chi-squared with $p^*$ degrees of freedom. Since the expected value of a central chi-squared distribution is equal to the degrees of freedom,

$$\underset{V}{\mathscr{E}} \, (s_V - \sigma_0)' \, \Gamma_0^{-1}(s_V - \sigma_0) \approx n_V^{-1} p^* \, . \qquad [A12]$$

Use of Equation A4 with $\hat{\Sigma}_C$ replacing $\hat{\Sigma}$, and substitution of (A12) and

$$\underset{V}{\mathscr{E}} \, (s_V - \sigma_0) = 0$$

into Equation A11 yields A10. ☐

## References

Akaike, H. (1973). Information theory and an extension of the maximum likelihood principle. In B. N. Petrov & F. Csaki (Eds.), *Second International Symposium on Information Theory.* Budapest: Akademiai Kiado.

Bollen, K. A. (1989). *Structural equations with latent variables.* New York: John Wiley.

Browne, M. W. (1974). Generalised least squares estimators in the analysis of covariance structures. *South African Statistical Journal, 8,* 1-24.

Browne, M. W. (1984). Asymptotically distribution-free methods in the analysis of covariance structures. *British Journal of Mathematical and Statistical Psychology, 37,* 62-83.

Browne, M. W. (1991). *FITMOD: A computer program for calculating point and interval estimates of fit measures.* Unpublished manuscript.

Browne, M. W., & Cudeck, R. (1989). Single sample cross-validation indices for covariance structures. *Multivariate Behavioral Research, 24,* 445-455.

Browne, M. W., & Du Toit, S. H. C. (1991). Models for learning data. In L. M. Collins & J. L. Horn (Eds.), *Best methods for the analysis of change* (pp. 47-68). Washington, DC: American Psychological Association.

Browne, M. W., & Du Toit, S. H. C. (1992). Automated fitting of nonstandard models. *Multivariate Behavioral Research, 27,* 269-300.

Browne, M. W., & Shapiro, A. (1988). Robustness of normal theory methods in the analysis of linear latent variate models. *British Journal of Mathematical and Statistical Psychology, 41,* 193-208.

Cudeck, R., & Browne, M. W. (1983). Cross-validation of covariance structures. *Multivariate Behavioral Research, 18,* 147-167.

Cudeck, R., & Henly, S. J. (1991). Model selection in covariance structures analysis and the "problem" of sample size: A clarification. *Psychological Bulletin, 109,* 512-519.

Ding, C. G. (1987). *Computational tools for interval testing.* Unpublished doctoral dissertation, University of Georgia.

Farebrother, R. (1987). Algorithm AS 231: The distribution of a noncentral chi-square variable with nonnegative degrees of freedom. *Applied Statistics, 36,* 402-405.

Hauser, R. M., Tsai, S. L., & Sewell, W. H. (1983). A model of stratification with response error in social and psychological variables. *Sociology of Education, 56,* 20-46.

Jöreskog, K. G. (1978). Structural analysis of covariance and correlation matrices. *Psychometrika, 43,* 443-477.

Linhart, H., & Zucchini, W. (1986). *Model selection.* New York: John Wiley.

McDonald, R. P. (1989). An index of goodness of fit based on noncentrality. *Journal of Classification, 6,* 97-103.

McGaw, B., & Jöreskog, K. G. (1971). Factorial invariance of ability measures in groups differing in intelligence and socioeconomic status. *British Journal of Mathematical and Statistical Psychology, 24,* 154-168.

Moschopoulos, P. G. (1983). On a new transformation to normality. *Communications in Statistics A, 12,* 1873-1878.

Mulaik, S. A., James, L. R., Van Alstine, J., Bennett, N., Lind, S., & Stillwell, C. D. (1989). An evaluation of goodness of fit indices for structural equation models. *Psychological Bulletin, 105,* 430-445.

Naglieri, J. A., & Jensen, A. R. (1987). Comparison of black-white differences on the WISC-R and K-ABC: Spearman's hypothesis. *Intelligence, 11,* 21-43.

Shapiro, A. (1985). Asymptotic equivalence of minimum discrepancy function estimators to GLS estimators. *South African Statistical Journal, 19,* 73-81.

Steiger, J. H. (1989). *EzPATH: A supplementary module for SYSTAT and SYGRAPH.* Evanston, IL: SYSTAT.

Steiger, J. H. (1990). Structural model evaluation and modification: An interval estimation approach. *Multivariate Behavioral Research, 25,* 173-180.

Steiger, J. H., & Lind, J. M. (1980). *Statistically based tests for the number of common factors.* Paper presented at the annual meeting of the Psychometric Society, Iowa City, IA.

Steiger, J. H., Shapiro, A., & Browne, M. W. (1985). On the multivariate asymptotic distribution of sequential chi-square statistics. *Psychometrika, 50,* 253-263.

# 7

# Bayesian Model Selection
## in Structural Equation Models

ADRIAN E. RAFTERY

The class of structural equation models is broad, and its very generality makes model selection difficult. This is especially so when the underlying theory does not allow one to specify the model structure fairly completely in advance. In that case, the number of models initially entertained can be very large, and some exploratory model selection strategy is necessary. A common approach is to use theory to specify an initial model, and then to use a sequence of tests based on $P$ values to decide whether the model should be simplified or expanded (e.g., Bollen, 1989; Long, 1983a, 1983b).

There are many difficulties with such a strategy. The theory of $P$ values was developed for the comparison of two nested models. In a typical structural equation model application, there may be hundreds of substantively meaningful models, many of them nonnested. Wheaton's (1978) model for the sociogenesis of psychological disorders contains about 20 parameters, or arrows in the corresponding graph, some of which could be removed (see also Long, 1983b, figure 4.1). Indeed, the key scientific issue may often be expressed in terms of *which* of the arrows can be removed. Thus there may be up to about $2^{20}$, or roughly

AUTHOR'S NOTE: This research was supported by NIH Grant 5R01HD26330-02. I am grateful to David Madigan for helpful discussions; to Ken Bollen, Herb Costner, Scott Long, and Michael Sobel for very useful comments; and to Sandy Welsh for excellent research assistance.

163

one million, competing models; this number will be smaller if theory or prior research enables us safely to assume in advance that some of the arrows are in or out, but will typically still be large. The sampling properties of the overall *strategy* in such circumstances is unknown and may be very different from the properties of the individual tests that make it up (Fenech & Westfall, 1988; Miller, 1984).

Perhaps most fundamentally, conditioning on a single selected model ignores model uncertainty and so leads to underestimation of the uncertainty about the quantities of interest. This underestimation can be large, as has been shown by Regal and Hook (1991) in the contingency table context and by Miller (1984) in the regression context. One bad consequence is that it can lead to decisions that are too risky (Hodges, 1987). Even when there are only two models, $M_0$ and $M_1$, and they are nested, it is not clear that the $P$ value is a suitable criterion for model comparison. Indeed, Berger and Sellke (1987) and Berger and Delampady (1987) have argued that $P$ values and evidence are actually often in *conflict* (the cited articles are highly recommended to the reader).

Also, I have argued elsewhere that significance tests based on $P$ values ask the wrong question (Raftery, 1986a). They ask whether the null model is "true," a question to which we already know the answer is no. A scientifically more relevant question is, Which model predicts the data better? (That is, under which model are the data more likely to have been observed?) This leads to a different approach, the Bayesian one. One consequence is that tests based on $P$ values tend to reject the null model frequently with large samples of the sizes typically met with in sociology, even when $M_0$ predicts the data well; see Raftery (1986a) for a dramatic example with $n = 110,000$. By the same token, when there are many models, specification searches that consist of multiple $P$-value-based tests tend to yield models that are overcomplicated.

An alternative that seems to overcome these problems is provided by the Bayesian approach, which is described in the next section. Then, the Bayesian approach is applied to structural equation modeling, model selection strategies are discussed, and an example is given. This approach is applicable whether the prior theory and research is strong, in which case the number of models considered will be small, or weak, in which case the number of models that could potentially be entertained is often enormous. In the latter case, the research is often exploratory.

The Bayesian approach tends to favor simpler, more parsimonious, models than the sequential $P$-value approach. This can lead to further simplification by allowing the removal of variables that now appear irrelevant to the research hypothesis, yielding less cluttered graphs and making interpretation easier. It has been said that structural equation modeling is a "castle built on sand," because it is based on models that are too complex for the data used to estimate them. On the other hand, structural equation models do correspond well to the actual research hypotheses of social scientists. They also implement the famous advice of R. A. Fisher for the analysis of observational data: "Make your theories elaborate," so as to minimize the possibility of observed associations being spurious (i.e., due to unobserved variables) rather than causal (see also Blalock, 1979). I believe that Bayesian model selection for structural equation models may give us the best of both worlds: simple and interpretable models that are well supported by the data, and yet reflect the real research hypotheses and are based on sufficiently "elaborate" theories.

## Bayesian Model Comparison

### Comparing Two Models: Bayes Factors

We first consider the artificial situation in which only two models, $M_0$ and $M_1$, are being compared. These may be any two competing structural equation models. This is relevant if, for example, we are interested in whether one particular parameter is zero or not, and we are prepared to assume that the model is otherwise well specified. The results are also useful as building blocks in the more general and realistic situation in which there are many models.

The posterior odds for $M_0$ against $M_1$ given data $D$ are

$$\frac{p(M_0 \mid D)}{p(M_1 \mid D)} = \left[\frac{p(D \mid M_0)}{p(D \mid M_1)}\right]\left[\frac{p(M_0)}{p(M_1)}\right] = B_{01}\lambda_{01} . \tag{1}$$

The first equality follows from Bayes's theorem. In Equation 1, $\lambda_{01} = p(M_0)/p(M_1)$ is the *prior odds* for $M_0$ against $M_1$; it is often taken to be unity, representing "neutral" prior information that does not favor either model. The quantity $B_{01} = p(D|M_0)/p(D|M_1)$ is the *Bayes factor*, or ratio of posterior to prior odds, and $p(D|M_k)$ ($k = 0, 1$) is the *marginal likelihood* defined by

$$p(D \mid M_k) = \int p(D \mid \theta_k, M_k)p(\theta_k \mid M_k)d\theta_k , \tag{2}$$

where $\boldsymbol{\theta}_k$ is the (vector) parameter of $M_k$, $p(\boldsymbol{\theta}_k|M_k)$ is the prior distribution of $\boldsymbol{\theta}_k$ and $p(D|\boldsymbol{\theta}_k, M_k)$ is the likelihood.

The marginal likelihood $p(D|M_k)$ is also the *predictive probability* of the data given the model $M_k$, and so it measures how well the model predicts the data, which I would argue is the right criterion for model evaluation. Thus the Bayes factor measures how well $M_0$ predicts the data relative to $M_1$, and so is just the right quantity on which to base model comparison. Note that this comparison does not depend on the assumption that either model is "true," unlike model comparisons based on $P$ values.

Finding $B_{01}$ involves the multiple integral in Equation 2, which is often of high dimension; this is not in general easy to evaluate analytically. However, good analytic approximations are available. A Taylor series expansion of the log-likelihood about the maximum likelihood estimator $\hat{\boldsymbol{\theta}}_k$ shows that

$$2\log p(D \mid M_k) \approx 2\log p(D \mid \hat{\boldsymbol{\theta}}_k, M_k) - \log \mid V_k \mid \qquad [3]$$

$$+ 2\log p(\hat{\boldsymbol{\theta}}_k \mid M_k) - \nu_k \log(2\pi) ,$$

with a relative error that is $O(n^{-3/2})$ (Chow, 1981). The first term on the right-hand side of Equation 3 is twice the maximized log-likelihood, the second term is minus the log of the determinant of $V_k$, the variance matrix of $\hat{\boldsymbol{\theta}}_k$, the third term is twice the log of the prior density at $\hat{\boldsymbol{\theta}}_k$, and the fourth term is $-\log(2\pi)$ times $\nu_k = \dim(\hat{\boldsymbol{\theta}}_k)$, the number of independent parameters in $M_k$. The first, second, and fourth terms are readily obtained from the standard output of most statistical model-fitting programs. The third term is readily calculated and is generally negligible in moderate to large samples. Slightly more accurate approximations are available using the Laplace method (Raftery, 1988), but these are harder to calculate.

The matrix $V_k/n$ tends to a constant matrix as $n \to \infty$, where $n$ is the number of independent (scalar) observations that contribute to the likelihood. Thus the determinant of $V_k/n$, namely, $|V_k/n| = |V_k|/n^{\nu_k}$, tends to a scalar constant, and so does its logarithm, $(\log|V_k| - \nu_k \log n)$. Thus, if we remove from the right-hand side of Equation 3 all the terms that do not tend to infinity as $n \to \infty$, we obtain the cruder but simpler approximation

$$2\log p(D \mid M_k) \approx 2\log p(D \mid \hat{\boldsymbol{\theta}}_k, M_k) - \nu_k \log n , \qquad [4]$$

with a relative error of $O(n^{-1})$.

We thus have two approximations to the Bayes factor, namely, by Equation 3,

$$-2\log B_{01} \approx L^2 - \log |V_0| + \log |V_1| \qquad [5]$$

$$- 2\log\left\{\frac{p(\hat{\theta}_0 \mid M_0)}{p(\hat{\theta}_1 \mid M_1)}\right\} + (v_1 - v_0)\log(2\pi),$$

where $L^2$ is the standard likelihood-ratio test statistic, and, by Equation 4,

$$-2\log B_{01} \approx L^2 - (v_1 - v_0)\log n = \text{BIC}_{01}. \qquad [6]$$

When $\text{BIC}_{01} > 0$, the criterion favors $M_1$, and when $\text{BIC}_{01} < 0$ it favors $M_0$. This result was first established by Schwarz (1978) for regression models and extended to log-linear models by Raftery (1986b). It is usually stated in terms of twice the logarithm because of the connection with the likelihood-ratio test statistic, but one can recover the approximate Bayes factor itself from the equation

$$B_{01} \approx e^{-\frac{1}{2}\text{BIC}_{01}}. \qquad [7]$$

In structural equation models, the Lagrange multiplier (LM) and Wald (W) tests are often used in place of the likelihood-ratio test because they can be much less expensive computationally.[1] The LM and W test statistics are asymptotically equivalent to $L^2$ (see Bollen, 1989, pp. 293-296), and so may be used, at least roughly, in place of $L^2$ in Equation 6. If $M_0$ is nested within $M_1$ and the only difference between them is that $M_0$ constrains one parameter of $M_1$ to be equal to zero, then the W test statistic is equal to $t^2$, where $t$ is the relevant $t$ statistic. Thus, in that case, $L^2$ may be replaced by $t^2$ in Equation 6.

For the comparison of two *nested* models, Jeffreys (1961, Appendix B) has suggested the following order of magnitude interpretation of the Bayes factor, $B_{01}$. (Corresponding approximate values of $\text{BIC}_{01}$ from Equation 7 are also shown.) If $B_{01} > 1$ ($\text{BIC}_{01} < 0$), the data favor $M_0$ and there is no evidence for the additional effects represented by $M_1$. If $1 \geq B_{01} > 10^{-1}$ ($0 \leq \text{BIC}_{01} < 4.6$), then there is weak evidence for $M_1$. If $10^{-1} \geq B_{01} > 10^{-2}$ ($4.6 \leq \text{BIC}_{01} < 9.2$), the evidence for $M_1$ is strong, while if $B_{01} \leq 10^{-2}$ ($\text{BIC}_{01} \geq 9.2$), the evidence for $M_1$ is conclusive. As

**Table 7.1** Approximate Minimum *t* Values for Different Grades of Evidence and Sample Sizes

| Evidence | Minimum BIC | $n$ | | | |
|---|---|---|---|---|---|
| | | 30 | 100 | 1,000 | 10,000 |
| Weak | 0 | 1.84 | 2.15 | 2.63 | 3.03 |
| Strong | 5 | 2.90 | 3.10 | 3.45 | 3.77 |
| Conclusive | 10 | 3.66 | 3.82 | 4.11 | 4.38 |

a rough rule of thumb, I use BIC values of 0, 5, and 10 as cutoff points for the different "grades of evidence." Of course, the interpretation depends on the context. For example, Evett (1991) has argued that for forensic evidence alone to be conclusive in a criminal trial one would require posterior odds for $M_1$ (guilt) against $M_0$ (innocence) of at least 1,000:1, rather than the 100:1 suggested by Jeffreys. This corresponds to a BIC value of about 14, but in such a matter one would also, presumably, want $B_{01}$ to be calculated more accurately than by the BIC approximation.

The approximate *t* values corresponding to different grades of evidence and different sample sizes are shown in Table 7.1. For minimal evidence this is $t = \sqrt{\log n}$, for "strong" evidence it is $t = \sqrt{\log n + 5}$, and for "conclusive" evidence it is $t = \sqrt{\log n + 10}$. Note that the critical values are larger than those based on *P* values, and also that they increase with $n$.

**Many Models: Accounting for Model Uncertainty**

Suppose now that instead of just two models there are $(K + 1)$ models $M_0, M_1, \ldots, M_K$. In most studies, there is one, or perhaps a small number of quantities of primary interest such as the coefficient associated with a particular arrow in the graph that represents the structural equation model; we denote such a quantity of interest by $\Delta$. The full Bayesian solution to inference about $\Delta$ takes account explicitly of model uncertainty and is as follows. First we form the *posterior distribution* of $\Delta$ under each model $M_k$, namely, the conditional distribution of $\Delta$ given the observed data $D$. If $\theta_k$ is the parameter of $M_k$ (consisting of the identified parameters in the eight matrices that define the structural equation model), then the posterior distribution of $\theta_k$ is

$$p(\theta_k \mid D, M_k) = \frac{p(D \mid \theta_k, M_k)p(\theta_k \mid M_k)}{\int p(D \mid \theta_k, M_k)p(\theta_k \mid M_k)d\theta_k}, \qquad [8]$$

and the posterior distribution of $\Delta$ is just the marginal distribution of $\Delta$ from Equation 8, obtained by integrating out the other components of $\theta_k$. The posterior distribution of $\Delta$ will usually be approximately normal if the sample size is reasonably large. It can often be well approximated by a normal distribution with mean $\hat{\Delta}_k$, the maximum likelihood estimator of $\Delta$ under $M_k$, and variance $V_k$, the (approximate) variance matrix of $\hat{\Delta}_k$; the precise form of the prior $p(\theta_k|M_k)$ often has little effect on the final inference. For further discussion of these results and the basic ideas of Bayesian inference, see, for example, Edwards, Lindeman, and Savage (1963), Box and Tiao (1973, chap. 1), and Cox and Hinkley (1974, chap. 10).

We then form the final posterior distribution of $\Delta$ as a weighted average of the posterior distributions of $\Delta$ under each of the models, weighted by their posterior model probabilities $p(M_k|D)$, namely,

$$p(\Delta \mid D) = \sum_{k=0}^{K} p(\theta_k \mid D, M_k) p(M_k \mid D) , \qquad [9]$$

where

$$p(M_k \mid D) = \frac{p(D \mid M_k)p(M_k)}{\displaystyle\sum_{k=0}^{K} p(D \mid M_k)p(M_k)} . \qquad [10]$$

If all the models have the same prior probability, then this may be approximated by

$$p(M_k \mid D) \approx \frac{e^{\frac{1}{2}BIC_{0k}}}{\displaystyle\sum_{k=0}^{K} e^{\frac{1}{2}BIC_{0k}}} , \qquad [11]$$

where $BIC_{00} = 0$ and $BIC_{0k}$ results from comparing $M_k$ with $M_0$, considered as a baseline model.

Note that Bayes factors and BIC values for comparing two models may, in general, be computed by comparing each with a different, third model. Suppose that we want to compare $M_1$ with $M_2$, and we compare each of them separately with $M_0$, then we have

$$B_{12} = \frac{B_{02}}{B_{01}}, \qquad\qquad [12]$$

and

$$BIC_{12} = BIC_{02} - BIC_{01}. \qquad\qquad [13]$$

An approximate combined point estimate and standard error can be calculated from the formulas,

$$E[\Delta \mid D] \approx \sum_{k=0}^{K} \hat{\Delta}_k p_k, \qquad\qquad [14]$$

$$\text{var}[\Delta \mid D] \approx \sum_{k=0}^{K} (V_k p_k + \hat{\Delta}_k^2 p_k) - E[\Delta \mid D]^2, \qquad\qquad [15]$$

where $p_k = p(M_k \mid D)$.

When the total number of models is very large, the sums over all models will be impractical to calculate. In Madigan and Raftery (1991), we argued that one should exclude from the sum (a) models that are much less likely than the most likely model—say, 10, 20, or 100 times less likely—corresponding to BIC differences of about 5, 6, or 10; and (b) models containing effects for which there is no evidence, that is, those that have more likely models nested within them. We refer to the models that are left as falling within *Occam's window,* a generalization of the famous Occam's razor, or principle of parsimony in scientific explanation.

### Application to Structural Equation Models

#### Bayes Factors for Structural Equation Models

The results in the above section apply quite generally to structural equation models. Note that in the definition of BIC, $n$ is equal to the total number of (scalar) observations, namely, $N(p + q)$ in the notation of Bollen (1989, table 2.2), where $N$ is the number of cases. Note also that for the calculation of BIC, most structural equation model software reports $L^2$ in terms of a comparison with the saturated model, $M_S$.

Suppose that we want to compare two models $M_1$ and $M_2$ and that for each model we have the likelihood ratio test statistic $L_k^2$ (relative to the saturated model), and the number of degrees of freedom, $df_k$, equal to $\frac{1}{2}(p + q)(p + q + 1) - \nu_k$ ($k = 1, 2$). Then we may compare each model in turn with the saturated model $M_S$ using

$$\text{BIC}_{kS} = L_k^2 - df_k \log [N(p + q)] .$$ [16]

Thus by Equation 13 we may compare $M_1$ with $M_2$ using

$$\text{BIC}_{12} = \text{BIC}_{1S} - \text{BIC}_{2S} .$$ [17]

In what follows, where BIC appears without subscripts it will refer to $\text{BIC}_{kS}$.

Note that $M_k$ will be preferred to $M_S$ if $\text{BIC}_{kS} < 0$. Thus $\text{BIC}_{kS}$ may be regarded as a kind of goodness-of-fit test of $M_k$ in the sense that if $\text{BIC}_{kS} > 0$, $M_k$ will be "rejected" in favor of the saturated model. Note also that the more accurate approximation in Equation 5 can be calculated fairly easily from the output of standard programs such as LISREL and EQS.

### Search Strategy

How should we carry out the search for good models? The number of possible models can be huge and, in principle, each new model considered must be checked for identifiability, a nontrivial task.

It seems that the search should be limited from the outset by substantive considerations. One way to do this might be as follows. First, develop one or several "encompassing" models that are sufficiently elaborate to include all the postulated effects, and check that each of these models is identified. Then specify which arrows have to be in all the models considered, for substantive reasons or in light of previous empirical results. Then the search would be restricted to models that are nested within the "encompassing" models and that contain the "essential" arrows. Since these are all nested within identified models, they are themselves quite likely to be identified. However, this is not necessarily the case and needs to be checked for the preferred models.[2] I will now outline two main types of search strategies.

#### Stepwise Strategies

Stepwise strategies have been used for many years for variable selection in regression, and have been extended to other contexts such as log-linear models (Goodman, 1971). They include forward selection, backward elimination, and strategies that combine features of both.

One possibility is a stepwise strategy that sequentially adds and deletes arrows in the structural equation model graph, with the criterion for making a change being that the Bayes factor (or BIC) favor the change. Probably the most convenient criterion for this purpose is the approximation to BIC obtained by replacing $L^2$ by $t^2$ in Equation 6 for deciding whether to remove an arrow, and the approximation that replaces $L^2$ by the LM test statistic or modification index (Bollen, 1989, p. 293) for deciding whether to add an arrow. A good starting model could be found by first estimating the "encompassing" model and including all the arrows that have $t$ values greater than the critical value for weak evidence, which, if BIC is used, is $\sqrt{\log n}$ (see Table 7.1).

Such a strategy should lead to the most likely single model, say, $M_{\max}$ (although this is not guaranteed). One could then attempt to find the other models that lie in Occam's window by comparing $M_{\max}$ with models that differ from it by at most a few arrows, and retaining those models $M_k$ such that $B_{\max,k}$ is less than some appropriate number such as 10, 20, or 100. Finally, models that have more likely models nested within them would be removed.

### The Down-Up Algorithm

This algorithm was proposed by Madigan and Raftery (1991) in the context of graphical models for contingency tables, and it seems also to be applicable to structural equation models. It is a direct and efficient way of finding all the models in Occam's window. It proceeds through model space from larger to smaller models and then back again in a series of pairwise comparisons of nested models.

It eliminates models by applying the principle that if a model is rejected, then its submodels (i.e., the models nested within it) are also rejected. All models that have not been rejected are included in Occam's window. In a pairwise comparison of $M_0$ with $M_1$, where $M_0$ is nested within $M_1$, $M_0$ (and all its submodels) is rejected if $B_{01} < C^{-1}$, $M_1$ is rejected if $B_{01} > 1$, and both models are retained if $C^{-1} \le B_{01} \le 1$. Here $C$ is a constant set equal to, for example, 10, 20, or 100. Generally, the smaller $C$ is, the fewer models there are in Occam's window, but we have found that the results tend to be fairly insensitive to the precise choice of $C$.

We now outline the search technique. The search can proceed in two directions: "up" from each starting model by adding arrows, or "down" from each starting model by dropping arrows. When starting from a nonsaturated, nonempty model, we first execute the down algorithm. Then we execute the up algorithm, using the models from the down algorithm as a starting point. Experience to date suggests that the ordering of these operations has little impact on the final set of models. Let $\mathcal{A}$ and $\mathcal{F}$ be subsets of model space $\mathcal{M}$, where $\mathcal{A}$ denotes the set of "acceptable" models and $\mathcal{F}$ denotes the models under consideration. For both algorithms, we begin with $\mathcal{A} = \varnothing$ and $\mathcal{F} = $ set of starting models.

*Down Algorithm*

(1) Select a model $M$ from $\mathcal{F}$.
(2) $\mathcal{F} \leftarrow \mathcal{F} - M$ (i.e., replace $\mathcal{F}$ by $\mathcal{F} - M$), and $\mathcal{A} \leftarrow \mathcal{A} + M$.
(3) Select a submodel $M_0$ of $M$ by removing an arrow from $M$.
(4) Compute $B = \frac{p(M_0 \mid D)}{p(M \mid D)}$.
(5) If $B > 1$ then $\mathcal{A} \leftarrow \mathcal{A} - M$ and if $M_0 \notin \mathcal{F}$, $\mathcal{F} \leftarrow \mathcal{F} + M_0$.
(6) If $C^{-1} \leq B \leq 1$ then if $M_0 \notin \mathcal{F}$, $\mathcal{F} \leftarrow \mathcal{F} + M_0$.
(7) If there are more submodels of $M$, go to 3.
(8) If $\mathcal{F} \neq \varnothing$, go to 1.

*Up Algorithm*

(1) Select a model $M$ from $\mathcal{F}$.
(2) $\mathcal{F} \leftarrow \mathcal{F} - M$ and $\mathcal{A} \leftarrow \mathcal{A} + M$.
(3) Select a supermodel $M_1$ of $M$ by adding an arrow to $M$.
(4) Compute $B = \frac{p(M \mid D)}{p(M_1 \mid D)}$.
(5) If $B < C^{-1}$ then $\mathcal{A} \leftarrow \mathcal{A} - M$ and if $M_1 \notin \mathcal{F}$, $\mathcal{F} \leftarrow \mathcal{F} + M_1$.
(6) If $C^{-1} \leq B \leq 1$ then if $M_1 \notin \mathcal{F}$, $\mathcal{F} \leftarrow \mathcal{F} + M_1$.
(7) If there are more supermodels of $M$, go to 3.
(8) If $\mathcal{F} \neq \varnothing$, go to 1.

Upon termination, $\mathcal{A}$ contains the set of potentially acceptable models. Finally, we remove all the models that have more likely submodels, and those models $M_k$ for which

$$\frac{p(M_{\max} \mid D)}{p(M_k \mid D)} > C . \tag{18}$$

$\mathcal{A}$ now contains the acceptable models, namely, those in Occam's window.

The algorithm has been coded for *discrete* recursive causal models and also for graphical log-linear models. It is very efficient, carrying out about 3,000 model comparisons per minute on a workstation. Efficient computer implementation of the algorithm for structural equation models remains to be done.

### *Example*

I will now outline how some of these ideas might apply in an example. The data considered are from Wheaton's (1978) study of the sociogenesis of psychological disorder (PD); these data were reanalyzed by Long (1983b). The main issue is whether low socioeconomic status (SES) leads to PD, PD leads to low SES, both, or neither. Low SES causing PD is referred to as *social causation,* while PD leading to low SES is called *social selection.* One of Wheaton's data sets consisted of $N = 603$ individuals in Illinois for whom SES was measured at three different time points; two indicators of PD were also measured at each of the last two time points. Father's SES was also used, giving a total of eight observed variables and $n = 603 \times 8 = 4,824$, so that $\log n = 8.48$. Figure 7.1, reproduced from Long (1983b), shows the main variables and represents Long's model $M_f$, which was close to his preferred model for the data.

Table 7.2 shows 22 models for the data. Long (1983b, table 4.2) fitted 6 models to the data, and the BIC values are shown in Table 7.2. Models $M_a$, $M_b$, and $M_c$ have positive BIC values, and so are unsatisfactory. Model $M_d$ does fit slightly better than the saturated model, but model $M_e$ fits much better. Model $M_e$ is preferred to model $M_f$, even though the evidence is weak. Also, $M_e$ is nested within $M_f$, so that if we considered only Long's six models to start with, only $M_e$ would be in Occam's window, and we would not need to average over models to make inference about individual parameters. Also, $M_e$ "fits" the data in the sense of being better than the saturated model (note that this is in conflict with the result based on $P$ values), but this does not preclude our search for better models.

The remaining 16 models document part of an implementation of the down algorithm starting from model $M_e$, so that $\mathcal{F} = \{M_e\}$. Here we take $C = 20$, by analogy with the popular 5% significance level for tests, so that $B_{01} < C^{-1}$ if $\text{BIC}_{01} > 6$. Thus we will reject the larger model $M_1$ if $\text{BIC}_{01} < \text{BIC}_{1S}$, while we will reject the smaller model, $M_0$, if the difference between the BIC values is greater than 6, that is, if $\text{BIC}_{01} = \text{BIC}_{0S} - \text{BIC}_{1S} > 6$. If

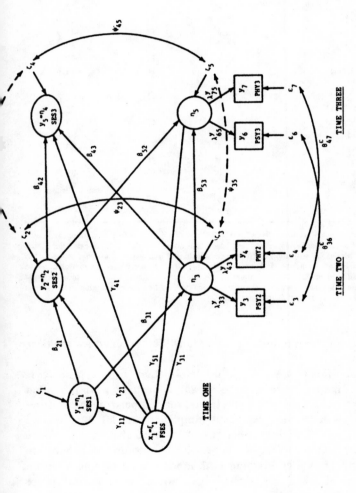

**Figure 7.1.** Model $M_f$ for data from Wheaton (1978). FSES = father's socioeconomic status; SES1 = socioeconomic status at time 1; SES2 = socioeconomic status at time 2; SES3 = socioeconomic status at time 3; PSY2 = number of psychological symptoms at time 2; PSY3 = number of psychological symptoms at time 3; PHY2 = number of psychophysiological symptoms at time 2; PHY3 = number of psychophysiological symptoms at time 23.

SOURCE: Reproduced from Long (1983b, figure 4.1).

175

**Table 7.2** Model Comparison for Wheaton's Data

| $k$ | Model | $L^2$ | $df$ | $BIC_{k}S$ |
|---|---|---|---|---|
| 1 | $M_a$ | 142.6 | 13 | 32.3 |
| 2 | $M_b$ | 147.5 | 15 | 20.3 |
| 3 | $M_c$ | 131.0 | 13 | 20.7 |
| 4 | $M_d$ | 89.9 | 11 | −3.4 |
| 5 | $M_e$ | 45.4 | 10 | −39.4 |
| 6 | $M_f$ | 40.8 | 9 | −35.5 |
| 7 | $M_e - \{\gamma_{31}\}$ | $45.4^t$ | 11 | −47.9 |
| 8 | $M_e - \{\gamma_{51}\}$ | $45.4^t$ | 11 | −47.9 |
| 9 | $M_e - \{\beta_{52}\}$ | $45.4^t$ | 11 | −47.9 |
| 10 | $M_e - \{\theta^5_{47}\}$ | $43.7^t$ | 11 | −49.6 |
| 11 | $M_e - \{\gamma_{31}, \gamma_{51}, \beta_{52}, \theta^5_{47}\}$ | 46.9 | 14 | −71.8 |
| 12 | $11 - \{\beta_{43}\}$ | 47.8 | 15 | −79.4 |
| 13 | $11 - \{\psi_{54}\}$ | 60.4 | 15 | −66.8 |
| 14 | $11 - \{\beta_{43}, \psi_{54}\}$ | 60.6 | 16 | −75.1 |
| 15 | $11$ with $\psi_{23} = \psi_{54}$ | 48.5 | 15 | −78.7 |
| 16 | $15 - \{\gamma_{21}\}$ | $49.5^t$ | 16 | −86.2 |
| 17 | $15 - \{\gamma_{41}\}$ | $52.5^t$ | 16 | −83.2 |
| 18 | $15 - \{\beta_{43}\}$ | $49.1^t$ | 16 | −86.6 |
| 19 | $15 - \{\gamma_{21}, \gamma_{41}\}$ | $55.0^M$ | 17 | −89.2 |
| 20 | $15 - \{\gamma_{21}, \beta_{43}\}$ | $50.2^M$ | 17 | −94.0 |
| 21 | $15 - \{\gamma_{41}, \beta_{43}\}$ | $53.3^M$ | 17 | −90.9 |
| 22 | $15 - \{\gamma_{21}, \gamma_{41}, \beta_{43}\}$ | 55.9 | 18 | −96.8 |

NOTE: The first six models are those fit in Long (1983b, Table 4.2). The "−{ }" notation indicates that the parameters inside the curly brackets have been constrained to equal zero. For example, Model 11 is the same as Model $M_e$ with the additional constraints that $\gamma_{31}$, $\gamma_{51}$, $\beta_{52}$, and $\theta^5_{47}$ are equal to zero. In the $L^2$ column, a superscript $t$ indicates that the quantity shown is an approximation equal to the $L^2$ value for a larger model plus the square of the relevant $t$ statistic, while the superscript $M$ indicates that the quantity shown is an approximation equal to the $L^2$ value for a smaller model minus the relevant LM test statistic or modification index.

$BIC_{01}$ is between 0 and 6, both $M_0$ and $M_1$ will be retained for the time being.

Model 7 specifies that $\gamma_{31} = 0$ in model $M_e$, that is, the $\gamma_{31}$ arrow is removed. This model is preferred to $M_e$ and is nested within it, so that $M_e$ is now rejected and Model 7 is retained for comparison with further models. Models 8-10 also represent simplifications of $M_e$ that are preferred to it; 13 other simplifications of $M_e$ were also tried but were rejected and are not shown in Table 7.2. The comparison between Models 11 and 13 is a case where both models were retained, with a BIC difference of 5 in favor of the larger model (although both were

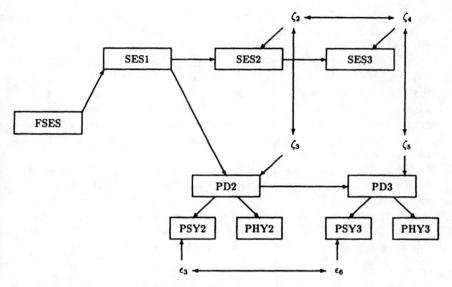

**Figure 7.2.** Model 22 from Table 7.2 for data from Wheaton (1978).

later rejected, Model 11 in favor of Model 15, and Model 13 in the final phase of the algorithm, in favor of the best model, Model 22).

In the end, only Model 22 is in Occam's window, so that the result is fairly clear-cut. All the parameters in Model 22 have highly significant $t$ values (all are greater than $\sqrt{\log(n + 6)} = 3.8$), none of the meaningful modification indices (LM test statistics) is significant according to BIC (i.e., greater than $\log n = 8.48$), and there are no outliers among the standardized residuals (each residual corresponds to one of the 36 sample covariances).

Model 22 is shown in Figure 7.2; it is considerably simpler than the model in Figure 7.1. Substantively, it leads to the conclusion that there is social causation but not social selection; the key feature that indicates this is the absence of $\beta_{43}$, the arrow from PD at Time 2 (PD2) to SES at Time 3 (SES3). Wheaton (1978) came to the same conclusion, but Long (1983b) points out that Wheaton's own model corresponds closely to model $M_d$, and that there $\beta_{43}$ is significant, supporting the social selection hypothesis.

Why this conflict? It seems that the significance of $\beta_{43}$ in $M_d$ is an artifact caused by the misspecification of $M_d$. As one moves toward better-fitting models, from $M_d$ to $M_e$ to Model 15, $\hat{\beta}_{43}$ goes from $-1.50$ to $-0.85$, to a nonsignificant $-0.47$ ($t = -0.8$), while in Models 16, 17, and 19, $\beta_{43}$ remains close to $-0.5$ and nonsignificant. The nonsignificance of $\beta_{43}$ is also indicated by the contrasts between Models 19 and 22, and between Models 15 and 18, which in each case favor the model that does not include $\beta_{43}$. In comparing $M_d$ with Model 22, note that Model 22 not only fits substantially better in terms of $L^2$, but also uses seven fewer parameters. The estimates of all the parameters that are present in the favored Model 22 remained quite stable across models, but this was not true for $\beta_{43}$.

A backward selection strategy starting from $M_e$ that uses a sequence of $P$-value-based significance tests at the 1% level would, like our approach, select Model 22. However, a similar strategy at the 5% level would choose Model 20 rather than Model 22, as would the AIC (Akaike, 1987). The only difference between the two models is that Model 20 includes $\gamma_{41}$ (the direct effect of father's SES on SES at Time 3), but Model 22 does not. The $P$ value for $\gamma_{41}$ in Model 20 is 0.017, and even if one wishes to use $P$ values, a reasonable balance between power and significance would suggest a lower significance level with such a large sample size. In addition, Model 20 is substantively unsatisfactory because it says that father's SES has a direct effect on SES at Time 3 but not at Time 2. In any event, Models 20 and 22 both lead to the same conclusions about the research question of primary interest.

## Discussion

An approach to Bayesian model selection and accounting for model uncertainty in structural equation models has been described. This seems to hold out the promise of selecting simpler and more interpretable models, without compromising the richness of the structural equation model framework for representing substantive research hypotheses. When appropriate, several models are selected, rather than just one. Thus ambiguity about model structure is pinpointed and taken into account when making inference about quantities of interest.

Another common approach to model selection consists of selecting a single model based on an information criterion such as AIC (Akaike, 1987; Bozdogan, 1987; Cudeck & Browne, 1983; Sclove, 1987). Note that BIC can be used in this way, as can the posterior probability or other approximations to it such as Equation 5, to select the single model with the best value of the criterion; however, this is not what is advocated here. A key difference between that approach and the one described here is that we select several models when appropriate and base inferences on all the selected models, thus taking account of uncertainty about model structure. While model uncertainty is not a crucial issue in the example discussed here, Madigan and Raftery (1991) give several examples with multivariate data where it is important. Failing to take account of model uncertainty leads to inferior predictive performance as well as reduced scientific insight.

## Notes

1. When there is one degree of freedom in the test, the LM test statistic is sometimes referred to as the modification index.
2. If a less restrictive model is identified, not all the models nested within it are identified. For example, the model given in Bollen (1989, pp. 244-245) with two indicators per latent variable and two latent variables is identified. However, if we form a nested model that specifies the two latent variables to be uncorrelated, it no longer is identified. I am grateful to Ken Bollen for pointing this out to me.

## References

Akaike, H. (1987). Factor analysis and AIC. *Psychometrika, 52*, 317-332.
Berger, J. O., & Delampady, M. (1987). Testing precise hypotheses (with discussion). *Statistical Science, 2*, 317-352.
Berger, J. O., & Sellke, T. (1987). Testing a point null hypothesis: The irreconcilability of *P* values and evidence (with discussion). *Journal of the American Statistical Association, 82*, 112-139.
Blalock, H. M. (1979). The presidential address: Measurement and conceptualization problems: The major obstacle to integrating theory and research. *American Sociological Review, 44*, 881-894.
Bollen, K. A. (1989). *Structural equations with latent variables*. New York: John Wiley.
Box, G. E. P., & Tiao, G. C. (1973). *Bayesian inference in statistical analysis*. Reading, MA: Addison-Wesley.
Bozdogan, H. (1987). Model selection and Akaike's information criteria (AIC): The general theory and its analytical extensions. *Psychometrika, 52*, 345-370.
Chow, G. C. (1981). A comparison of the information and posterior probability criteria for model selection. *Journal of Econometrics, 16*, 21-33.
Cox, D. R., & Hinkley, D. V. (1974). *Theoretical statistics*. London: Chapman & Hall.
Cudeck, R., & Browne, M. W. (1983). Cross-validation of covariance structures. *Multivariate Behavioral Research, 18*, 147-167.

180     Bayesian Model Selection

Edwards, W., Lindeman, H., & Savage, L. J. (1963). Bayesian statistical inference for psychological research. *Psychological Review, 70,* 193-242.

Evett, I. W. (1991). *Implementing Bayesian methods in forensic science.* Paper presented at the Fourth Valencia International Meeting on Bayesian Statistics.

Fenech, A., & Westfall, P. (1988). The power function of conditional log-linear model tests. *Journal of the American Statistical Association, 83,* 198-203.

Goodman, L. A. (1971). The analysis of multidimensional contingency tables: Stepwise procedures and direct estimation methods for building models for multiple classifications. *Technometrics, 13,* 33-61.

Hodges, J. S. (1987). Uncertainty, policy analysis and statistics (with discussion). *Statistical Science, 2,* 259-291.

Jeffreys, H. (1961). *Theory of probability* (3rd ed.). Oxford: Oxford University Press.

Long, J. S. (1983a). *Confirmatory factor analysis.* Beverly Hills, CA: Sage.

Long, J. S. (1983b). *Covariance structure models.* Beverly Hills, CA: Sage.

Madigan, D., & Raftery, A. E. (1991). *Model selection and accounting for model uncertainty in graphical models using Occam's window* (Tech. Rep. No. 213). Seattle: University of Washington, Department of Statistics.

Miller, A. J. (1984). Selection of subsets of regression variables (with discussion). *Journal of the Royal Statistical Society, Series A, 147,* 389-425.

Raftery, A. E. (1986a). Choosing models for cross-classifications. *American Sociological Review, 51,* 145-146.

Raftery, A. E. (1986b). A note on Bayes factors for log-linear contingency table models with vague prior information. *Journal of the Royal Statistical Society, Series B, 48,* 249-250.

Raftery, A. E. (1988). *Approximate Bayes factors for generalized linear models* (Tech. Rep. No. 121). Seattle: University of Washington, Department of Statistics.

Regal, R. R., & Hook, E. B. (1991). The effects of model selection on confidence intervals for the size of a closed population. *Statistics in Medicine, 10,* 717-721.

Schwarz, G. (1978). Estimating the dimension of a model. *Annals of Statistics, 6,* 461-464.

Sclove, S. L. (1987). Application of some model-selection criteria to some problems in multivariate analysis. *Psychometrika, 52,* 333-344.

Wheaton, B. (1978). The sociogenesis of psychological disorder. *American Sociological Review, 43,* 383-403.

# 8

# *Power Evaluations in Structural Equation Models*

WILLEM E. SARIS
ALBERT SATORRA

The introduction of the LISREL program (Jöreskog, 1973), which routinely provides a goodness-of-fit statistic, brought the testing of structural equation models back to the attention of researchers. Before that time, researchers had been concentrating on the estimation of effects rather than on testing. The testing had earlier been suggested by Simon (1954) and Blalock (1962). However, the standard use of the likelihood ratio test was soon criticized because of the effect of sample size on test statistics (e.g., Bentler & Bonett, 1980; Jöreskog & Sörbom, 1988; Wheaton, Muthén, Alwin, & Summers, 1977). Each of the above-cited authors, and many others besides, have proposed goodness-of-fit indices. The increasing number of goodness-of-fit indices, however, would appear to suggest that there is no general agreement on the usefulness of the existing procedures. One of the problems with these indices is that they measure misspecification at the level of covariances, and not at the level of the relevant structural parameters. This means that the relationship between the misspecification in the model and the fit index is not clear. Further, as Kaplan (1990) argues, the introduction

AUTHORS' NOTE: The help of F. Udina in computer assistance is gratefully acknowledged. We are also grateful to Kenneth Bollen and one reviewer for very helpful comments. The work reported here was partially supported by the Spanish research grant DGICYT PS89-0040.

of fit indexes has distracted attention from the more fundamental problem of power analysis. Besides, it has been shown that goodness-of-fit indices are also affected by sample size (Bollen, 1986).

Nevertheless, it is true that the same size of misspecification will lead to rejection of the model more frequently for large samples than for small samples. In fact, Saris, den Ronden, and Satorra (1987) have shown that for articles published in social science journals between 1979 and 1982 there is indeed a nearly perfect relationship between sample size and the acceptability of the model. But they also point out that the relationship is not so simple that only the sample size plays a role. From a previous study by Saris, de Pijper, and Zegwaart (1979) it had already become clear that there were more problems with the LISREL goodness-of-fit test. In this study, using simulated data and equal sample sizes, misspecified models were frequently not rejected and the frequency of detection of the same size of misspecification depended on the specific model studied. This finding suggests that the problem is more general than one of sample size. The authors came to the conclusion that one cannot use the LISREL goodness-of-fit test without some knowledge of the power of the test.

Therefore, a study was started concerning the power of the model test for structural equation models. Satorra and Saris (1983, 1985) developed a procedure to evaluate the power of the goodness-of-fit test against specific deviations from the hypothesized model, also called *null model* or $H_0$. This approach has been demonstrated for several examples by Saris and Stronkhorst (1984) and Saris et al. (1987). The disadvantage of this approach is that one has to specify fully an alternative value of the parameter vector to obtain information about the power of the test. Satorra (1989) has considered several procedures to evaluate the power of the test for specific deviations from the null model, and Satorra, Saris, and de Pijper (1991) have compared different asymptotically equivalent procedures to compute the power of the test.

In this chapter, we present a new approach that allows something to be said about the power of the test without the need to choose specific alternative values of the parameter vector. In this new approach, one has only to specify a null model $H_0$ that is the model of interest and a less restricted model that is assumed to be correct on a priori grounds. This less restricted model will be called the *maintained model* H. The approach discussed here will provide information about the power of the test for the extra restrictions that differentiate $H_0$ from H. Note that here the models $H_0$ and H are nested models.

We start with a brief introduction to the testing of structural equation models. We then introduce the power of the goodness-of-fit test as well as alternative procedures to evaluate the power. We go on to discuss a new procedure for evaluating the power of the test, and then discuss some of the limitations of the new approach. The chapter ends with a discussion of the results.

## The Goodness-of-Fit Test

The structural equation modeling approach implies that the covariance matrix $\Sigma$ of the observed variables is expressed as a function of a vector ($\theta$) containing the fixed and free model parameters. That is,

$$\Sigma = \Sigma(\theta) , \qquad [1]$$

where $\theta$ is a partitioned vector with $q$ free parameters ($\theta_{fr}$) for which a priori no value is specified and a vector with $p$ fixed parameters ($\theta_{fi}$) for which the values are restricted a priori according to the null model ($H_0$).

Although this approach can be used for any type of structural model, with or without latent variables, we will use as an example a very simple measurement or factor analysis model. In this example, discussed frequently in the literature (e.g., see Bollen & Grandjean, 1981; Jöreskog, 1971; Saris, 1982), there are two latent and several observed variables. A possible model for such a situation is specified in the path diagram presented in Figure 8.1. In this diagram, $\eta_1$ and $\eta_2$ are the latent variables and $y_1$ to $y_4$ are the observed variables.

A typical research task is to test whether the two latent variables in fact measure the same variable. In this model, if this were the case, the correlation between $\eta_1$ and $\eta_2$ would be 1. In carrying out this test, it is in general also assumed that each latent variable affects only some observed variables, and that the error terms are uncorrelated with each other and with the latent variables.

The model shown in Figure 8.1 is a specific case of the more general class of factor analysis models for which the following model specification holds:

$$\Sigma = \Gamma \Phi \Gamma' + \Psi \qquad [2]$$

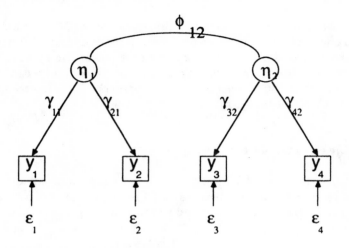

**Figure 8.1.** Two-indicator two-factor model.

where $\Sigma$ is the variance-covariance matrix or VC-matrix for the observed variables, $\Phi$ is the VC-matrix for the latent variables, $\Psi$ is the VC-matrix for the measurement errors, and $\Gamma$ is the matrix of the loadings.

The model $H_0$ in Figure 8.1 specifies the following restrictions in the matrices mentioned in Equation 2:

$$\Gamma = \begin{pmatrix} \gamma_{11} & 0 \\ \gamma_{21} & 0 \\ 0 & \gamma_{32} \\ 0 & \gamma_{42} \end{pmatrix}, \quad \Phi = \begin{pmatrix} 1 & \varphi_{12}=1 \\ \varphi_{21}=1 & 1 \end{pmatrix} \tag{3}$$

$$\Psi = \begin{pmatrix} \psi_{11} & 0 & 0 & 0 \\ 0 & \psi_{22} & 0 & 0 \\ 0 & 0 & \psi_{33} & 0 \\ 0 & 0 & 0 & \psi_{44} \end{pmatrix}$$

In these three matrices some parameters have been given fixed values. These fixed values represent restrictions, according to the null model, on the general model specified in Equation 2. The fixed values of these parameters are the elements of the vector $\theta_{fi}$ of Equation 1. Other parameters are represented by a symbol. These parameters are the $q$ free parameters ($\theta_{fr}$) of the model that have to be estimated.

Misspecifications in the model can exist for the main hypothesis to be investigated (i.e., the correlation between the latent variables) or for all the restrictions introduced in the model. In this model this would mean that there could be correlated error terms such as $\psi_{21} \neq 0$ or $\psi_{31} \neq 0$.

It is common practice to estimate the parameters of a model as specified in Equations 2 and 3 by minimizing the following function with respect to the free parameters in $\theta$:

$$F[S, \Sigma(\theta)] = \ln | \Sigma(\theta) | + \text{tr}[S\Sigma(\theta)^{-1}] - \ln | S | - m, \qquad [4]$$

where $S$ is the usual sample covariance matrix and $m$ is the number of observed variables.

If the observed variables have a multivariate normal distribution, it can be shown that

$$-(n/2)F[S, \Sigma(\theta)] = \ln[L(\theta)], \qquad [5]$$

where $n = (N - 1)$ and $N$ is the sample size while $\ln L(\theta)$ is the corresponding log-likelihood function of the sample except for an additive constant. That is, the minimization of Equation 4 provides maximum likelihood estimates for the free parameters in $\theta$. It can also be shown that the likelihood ratio test statistic corresponding to the test of the specified null model against a model that does not restrict the covariance matrix is given by (Jöreskog, 1971):

$$T = nF_0, \qquad [6]$$

where $F_0$ is the minimum of function 4 under the specified null model.

This statistic $T$ is called the chi-square goodness-of-fit test statistic for the whole model in programs for structural equation models. It is used as an "overall goodness-of-fit" statistic or as a "model test" statistic.

If the null model under scrutiny is correct and the observed variables have a multivariate normal distribution—or weaker assumptions, as discussed, for example, by Satorra (1990)—then it can be derived that the test statistic $T$ is asymptotically distributed as a $\chi^2$ variable with degrees of freedom (df) equal to the number of independent elements in the VC-matrix minus the number of parameters of the model ($H_0$), which has to be estimated.

On the basis of this result a test, commonly used for testing structural equation models, is specified as follows. The model $H_0$ is rejected if

**Table 8.1** Covariance Matrix Computed for the Model Shown in Figure 8.1 With Loadings .7 and $\varphi_{21} = .9$

|     | $y_1$ | $y_2$ | $y_3$ | $y_4$ |
|-----|-------|-------|-------|-------|
| $y_1$ | 1.00 |      |      |      |
| $y_2$ | .49  | 1.00 |      |      |
| $y_3$ | .44  | .44  | 1.00 |      |
| $y_4$ | .44  | .44  | .49  | 1.00 |

$$T > c_\alpha , \qquad [7]$$

where $c_\alpha$ is the value of the $\chi^2$ variable for which

$$\Pr(\chi^2_{df} > c_\alpha) = \alpha . \qquad [8]$$

In this formulation, $c_\alpha$ is called the critical value of the test and $\alpha$ the (nominal) significance level of the test. In general, $\alpha$ is chosen to be .05. Given this choice, the critical value $c_\alpha$ can be obtained from the $\chi^2$ table.

Although in this section the test statistic $T$ has been derived using the maximum likelihood fitting function, similar types of test statistics can be derived with any other commonly used fitting functions (see, e.g., Satorra, 1989).

The above test is commonly employed in the way described above. This approach, however, is not without serious limitations, since one would like to have a test that would detect the same size of error equally well in various kinds of models and studies. The test described here cannot do this. We would like to illustrate this point with a simple example. If we suppose that in the model specified in Equations 2 and 3 the $\gamma$-coefficients are .7, the error variances are equal to .51 and the correlation between the standardized latent factors is .9, then the covariance matrix for the observed variables ($y_1$ to $y_4$) can be computed. The results of these calculations are presented in Table 8.1.

If this (population) covariance matrix is analyzed with the model $H_0$ specified in Equations 2 and 3, it is clear that we have introduced a misspecification into the model, because the covariance matrix has been obtained with $\varphi_{21} = .9$ while the analyzed model specifies $\varphi_{21} = 1$. Therefore, the obtained value $T$ in Equation 6 will deviate from zero

**Table 8.2** Values of $T$ for Different Combinations of Values of Loadings and Sample Size

| | Loading Values | | | |
| Sample Size | .95 | .90 | .80 | .70 |
|---|---|---|---|---|
| 25 | 9.46 | 3.21 | .76 | .26 |
| | (.79) | (.34) | (.11) | (.07) |
| 50 | 19.31 | 6.56 | 1.56 | 0.51 |
| | (.98) | (.63) | (.18) | (.09) |
| 100 | 39.10 | 13.25 | 3.15 | 1.04 |
| | (.99) | (.91) | (.33) | (.14) |
| 200 | 78.43 | 26.63 | 6.33 | 2.09 |
| | (1.00) | (.99) | (.61) | (.23) |
| 300 | 117.84 | 40.01 | 9.50 | 3.13 |
| | (1.00) | (1.00) | (.79) | (.33) |
| 600 | 236.08 | 80.16 | 19.05 | 6.26 |
| | (1.00) | (1.00) | (.98) | (.60) |

NOTE: $\varphi_{21} = .9$ was used; in the null model this coefficient is assumed to be 1. Power of the test is shown in parentheses.

because of the misspecification on $\varphi_{21} = 1$. In this specific case, with a sample size of 600 cases, the value of $T$ was equal to 6.26.

In order to illustrate what happens to the value $T$ under different conditions, Satorra and Saris (1983) have done such computations with two indicator models not only for loadings of .7 but also for loadings of .8, .9, and .95 and for different sample sizes. Table 8.2 presents the resulting values of $T$.

First, we see in the last column of the table, under the loading value .70, that for these parameter values and a sample size of 600 the value of $T$ is 6.26. This is the result obtained by analyzing the covariance matrix as shown in Table 8.1 with the misspecified null model that set $\varphi_{21} = 1$. If the sample size decreases, the test statistic also decreases, up to a value of .26 for a sample size of 25 cases. On the other hand, we also see in the second column of the table that, using the same procedure for loadings of .95, the value of $T$ is 9.46 with a sample size of 25 cases.

Bearing in mind that the test is usually done with a fixed critical value ($c_\alpha = 3.84$ in the case of df = 1 and $\alpha = .05$), it is clear that conclusions on whether there is a misspecification in the model differ considerably with the size of the loadings and the size of the sample. This is so even though the size of the misspecification in the $\varphi_{21}$ is exactly the same in all the cells of the table.

The problem in testing structural equation models with a fixed critical value is that the testing procedure completely ignores the power of the test. The power of the test is defined as the probability that an incorrect model will be rejected. In the next section we will discuss different procedures for computing the power of the goodness-of-fit test, and then we will suggest different procedures for power evaluation. After this discussion, we will come back to explain the results in Table 8.2.

### Procedures for Calculating the Power of the Test

It can be derived that for an incorrect but not highly misspecified model $H_0$, the test statistic $T$ is asymptotically distributed as a noncentral $\chi^2$ variable with noncentrality parameter $\lambda$. The noncentral $\chi^2$ distribution with degrees of freedom (df) and noncentrality parameter $\lambda$ will be denoted by $\chi^2_{df}(\lambda)$. Once an alternative value of $\theta$—say, $\theta_A$—has been specified, the value of $\lambda$ can be computed according to various procedures (Satorra, 1989). If $\lambda$ has been determined, the power ($\pi$) of the test can be obtained by various programs or from the tables (Haynam, Govindarajulu, & Leone, 1973; Saris & Stronkhorst, 1984, Appendices C, D) for the $\chi^2_{df}(\lambda)$ in the following way:

$$\pi = \Pr[\chi^2_{df}(\lambda) > c_\alpha] .$$    [9]

In Figure 8.2 we present the central $\chi^2$ distribution with 9 degrees of freedom and the noncentral $\chi^2$ distribution with 9 degrees of freedom and $\lambda$ equal to 20. The larger the noncentrality parameter (the noncentrality parameter is the difference between the expected values of the two distributions), the further the noncentral $\chi^2$ distribution moves to the right. The power of the model test is the area of the noncentral $\chi^2$ distribution that is to the right of the critical value ($c_\alpha$) of the test. It will be clear that the larger the noncentrality parameter, the greater the power of the test. Therefore, the evaluation of the power of the test is in fact an evaluation of the noncentrality parameter $\lambda$.

In the literature, several procedures to compute $\lambda$ have been mentioned (Satorra, 1989; Satorra et al., 1991). We restrict the discussion to the two most convenient ones from a computational point of view.

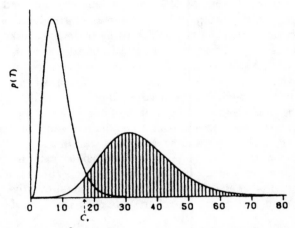

**Figure 8.2.** The central $\chi^2$ distribution with 9 degrees of freedom and the noncentral $\chi^2$ distribution with 9 degrees of freedom and noncentrality parameter 20.

The first procedure was introduced by Satorra and Saris (1983, 1985) and can be described formally as follows:

$$\lambda = \text{Min}_{\theta \in H_0} nF[\Sigma(\theta_A), \Sigma(\theta)] . \qquad [10]$$

In this approximation the power of the test is evaluated at a specific alternative parameter value denoted by $\theta_A$. The form above shows that the noncentrality parameter is the value of the fitting function (test statistic $T$) if the covariance matrix $\Sigma(\theta_A)$ computed for the specific alternative ($\theta_A$) is analyzed with the null model.

This is exactly what we did at the end of the last section to produce the values of $T$ given in Table 8.2. This means that the values of $T$ in Table 8.2 are in fact values of the noncentrality parameter $\lambda$ for different combinations of sample size and size of the loadings. Given a specific choice of $\alpha$, we can easily compute the power of the test for each cell of the table using the standard tables for the noncentral $\chi^2$ distribution (see Equation 9). These power values are presented in Table 8.2, in parentheses below the values of $T$. In this example, two indicators are used for each factor, which means that the degrees of freedom are equal to 2 and the $\alpha$ level was chosen to be .05. Given the choice of $\alpha$, a value of a noncentrality parameter of 6.26 (last row, last column of Table 8.2) leads to a power value of .60. This value was obtained from the noncentral $\chi^2$ distribution with two degrees of freedom. In the same way, all other values can be derived using the standard tables. These power values make it very clear that in some situations the goodness-of-fit test will hardly ever detect the misspecification in the model, while in other situations the misspecification will nearly always lead to rejection of the model. This is so even though the specification error of $H_0$ is exactly the same in all cells of the table.

The advantage of this approach to evaluating the noncentrality parameter is that the power can be computed with the standard programs available. On the other hand, it will be clear that this procedure, although intuitively clear, has its disadvantages. The major disadvantages are that one has to be willing to specify an alternative parameter value ($\theta_A$) and, further, that the alternative covariance matrix $\Sigma(\theta_A)$ has to be analyzed under the null model.

The second procedure for computing the noncentrality parameter tries to avoid these two complications. This procedure uses the quadratic expression of the noncentrality parameter derived by Wald (1943) and discussed in the context of structural equations models by Satorra and Saris (1985, p. 85):

$$\lambda = n(\theta_A - \theta_0)'M(\theta_A - \theta_0) , \qquad [11]$$

where

$$M = [\partial\sigma(\theta_0)/\partial\theta_H{}']'R[\partial\sigma(\theta_0)/\partial\theta_H{}'] ,$$

$$R = (\partial^2 F/\partial\sigma\partial\sigma') - (\partial^2 F/\partial\sigma\partial\theta_{fr}{}')(\partial^2 F/\partial\theta_{fr}\partial\theta_{fr}{}')^{-1}(\partial^2 F/\partial\theta_{fr}\partial\sigma') ,$$

$\sigma$ denotes the vector of distinct elements of the covariance matrix $\Sigma$, $\theta_H$ denotes the vector of free elements of $\theta$ under the maintained model H, and $\theta_0$ is a hypothesized (usually estimated) value of $\theta$ under the null model $H_0$. Note that $\theta_{fr}$ is a subvector of $\theta_H$ and that both $\theta_{fr}$ and $\theta_H$ are subvectors of $\theta$. Here $\theta_A$ is a specific value of $\theta$ satisfying the maintained model H (this $\theta_A$ may differ from $\theta_0$ in several components).

If the matrix $S$ has been analyzed with the null model, then all elements of the matrices can be known through simple substitution of sample estimates for population values. Therefore, without calculating a new covariance matrix or running the program again, the power of the test for any $\theta_A$ can be obtained with this approach. In cases where $\theta_0$ and $\theta_A$ differ by only one parameter at a time, one could produce with the above expression of $\lambda$ the power function of the test for different sizes of single-parameter misspecification. The same type of power function could be considered for simultaneous misspecification of several parameters. Problems arise, however, with the presentation of the multiparametric power functions and the possible use of them. We will return to this point later.

Aside from the computational aspects and the problem of choosing a specific alternative, the question of the quality of the different approximations of $\lambda$ also arises. The two above-mentioned approximations of $\lambda$ have been justified asymptotically under the technical assumption of a sequence of local alternatives (Satorra & Saris, 1985). In practice, this assumption means that these approximations may not be very accurate for large misspecifications and/or small sample sizes. On the other hand, both procedures for computing the noncentrality parameter give similar results in the case of small misspecifications and large samples. Satorra and Saris (1983) have shown in a large Monte Carlo experiment for a specific type of model that their procedure can be accurate for all practical purposes even for sample sizes as small as 25 cases.

Keeping the limitations of the procedures in mind, we will now present some different ways in which the information about the noncentrality parameter and the power of the test can be used in practice.

## Power Evaluation of the Model Test

Having addressed the need for power analysis of a test and the procedures by which the power can be calculated, we will now discuss how this information can be used to determine whether a model should be rejected or not. In order to make such decisions, one has to take into account the value of the test statistic and the power of the test—a recommendation more frequently heard than practiced. In principle, the argument is quite simple. Four different situations can be distinguished, as indicated in Table 8.3.

If the test statistic is smaller than the critical value $c_\alpha$ and the power is high, then the model can be accepted, because any serious misspecification would be detected by the test. If the test statistic is smaller than the critical value $c_\alpha$ and the power is low, then no decision can be made

**Table 8.3** Four Different Testing Situations

| test statistic | Power of the Test | |
| | Low | High |
| --- | --- | --- |
| $T < c_\alpha$ | ? | accept model |
| $T > c_\alpha$ | reject model | ? |

because we do not know whether the low value of the test statistic is caused by the correctness of the model or the lack of sensitivity of the test to misspecifications.

If the test statistic is larger than the critical value $c_\alpha$ and the power is high, then no decision can be made, because we do not know whether the high value of the test statistic is caused by the fact that the model is misspecified or the high sensitivity of the test to very small errors in the model. If the test statistic is larger than the critical value $c_\alpha$ and the power is low, then the model can be rejected, because a small misspecification would not be detected by the test. Therefore, given the large value of the test statistic, the model must be wrong. In order to be able to use these arguments in practice, one has to know how to determine the situation of high power and low power for the model test.

Power evaluations can be done in two very distinct ways. The first approach is to evaluate the power of the model test for several specific alternative parameter values. The second possibility is to describe the variation of the power of the model test for deviations of the null model in all directions. We will start with a discussion of the first approach.

### Power Analysis Using Specific Alternatives

Saris and Stronkhorst (1984) developed a procedure for formulating tests of structural equation models if a researcher is willing to specify a specific alternative. Saris et al. (1987) applied this procedure to several examples. In all the examples the power of the model test was evaluated for alternatives that deviated from the null model in only one restriction. Here, we will use the earlier model specified in Equations 2 and 3. In that case we evaluated the power of the .05 level test for the alternative that the correlation between the factors was not 1.0 but .9, keeping all other values of the parameters the same as in Bollen and Grandjean's study (including three correlated errors). As we did above, we calculated the covariance matrix for this specific alternative and analyzed this covariance matrix with the null model, assuming that the correlation between the factors ($\varphi_{21}$) was equal to 1. The value of $T$ in that run was 14.36. As we have mentioned, this value is the noncentrality parameter corresponding to the test of the model with the restriction that the correlation between the factors is 1. Using the tables for the noncentral $\chi^2$ and taking into account that df = 6 and an $\alpha$ level of .05, we found that the power of the model test would be .59. This is a rather high power value given the sample size of 113 cases. This result suggests that in this model a deviation from 1 larger than .1 for this correlation coefficient would have a quite high probability ($F$ at least 59%) of being detected by the goodness-of-fit test. In this specific case, the test had quite high power and the test statistic (5.5 with df = 6) was smaller than the critical value. So it was concluded, following Table 8.3, that the hypothesis that the correlation between the latent variables was not smaller than .9 could not be rejected. One can therefore say that the two latent variables are very similar, if not the same.

Several other examples are given by Saris et al. (1987), although not all of them are as simple as this one. It is possible that the power is too low or too high and that no decision can be made. In such cases the tests can be adjusted. The power of the test can be improved by increasing the sample size or improving the quality of the measurement, as we have shown in Table 8.2 (see also Matsueda & Bielby, 1986; Saris & Satorra, 1987). If the power is too high, the $\alpha$ level can be adjusted. We will not repeat these arguments here. The interested reader is referred to Saris et al. (1987), where these procedures are spelled out and where it is shown that one can design a model test balancing significance level and power for single-parameter alternatives, that is, for alternatives that deviate from the null model in a single parameter.

In the rest of this section we would like to concentrate on another aspect of this test. Looking at this testing procedure, it should be clear that the power of the test is evaluated for the misspecification of only one parameter, assuming all the other restrictions in the model to be correct. If there are other misspecifications in the model, they will also contribute to the value of the test statistic. It is even possible that the test will lead to rejection of the model while the hypothesis one would like to test is correct but another restriction is incorrect. This is exactly what would happen if one were to analyze Bollen and Grandjean's data without correlated errors. There are many restrictions made in the example we have used that may be incorrect. For example, the error terms may be correlated or an extra effect may exist between a factor and an observed variable. This means that one of the conditions for using this test is that one must be sure that the other restrictions in the model are correct. But how can one be sure about this? It seems that one needs to evaluate power for simultaneous misspecifications on several parameters (multiparameter power evaluation) instead of the described single-parameter power evaluation. For example, one would like to test if $\varphi_{21} = 1$ and $\psi_{21} = \psi_{41} = 0$, given that one has doubts about these three parameters but is sure about all the others.

Also, for multiparametric alternatives—that is, alternatives that deviate from the null model on several parameters—the Satorra-Saris procedure can be used to compute the power of the test. However, when one considers more than one restriction simultaneously, the problem in practice is how to choose one of these specific multiparametric alternatives, since there are so many possibilities. An alternative approach that avoids some of these complications will be discussed in the next section.

**Power Analysis Without Using Specific Alternatives**

If one is not willing to specify a specific value for the alternative, the procedure outlined above is not possible. But if the discussion is restricted to deviations from the null model in a single restriction only, then the power can be evaluated for different values of the single-parameter misspecification. Such a power function could be obtained using the Satorra-Saris procedure for power calculations, but it is more efficient to use the quadratic form (Equation 11) of $\lambda$.

The advantage of using the quadratic expression of $\lambda$ is that it does not require a run of the program for each alternative considered; one can calculate the power of the test for any value of $\theta_A$ once the analysis of $S$ using the null model has been performed. This means that it is easy to calculate the power of the test as a function of the values of the vector $\theta_A$. In LISREL 7 this can be done for each single parameter separately using the PL plot procedure. These plots indicate the increase or decrease in the noncentrality parameter (or expected $\chi^2$ value) if a single parameter changes its value. Similar results can be obtained even more efficiently using the estimated parameter change and the modification index (Saris, Satorra, & Sörbom, 1987), but description of these procedures is outside the scope of this chapter.

It should be clear that in this case the information obtained on power sensitivity of the test is specific for each restriction separately, assuming the other restrictions are correct. Misspecification, however, may come from several restrictions at the same time. Therefore, we should evaluate the power when there is misspecification on several restrictions at the same time.

Motivated by the work of Andrews (1989), we propose to evaluate the power of the test when there is misspecification on several restrictions at the same time by using what we call *isopower contours*. An isopower contour is a set of (alternative) parameter values at which the power of the test is constant. Since we compute power using the non-centrality parameter of Equation 11, an isopower contour in the neighborhood of $\theta_0$ will be those values of $\theta$ for which

$$n(\theta - \theta_0)'M(\theta - \theta_0) = K, \qquad [12]$$

where $K$ is a constant that depends on the power value at the contour, the degrees of freedom, and the $\alpha$ level of the test.

For given values of the free parameters ($\theta_{fr}$) of the model, the values of $\theta$ satisfying Equation 12 define an ellipse. The principal axis of the ellipse is the direction of low power sensitivity (LS) of the test, since the two cutting points of the isopower contour with the axis are points further away from $\theta_0$ than any other point on the isopower contour. The minor axis of the ellipse corresponds to the high sensitivity (HS) direction of the test because the cutting points of this axis with the isopower contour gives the points that are the closest to $\theta_0$ of all points on the isopower contour.

In order to obtain the values of $\theta$ on the isopower contour, one has to choose a power level $\pi$ and an $\alpha$ level, and one has to use the degrees of freedom associated with the model test under consideration. Given these values, the noncentrality parameter $\lambda$ can be obtained using the statistical tables of the noncentral $\chi^2$ distribution. This derived value is the value $K$ in Equation 12. Since the LS points are the most distant points from $\theta_0$ on the isopower contour, the values of $\theta_{LS}$ for which LS is obtained can be found by computing the nonnull eigenvalues ($\tau_1$ to $\tau_k$) corresponding to the normalized eigenvectors ($u_1$ to $u_k$) of the matrix $M$. If the eigenvalues are ordered in decreasing order of magnitude from 1 to $k$ and the associated eigenvectors are ordered in the same way, then the values of $\theta_{LS}$ are

$$\theta_{LS} = \theta_0 \pm u_k(\lambda/n\tau_k)^{1/2}. \qquad [13]$$

The values for which HS of the test is obtained can be found by using $u_1$ and $\tau_1$ instead of $u_k$ and $\tau_k$ in the computations.

The chosen power level determines whether high power (HP) or low power (LP) is obtained. Unfortunately, the procedure specified here is not yet available in the statistical packages LISREL and EQS. They can, however, be implemented easily in these programs, which routinely use the matrices and vectors mentioned in Equation 12. All calculations in this chapter have been made using the MatLab program "Power" of Satorra. For more details on this approach, we refer the reader to Satorra and Saris (1991). In the appendix to this chapter, we give an example showing the details of the computations involved in obtaining an isopower contour.

The reason we have chosen the two directions of low sensitivity and high sensitivity is that this information allows the power characteristic of a multiparameter test to be specified. Let us consider a high power contour, for example, a $\pi = .9$ power contour, and look at the low sensitivity point (HPLS). If this point is substantively close to the null model, then the model test has high power because high power is obtained in the low sensitivity direction. That means that in all other directions the power (for points as deviant from $\theta_0$) is even higher. Thus the distance of the HPLS point from $\theta_0$ can be used to determine whether the power is high or not (see Figure 8.3).

Let us now consider a low power contour, for example, a $\pi = .1$ power contour, and look at the high sensitivity point (LPHS). If this point is substantively far from the null model, then the model test has low power because low power is obtained in the high sensitivity direction. That means that in all other directions (for points as deviant from $\theta_0$) the power is even lower. Thus the distance of the LPHS point from $\theta_0$ can be used to determine whether the power is low or not. There are, of course, also situations in which the power status of the test is between these two extremes. We will discuss examples of this below.

Although we have indicated in general terms how one can evaluate the power of a test, we have not formulated precisely what we mean by the terms *high power* and *low power*. The precise values of *high* and *low* will depend on the precision of the theory under discussion. In some disciplines it is important that even very small errors be detected, whereas in others one can afford to be less precise.

In order to illustrate this approach, we offer the following examples. These use the same null model we have used before to evaluate the power of the test against deviations from the null model for the restrictions on the parameters $\varphi_{21}$, $\psi_{21}$, and $\psi_{41}$. That is, we evaluate the power

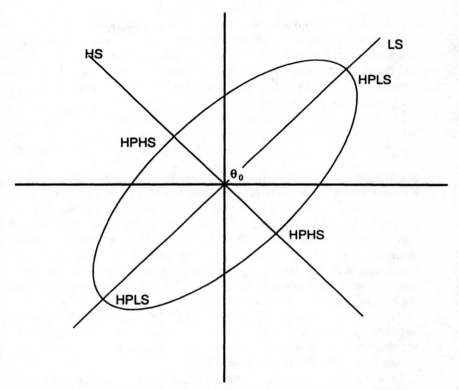

**Figure 8.3.** An isopower contour (of high power, HP) with the directions of extreme sensitivity (low sensitivity, LS, and high sensitivity, HS) and the HPLS and HPHS points.

of the test of the null model when the maintained model has as extra parameters $\varphi_{21}$, $\psi_{21}$, and $\psi_{41}$.

The first situation we want to describe is one of low power. This situation occurs for the specified model if the loadings are low (for example, .5). In this case, the relevant parameters should deviate greatly from the values in the null model to lead to high power: For these parameters the HPHS point gives values for the correlations of .42 for $\varphi_{21}$, .99 for $\psi_{21}$, and .99 for $\psi_{41}$. If such large values are necessary in the high sensitivity direction and even higher values in all other directions, it is clear that this test has very low power. In such a situation the fact that one finds a nonsignificant test statistic cannot be taken to mean that the model has no misspecifications. It is equally possible that the model is wrong but the test cannot detect the errors. On the other hand, if a significant test statistic is obtained in the case of low power, one can be sure that the model is wrong, because only if the model is very wrong will it lead to rejection of the model. Any other explanation is very unlikely, given the low power.

Let us now look at a model where all loadings are .95. In this case the analysis leads to the following values for the HPLS point: .99 for $\varphi_{21}$, .96 for $\psi_{21}$, and .66 for $\psi_{41}$. This result suggests that in the direction of lowest sensitivity a very small deviation from 1 for the correlation coefficient $\varphi_{21}$ in combination with a large correlation (.96) for $\psi_{21}$ and a moderate correlation (.66) for $\psi_{41}$ will have high power. In this case one value is very small and the others are large, and therefore one cannot conclude that the test has high power in all possible directions, so no conclusions can be drawn with certainty. Looking at the univariate information where high power is obtained for $\varphi_{21}$ for a value of .98, we can conclude that the test is in general very sensitive for deviations from 1 for this parameter and much less so for the other parameters. Thus if the test statistic is smaller than the critical value one can be quite certain that the correlation between the factors is not very different from unity, but one cannot be sure that there are not very large deviations from zero for the other two parameters. In this case, a firm conclusion can be drawn for only a part of the model.

These two examples indicate that the proposed procedure can be used to make decisions. In the case of high power similar arguments can, of course, be used. We would also like to point out that the power evaluations do not depend on the sample data. All evaluations of the tests can be made in advance, and the test can be adjusted if the power evaluation indicates that the test does not satisfy the requirements of the user.

### Power and the Maintained Hypothesis

Before we end this chapter, we have to point out that given a null model $H_0$, the power evaluation results provided by the above suggested procedure depend on the null model specified and the choice of $\theta_0$ and the maintained hypothesis H. That is, the extra restrictions made in the null model compared with the maintained model will very heavily influence the results of all power calculations. It means that one has to be very certain about a large part of the model before relying on the

**Table 8.4** The High Power High Sensitivity Values for Three Parameters of the Factor Model Shown in Figure 8.1

| Models | *HPHS Points for Different Models* | | |
|--------|----------|-----------|-----------|
| | $\varphi_{21}$ | $\psi_{21}$ | $\psi_{41}$ |
| 1a | .022 | — | — |
| 1b | — | .098 | — |
| 1c | — | — | .098 |
| 2a | .021 | −.005 | — |
| 2b | .021 | — | .003 |
| 2c | — | −.031 | .031 |
| 3 | .021 | .002 | .001 |

power analysis. It also suggests that the commonly used procedure, where one concentrates on only one extra parameter at a time, is questionable. This point can be illustrated easily by the example used in this chapter. In Table 8.4 we provide high power values for the restricted parameters discussed before, $\varphi_{21}$, $\psi_{21}$, and $\psi_{41}$. The choice of these parameters is arbitrary but illustrative. The high power values for the parameters have been calculated for three models with a maintained model H with one extra parameter (1a, 1b, 1c), three models with two extra parameters (2a, 2b, 2c), and one model with three extra parameters (3). In all cases the loadings are identical (.95) and $\varphi_{21} = 1$.

Table 8.4 illustrates that the values for which high power is reached depend very heavily on the maintained hypothesis, that is, the restrictions that are simultaneously evaluated with respect to power. The value of $\varphi_{21}$ for which power .9 is obtained does not vary much, but the values of the other two parameters vary in correlation between nearly zero and nearly 1 (the reported values are covariances). For the models where only one extra parameter is introduced, the power is high if these correlations are very close to 1; in the other models the power is high if coefficients are much smaller, because the misspecification occurs in two or more coefficients instead of only one.

The effects that have been demonstrated here can be found for other models as well. For another example, we refer the reader to Satorra and Saris (1991). Only if there is complete separability between the parameters (independence) do these differences in values across models not occur. This phenomenon indicates that a lot of prior knowledge is necessary also for power evaluation. On the other hand, it is a warning not to accept or reject a model too easily on the basis of minimal information.

### Discussion

In this chapter we have given an overview of the developments in the field of testing structural equation models, especially with respect to the evaluation of the power of the test. It is clear that there are problems with the most commonly used testing procedure, which ignores the power of the test. Not only is there a problem of sample size, there is also the general problem that model characteristics influence the power of the test very strongly. In our opinion, the amount of attention given in the literature to goodness-of-fit indices is not justified, because the required information cannot be provided.

Given the need to take into account simultaneous misspecification in several restrictions, we have presented a procedure for evaluating the power of the goodness-of-fit test for multiparameter restrictions. It transpires that the low and high power sensitivity directions will be useful for determining whether a test has high or low power. We have shown by argument and by example that one can use this information to make decisions with respect to the acceptance or rejection of models, even if the test does not have high power in all directions.

Finally, we have shown the importance of a priori knowledge in the testing procedure, since all the results on power evaluation depend on the division made between restrictions to be tested and restrictions that are accepted without a test. This result emphasizes that one should be very careful about drawing conclusions on the correctness (or incorrectness) of a model. One should be especially careful with the traditional approach of single-parameter power evaluations when there is doubt about the correctness of several restrictions in the model.

## APPENDIX

This appendix sketches the computation of an isopower contour in the context of a specific example. For the sake of ease of illustration, the example chosen is a very simple one. We consider the null model $H_0$ represented in Figure 8.1

with loadings and correlation among factors restricted to be 1. That is, $H_0$ is a two-factor, two-indicator model with correlation 1 among factors and with the error variances (the $\psi_{ii}$s) as the free parameters of the model. Since there are 10 variances and covariances and 4 parameters to be estimated, the degrees of freedom associated with this model are equal to 6. The maintained model H is chosen to be the model $H_0$, with $\varphi_{12}$ and $\psi_{13}$ as additional free parameters. Sample size in this example is 100. The isopower contour of power level $\pi = .9$ will be considered.

We choose $\theta_0$ to be the parameter value for which the free parameters of the model $H_0$ are equal to .36. This $\theta_0$ gives the following covariance matrix under $H_0$:

$$\Sigma = \begin{pmatrix} 1.36 & 1.00 & 1.00 & 1.00 \\ 1.00 & 1.36 & 1.00 & 1.00 \\ 1.00 & 1.00 & 1.36 & 1.00 \\ 1.00 & 1.00 & 1.00 & 1.36 \end{pmatrix}.$$

Given the above-specified maintained model H, the matrix $M$ of Equation 11 can be seen to be

$$M = \begin{pmatrix} 0 & 0 & 0 & 0 & 0 & 0 \\ 0 & 0 & 0 & 0 & 0 & 0 \\ 0 & 0 & 0 & 0 & 0 & 0 \\ 0 & 0 & 0 & 0 & 0 & 0 \\ 0 & 0 & 0 & 0 & 10.47 & 2.61 \\ 0 & 0 & 0 & 0 & 2.61 & 3.17 \end{pmatrix},$$

where, in the computations to obtain this matrix, we have used the standard results of ML estimation that $(\partial^2 F/\partial\sigma\partial\sigma') = 2^{-1}D'(\Sigma^{-1} \otimes \Sigma^{-1})D$, where $D$ is the 0-1 duplication matrix. Note also that $(\partial^2 F/\partial\theta_{fr}\partial\theta_{fr}') = \Delta'(\partial^2 F/\partial\sigma\partial\sigma')\Delta$ and $(\partial^2 F/\partial\sigma\partial\theta_{fr}') = (\partial^2 F/\partial\sigma\partial\sigma')\Delta$, where $\Delta = [\partial\sigma(\theta_0)/\partial\theta_{fr}']$ evaluated at $\theta_0$. The derivative matrix $[\partial\sigma(\theta_0)/\partial\theta_H']$ was also needed in order to compute $M$.

The singular value decomposition of $M$ gives the following eigenvectors and eigenvalues of $M$:

| | | eigenvectors | | | |
|---|---|---|---|---|---|
| $u_1$ | $u_2$ | $u_3$ | $u_4$ | $u_5$ | $u_6$ |
| 0 | 0 | 1.0 | 0 | 0 | 0 |
| 0 | 0 | 0 | 1.0 | 0 | 0 |
| 0 | 0 | 0 | 0 | 1.0 | 0 |
| 0 | 0 | 0 | 0 | 0 | 1.0 |
| 0.95 | −0.30 | 0 | 0 | 0 | 0 |
| 0.30 | 0.95 | 0 | 0 | 0 | 0 |
| | | eigenvalues, $\tau_i$s | | | |
| 11.31 | 2.33 | 0 | 0 | 0 | 0 |

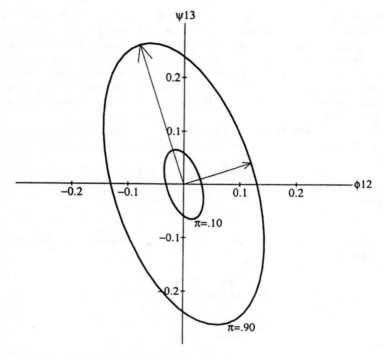

**Figure A.1.** Contours of power levels .10 and .90.

Note that the rank of **M** is two, since $H_0$ imposes only two restrictions on H. The goodness-of-fit test, however, has df = 6, since we consider the test of $H_0$ against an unrestricted covariance matrix.

Choosing power levels $\pi = .10$ and $\pi = .90$, and given that df = 6, the corresponding noncentrality parameters are (see the tables of the noncentral chi-square distribution) $\lambda = 1.13$ and $\lambda = 17.42$, respectively.

The shifts from $\theta_0$ corresponding to the points HPHS and HPLS points (where high power means $\pi = .90$), that is, the vectors $u_k(\lambda/n\tau_k)^{1/2}$ of Equation 13, will then be

|  | HPHS | HPLS |
|---|---|---|
| $\psi_{11}$ | 0 | 0 |
| $\psi_{22}$ | 0 | 0 |
| $\psi_{33}$ | 0 | 0 |
| $\psi_{44}$ | 0 | 0 |
| $\varphi_{12}$ | 0.12 | −0.08 |
| $\psi_{13}$ | 0.04 | 0.26 |

up to an indeterminacy of a change of sign. That is, we have an ellipse contour where at the points HPHS ($\varphi_{12} = 0.12$, $\psi_{13} = 0.04$) and HPLS ($\varphi_{12} = -0.08$, $\psi_{13} = 0.26$) the goodness-of-fit test has power value .90. Multiplying the above values by 0.255 [= $(1.13/17.42)^{1/2}$], we obtain the corresponding points at the contour of power level .10. The isopower contours of this example are shown in Figure A.1.

Note that in this case there is nearly separability between $\varphi_{12}$ and $\psi_{13}$ (for each HPHS and HPLS point one of the components $\varphi_{12}$ or $\psi_{13}$ is nearly zero).

If it is the case that the maintained model differs from $H_0$ in a single parameter, say, $\varphi_{12}$ (idem $\psi_{12}$), then power .90 is attained for $\varphi_{12} = \pm0.13$ (idem $\psi_{13} = \pm23$).

## References

Andrews, W. K. (1989). Power in econometric applications. *Econometrica, 75,* 1059-1090.

Bentler, P. M., & Bonett, D. G. (1980). Significance tests and goodness of fit in the analysis of covariance structures. *Psychological Bulletin, 88,* 588-606.

Blalock, H. M. (1962). Four variable causal models and partial correlations. *American Journal of Sociology, 68,* 182-194.

Bollen, K. A. (1986). Sample size and Bentler and Bonett's nonnormed fit index. *Psychometrika, 51,* 375-377.

Bollen, K. A., & Grandjean, B. (1981). The dimensions of democracy. Further issues in the measurement and effects of political democracy. *American Sociological Review, 46,* 651-659.

Haynam, G. E., Govindarajulu, Z., & Leone, F. C. (1973). Tables of the cumulative non-central chi-square distribution. In H. L. Harter & D. B. Owen (Eds.), *Selected tables in mathematical statistics* (Vol. 1, pp. 1-78). Providence, RI: Mathematical Statistical Society.

Jöreskog, K. G. (1971). Statistical analysis of sets of congeneric tests. *Psychometrika, 36,* 109-133.

Jöreskog, K. G. (1973). A general method for estimating a linear structural equation system. In A. S. Goldberger & O. D. Duncan (Eds.), *Structural equation models in the social sciences* (pp. 85-107). New York: Seminar.

Jöreskog, K. G., & Sörbom, D. (1988). *LISREL 7: A guide to the program and applications.* Chicago: SPSS.

Kaplan, D. (1990). Evaluating and modifying covariance structure models: A review and recommendation. *Multivariate Behavioral Research, 25,* 285-305.

Matsueda, R. L., & Bielby, W. T. (1986). Statistical power in covariance structure models. In N. B. Tuma (Ed.), *Sociological methodology 1986* (pp. 120-158). San Francisco: Jossey-Bass.

Saris, W. E. (1982). Different questions, different variables? In Fornell (Ed.), *A second generation of multivariate analysis* (Vol. 2, pp. 78-95). New York: Praeger.

Saris, W. E., de Pijper, W. M., & Zegwaart, P. (1979). Detection of specification errors in linear structural equation models. In K. F. Schuessler (Ed.), *Sociological methodology 1979.* San Francisco: Jossey-Bass.

Saris, W. E., den Ronden, J., & Satorra, A. (1987). Testing structural equation models. In P. Cuttance & R. Ecob (Eds.), *Structural modeling by example* (pp. 202-221). Cambridge: Cambridge University Press.

Saris, W. E., & Satorra A. (1987). Characteristics of structural equation models which affect the power of the likelihood ratio test. In W. E. Saris & I. N. Gallhofer (Eds.), *Sociometric research* (Vol. 2). London: Macmillan.

Saris, W. E., Satorra, A., & Sörbom, D. (1987). The detection and correction of specification errors in structural equation models. In C. C. Clogg (Ed.), *Sociological methodology 1987*. San Francisco: Jossey-Bass.

Saris, W. E., & Stronkhorst, L. H. (1984). *Causal modelling in nonexperimental research: An introduction to the LISREL approach*. Amsterdam: Sociometric Research Foundation.

Satorra, A. (1989). Alternative test criteria in covariance structure analysis: A unified approach. *Psychometrika, 54*, 131-151.

Satorra, A. (1990). Robustness issues in structural equation modeling: A review of recent developments. In W. E. Saris (Ed.), Structural equation modelling [Special issue]. *Quality and Quantity, 24*, 367-387.

Satorra, A., & Saris, W. E. (1983). The accuracy of a procedure for calculating the power of the likelihood ratio test as used within the LISREL framework. In C. O. Middendorp (Ed.), *Sociometric research 1982* (pp. 129-190). Amsterdam: Sociometric Research Foundation.

Satorra, A., & Saris, W. E. (1985). The power of the likelihood ratio test in covariance structure analysis. *Psychometrika, 50*, 83-90.

Satorra, A., & Saris, W. E. (1991). *On the goodness of fit test in structural equation models: Extremal directions of power*. Paper presented at the 9th European Meeting of the Psychometric Society, Trier, Germany.

Satorra, A., Saris, W. E., & de Pijper, W. M. (1991). Several approximations to the power function for the likelihood ratio test in covariance structure analysis. *Statistica Neerlandica, 45*, 173-185.

Simon, H. A. (1954). Spurious correlation: A causal interpretation. *Journal of the American Statistical Association, 49*, 467-479.

Wald, A. (1943). Tests of statistical hypotheses concerning several parameters when the number of observations is large. *Transactions of the American Mathematical Society, 54*, 426-482.

Wheaton, B., Muthén, B., Alwin, D., & Summers, G. (1977). Assessing reliability and stability in panel models. In D. R. Heise (Ed.), *Sociological methodology 1977* (pp. 84-136). San Francisco: Jossey-Bass.

# 9

# Goodness of Fit With Categorical and Other Nonnormal Variables

## BENGT O. MUTHÉN

With continuous-normal variables, the testing of a structural model involves testing the fit of the restrictions imposed on the covariance matrix. Testing of structural models for categorical data involves additional considerations compared with those for normal data. Since these considerations are similar to testing with nonnormal continuous variables, the case of nonnormal continuous variables will also be discussed in this chapter and will thereby provide a convenient connection with the continuous-normal case discussed in other chapters.

For continuous-normal variables, the sample covariance matrix is a natural choice of statistic to analyze, and testing the model involves testing restrictions on the covariance matrix. Structural models for categorical data have no such natural choice of sample statistics, and testing the model can be done in more than one way. The structural models for categorical data considered here use a model specification that can be expressed as a certain model family for the observed variables, where the parameters of this model family are further restricted in terms of a smaller number of structural parameters. As an example, we may consider a model with four binary variables. With an assumption of nor-

AUTHOR'S NOTE: This research was supported by Grant AA 08651-01 from NIAAA for the project Psychometric Advances for Alcohol and Depression Studies and by National Science Foundation Grant SES-8821668. Albert Satorra provided stimulating discussions. I thank Ginger Nelson and Kathleen Wisnicki for helpful research assistance.

mality for continuous variables underlying the observed variables, the natural statistics to analyze are the correlations among the underlying variables, the tetrachoric correlations. As a structural model for the correlations among the underlying variables we may consider a standard one-factor model. In this example, the model family for the observed variables is one that specifies multivariate normality for the underlying variables. Only if this model family is accepted should tetrachorics be used. Having accepted the model family, the testing of the structural model proceeds with testing the restrictions it imposes on the tetrachorics. Since in this way variances are not considered, the usual residual variance parameters of covariance structure analysis are disregarded. In this way, the degrees of freedom for $p$ variables are obtained as $p(p - 1)/2$, the number of parameters in the unrestricted model, minus the number of free parameters. With four variables, the unrestricted model has as many parameters as there are correlations, in this case six, while a one-factor model uses four parameters to generate the correlations. In this way, the structural model implies that two restrictions are imposed on the correlations. Note, however, that the choice of model family, and hence of statistics to analyze, is not unambiguous. The use of the tetrachoric family implies accepting a model for the probabilities of the cells of the $2 \times 2 \times 2 \times 2$ table for the four binary variables. Testing of this model will be discussed below. It is interesting to contrast the incorrect acceptance of the normality assumption of the tetrachoric family with the incorrect use of normal theory estimators and tests for continuous, nonnormal variables. In the latter case, it is well known that the estimators will produce consistent estimates of structural model parameters and that only chi-square tests and standard errors are affected. In the former case, however, using the wrong model family results in using the wrong statistics, and inconsistent estimation of structural model parameters results.

   In testing structural models for categorical data one may therefore consider two levels of goodness of fit: (a) the fit of the observed variable model family to the observed data where no further restrictions of model family parameters are made and (b) the fit of the structural model to the model family. As will be discussed, it is often hard to test the structural model directly against observed categorical data, and the two levels of fit may instead be considered in these two steps. The second level of testing corresponds most closely to the conventional testing for continuous variables. The first level of testing has no counterpart in normal theory analysis and it is unfortunately often ignored in structural analysis of categorical data. Examples of the first level of testing will be discussed in terms of logit and probit regression for binary dependent variables, regression with ordered polytomous response, analysis with polychoric correlation coefficients, analysis with tetrachoric correlations, and analysis with mixtures of continuous and categorical variables. Examples of the second level of testing will be discussed only briefly in terms of factor analysis and structural equation modeling of binary variables. Structural modeling with latent variables runs the risk of removing interpretations of the model too far from the observed data; this is perhaps particularly true for categorical data. A final section discusses how this can be avoided by complementing the two levels of testing by explicating predictions from the structural model for the observed data.

A general structural equation model will first be presented. Checking the appropriateness of model families against the data will then be discussed, followed by testing of underlying structure and how this structure can be tied back to the data.

## The Structural Model

As in the LISCOMP program (Muthén, 1978, 1979, 1983, 1984, 1987, 1989b), a variety of response models for categorical and other nonnormal data can be put into a unifying framework by the use of latent continuous response variables. These $y^*$ variables may be observed as $y$ variables in a variety of forms. In the conventional case, the $y^*$s may be directly observed as continuous-unlimited $y$ variables, whether they are normal or nonnormal (Muthén, 1989c). The $y^*$ variables may also be observed as censored continuous variables (Muthén, 1987, 1989d) and as ordered categorical variables, including binary variables. Recently, such modeling has also been provided within the framework of Jöreskog and Sörbom's (1988, 1989) PRELIS and LISREL programs. Thus the estimation and testing procedures to be discussed are widely available.

This chapter will focus on the ordered categorical case,

$$y = c, \qquad \text{if } \tau_c < y^* < \tau_{c+1}, \qquad\qquad [1]$$

where $y^*$ is an underlying continuous variable with thresholds $\tau$ as parameters for the categories $c = 0, 1, 2, \ldots, C - 1$, for a variable with $C$ categories, and where $\tau_0 = -\infty$, $\tau_C = \infty$. In the binary case, there is a single $\tau$ parameter and it is equivalent to the negative of the intercept of conventional probit regression. If continuous variables $y$ are present, this is taken to mean that the underlying variable is directly observed, $y = y^*$.

The LISCOMP model involves a measurement model

$$y^* = \Lambda\eta + \epsilon ,$$    [2]

and a structural model

$$\eta = B\eta + \Gamma x + \zeta .$$    [3]

Here, $\epsilon$ is a random vector of measurement errors with zero means and covariance matrix $\theta_\epsilon$, $\eta$ is a random vector of constructs with zero means, $x$ is a random vector of observed background variables, and $\zeta$ is a random vector of residuals with zero means and covariance matrix $\Psi$. The vectors $\epsilon$ and $\zeta$ are assumed to be independent of each other and of $\eta$. For simplicity, arrays related to intercepts and means are left out in the present discussion and so are multiple-group specifications and scaling issues. The model parts of Equations 2 and 3 lead to the model structure for the conditional distribution of $y^*$ given $x$,

$$E(y^*|x) = \Pi x ,$$    [4]

$$V(y^*|x) = \Omega ,$$    [5]

where

$$\Pi = \Lambda(I - B)^{-1}\Gamma ,$$    [6]

$$\Omega = \Lambda(I - B)^{-1}\Psi\Lambda'(I - B)^{-1\prime} + \Theta_\epsilon .$$    [7]

The $\Pi$ structure constitutes LISCOMP's model part 2, while the $\Omega$ structure constitutes LISCOMP's model part 3. Mean and threshold structures would be included in part 1. When categorical $y$ variables are present, the corresponding diagonal elements of $\Omega$ are not identifiable and are not included in the LISCOMP analysis. In the modeling such diagonal elements are taken to be unity. For categorical variables, the PRELIS/LISREL system also involves the $\Omega$ structure, but the threshold structure of part 1 and the $\Pi$ structure of part 2 have no counterparts in the current PRELIS/LISREL system.

For categorical and other nonnormal $y$ variables, generalized least squares (GLS) estimation is used to estimate the model parameters in LISCOMP and PRELIS/LISREL (see also Jöreskog, 1991). LISCOMP has the special feature that when $x$ variables are present, GLS estimation is done by fitting $\Pi$ and $\Omega$ elements to the vector of sample statistics corresponding to the multivariate regression slopes and residual covariances (see Muthén, 1987). The advantage is that the calculation of these regression-based statistics draws only on the assumption of conditional normality for $y^*$ given $x$, while the customary use of correlations would entail joint normality of $y^*$ and $x$. When $x$ variables are not present, the conditioning on $x$ is vacuous, the $\Pi$ matrix does not exist, and the $\Omega$ elements are fitted to a sample statistics matrix of underlying variable correlations and/or covariances. This includes tetrachoric, polyserial, and polychoric correlations as well as correlations and covariances for censored variables. In all cases, the sample statistics are calculated in two steps using univariate and bivariate response variable information and maximum likelihood (ML) estimation.

## Testing of the First Level: The Fit to the Data

In this section the fitting of the model is related to the sampling scheme under which the data were observed. For categorical data, product-multinomial or multinomial sampling schemes are relevant (see, e.g. Agresti, 1990; Bock, 1975, chap. 8). The just-identified, or saturated, model then has the corresponding probabilities as parameters and the ML estimates are the observed proportions. Checking the model involves an investigation of how these estimated probabilities are reproduced by our model. The general point of this section is that this first-level model testing stage is often ignored, despite the fact that a host of model checking techniques are available. By means of a series of examples, this testing is shown to contribute crucially to the understanding of the data. Examples of the first level of testing will be discussed in terms of logit and probit regression for binary dependent variables, regression with ordered polytomous response, analysis with polychoric correlation coefficients, analysis with tetrachoric correlations, and analysis with mixtures of continuous and categorical variables.

**Regression With a Binary Dependent Variable**

The first two examples discuss regression analysis with categorical dependent variables. As a starting point, consider the simple case of regression of a binary dependent variable $y$ on an $x$ variable. In terms of the general model of the previous section, probit regression is obtained with $\Lambda = I$, $\Theta_\epsilon = 0$, $B = I$, so that

$$y^* = \gamma x + \zeta,$$ 
[8]

obtaining the ML-estimated probit slope of $\Pi$ in Equation 6 as $\gamma$. The variance of the residual $\zeta$ is standardized to one so that $\Omega$ of Equation 7 is the scalar 1. The model expresses the conditional probability of $y$ given $x$ as the probability that $y^*$ exceeds the threshold $\tau_c$ in Equation 1,

$$P(y = 1 \mid x) = \int_{\tau - \gamma x}^{\infty} \varphi(t)dt,$$
[9]

where $\varphi$ denotes the univariate standard normal density. Equivalently, conventional probit regression parameterization expresses the negative of $\tau$ as an intercept, while $\gamma$ is the conventional slope.

$$P(y = 1 \mid x) = \Phi(-\tau + \gamma x)$$
[10]

$$= \Phi(\alpha + \beta x),$$

where $\Phi$ is the standard normal distribution function.

*Example 1: Probit Regression*

Table 9.1 gives British coal miner data taken from Ashford and Sowden (1970). The $x$ variable is age and the binary $y$ variable is breathlessness. This is a case of grouped data in the sense that each distinct $x$ value in the sample has more than a single observation. The sampling scheme may be considered as product-binomial so that the conditional probabilities of $y$ given $x$ are modeled. There are 9 different $x$ values and for each $x$ value a binomial variable is observed. Hence the unrestricted $H_1$ model for the data has one parameter, a probability, for each of 9 $x$ values, giving a total of 9 parameters. In contrast, the linear probit

**Table 9.1** Example 1: British Coal Miner Data

| Age (x) | N | N Yes | Proportion Yes | Probit Estimated Probability | Logit Estimated Probability | OLS Estimated Probability |
|---------|---|-------|----------------|------------------------------|-----------------------------|---------------------------|
| 22 | 1,952 | 16 | 0.008 | 0.009 | 0.013 | −0.053 |
| 27 | 1,791 | 32 | 0.018 | 0.018 | 0.022 | −0.004 |
| 32 | 2,113 | 73 | 0.035 | 0.034 | 0.036 | 0.045 |
| 37 | 2,783 | 169 | 0.061 | 0.060 | 0.059 | 0.094 |
| 42 | 2,274 | 223 | 0.098 | 0.100 | 0.095 | 0.143 |
| 47 | 2,393 | 357 | 0.149 | 0.156 | 0.148 | 0.192 |
| 52 | 2,090 | 521 | 0.249 | 0.231 | 0.225 | 0.241 |
| 57 | 1,750 | 558 | 0.319 | 0.322 | 0.327 | 0.290 |
| 62 | 1,136 | 478 | 0.421 | 0.425 | 0.448 | 0.339 |
| | 18,282 | 2,427 | 0.130 | | | |

SOURCE: Data from Ashford and Sowden (1970).

model has two parameters, $\tau$ and $\gamma$. The latter model is nested within the former. This can be seen by considering a transformation of the 9 probability parameters $\pi_j$, $j = 1, 2, \ldots, 9$, into 9 (probit) parameters, $z_j$, where $\pi_j = \Phi(z_j)$: The probit model restricts the 9 $z_j$s to be a linear function of $x$. In this way, a Pearson or likelihood ratio chi-square test of fit has 7 degrees of freedom. If a multinomial sampling scheme is instead considered, the result is the same. The unrestricted model then has 17 parameters because there are $9 \times 2$ cells of probabilities and these have to add to one. As is the case in log-linear modeling, 8 of these parameters correspond to the marginal distribution of $x$ and should be added to the $H_0$ model. However, in line with ordinary regression, the marginal distribution of $x$ is not restricted here. The likelihood ratio chi-square value is 5.19 with 7 degrees of freedom and the model is not rejected despite the huge sample size. Note that this may be considered a test against the data of the probit model family for the relationship between $y$ and $x$. The corresponding test of the logit family results in a likelihood ratio chi-square of 17.13, which is not significant on the 1% level. Table 9.1 also gives the fitted, or predicted, probabilities of breathlessness for each $x$ value. It can be seen that the probit family captures the observed proportions better than the logit family at low and high $x$ values. In Example 1 there is no further structure imposed on the linear probit model parameters, but this could be envisioned as a case of testing $\gamma = 0$, or equality of $\gamma$ slopes with more than one $x$ variable. Such a test can be performed using as the alternative hypothesis the probit/logit model with unrestricted slopes. In this way, the test is done on the second level without involving the unrestricted multinomial model.

If data are not grouped as in Example 1, model testing against the data is more difficult, because the chi-square approximation may be poor, with many cells having zero or very low expected frequencies. This is the more common case and illustrates the difficulty of testing the categorical variable model against the data directly. Standard computer packages offer a "model test" also in this case, but it refers to the $H_0$ hypothesis of $\gamma$s all being zero tested against the $H_1$ hypothesis of the $\gamma$s not being zero. Such a test is what is here termed a *second-level test*. Although it is interesting to know that your predictors have significant influence on $y$, this procedure does not offer the desired test of the probit/logit family against the data. For ungrouped data, Agresti (1990) discusses more suitable goodness-of-fit tests related to residuals.

**Regression With an Ordered Polytomous Dependent Variable**

*Example 2: Ordered Polytomous Regression*

Muthén (1987) considered an example of alcohol consumption where $y$ corresponds to the number of drinks a person has per day on average and the $x$s are age and income. The $y$ categories are 0 (nondrinker), 1 (1-2 drinks per day), 2 (3-4 drinks per day), and 3 (5 or more drinks per day). A U.S. general population sample of 713 males with regular physical activity levels was considered. In this example there are four ordered response categories, where

$$P(y = 0 \mid x) = \Phi(\tau_1 - \gamma' x), \qquad\qquad [11]$$

$$P(y = 1 \mid x) = \Phi(\tau_2 - \gamma' x) - \Phi(\tau_1 - \gamma' x),$$

$$P(y = 2 \mid x) = \Phi(\tau_3 - \gamma' x) - \Phi(\tau_2 - \gamma' x),$$

$$P(y = 3 \mid x) = \Phi(-\tau_3 + \gamma' x).$$

The arguments of $\Phi$ are called (population) probits and are linear in the $x$s. For example, $(-\tau_3 + \gamma' x)$ is the probit for $P(y = 3 \mid x)$. The conditional

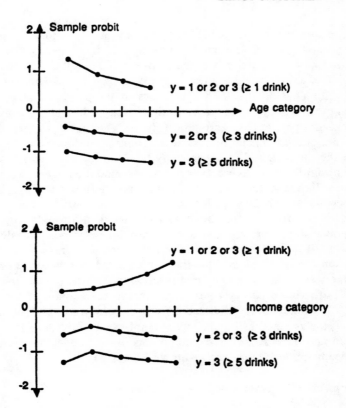

**Figure 9.1.** Example 2: Sample probit plots for alcohol data.

probabilities of the response categories imply that the probits are linear in the $x$s when the probabilities for the following three events are considered: $y = 3$, $y = 2$ or $3$, $y = 1$ or $2$ or $3$. As an example, consider the event $y = 2$ or $3$. Noting that $1 - \Phi(z) = \Phi(-z)$, the probit for this event is $-\tau_2 + \gamma'x$. The probits for these three events also have the same $x$ slopes $\gamma$. These facts can be used to test the goodness of fit for the family of ordered four-category probit models against the data. Using grouped data, the corresponding sample probits based on observed proportions can be plotted against the $x$ variables. Figure 9.1 shows the plots where age has been categorized into four categories and income has been categorized into five categories.

The top panel of Figure 9.1 shows three probit functions corresponding to the three events plotted against age. If the ordered probit model
is correct, these functions should be linear and parallel, and this seems
to hold to a reasonable degree of approximation. For income, however,
the bottom panel indicates that the lines are not parallel. The probit for
drinking at all appears to have a positive slope, while larger amounts of
drinking appear to have zero probit slopes. These plots suggest that the
ordered polytomous probit model is inappropriate for these data. Note
that the plots should more properly be done for each variable while
conditioning on the other, using, say, the modal category. This, however, will drastically reduce the sample sizes used for the plots, and the
distortion may not be large if the $x$s are approximately normally distributed. ML estimation of the model results in a strongly significant
negative slope for age and a weakly significant positive slope for
income. If instead the $y$ variable is dichotomized as nondrinker versus
drinker, the age slope is about the same and the income slope becomes
strongly significant, with a large positive value. The conclusion is that
while drinking is strongly related to income, the amount of drinking is
not. This outcome is predictable from the probit plots. The example
shows the value of testing the model family against the data. If one goes
ahead and uses the ordered polytomous probit model for these data,
misleading conclusions can be drawn.

### Regression With Several Dependent Variables

With multivariate categorical dependent variables, the testing and
model checking becomes more complex. As an example of the increasing complexity, consider the case of bivariate, binary response. As a
special case of the general model of Equations 2 and 3, Muthén (1979)
studied a bivariate probit model with two indicators of a single factor,
where the factor was regressed on a set of exogenous variables. Leaving
the fit of the underlying latent variable structure aside, checking the
appropriateness of the family of bivariate probit models against the data
involves checking a $2 \times 2$ table for each distinct combination of values
on the $x$ variables. Unless data are grouped and a large sample is
available, this is intractable. More informal model checking is, however, possible in line with the probit plots of the previous example. For
bivariate binary responses, a probit plot is first carried out for each
variable and checked for linearity in line with the previous example. In
addition, a probit plot needs to be inspected for the joint event $y_1 = 1$,

$y_2 = 1$. This requires transforming the sample proportion by use of a bivariate normal distribution function.

## Correlations Between Ordered, Polytomous Variables

Multivariate response with a structural model is a special case of the general model of Equations 2 and 3 where $x$s are not present and $\Gamma = 0$. Here, the assumption of conditional normality for $y^*$s given $x$s is replaced by the assumption of normality of the $y^*$s themselves. In particular, this occurs when the latent variables of $\eta$ as well as the measurement errors $\epsilon$ are normal. Assuming normally distributed $y^*$ variables and using only bivariate information from pairs of variables leads to the analysis of latent correlations such as tetrachorics, polychorics, and polyserials, as is done in LISCOMP and PRELIS/LISREL. The use of such correlations implies the acceptance of a model in itself, the model of underlying normality of $y^*$s. This is different from the case of continuous variables where Pearson product-moment (PPM) correlations are used. For categorical variables, underlying $y^*$ variables have to be assigned a distribution, although not necessarily normal (see, e.g., Jöreskog, 1991), in order to enable the estimation of latent correlations. For continuous variables, a linear relationship between the two variables is assumed for a PPM correlation, but the full distribution of the two variables need not be given. If the two variables are not bivariate normal this does not invalidate the use of the PPM correlation as it does the latent correlation. The next two examples consider the goodness of fit of underlying normality models to data.

### Example 3: Polychoric Correlations

Muthén, Huba, and Short (1985) analyzed quality of life data measured on seven-category Likert scales for 1,814 individuals. Questions referred to satisfaction with a person's house, leisure, family life, standard of living, and savings, among other factors. The scale steps ranged from "very satisfied" to "very dissatisfied," with the fourth category being neutral. Underlying normality for a pair of variables can be assessed by a chi-square test. With seven-category variables the pairwise chi-square tests have 35 degrees of freedom, obtained as the difference of 48 parameters in the unrestricted multinomial model for the 49 cells and $6 + 6 + 1 = 13$ parameters in the normality model (6 thresholds for each variable and 1 correlation). The latter model may

**Table 9.2** Example 3: Polychoric Versus Pearson Correlations: Quality of Life Data ($N$ = 1,814; seven-category Likert)

| | *Pairwise Chi-Square Tests of Normality (35 df)* | | | | |
| | *Neighborhood* | *House* | *Leisure* | *Family* | *Standard* |
|---|---|---|---|---|---|
| House | 160.7 | | | | |
| Leisure | 117.8 | 145.7 | | | |
| Family | 73.7 | 88.2 | 197.5 | | |
| Standard | 115.0 | 173.3 | 181.3 | 123.2 | |
| Savings | 93.6 | 139.8 | 120.1 | 92.0 | 173.7 |

| | *Correlations:* | *Pearson* | | | |
| | | *Polychoric* | | | |
|---|---|---|---|---|---|
| House | .454 | | | | |
| | .515 | | | | |
| Leisure | .249 | .285 | | | |
| | .309 | .335 | | | |
| Family | .188 | .230 | .376 | | |
| | .249 | .291 | .437 | | |
| Standard | .323 | .384 | .376 | .305 | |
| | .373 | .431 | .432 | .355 | |
| Savings | .226 | .296 | .330 | .287 | .578 |
| | .261 | .336 | .373 | .330 | .632 |

SOURCE: Data from Muthén, Huba, and Short (1985).

be seen as nested within the former as follows. The unrestricted model parameters can be transformed into bivariate probit parameters. The normality model restricts these parameters so that they increase or decrease monotonically both horizontally and vertically in the table, reflecting the ordered nature of the pair of variables at hand.

The top panel of Table 9.2 shows the results of this chi-square testing using Pearson chi-squares. In my experience, the rejections of the normality model observed in this example are frequently found, but these rejections are often to a large extent caused by cells with low expected frequencies (see, e.g., Benson & Muthén, 1992). For cells with large enough numbers, however, there are often interesting information and ideas to be found in such testing. A particularly common outcome is one where "outlier" responses, or responses by a heterogeneous subpopulation, contribute to the rejection. In the quality of life example, certain individuals are very satisfied with one aspect of life and very dissatisfied with another, related, aspect. An example is given in Table 9.3

**Table 9.3** Quality of Life, Neighborhood, Savings

|   | 1 | 2 | 3 | 4 | 5 | 6 | 7 |
|---|---|---|---|---|---|---|---|
| | | | | *Observed Table* | | | |
| 1 | 134 | 139 | 111 | 118 | 64 | 52 | 86 |
| 2 | 37 | 95 | 97 | 75 | 76 | 43 | 62 |
| 3 | 13 | 26 | 64 | 39 | 59 | 19 | 34 |
| 4 | 15 | 17 | 26 | 43 | 34 | 34 | 34 |
| 5 | 2 | 10 | 12 | 16 | 21 | 14 | 17 |
| 6 | 0 | 4 | 7 | 5 | 7 | 9 | 6 |
| 7 | 3 | 1 | 2 | 6 | 9 | 6 | 11 |
| | | | | *Expected Table (rounded)* | | | |
| 1 | 115 | 139 | 135 | 113 | 90 | 52 | 59 |
| 2 | 49 | 77 | 87 | 84 | 75 | 48 | 64 |
| 3 | 20 | 35 | 43 | 44 | 42 | 29 | 42 |
| 4 | 13 | 24 | 32 | 34 | 34 | 25 | 40 |
| 5 | 4 | 9 | 13 | 15 | 16 | 12 | 22 |
| 6 | 2 | 3 | 5 | 6 | 7 | 5 | 10 |
| 7 | 1 | 3 | 4 | 6 | 7 | 6 | 12 |
| | | | | *Chi-Square Elements (rounded)* | | | |
| 1 | 3 | 0 | 4 | 0 | 8 | 0 | 13 |
| 2 | 3 | 4 | 1 | 1 | 0 | 1 | 0 |
| 3 | 2 | 2 | 11 | 1 | 7 | 3 | 2 |
| 4 | 0 | 2 | 1 | 2 | 0 | 3 | 1 |
| 5 | 1 | 0 | 0 | 0 | 2 | 0 | 1 |
| 6 | 1 | 0 | 1 | 0 | 0 | 3 | 2 |
| 7 | 3 | 1 | 1 | 0 | 1 | 0 | 0 |

for the pair of variables Neighborhood and Savings. Consider first cell 1, 7, in the top panel. Here, 86 individuals are very satisfied with their neighborhoods and very dissatisfied with their savings. One may suspect either that certain individuals have made sloppy responses or that for these individuals the two matters have become negatively related, perhaps because of a recent house purchase. Consider next cell 3, 3, corresponding to a point on the response scale that is one step away from neutral toward the satisfied end. While 64 individuals respond in this way, the model estimates a lower number of 43. Perhaps the higher number of observed individuals can be explained by a noncommittal response style, where the individual perhaps responds to most questions in a somewhat positive way although he or she has different true feelings. In any case, the bottom panel shows that these two cells contribute in a major way to the rejection of the underlying normality model. It is possible that retaining the model and using its polychoric correlation gives a smoothed estimate of association that is less influenced by outlier behavior than, say, PPM correlations. Such speculations can be made plausible only by in-depth analysis using additional information from other variables. A comparison of regular PPM correlations and polychoric correlations is given in Table 9.2. The testing of underlying normality in conjunction with polychoric correlations can be done in both LISCOMP and PRELIS/LISREL.

**Correlations Between Binary Variables**

While testing of underlying normality is possible for a pair of poly-tomous variables, the case of a $2 \times 2$ table results in a just-identified model that cannot be tested. As suggested in Muthén and Hofacker (1988), this fact may have contributed to the long-standing debate about whether or not to use tetrachoric correlations. Usually, parameter esti-mates, such as tetrachorics, are used only when the model from which they are derived fits the data well. But the customary way of computing tetrachorics from $2 \times 2$ tables does not provide such a test. In principle, one could attempt to use full information from the $2^P$ cells, but, as already noted, this leads to problems of small cell frequencies. Muthén and Hofacker propose a compromise using information from three variables at a time. The unrestricted model for a $2 \times 2 \times 2$ table has 7 probability parameters. Since the trivariate normality model has three threshold and three correlation parameters, this gives a single-degree-of-freedom chi-square test of underlying normality. This triplet testing approach is suggested by Muthén and Hofacker (1988) for assessing the suitability of using tetrachoric correlations for dichotomous data. This technique is currently available only in LISCOMP.

*Example 4: Triplet Testing of Tetrachorics*

Consider panel data for a dichotomous variable observed at three time points. This example relates to attempts by Alwin (1992) to establish a quality declaration of attitudinal items by studying their correlation over time. This longitudinal model is shown in Figure 9.2 using the notation of the general framework of Equations 2 and 3. As in this

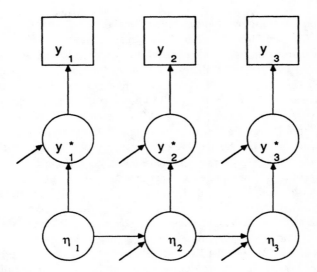

**Figure 9.2.** Example 4: Three-wave panel model for binary variables.

framework, the paths involving the continuous variables of $y^*$ and $\eta$ are linear regression among latent variables. In line with Heise (1969), Alwin (1989) considered the case of standardized factors $\eta$ and denoted the slope of $\eta_2$ on $\eta_1$ and the slope of $\eta_3$ on $\eta_2$ as stability coefficients. Standardizing the $y^*$ variances to unity, the squared slopes (loadings) of the regressions of each $y^*$ on the respective $\eta$ then corresponds to the reliability of that $y^*$ variable. Since $y$ can be viewed as a crude measurement of $y^*$, this reliability may be viewed as the maximum attainable reliability under optimal measurement circumstances. In addition, the size of this reliability is directly related to how precisely the stability coefficients can be estimated. Following Heise's approach of assuming time-invariant reliabilities, the common reliability may be obtained as an estimate of the ratio $\rho_{21}\rho_{32}/\rho_{31}$, where in this case $\rho$s denote correlations between the $y^*$s, estimated as the tetrachoric correlations for the $y$s. Under this structural model, there are three parameters: the common loading and the two stability coefficients. The structural model measurement error and residual variances are not free parameters, but are restricted to yield unit $y^*$ and $\eta$ variances. The structural model is therefore just-identified in terms of the three correlations. In this way, the second-level testing of the structure is not possible. The first-level testing of underlying normality of the $y^*$ variables, however, is possible using the Muthén-Hofacker triplet testing approach.

As an illustration, data were generated according to this model using stabilities of 0.7 and reliabilities of 0.64. A "population" was created by using LISCOMP to generate 100,000 trivariate normal $y^*$ observations that were dichotomized at 0.25 to give 40% "1" responses at each time point. A random sample of 1,500 observations was then drawn from this population. For this sample, the one-degree-of-freedom likelihood ratio chi-square value was obtained as 0.003 with an estimated reliability of 0.64. Hence the sample reflects the population very well in that normality is not rejected and the true reliability value is obtained. The true situation is then distorted in order to violate underlying normality. This is done by assuming that after the first wave, 20% of those with true minority opinions ($y^* > \tau$) change their responses to the majority opinion ($y = 0$). In this way, 20% of the response pattern frequencies for 101, 110, and 111 are changed to response pattern 100. The triplet test for this new data set obtained a likelihood ratio chi-square value of 7.87, which exceeds the 1% critical value of 6.64 so that the tetrachoric model is rejected. The rejection is fortunate, since for these distorted data the estimated reliability is 0.93, which is a severe overestimation of the true value of 0.64. If only 10% are changed, the chi-square value is 2.24, so that the model is not rejected at the 5% level (critical value 3.84). In this case, however, the estimated reliability of 0.74 is closer to the true value.

This artificial example suggests that lack of first-level goodness of fit can have important consequences for inference on structural parameters. Very little is known about the interaction between first-level misfit and structural modeling, however. Muthén and Hofacker (1988) performed triplet testing of data on attitudes toward abortion. For six abortion items, there were 20 triplets to be tested. Four of the 20 triplets were rejected at the 5% level from a sample of 3,921. One item, RAPE, was involved in all four triplets. Factor analysis of tetrachoric correlations using all six items versus five items deleting RAPE gave very similar results, however. Muthén and Hofacker (1988) also provided an artificial example where response consistency effects were generated for the last three of a set of 12 items following a one-factor model. Triplet testing correctly identified the misfitting items. Incorrectly using tetrachoric correlations for all 12 items led to a two-factor model where the last three items were incorrectly taken to measure a second factor.

### Correlations Between Ordered Polytomous and Continuous-Normal Variables

Given a mixture of ordered categorical variables and continuous variables, both polychoric and polyserial correlations are computed. For polyserial correlations, the underlying normality assumption pertains to the bivariate distribution of the $y_j^*$ for the categorical variable and the continuous $y_k$ variable. This case has been studied by Jöreskog (1985). Testing of underlying bivariate normality is available in PRE-LIS, but not in LISCOMP. Traditionally, polyserial correlations have been estimated by considering the product of the likelihood for the continuous $y_k$ variable and the likelihood of the conditional distribution of $y_j^*$ given $y_k$. Jöreskog (1985) points out that there is a strong computational advantage to considering instead the product of the marginal distribution of $y_j$ and the conditional distribution of $y_k$. Approaching the estimation in this way, the individual data points on $y_k$ are not needed because the means and variances of $y_k$ for each category of $y_j$ are sufficient statistics. This approach also provides a likelihood ratio chi-square test of underlying bivariate normality that is readily interpretable as follows.

The model of bivariate normality has $C + 2$ parameters: $C - 1$ threshold parameters (for a $y_j$ with $C$ categories), one mean and one variance parameter for the continuous $y_k$, and one correlation between $y_j^*$ and $y_k$. This model expresses the $C$ conditional means and $C$ conditional variances for $y_k$ given each $y_j$ category in terms of only three parameters (the mean, the variance, and the correlation). In contrast, the unrestricted model uses the $2C$ mean and variance parameters, which together with the $C - 1$ probability parameters for the marginal distribution of $y_j$, gives a total of $3C - 1$ parameters. It follows that the chi-square test has $3C - 1 - (C + 2) = 2C - 3$ degrees of freedom (Jöreskog, 1985). The test is clearly applicable also when the categorical variable is binary, yielding 3 degrees of freedom.

To conclude the section on first-level testing of the observed variable model family against the data, one may safely say that much more research is warranted. First of all, not all cases have been covered. As an example, censored variables and mixtures of such variables and categorical variables have not been covered. Second, and perhaps more important, there is almost no research on how goodness-of-fit assessment on the first level interacts with structural inference. It is largely unknown how serious the consequences of lack of fit on the first level are for estimation and testing of structural models. Nevertheless, the techniques that are available today appear to be underutilized in terms of providing insights about the data.

### Testing of the Second Level:
### The Structural Model Fit

This section discusses inferential procedures for structural models not only in cases with categorical variables, but also in those with continuous, nonnormal variables. It will be shown that testing techniques for nonnormal continuous variables are closely related to those for categorical data; this development ties the present discussion to that of other chapters for continuous variables. For simplicity, the general modeling framework of Equations 2 and 3 will be considered for the special case of no $x$s. The case of binary variables will be emphasized as an illustration of the ideas, focusing on the fitting of tetrachoric correlations. However, the general discussion carries over to polytomous and censored variables as well as to models with $x$s and fitting models to regression statistics.

Testing of a structural model in terms of summary sample statistics such as correlations involves the use of test statistics that under certain conditions are asymptotically distributed as chi-square. As is well known, such testing often leads to rejection of a hypothesized model. A primary suggested cause of this is overwhelming power due to large sample size. Many alternative fit indices have been proposed and some are discussed elsewhere in this book. In my opinion, however, there are good reasons for not discarding the chi-square approach for a test of overall model fit. Power issues can be directly addressed (see Saris & Satorra, Chapter 8, this volume). In situations where power is difficult to assess, there are practical ways of checking ill effects of large sample sizes. First, respecifications of the model as suggested by modification indices can be carried out until a nominally well-fitting model is approached. Second, the importance of these respecifications can be checked in terms of practical significance of the new parameter estimates and in terms of the change in the estimates of the original parameters of central interest. If, practically speaking, these changes are not large, then the original fit may be deemed sufficient. There are two important caveats to this approach. One is that the researcher must have started out in a modeling framework that is close enough to the true model for model modifications to be able to lead in the right direction. Second, the chi-square value itself must be trustworthy. It is this second point on which the following discussion centers.

In Equation 5, the covariance matrix of the $y^*$ variables is expressed in terms of structural model parameters. In the continuous case, the $y^*$ variables are directly observed as $y$s and the sample matrix is a conventional covariance or correlation matrix. In the binary case, the $y^*$ variables are indirectly observed by the $y$s and the sample matrix is a tetrachoric correlation matrix. If the continuous variables are not multivariate normal, the use of the sample covariance matrix to fit the model represents a limited information estimation approach. This is also the case when using tetrachoric correlations. In both cases, the sample matrix is created using only bivariate information from pairs of variables.

### Estimation and Testing for Continuous Variables: A Brief Overview

Under the conventional assumption of IID observations on a $p$-variate vector $y$ and assuming normality for $y$, the sample covariance matrix $S$ contains sufficient statistics for estimating the structural model parameters of $\theta$, say. In this case, two common fitting functions are normal theory maximum likelihood (NTML) and normal theory GLS (NTGLS),

$$F_{NTML} = \ln | \Sigma | + \text{tr}(\Sigma^{-1}S) - \ln | S | - p , \qquad [12]$$

$$F_{NTGLS} = \text{tr}[(\Sigma - S)S^{-1}]^2 , \qquad [13]$$

where $\Sigma$ is the population covariance matrix for $y$. The expression for $F_{NTGLS}$ is a special case of the general weighted least squares fitting function

$$F_{WLS} = (s - \sigma)' W^{-1}(s - \sigma) , \qquad [14]$$

where $s$ and $\sigma$ refer to the $p(p + 1)/2$ vectors of distinct elements of $S$ and $\Sigma$, respectively. If in Equation 14 $W$ is taken as a consistent estimator of the asymptotic covariance matrix of $s$, then $F_{WLS}$ is referred to as a generalized least squares estimator or minimum chi-square analysis (Ferguson, 1958; Fuller, 1987, sec. 4.2). In the special case of multivariate normality for $y$, the asymptotic covariance matrix of $s$ has a particularly simple structure, depending only on second-order moments,

$$2K_p' (\Sigma \otimes \Sigma)K_p , \qquad [15]$$

where $K_p'$ is given in Browne (1974, p. 210) and $\otimes$ denotes the Kronecker product. A consistent estimator of Equation 15 is obtained by replacing $\Sigma$ with $S$. This simplification of Equation 14 leads to Equation 13.

For arbitrary distributions, the asymptotic covariance matrix of $s$, $\Gamma$, say, has elements

$$\gamma_{ijkl} = \sigma_{ijkl} - \sigma_{ij}\sigma_{kl} \qquad [16]$$

(see, e.g., Browne, 1982), when these moments exist. (Note that this $\Gamma$ matrix is not the same as in equation 3.) Define the $p(p + 1)/2$ data vector $d_i$ for observation $i$,

$$d_i = \begin{pmatrix} (y_{i1} - \bar{y}_1)(y_{i1} - \bar{y}_1) \\ (y_{i2} - \bar{y}_2)(y_{i1} - \bar{y}_1) \\ (y_{i2} - \bar{y}_2)(y_{i2} - \bar{y}_2) \\ \cdots \\ (y_{ip} - \bar{y}_p)(y_{ip} - \bar{y}_p) \end{pmatrix} , \qquad [17]$$

where $y_{iv}$ is the $i$th observation on variable $v(v = 1, 2, \ldots , p)$ and $\bar{y}_v$ is the sample mean for variable $v$, so that summing over the $n$ sample units,

$$(n - 1)^{-1}\sum_{i=1}^{n} d_i = s . \qquad [18]$$

A consistent estimator of $\Gamma$ is obtained via the sample covariance matrix of $d_i$, involving fourth-order moments (see, e.g., Browne, 1982, 1984; Chamberlain, 1982),

$$\hat{\Gamma} = (n - 1)^{-1}\sum_{i=1}^{n} (d_i - \bar{d})(d_i - \bar{d})' \qquad [19]$$

so that the estimator of the asymptotic covariance matrix of $s$ is $n^{-1}\hat{\Gamma}$. Taking $\hat{\Gamma}$ as $W$ in the weighted least squares fitting function of Equation 14 gives the asymptotically distribution free (ADF) estimator proposed by Browne (1982) for covariance structure analysis of nonnormal continuous variables.

Consider now standard errors of parameter estimates and tests of model fit. Let $p^* = p(p + 1)/2$ and define the $p^* \times q$ derivative matrix

$$\Delta = \partial\boldsymbol{\sigma}(\boldsymbol{\theta})/\partial\boldsymbol{\theta} \ . \tag{20}$$

Estimating $\boldsymbol{\theta}$ with the weighted least squares fitting function of Equation 14, it is well known that a Taylor expansion gives the asymptotic covariance matrix,

$$nV(\hat{\boldsymbol{\theta}}) = (\Delta'W^{-1}\Delta)^{-1}\Delta'W^{-1}\Gamma W^{-1}\Delta(\Delta'W^{-1}\Delta)^{-1} \tag{21}$$

(see, e.g., Browne, 1984; Ferguson, 1958; Fuller, 1987; Satorra, 1989). This matrix may be consistently estimated by inserting the estimated $\boldsymbol{\theta}$ in $\Delta$ and using the estimated $\Gamma$. It is common to set the weight matrix $W = \hat{\Gamma}$ so that the estimated asymptotic covariance matrix of the parameter estimates simplifies to

$$n\widehat{V(\hat{\boldsymbol{\theta}})} = (\hat{\Delta}'W^{-1}\hat{\Delta})^{-1} \ . \tag{22}$$

Note that this expression is commonly used for both NTGLS and ADF. Satorra (1989) shows that asymptotically the same expressions hold for NTML. The expression in Equation 21 points to the fact that $W$ need not be the same as $\hat{\Gamma}$. For example, $W$ may be calculated via the computationally simple normal theory expression of Equation 15 to give normal theory parameter estimates. Using the general $\hat{\Gamma}$ expression of Equation 19 in Equation 21 provides the proper covariance matrix for these estimates even under nonnormality. Under nonnormality the estimates then have somewhat larger asymptotic variability than for ADF, but such an approach is strongly preferable to ADF from a computational point of view when the number of variables is large. In contrast to the ADF approach, Equation 21 shows that the large $\hat{\Gamma}$ matrix need not be inverted to obtain the standard errors of the estimates.

Under normal theory, the conventional model test of fit of $H_0$ against an unrestricted covariance matrix is obtained as the likelihood ratio statistic $nF$, where $F$ is the optimum value of the fitting functions in Equations 12 and 13. For Equation 14, a corresponding Wald statistic is obtained. This quantity is distributed as chi-square with $p^* - q$ degrees of freedom. Relaxing the restriction of normality, Browne (1984) gives a more general expression for a chi-square test of model fit. Consider the residual expression,

$$nT = (s - \hat{\boldsymbol{\sigma}})'A(s - \hat{\boldsymbol{\sigma}}) ,$$ [23]

where $\hat{\boldsymbol{\sigma}}$ is the estimated covariance structure and $A$ is a consistent estimator of

$$V - V\Delta(\Delta'V\Delta)^{-1}\Delta'V = \Delta_\perp(\Delta_\perp' V^{-1}\Delta_\perp)^{-1}\Delta_\perp' ,$$ [24]

where $\Delta_\perp$ is an orthogonal complement of $\Delta$ (see Satorra, 1992, p. 7). Robustness to nonnormality is obtained by using $V^{-1} = \hat{\Gamma}$ of Equation 19. Satorra (1989) shows that this also holds when the optimum of $F$ is obtained via NTML. In line with Bartlett (1937), a simpler, mean-corrected expression is the scaled chi-square, $nF/\alpha$, where

$$\alpha = \text{tr}[(W - W\Delta(\Delta'W\Delta)^{-1}\Delta' W)\Gamma]/r ,$$ [25]

where $r$ is the degrees of freedom of the model. A mean- and variance-corrected chi-square may also be computed (see, e.g., Satorra & Bentler, 1990; Satterthwaite, 1941).

To summarize estimation and testing for continuous variables, three types of analysis approaches can be distinguished. First, *normal theory analysis* refers to obtaining model estimates by the NTML or NTGLS fitting functions and computing standard errors and chi-square test of model fit by the conventional formulas of Equation 22 and $nF$. Second, *ADF analysis* refers to obtaining parameter estimates by the weighted least squares fitting function of Equation 14, setting $W$ to the ADF-type $\hat{\Gamma}$ of Equation 19, computing standard errors via Equation 22, and a chi-square model test as $nF$. Third, *robust normal theory analysis* refers to obtaining estimates by the NTML or NTGLS estimators. Using the normal theory $W$ and the ADF-type $\hat{\Gamma}$, standard errors are computed via Equation 21, and the chi-square test of model fit is computed either as the residual chi-square of Equations 23 and 24 or as the scaled chi-square of Equation 25.

Muthén and Kaplan (1985, 1992) carried out Monte Carlo studies of normal theory analysis and ADF analysis using factor analysis on nonnormal data. They found that normal theory analysis gave good inference for small models (around five variables), but inflated chi-square values and a downward bias of standard errors for larger models (ten or more variables). ADF analysis gave good standard errors and chi-square tests for small models and large samples (at least 1,000), but larger models did not show good results. Larger models produced inflated chi-square values and a downward bias of standard errors that was comparable to or worse than that of normal theory analysis. Apparently the asymptotic properties of ADF are not realized for the type of models and the finite sample sizes often used in practice. The method is also computationally heavy with many variables. This means that while ADF analysis may be theoretically optimal, it is not a practical method. Robust normal theory analysis appears to be an attractive alternative. To date, however, there is very limited experience with this type of analysis. Muthén and Kaplan (1985, 1992) have demonstrated that normal theory estimates usually show very little bias, even under nonnormality. A few studies with small models have recently reported promising results with regard to the robust standard errors and robust chi-square for nonnormal data (see, e.g., Chou, Bentler, & Satorra, 1991; Satorra, 1992; Satorra & Bentler, 1990), but nothing has been reported for realistic-sized models. Robust normal theory analysis appears to warrant further study.

The previous discussion considered second-level testing using chi-square statistics to investigate the fit of a model to sample variances and covariances. At issue was the trustworthiness of the chi-square value itself, and it was noted that robust procedures seem to offer better results in this regard. Some investigations of robustness will now be presented in connection with binary data.

## Correlation Structure Analysis With Dichotomous Variables

The robust standard errors and chi-square tests of model fit can be extended to analysis of statistics other than the sample covariance matrix $S$ for continuous variables, for example, the use of tetrachoric correlations in the factor analysis of binary items. In Muthén (1978, 1984), a weighted least squares procedure was proposed for the estimation and calculation of standard errors and chi-square test of model fit. An estimated $\Gamma$ matrix was computed as a consistent estimate of the asymptotic covariance matrix of the sample thresholds and tetrachoric correlations (see Muthén, 1978),

$$\Gamma = (\partial \pi / \partial \sigma)^{-1} V(p)(\partial \pi / \partial \sigma)^{-1}, \qquad [26]$$

where $\pi$ denotes the vector of univariate and bivariate marginal probabilities, $\sigma$ denotes the vector of population thresholds and tetrachoric correlations, and $V(p)$ denotes the covariance matrix of the vector of univariate and bivariate marginal sample proportions, consisting of sample moments up to the fourth order. In this way, the Muthén (1978) estimator is analogous to the ADF analysis for continuous variables. In both cases, fourth-order moments are used in computing $\Gamma$. In practice, the method suffers from the same type of computational and statistical limitations for large models as does ADF, as described previously. Here, a counterpart to robust normal theory analysis will be discussed that avoids these limitations. I have recently proposed this method elsewhere (Muthén, 1992).

In the dichotomous case, correlations are analyzed and there is no issue of scale dependency. Because of this, a simple analogue to robust normal theory analysis for continuous variables is to obtain model parameter estimates by unweighted least squares, using $W = I$ for estimation, standard errors, and tests by Equations 14, 21, and 25. This new approach to the analysis of tetrachoric correlations shows promise for a computationally efficient way of obtaining more robust standard errors and chi-square tests of model fit. The approach has a further advantage as well. For strongly skewed dichotomous variables, the weight matrix is often singular, even with large samples. This was frequently found in analysis of symptom items for depression and alcohol, as in Muthén (1989a) and Muthén, Wisnicki, and Hasin (1991), owing to the fact that these items have small frequencies for $y = 1$ even with large samples. In these cases, the conventional weighted least squares estimator cannot be used, because the weight matrix cannot be inverted. The new approach, however, does not rely on the inversion of a weight matrix and provides standard errors and chi-square by Equations 21 and 25 even for a singular $\hat{\Gamma}$.

As shown in Muthén and Kaplan (1992), the size of the model is a crucial factor in testing structural models for categorical and other nonnormal data. The larger the model, the larger the sample size needed for the asymptotic properties of the chi-square approximations to hold to a reasonable degree. The importance of this may not be fully realized among practitioners. In particular, the fact that the chi-square value is inflated by a too small sample size may come as a surprise. Also, methodologists demonstrating the sampling behavior of new testing procedures are wise not to limit their study to the common choice of small-sized models of around five variables. Although such studies are valuable, they may seriously misrepresent results for larger models. These issues are illustrated in the next example.

*Example 5: Size of the Model in Testing*
*Skewed Likert Scale and Dichotomous Data*

In this study, standard errors and chi-square tests of model fit are contrasted for a small model of 5 variables and a medium-sized model of 15 variables. Strongly skewed 5-category and 2-category scales were studied, each case generated as categorized multivariate normal data with a single-factor structure. The 5-category case was the same as "Case 4" in Muthén and Kaplan (1985), where category percentages for the variables were 5, 5, 5, 10, and 75. The 2-category case used 75%/25% splits for each variable, which may be viewed as dichotomizing the 5-category variables. The 5-category data were treated as continuous variables scored 0-4 and analyzed by regular sample covariance matrices, while the 2-category data were treated as binary and analyzed via tetrachoric correlation matrices. The different technologies for continuous and binary data are discussed together here because it turns out that they produce analogous results.

In both cases, the categorized data follow the postulated model of a single factor. Equal loadings were chosen to give correlations of 0.5 and reliabilities of 0.5. Two sample sizes were studied. Because such skewed variables were analyzed, these sizes were set at large values, using $N = 1,000$ and $4,000$, representing large-scale surveys of rare phenomena. The Monte Carlo study was carried out with 500 replications. For each data set, the conventional inference method as well as the robust inference method was used. The two methods will be referred to as MI and MII, respectively. In this way, the 5-category data were analyzed by conventional nonnormal variable GLS (ADF) using the estimator of Equation 14, standard error calculations as in Equation 22, and chi-square computed as $nF$ (MI). The 5-category data were also analyzed by robust normal theory analysis of Equation 12, using $W$ based on Equation 15, calculating the standard errors by Equation 21, and computing the mean-corrected chi-square as in Equation 25 (MII). The 2-category data were analyzed by the conventional GLS estimator of Equation 14 applied to tetrachorics, standard errors as in Equation 22, and chi-square as $nF$ (MI). The 2-category data were also analyzed by ULS, using the standard error formula of Equation 21, $W = I$, and chi-square as in Equation 25 (MII; see Muthén, 1992, for technical details).

Table 9.4 presents results for both 5-category (labeled continuous) and 2-category (labeled dichotomous) data, contrasting the small model (5 variables) with the medium-sized model (15 variables), the smaller

**Table 9.4** Example 5: Size of the Model in Testing Skewed Likert Scale and Dichotomous Data

| N = 1,000 | | | | N = 4,000 | | | |
| Continuous | | Dichotomous | | Continuous | | Dichotomous | |
| MI | MII | MI | MII | MI | MII | MI | MII |
|---|---|---|---|---|---|---|---|
| | | | 5 Variables (5 df) | | | | |
| | | | Standard Error Bias % | | | | |
| -7 | -5 | 1 | 2 | -6 | -5 | -4 | -4 |
| | | Chi-square (mean, variance, 5%, 1%) | | | | | |
| 4.97 | 4.49 | 4.86 | 4.83 | 4.90 | 4.45 | 5.18 | 5.18 |
| 8.70 | 7.29 | 8.88 | 8.82 | 9.30 | 7.73 | 11.37 | 11.29 |
| 4.8 | 2.4 | 4.4 | 4.0 | 4.0 | 2.6 | 6.0 | 5.6 |
| 0.2 | 0.4 | 0.0 | 0.6 | 1.0 | 0.6 | 1.0 | 0.8 |
| | | | 15 Variables (90 df) | | | | |
| | | | Standard Error Bias % | | | | |
| -19 | 1 | -13 | -2 | -5 | -2 | -8 | -4 |
| | | Chi-square (mean, variance, 5%, 1%) | | | | | |
| 103.8 | 91.2 | 98.99 | 90.86 | 94.21 | 90.18 | 92.72 | 90.72 |
| 195.4 | 163.3 | 225.9 | 196.0 | 189.6 | 172.1 | 196.8 | 176.6 |
| 26.2 | 3.8 | 17.2 | 7.2 | 9.8 | 4.2 | 9.4 | 6.4 |
| 8.2 | 1.0 | 7.8 | 1.4 | 1.8 | 0.2 | 2.4 | 0.6 |

sample ($N = 1,000$) with the larger sample ($N = 4,000$), and the conventional inference method (MI) with the more robust inference method (MII). The table reports standard error bias percentage in the loadings, where bias is calculated as $(a - b)/b$, where $a$ is the mean estimated standard error over the 500 replications and $b$ is the standard deviation of the estimates over the replications. The table also reports chi-square test results. The four entries are mean value over the replications, variance over the replications, proportion of the replications leading to model rejection at the 5% level, and proportion of replications leading to model rejection at the 1% level.

Table 9.4 shows that for the smaller model of 5 variables the conventional method of MI works well at the lower sample size of 1,000 for both the continuous case and the dichotomous case. No adjustments seem needed. In fact, judging by the 5% rejection proportion, the more robust chi-square procedures of MII seem to overcorrect slightly in the continuous case. For the larger model of 15 variables the conventional methods of MI do not work well at the smaller sample size of 1,000, and can be said to be only marginally acceptable at sample size 4,000. For this model size, the more robust procedures of MII give a marked improvement at sample size 1,000. It is interesting to note that the standard errors computed for MII by Equation 22 in all cases outperform the conventional standard errors.

The preceding analyses have shown that robust model testing methods are needed for models with categorical data whenever the model is not small. The new robust method for the analysis of dichotomous variables shows a marked improvement over the older method, particularly in terms of the chi-square test of model fit. In this way, a more trustworthy tool is provided for the second-level model testing.

### Discussion

With continuous variables, the testing of a structural model involves testing the model's fit to its sample statistics, the sample covariance matrix. If techniques are used that are robust to deviations from normality, no further testing against the data seems essential. It is true, however, that checks of linear relations among variables should be carried out. Also, with strongly skewed variables it may be argued that a nonlinear model, using different sample statistics, may be more appropriate—for example, a "tobit" factor analysis model for censored variables (see Muthén, 1989d). For the categorical variables techniques that we have discussed, however, first-level testing of the model family against the data is an essential augmentation to second-level testing of the structural model. This is because first-level testing may affect the very choice of sample statistics.

If efficient estimates are obtained for the cell probabilities, first- and second-level testing can be replaced by a chi-square test of a structural model directly against the data by comparing it to the unrestricted multinomial alternative. To this end, full-information estimation via ML can be carried out, such as in the Bock and Aitkin (1981) approach to the exploratory factor analysis of dichotomous items. Such a direct test of a factor model against the unrestricted multinomial alternative is often problematic, however, because the chi-square approximation is poor in the typical situation of many cells having small or zero frequencies.

While informative, the combined use of first- and second-level testing proposed here poses the question of how to assess the seriousness of first-level misfits for inferences about structural models that have good second-level fits. Muthén and Hofacker's (1988) abortion example suggests a certain amount of robustness for first-level misfit, whereas the artificial three-wave panel example suggests that important structural parameters may be misestimated.

It is also important that a model be assessed in a way that is relevant for its ultimate use. To augment first-level and second-level testing, a useful approach would be to deduce predictions from the structural model to the observed data. Take as an example MIMIC modeling as discussed in Muthén (1989b). Here the MIMIC model was used to capture mean differences in factors and items for various sociodemographic groups by including group membership variables as dummies among the exogenous "multiple causes" variable set. This modeling was suggested as an alternative to multiple-group structural modeling with one group for each sociodemographic cross-classification. The multiple-group approach is unattractive because of small group sizes when there are many cells in the cross-classification, particularly when the $y$ variables, the "multiple indicators," are strongly skewed, as in modeling of dichotomous alcohol dependence or depression symptom items. The MIMIC approach avoids these problems, but assumes instead that the factor variances and the loadings are invariant across groups. If the use of the model is to predict group differences in levels, a relevant test is to check how close the set of predicted item means are to the observed ones for as fine a sociodemographic grouping as possible. This sort of model check also ties the implications of the structural model back to the data.

## References

Agresti, A. (1990). *Categorical data analysis*. New York: Wiley.

Alwin, D. F. (1989). Problems in the estimation and interpretation of the reliability of survey data. *Quality and Quantity, 23*, 277-331.

Alwin, D. F. (1992). Information transmission in the survey interview: Number of response categories and reliability of attitude measurement. In P. Marsden (Ed.), *Sociological methodology 1992*. Washington, DC: American Sociological Association.

Ashford, J. R., & Sowden, R. R. (1970). Multivariate probit analysis. *Biometrics, 26*, 535-546.

Bartlett, M. S. (1937). Properties of sufficiency and statistical tests. *Proceedings of the Royal Society A, 160*, 268-282.

Benson, J., & Muthén, B. (1992). *Testing the factor structure invariance of the Test Anxiety Inventory using categorical variable methodology*. Unpublished manuscript.

Bock, R. D. (1975). *Multivariate statistical methods in behavioral research.* New York: McGraw-Hill.
Bock, R. D., & Aitkin, M. (1981). Marginal maximum likelihood estimation of item parameters: Application of an EM algorithm. *Psychometrika, 46,* 443-459.
Browne, M. W. (1974). Generalised least squares estimates in the analysis of covariance structures. *South African Statistical Journal, 8,* 1-24.
Browne, M. W. (1982). Covariance structures. In D. M. Hawkins (Ed.), *Topics in applied multivariate analysis.* Cambridge: Cambridge University Press.
Browne, M. W. (1984). Asymptotically distribution-free methods for the analysis of covariance structures. *British Journal of Mathematical and Statistical Psychology, 37,* 62-83.
Chamberlain, G. (1982). Multivariate regression models for panel data. *Journal of Econometrics, 18,* 5-46.
Chou, D., Bentler, P. M., & Satorra, A. (1991). Scaled test statistics and robust standard errors for non-normal data in covariance structure analysis: A Monte Carlo study. *British Journal of Mathematical and Statistical Psychology, 44,* 347-357.
Ferguson, T. S. (1958). A method of generating best asymptotically normal estimates with application to the estimation of bacterial densities. *Annals of Mathematical Statistics, 29,* 1046-1062.
Fuller, W. A. (1987). *Measurement error models.* New York: John Wiley.
Heise, D. R. (1969). Separating reliability and stability in test-retest correlations. *American Sociological Review, 34,* 93-101.
Jöreskog, K. G. (1985, July 2-5). *Estimation of the polyserial correlation from summary statistics.* Paper presented at the Fourth European Meeting of the Psychometric Society, Cambridge, England.
Jöreskog, K. G. (1991, July 15-17). *Latent variable modeling with ordinal variables.* Paper presented at the International Workshop on Statistical Modeling and Latent Variables, Trento, Italy.
Jöreskog, K. G., & Sörbom, D. (1988). *PRELIS: A program for multivariate data screening and data summarization. A preprocessor for LISREL* (2nd ed.). Chicago: Scientific Software.
Jöreskog, K. G., & Sörbom, D. (1989). *LISREL 7: A guide to the program and applications* (2nd ed.). Chicago: SPSS.
Muthén, B. (1978). Contributions to factor analysis of dichotomous variables. *Psychometrika, 43,* 551-560.
Muthén, B. (1979). A structural probit model with latent variables. *Journal of the American Statistical Association, 74,* 807-811.
Muthén, B. (1983). Latent variable structural equation modeling with categorical data. *Journal of Econometrics, 22,* 48-65.
Muthén, B. (1984). A general structural equation model with dichotomous, ordered categorical, and continuous latent variable indicators. *Psychometrika, 49,* 115-132.
Muthén, B. (1987). *LISCOMP: Analysis of linear structural equations with a comprehensive measurement model. Theoretical integration and user's guide.* Mooresville, IN: Scientific Software.
Muthén, B. (1989a). Dichotomous factor analysis of symptom data. In M. Eaton & G. W. Bohrnstedt (Eds.), Latent variable models for dichotomous outcomes: Analysis of data from the Epidemiological Catchment Area Program [Special issue]. *Sociological Methods & Research, 18,* 19-65.

Muthén, B. (1989b). Latent variable modeling in heterogeneous populations: Presidential address to the Psychometric Society, July 1989. *Psychometrika, 54,* 557-585.

Muthén, B. (1989c). Multiple-group structural modeling with non-normal continuous variables. *British Journal of Mathematical and Statistical Psychology, 42,* 55-62.

Muthén, B. (1989d). Tobit factor analysis. *British Journal of Mathematical and Statistical Psychology, 42,* 241-250.

Muthén, B. (1992, April). *A new inference technique for factor analyzing binary items using tetrachoric correlations.* Paper presented at the annual meeting of the American Educational Research Association, San Francisco.

Muthén, B., & Hofacker, C. (1988). Testing the assumptions underlying tetrachoric correlations. *Psychometrika, 53,* 563-578.

Muthén, B., Huba, G., & Short, L. (1985). *Applications of LISCOMP structural equation modeling for ordered categorical variables.* Paper presented at the annual meeting of the American Psychological Association, Los Angeles.

Muthén, B., & Kaplan, D. (1985). A comparison of some methodologies for the factor analysis of non-normal Likert variables. *British Journal of Mathematical and Statistical Psychology, 38,* 171-189.

Muthén, B., & Kaplan, D. (1992). A comparison of some methodologies for the factor analysis of non-normal Likert variables: A note on the size of the model. *British Journal of Mathematical and Statistical Psychology, 45,* 19-30.

Muthén, B., Wisnicki, K. S., & Hasin, D. (1991). *Factor analysis of ICD-10 symptom items in the 1988 National Health Interview Survey on Alcohol Dependence.* Unpublished manuscript.

Satorra, A. (1989). Alternative test criteria in covariance structure analysis: A unified approach. *Psychometrika, 54,* 131-151.

Satorra, A. (1992). Asymptotic robust inferences in the analysis of mean and covariance structures. In P. Marsden (Ed.), *Sociological methodology 1992.* Washington, DC: American Sociological Association.

Satorra, A., & Bentler, P. M. (1990). Model conditions for asymptotic robustness in the analysis of linear relations. *Computational Statistics & Data Analysis, 10,* 235-249.

Satterthwaite, F. E. (1941). Synthesis of variance. *Psychometrika, 6,* 309-316.

# 10

# Some New Covariance Structure Model Improvement Statistics

## P. M. BENTLER
## CHIH-PING CHOU

A standard methodology for improving an ill-fitting structural equation or covariance structure model is to remove parameter restrictions (e.g., to free up previously fixed parameters). The Lagrange Multiplier (LM) or score test was developed to evaluate hypotheses on whether a restriction is statistically inconsistent with the data (Lee & Bentler, 1980; Satorra, 1989; Sörbom, 1989). Another method suggests evaluating the estimated value, or estimated parameter change (EPC), that a specific fixed parameter may take if it is freed (Saris, Satorra, & Sörbom, 1987). In this chapter, we propose extending the ideas behind these model improvement methods and develop three other criteria that concentrate on the impacts to the current model of reducing constraints. As each restriction is removed, or a fixed parameter is freed, from the current model, it may cause changes in parameter estimates as well as an increment in the estimated sampling variabilities of the free parameters (Bentler & Mooijaart, 1989). Without reevaluating the model, statistics reflecting these features can be computed based on the existing model.

AUTHORS' NOTE: This research was supported by grants DA01070, DA00017, and DA03976 from the National Institute on Drug Abuse, and was reported at the Joint Statistical Meetings of the American Statistical Association and Biometric Society, Anaheim, CA, August 1990. The helpful comments of several anonymous reviewers and the editors are gratefully acknowledged.

The average change in parameter estimates and standard errors (or variances) of the free parameters and the significance of these parameter changes associated with removing restrictions provide three new criteria for selecting fixed parameters to be considered for freeing to yield a new, less restricted, model. We also relate our statistics to the LM and EPC statistics, and develop a new $\chi^2$ test for a multivariate EPC statistic that deals with the anticipated effects of freeing a previously fixed parameter. We emphasize, but do not discuss further, the overridingly important idea that model modifications of any sort should be carried out within an appropriate substantive theory that guides the choice of modification to consider.

Although we propose several new statistics, we do not have definitive recommendations regarding their use. We shall illustrate their use in two examples, and draw some conclusions. However, we suspect that substantial additional experience will be needed before unambiguous recommendations regarding the role of these statistics in model modification can be made.

### Statistical Background

#### Covariance Structure Analysis

In covariance structure analysis, a model $\Sigma(\theta)$ is hypothesized for the $p \times p$ population covariance matrix $\Sigma$, based on a set of $q$ unknown or free parameters arranged in the vector $\theta$. For example, $\Sigma = \Lambda\Phi\Lambda' + \Psi$ is the well-known confirmatory factor analysis model, where the elements of $\theta$ are the unknown parameters in $\Lambda$, $\Phi$, and $\Psi$. In practice, one does not study a single model. Typically, there is a sequence of nested models in which parameters that are fixed in one model—say, at zero—might be considered to be free or unknown in another model. Estimation and evaluation of this sequence of nested models may be driven by theory, which is the ideal case, or by empirical model modification procedures. The focus of this chapter is on the estimated changes in the free parameters due to model modification.

An optimization criterion is used in estimating and evaluating a particular model $\Sigma(\theta)$. Let $F$ be a fit function of the unknown parameters, that is, $F = F(\theta)$, to be minimized given a sample covariance matrix $S$, based on a sample of size $N$. Typical fit functions used in covariance structure analysis are $F_1 = \log|\Sigma| + \text{tr}(S\Sigma^{-1}) - \log|S| - p$, $F_2 = \frac{1}{2}\text{tr}[(S - \Sigma)S^{-1}]^2$, and $F_3 = \text{Vecs}(S - \Sigma)'W\text{Vecs}(S - \Sigma)$, where $\text{Vecs}(.)$ yields the vector of lower triangular elements in (.), and $W$ is a positive definite weight matrix. Other fit functions are discussed, for example, by Kano, Berkane, and Bentler (1990). Under standard regularity conditions, $F_1$ is a function that yields normal theory maximum likelihood estimators, $F_2$ is a function that yields asymptotically equivalent generalized least squares estimators, and, under an appropriate choice of weight matrix, $F_3$ yields asymptotically distribution-free estimators. Where the free parameters $\theta$ are not subject to constraints, an overall goodness-of-fit test for the model is typically based on $(N - 1)\hat{F}$, where $\hat{F}$ is the value of the appropriate function at the minimizing estimator $\hat{\theta}$. This test is evaluated with reference to the $\chi^2$ distribution with degrees of freedom $p(p + 1)/2 - q$ (see, e.g., Bentler & Dijkstra, 1985; Browne, 1984; Jöreskog & Sörbom, 1988; Satorra, 1989). An evaluation of the performance of the various test statistics under conditions that include violation of assumptions is given by Hu, Bentler, and Kano (1992).

## LM Statistic

The LM test is one of three test statistics that are classically used in multivariate analysis, namely, the likelihood ratio, LM, and Wald statistics. The likelihood ratio statistic (or, more generally, the $\chi^2$ difference test) requires estimation of both a restricted and a more general model, the LM statistic requires estimation of only the restricted model, and the Wald statistic requires estimation of only the more general model. Under the same null hypothesis, these tests are asymptotically equivalent and can be used interchangeably. Good overviews of these tests are given by Buse (1982) in the context of statistics, Engle (1984) in the context of econometrics, and Satorra (1989) in the context of covariance structure analysis. Because of the economy in estimation, and because practice frequently involves moving from an inadequate restricted model to a more general, less restricted, model, in this chapter we concentrate on the restricted model and some resulting statistics, including the LM statistic. The estimated change in the free parameters due to model modification can be derived from the concepts of the LM and EPC statistics for the fixed parameters.

The LM statistic has a long history in the context of maximum likelihood estimation. Developed by Rao (1947) and Aitchison and Silvey (1958), it is sometimes known in this context as Rao's score test. It was brought into covariance structure analysis by Lee and Bentler

(1980), who developed the test's asymptotic properties in the context of generalized least squares estimation with functions such as $F_2$. See also Sörbom (1989). In this chapter, following Bentler (1989) and Satorra (1989), the LM statistic and its relatives and derivatives are obtained for any relevant covariance structure fit function $F$. It is assumed that the usual technical regularity conditions for these tests, such as continuity of $\partial \Sigma / \partial \theta$, model identification, positive definiteness of $\Sigma$, and constraints that are not linearly dependent, are met (see, e.g., Lee & Bentler, 1980; Satorra, 1989).

We are concerned with estimation of the model under various restrictions. Assume that $\hat{\theta}$ is the vector of constrained estimators of $\theta$ that satisfies the $r < q$ constraints $h(\theta) = 0$, while minimizing $F$. There exists a vector of Lagrange multipliers, $\lambda$, and matrices of derivatives $g = (\partial F / \partial \theta)$ and $L' = (\partial h / \partial \theta)$, assumed full rank and evaluated at $\hat{\theta}$ such that

$$\hat{g} + \hat{L}'\hat{\lambda} = 0 \quad \text{and} \quad \hat{h}(\hat{\theta}) = 0 . \quad [1]$$

Let $H = H(\theta)$ be the information matrix of $\theta$ in the case of maximum likelihood estimation, or the matrix of expected values of second partial derivatives of $F$ with respect to $\theta$ otherwise, assumed full rank. Let $n = (N - 1)$. We assume that this "information matrix" is scaled such that if there were no constraints, the large sample variance-covariance matrix of the estimated parameters $\sqrt{n}(\hat{\theta} - \theta)$ would be given by $H^{-1}$. In the context of constraints, the asymptotic covariance matrix can be obtained from a matrix that is based on $H$, augmented by the matrix of derivatives $L$ and a null matrix $O$. Specifically, if we define

$$[2]$$
$$\begin{bmatrix} H & L' \\ L & O \end{bmatrix}^{-1} = \begin{bmatrix} H^{-1} - H^{-1}L'(LH^{-1}L')^{-1}LH^{-1} & H^{-1}L'(LH^{-1}L')^{-1} \\ (LH^{-1}L')^{-1}LH^{-1} & -(LH^{-1}L')^{-1} \end{bmatrix} = \begin{bmatrix} M & T' \\ T & -R \end{bmatrix},$$

then the matrix $M$ gives the asymptotic covariance matrix of the constrained estimator $\sqrt{n}(\hat{\theta} - \theta)$, while $R$ gives the covariance matrix of the Lagrange multipliers $\sqrt{n}(\hat{\lambda} - \lambda)$. The standard regularity conditions assure that the inverses in the expression exist.

Under appropriate regularity conditions and the null hypothesis $h(\theta) = 0$, the multivariate LM statistic $T_{LM}$ is distributed asymptotically as a central chi-square variate

$$T_{LM} = n\hat{\lambda}'\hat{R}^{-1}\hat{\lambda} \quad \sim \chi_r^2 , \quad [3]$$

where $r$ is the number of nondependent constraints, and

$$\hat{\lambda} = -(\hat{L}\hat{H}^{-1}\hat{L}')^{-1}\hat{L}\hat{H}^{-1}\hat{g} \qquad [4]$$

(see Bentler, 1989, eq. 10.51). Expression 3 is sometimes written in a form in which the sample size multiplier $n$ does not appear. The particular form of this expression depends on the definition of $\hat{\lambda}$ and $R$. See Satorra (1989) and Bentler (1989) for generalized definitions of the LM statistic that hold under violation of distributional assumptions.

## Changes in Parameter Estimates

In order to provide a clear presentation of the new statistics, we will discuss only one type of constraint: fixing a set of parameters to a constant. The new statistics could, however, be applied in situations where more general constraints are imposed. In this simple situation, $\theta' = [\theta_f', \theta_r']$, where $\theta_f$ is the $f = (q - r)$ vector of truly free parameters, and the remaining $r$ parameters in the vector $\theta_r$ take on known values $\theta_r = c$. We shall develop the case where $\theta_f$ has no constraints, and all constraints are on $\theta_r$. We shall call $\theta_r$ the *fixed* parameters, though in the setup they are treated as free to be estimated, subject to the constraint $\theta_r = c$. Under this ordering of parameters, and under these simple constraints,

$$\theta_f = G\theta \quad \text{and} \quad \theta_r = L\theta, \qquad [5]$$

where $G = [I_f, 0]$ is an $(f \times q)$ selection matrix of known 0-1 elements, $L = [0, I_r]$ is an $(r \times q)$ selection matrix of 0-1 elements, and $[G', L'] = I_q$. In this simple situation, $L$ in Expression 5 equals $\hat{L}$ given in Equations 1 and 4. Of course, $g$ and $H$ are similarly permuted so that their components corresponding to free parameters precede those corresponding to the constrained (fixed) parameters.

Our development for parameter change estimates is based on Bentler and Dijkstra's (1985) concept of improved estimation via linearization. Let $\hat{\theta}$ be the initial consistent estimator, for example, the estimator that optimizes $F$ under the constraints. This might be the constrained maximum likelihood estimator, for instance. We are interested in determining $\bar{\theta}$, the optimal estimator that would be obtained if $\theta_r$ were unrestricted. One way to obtain $\bar{\theta}$ is to reestimate the model without the constraints. But, based on Bentler and Dijkstra (1985, eq. 2.1.10), in this instance, a linearized estimator is given by

$$\bar{\theta} = \hat{\theta} - \hat{H}^{-1}\hat{g}, \tag{6}$$

where all terms on the right-hand side are evaluated at $\hat{\theta}$, the constrained estimator. (In the more general case, see Bentler & Dijkstra, 1985, eq. 2.1.4.) In this simple setup, in view of Equations 5 and 6,

$$(\bar{\theta} - \hat{\theta}) = \begin{pmatrix} \hat{\delta} \\ \hat{\pi} \end{pmatrix} = \begin{pmatrix} G\,(\bar{\theta} - \hat{\theta}) \\ L\,(\bar{\theta} - \hat{\theta}) \end{pmatrix} \tag{7}$$

gives the estimated parameter changes. Specifically, $\hat{\delta}$ is the $f \times 1$ vector of estimated changes in free parameters as introduced here, and $\hat{\pi}$ is the $r \times 1$ vector of estimated changes in fixed parameters that is a multivariate version of the EPC introduced in Saris et al. (1987) (see Bentler, 1989, p. 220).

### Estimates and Tests

The estimated changes in parameter estimates are linear combinations of the Lagrange multipliers $\hat{\lambda}$. The multivariate version of the estimated change in fixed parameters introduced in Saris et al. (1987), the multivariate EPC for the fixed parameters (Bentler, 1989; Satorra, 1989), therefore, is

$$\hat{\pi} = -L\hat{H}^{-1}\hat{g} \tag{8}$$

$$= -(L\hat{H}^{-1}L')(L\hat{H}^{-1}L')^{-1}L\hat{H}^{-1}\hat{g}$$

$$= \hat{R}^{-1}\hat{\lambda},$$

in view of Equation 4. The vector $\sqrt{n}(\hat{\pi} - \pi)$ is asymptotically normally distributed with full rank covariance matrix $R^{-1}$. Thus, under the null hypothesis,

$$n\hat{\pi}'\hat{R}\hat{\pi} \sim \chi_r^2 \tag{9}$$

is an asymptotic $\chi^2$ variate. However, in view of Equation 8, and since the asymptotic covariance matrix of $\sqrt{n}(\hat{\lambda} - \lambda)$ is given by $R$, Equation 9 can be written as Equation 3; that is, no new overall statistical information is gained by evaluating the fixed parameter changes via Equation 9 that is not available in the LM test $T_{LM}$. Nonetheless, a subset of the changes $\hat{\pi}_a$ can be tested in a way that is not synonymous with the LM test.

Let $\hat{\pi}_a = A\hat{\pi}$, where $A$ is a known $(a \times r)$ matrix, with $(a < r)$. Thus asymptotically $\sqrt{n}(\hat{\pi}_a - \pi_a)$ has covariance matrix $AR^{-1}A'$, and, under the null hypothesis $h(\theta) = 0$,

$$T_\pi = n\hat{\pi}_a' (A\hat{R}^{-1}A')^{-1}\hat{\pi}_a \sim \chi_a^2 \qquad [10]$$

provides a test on the changes in a subset of fixed parameters. $T_\pi$ is a new statistic that does not appear to have been studied previously. Taking this rationale to a single fixed parameter, the univariate LM and EPC for a specific fixed parameter, say, $\theta_i$, can be obtained as

$$T_{LM_i} = n\hat{\lambda}_i^2/\hat{R}_{ii} \sim \chi_1^2 \qquad [11]$$

and

$$\hat{\pi}_i = \hat{\lambda}_i/\hat{R}_{ii}, \qquad [12]$$

where $\hat{R}_{ii}$ is the $i$th diagonal of the $\hat{R}$ matrix. See Saris et al. (1987) for a rationale toward the use of Equations 11 and 12 in the practice of model modification.

Our main interest is in the parameter changes $\hat{\delta}$, which have not been discussed previously. From Equations 6 and 7,

$$\hat{\delta} = -G\hat{H}^{-1}\hat{g}. \qquad [13]$$

In view of Equation 1, Equation 13 can also be written as

$$\hat{\delta} = G\hat{H}^{-1}L'\hat{\lambda} \qquad [14]$$

$$= G\hat{H}^{-1}L'(L\hat{H}^{-1}L')^{-1}(L\hat{H}^{-1}L')\hat{\lambda}$$

$$= G\hat{T}'\hat{R}^{-1}\hat{\lambda}.$$

These multivariate estimated changes in the estimated free parameters resulting from the release of a set of restrictions, or the freeing of fixed parameters, are linear combinations of Lagrange multipliers. Consequently, under the null hypothesis, the vector $\sqrt{n}(\hat{\delta} - \delta)$ is asymptotically normally distributed with mean $\boldsymbol{0}$ and covariance matrix $\Sigma(\delta) = GT'R^{-1}TG'$. Although this covariance matrix is of dimension $(f \times f)$, its rank is only $r < f$. Thus not all changes in free parameters can be evaluated simultaneously.

There is an explicit relation between the estimated changes in fixed and free parameters. In view of Equations 8 and 14,

$$\hat{\delta} = G\hat{T}'\hat{\pi}. \tag{15}$$

Thus changes in $\hat{\pi}$ are propagated to changes in the free parameters $\hat{\delta}$. If the fixed parameters are estimated not to change, neither will the free parameters. But changes in $\hat{\pi}$ will affect the specific free parameters, $\hat{\delta}_i$, differentially. In fact, it would be possible to manipulate Equation 15 to see the effect on $\hat{\delta}$ of a particular fixed parameter change, say, $\hat{\pi}_i$.

It is somewhat difficult to interpret the estimated parameter changes $\hat{\delta}$ and $\hat{\pi}$ in an absolute way, since the relative size of these estimates can easily depend on arbitrary features of a model. A parameter that seems to be large in the context of one set of identification constraints on a model may be relatively small in the context of another, but equivalent, set of identification constraints. This type of a paradox will not occur if the parameters have an equivalent interpretation owing to the fact that they are all standardized regression coefficients (see, e.g., Chou & Bentler, in press; Kaplan, 1989). When comparing alternative model modifications on the same set of free parameter changes, this paradox does not occur. Thus we shall study the mean absolute parameter change

$$m(\hat{\delta}) = f^{-1} \sum_{i=1}^{f} | \hat{\delta}_i |, \tag{16}$$

recognizing that in some contexts there may be an ambiguity in its meaning.

By the theory of quadratic forms in possibly degenerate asymptotically normal variates, a significance test of the null hypothesis that $\delta = \boldsymbol{0}$ can be evaluated by the quadratic form

$$n\hat{\delta}'(\hat{G}\hat{T}'\hat{R}^{-1}\hat{T}\hat{G}')^{-}\hat{\delta} \sim \chi_r^2, \tag{17}$$

where $r$ is the rank of $(GT'R^{-1}TG')$ and $(GT'R^{-1}TG')^{-}$ is the generalized inverse of $(GT'R^{-1}TG')$. This statistic is, in fact, again the same as the multivariate LM statistic $T_{LM}$ given in Equation 3. Thus overall tests on $\hat{\delta}$ reveal no new statistical information. However, a new variant of this statistic can be constructed when interest focuses on only a subset of the free parameters. For example, one might want to determine which parameters account for the rejection of the global null hypothesis $\delta = 0$, or one might be interested in changes in factor regressions, but not in estimates associated with error variables. In such a case, the vector $\hat{\delta}$ can be reduced with an $(a \times f)$ selection matrix $A$ to concentrate on the changes in a specific set of $a$ free parameters, where $a < r$. These estimated parameter changes are given as $\hat{\delta}_a = (A\hat{\delta})$. Let $G_a = AG$. Then $\hat{\delta}_a = G_a T'R^{-1}\hat{\lambda}$. The asymptotic covariance matrix of $\sqrt{n}(\hat{\delta}_a - \delta_a)$ is $G_a T'R^{-1}TG_a$. Thus a new statistic, $T_\delta$, which evaluates the null hypothesis that $\delta_a = 0$, can be expressed as

$$T_\delta = n\hat{\delta}_a{}'(G_a\hat{T}'\hat{R}^{-1}\hat{T}G_a')^{-1}\hat{\delta}_a \sim \chi_a^2. \qquad [18]$$

Changes in the selected existing parameters can be considered to be significantly different from zero if the statistic $T_\delta$ exceeds the tabled cutoff value in the $\chi_a^2$ distribution. Under appropriate conditions (see Satorra, 1989), the statistic is noncentrally rather than centrally $\chi^2$ distributed.

## Change in Estimated Variances

In general, increasing the number of parameters in a model results in increased statistical instability; that is, the variances of parameter estimates are increased (e.g., Bentler & Mooijaart, 1989; DeLeeuw, 1988). The changes in sampling variability and covariation among estimates of the free parameters associated with the removal of all $r$ fixed parameters is given by the matrix $\Sigma(\hat{\delta})$. Various quantities based on this matrix can provide a summary of changes in sampling variability. The diagonal of this matrix reflects the changes in variances, which are probably of major interest. Specifically, the estimated change in sampling variances of existing parameters associated with releasing a set of constraints can be defined as

$$\hat{\Delta} = \text{Diag}(\hat{G}\hat{T}'\hat{R}^{-1}\hat{T}\hat{G}')/n. \qquad [19]$$

A simple summary is then given by

$$m(\hat{\Delta}) = f^{-1} \sum_{i=1}^{f} \hat{\Delta}_i \,. \qquad [20]$$

## Practical Implications

In practice, the above equations can be utilized in many ways. For example, they could be studied in a stepwise fashion by comparing the changes caused by each restriction. Thus we could choose to remove the restriction on the fixed parameter that causes the maximum $\chi^2$ increment in the LM statistic $T_{LM}$ (Equation 3), the maximum increment in the $T_\pi$ (Equation 10), the minimum average absolute estimated parameter change $m(\hat{\delta})$ (Equation 16) (or, perhaps, the maximum change, depending on one's interest), the minimum average increment in the sampling variability $m(\hat{\Delta})$ (Equation 20), or the maximum $\chi^2$ increment associated with test statistic $T_\delta$ (Equation 18) that evaluates the significance of $\hat{\delta}$.

Our tentative recommendations are based on relatively minimal practical experience with these new statistics. We take into account both substantive and statistical considerations, and again we note that theoretical meaningfulness is a prerequisite of incorporating any model modifications. In general, the LM statistic must provide the most important statistical information. The set of constrained parameters associated with the largest LM statistic is the one that would lead, when included in a new model, to the statistically most significant model improvement, that is, the potentially largest drop in goodness-of-fit $\chi^2$. After all, if a model is acceptable from a statistical point of view, there is usually little reason to consider empirical model modification procedures. Saris et al. (1987) and Kaplan (1989) have argued that the EPC, or here its generalized analogue $\hat{\pi}$, for the fixed parameters ought to be considered simultaneously with the LM test. They argue that there is not much point to freeing a parameter that, while statistically significant due perhaps to unusual power circumstances, may be very small in magnitude (especially when considered in a standardized metric). However, we would argue that there is not much point to freeing a parameter that shows a large EPC yet does not have much impact on the statistical fit of the model. So the new statistic $T_\pi$ may be useful here. A subset of parameters that yields a high $T_\pi$ statistic would be a subset that yields a simultaneously large set of EPCs and also makes a statistically significant difference to model fit.

Suppose next that one realizes that a current model may be misspecified, but hopes that the misspecification is in parts of the model that do not matter too much from an interpretive point of view. Then one would hope that parameters that are added a posteriori should not create appreciable changes in the parameters originally hypothesized, especially the ones based on substantive theory. More specifically, if adding a missing parameter significantly reduces the $\chi^2$, yet does not change any of the important preexisting free parameters, one can conclude that adding the new parameter made no significant difference to the substantively meaningful part of the model. In that case, the original misspecification would be technical in nature, but not especially substantive. From a substantive point of view, it would not matter much whether the parameter were included or excluded, since all parameter interpretations would be the same. An example in which small changes are expected in key parameters is the typical situation where correlated errors are added to an a priori model. The correlated errors are added primarily to reduce $\chi^2$ goodness-of-fit value rather than for any substantive consideration, so one would hope that the meaningful parameters, such as factor regressions, should not be affected as a result. On the other hand, big estimated changes in substantively important free parameters would suggest that the misspecification really mattered in the part of the model under focus. And in view of the somewhat arbitrary nature of the size of some parameters, the significance test associated with $T_\delta$ can be helpful, although it must be recalled that only a subset of the free parameters $\hat{\delta}$ can be tested for significant change at one time.

It seems hard to establish a definitive criterion for how to use the information on the increment of sampling variability in free parameters. No statistical test is available. However, in a basically satisfactory model, variance changes are usually not expected to be large. In general, it is known that for a fixed mean squared error in estimation, there is a trade-off between bias and variance; that is, variance can be reduced at the cost of an increase in bias, and vice versa. Having too low variance may suggest substantial bias in estimates, so that an increase in variance may be desirable. Alternatively, "an estimate with a small bias and a small variance will be preferable to one with a zero bias and large variance" (Cox & Hinkley, 1974, p. 253), so keeping variance small is probably a valuable goal. This is also true because mean squared error is not really fixed in this context, and an increase in variance may imply

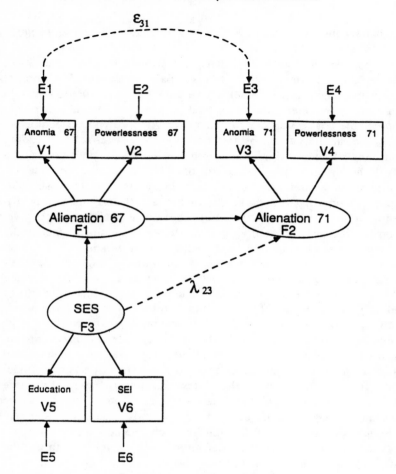

**Figure 10.1.** Model 1, from Jöreskog and Sörbom (1988).

poorer mean square error as well. In fact, large variances are frequently associated with unstable, nearly empirically underidentified, solutions. So a substantial increase in variance could be a good thing (reducing bias) or a bad thing (model instability), depending on the size of the increase and final variance estimates.

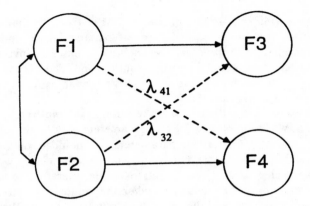

**Figure 10.2.** Model 2, from MacCallum (1986).

## Illustrative Application

### Methodology

In this study, we illustrate the performance of the four new statistics—the average absolute change of free parameter estimates [$m(\hat{\delta})$], Equation 16; the average change of sampling variability [$m(\hat{\Delta})$], Equation 20; the $\chi^2$ statistics for changes in free parameters ($T_\delta$), Equation 18; and changes in fixed parameters $T_\pi$, Equation 10—with the multivariate LM statistic ($T_{LM}$), Equation 3. Two covariance structure models are investigated to evaluate how the above criteria might perform—for example, which one might be more capable of finding the missing but presumably "correct" parameters, that is, those missing or fixed parameters that are part of a larger model that is used to generate the population covariance matrix. The first model and data, based on $N = 932$, were obtained from Jöreskog and Sörbom (1988). The path diagram is presented in Figure 10.1. The parameters needed to be freed to yield the "correct" model are $\lambda_{23}$ and $\epsilon_{31}$, which are depicted by dotted lines in Figure 10.1. The second model was obtained from MacCallum (1986), and is shown in Figure 10.2. One sample with $N = 100$ was generated based on the "true" model. The missing parameters that are omitted from the more complete "true" model are the regression weights, $\lambda_{32}$ and $\lambda_{41}$.

For each model only the fixed parameters with significant univariate LM statistics (Equation 11) are considered to be freed. This is an arbitrary but effective way to define the set of fixed parameters to evaluate. Note that if a fixed parameter that should truly be freed were not associated with a significant univariate LM statistic, further analyses would focus upon the "wrong" set of parameters. All possible subsets containing up to three parameters are evaluated to investigate the performance of each model improvement method. The five statistics are displayed only for the top five subsets with the largest multivariate LM statistics at each set size (1, 2, or 3).

As noted above, the statistic, $T_\delta$, is the same as the multivariate LM statistic, $T_{LM}$, when the number of free parameters, $f$, is larger than the number of restrictions or fixed parameters, $r$, included in the test procedure. This problem does not occur when a subset of $a < r$ free parameters is selected a priori. In this example, therefore, two free parameters are chosen. Consequently, when the number of restrictions to be released is one or two, the resulting $T_\delta$ statistic will be the same as the LM statistic, but when three restrictions are evaluated, it will be different. In Model 1, for example, changes in regression weights, $\hat{\lambda}_{13}$ and $\hat{\beta}_{21}$, are chosen, and observed for change in estimates. The test of free parameter change ($T_\delta$), therefore, concentrates only on these two parameters, rather than on the whole set of free parameters. In Model 2, we also evaluate the significance of a single parameter change.

### Results

#### Model 1

In Model 1, nine parameters were significantly different from zero by the univariate LM statistics. These nine fixed parameters, when considered jointly, had linearly dependent Lagrange multipliers (Equation 4), and the statistic $T_\pi$ in Equation 10 could not be computed for any set of selected parameters. This result highlights a practical weakness in this statistic. It is applicable only when the restrictions are not redundant; that is, the matrix $R$ in Equation 10 is invertible. The remaining statistics could be computed.

Table 10.1 summarizes the four statistics for the subsets of parameter restrictions associated with the five largest LM statistics at three different set sizes, namely, one, two, and three possible restrictions to be removed as shown in the first column of the table. The second column of Table 10.1 shows that the $T_{LM}$ statistic increases as the number of restrictions to be removed increases from one to two to three, as is expected, and that at each number, there is some variation in values of the statistic for evaluating different restrictions. At the evaluation of a

**Table 10.1**  Summary of Four Statistics[a] for Model 1

| Subset of Free Parameters | $T_{LM}$ | $m(\hat{\delta})$ | $m(\hat{\Delta})$ | $T_{\delta}$[b] |
|---|---|---|---|---|
| $\epsilon_{51}$ | 10.833 | 1.083 | 1.146 | 10.833 |
| $\epsilon_{42}$ | 32.655 | 0.283 | 0.006 | 32.655 |
| $\epsilon_{31}$ | 52.469 | 0.344 | 0.005 | 52.469 |
| $\epsilon_{41}$ | 54.531 | 0.379 | 0.006 | 54.531 |
| $\epsilon_{32}$ | 56.067 | 0.346 | 0.005 | 56.067 |
| $(\epsilon_{32}, \epsilon_{54})$ | 67.944 | 0.623 | 0.070 | 67.944 |
| $(\epsilon_{41}, \epsilon_{51})$ | 71.850 | 1.769 | 1.168 | 71.850 |
| $(\epsilon_{31}, \beta_{12})$ | 73.086 | 0.664 | 0.089 | 73.086 |
| $(\epsilon_{31}, \lambda_{23})$[c] | 73.087 | 0.385 | 0.007 | 73.087 |
| $(\epsilon_{21}, \epsilon_{31})$ | 73.087 | 0.783 | 0.057 | 73.087 |
| $(\epsilon_{32}, \epsilon_{41}, \epsilon_{42})$ | 74.128 | 0.444 | 0.074 | 12.627 |
| $(\epsilon_{31}, \epsilon_{42}, \beta_{12})$ | 74.362 | 0.603 | 0.115 | 29.855 |
| $(\epsilon_{31}, \epsilon_{42}, \lambda_{23})$ | 74.362 | 0.297 | 0.033 | 33.596 |
| $(\epsilon_{21}, \epsilon_{31}, \epsilon_{42})$ | 74.363 | 0.694 | 0.083 | 18.615 |
| $(\epsilon_{32}, \epsilon_{41}, \epsilon_{51})$ | 74.577 | 1.290 | 1.511 | 58.107 |

NOTES: a. $T_{LM}$: Lagrange multiplier statistic, Equation 3. $m(\hat{\delta})$: average absolute change of free parameter, Equation 16. $m(\hat{\Delta})$: average change of sampling variability, Equation 20. $T_{\delta}$: $\chi^2$ statistic for change of free parameters, Equation 18.
b. $T_{\delta}$ is based on the free parameters, $\lambda_{13}$ and $\beta_{21}$.
c. The "correct" set of fixed parameters to be selected.

single parameter, the $T_{LM}$ statistics are highly divergent, and $T_{LM}$ points to the restricted parameter $\epsilon_{32}$ as the one that would yield the highest improvement in model fit if only one restriction were released. At two or three parameters, the $T_{LM}$ statistic can hardly distinguish among several alternative sets of parameters that might fruitfully be freed. The supposed "correct" set of restrictions to be released is associated with a $T_{LM}$ statistic of 73.087, but the LM test shows other combinations of parameters that could be released with a virtually identical predicted effect in model improvement. In addition, the increment in $\chi^2$ in going from two to three restrictions to release is very small, so that three restrictions would typically not be entertained by this test (Bentler, 1989), though clearly one can do significantly better by removing more than just one restriction.

The statistic $m(\hat{\delta})$, the average absolute change in estimates for all free parameters, yielded an interesting result, as shown in the next column of Table 10.1. The smallest parameter change overall (.283) is associated with an error covariance that is meaningful (same variable repeatedly measured), although it is not a member of the "correct" set. The next smallest change (.297) occurs when this error covariance is included along with the correct set to yield three restrictions to remove. At two restrictions, the smallest change is associated with the "correct" set (as indicated), although the value of the changes (.385) is somewhat larger than with one or three restrictions to be released. However, while the $T_{LM}$ statistic at two restrictions cannot differentiate among three possible sets of parameters to modify, the next largest change in existing parameters is .664, substantially higher than the correct set to release. In this example, it would seem that $m(\hat{\delta})$ provides very useful additional information to the LM test in model modification, since it clearly homes in on the appropriate set of two restrictions to release. Of course, from the heavy history of study on this model, Model 1 is a very developed model. Model improvement is therefore not expected to cause appreciable change in the original structure.

The statistic $m(\hat{\Delta})$, representing the average change in sampling variability, shows in the next column of Table 10.1 that 4 of the 5 choices at 1 parameter to release create a very low (.005 − .006) increase in estimated variance, while one creates quite a substantial increase (1.146) in variance. At 2 restrictions to be evaluated, $m(\hat{\Delta})$ clearly shows that the "correct" set of restrictions are associated with the least increase in sampling variance (.007), while any other combination yields one or two orders of magnitude larger increase. At 3 parameters to consider, the correct set is again flagged, with the value (.033) being almost a third as large as any other set that might be considered. Again, $m(\hat{\Delta})$ seems able to provide useful adjunct information to the LM test. In this case, the apparently correct model is the one that leads to the smallest increment in sampling variability of the estimated free parameters.

As shown in the last column of Table 10.1, the $\chi^2$ statistic $T_\delta$ has the expected property of mirroring the $T_{LM}$ statistic at set sizes of 1 and 2, yielding no new information. However, at set size 3, the $T_\delta$ statistic is not equivalent to the $T_{LM}$ test, as expected. At this set size, furthermore, the set containing the "correct" restrictions to release is associated with only an intermediate $\chi^2$ value (33.596), so that this statistic would not, when used within set size, yield a very meaningful result. However, when the entire set of numbers in the last column of Table 10.1 is considered, it is apparent that the overall largest value of $T_\delta$ is given by the value 73.087 (and 73.086, no doubt a rounding equivalent). One of these values is associated with the correct restriction. The contribution of $T_\delta$ as an adjunct to the $T_{LM}$ test seems to be that it can help to locate overfitting, in that the statistic can decrease with tests on larger parameter sets.

**Table 10.2** Summary of Four Statistics[a] for Model 2

| Subset of Free Parameters | $T_{LM}$ | $m(\hat{\delta})$ | $m(\hat{\Delta})$ | $T_\delta$[b] | $T_\delta$[b] | $T_\pi$ |
|---|---|---|---|---|---|---|
| $\epsilon_{63}$ | 6.463 | 0.002 | 0.000 | 6.463 | 6.463 | 3.749 |
| $\beta_{43}$ | 7.497 | 0.009 | 0.000 | 7.497 | 7.497 | 0.000 |
| $\lambda_{41}$ | 10.210 | 0.015 | 0.000 | 10.210 | 10.210 | 0.000 |
| $\beta_{34}$ | 10.412 | 0.009 | 0.000 | 10.412 | 10.412 | 0.000 |
| $\lambda_{32}$ | 18.561 | 0.019 | 0.000 | 18.561 | 18.561 | 0.000 |
| $(\epsilon_{92}, \lambda_{32})$ | 22.862 | 0.019 | 0.000 | 22.862 | 20.423 | 4.186 |
| $(\epsilon_{41}, \lambda_{32})$ | 23.260 | 0.020 | 0.000 | 23.260 | 6.092 | 3.421 |
| $(\epsilon_{63}, \lambda_{32})$ | 23.841 | 0.019 | 0.000 | 23.841 | 9.344 | 3.750 |
| $(\lambda_{32}, \beta_{43})$ | 24.319 | 0.026 | 0.000 | 23.319 | 24.298 | 7.850 |
| $(\lambda_{32}, \lambda_{41})$[c] | 28.771 | 0.034 | 0.001 | 28.771 | 28.462 | 14.230 |
| $(\epsilon_{41}, \lambda_{32}, \beta_{43})$ | 28.972 | 0.026 | 0.000 | 24.165 | 10.760 | 11.802 |
| $(\epsilon_{63}, \lambda_{32}, \beta_{43})$ | 29.540 | 0.025 | 0.000 | 22.975 | 14.659 | 12.432 |
| $(\epsilon_{41}, \lambda_{32}, \lambda_{41})$ | 32.959 | 0.034 | 0.001 | 28.072 | 14.976 | 18.532 |
| $(\epsilon_{92}, \lambda_{32}, \lambda_{41})$ | 33.072 | 0.033 | 0.001 | 26.425 | 30.171 | 18.995 |
| $(\epsilon_{63}, \lambda_{32}, \lambda_{41})$ | 33.322 | 0.032 | 0.001 | 26.767 | 18.716 | 19.372 |

NOTES: a. $T_{LM}$: Lagrange multiplier statistic, Equation 3. $m(\hat{\delta})$: average absolute change of free parameter, Equation 16. $m(\hat{\Delta})$: average change of sampling variability, Equation 20. $T_\delta$: $\chi^2$ statistic for change of free parameters, Equation 18. $T_\pi$: $\chi^2$ statistic for change of fixed parameters, Equation 10.
b. The first $T_\delta$ is based on parameter set $\lambda_{31}$ and $\lambda_{42}$; the second $T_\delta$ is based on parameter $\varphi_{21}$.
c. The "correct" set of fixed parameters to be selected.

## Model 2

The results from a sample simulated under Model 2 are summarized in Table 10.2, which has a format equivalent to that of Table 10.1. In addition, however, there are two columns for $T_\delta$, corresponding to two implementations of $T_\delta$. As stated in the table notes, the first $T_\delta$ statistic is based on evaluating the effect of releasing the restrictions on existing parameters $\lambda_{31}$ and $\lambda_{42}$, while the second statistic is based on evaluating the effect on $\varphi_{21}$ only. Unlike Table 10.1, Table 10.2 also reports in the last column on the performance of the statistic $T_\pi$, which could be computed in all cases considered. Thus the limitations of $T_\pi$ found for Model 1, as implemented, were not found here.

The magnitude of the LM statistic $T_{LM}$ increases with the number of restrictions to be considered, as shown in the second column of Table 10.2. At 2 parameters, the largest $T_{LM}$ statistic (28.771) points to the correct set to release. However, adding a third parameter makes a significant increment in $\chi^2$, so the LM test would overfit in this instance.

A tendency to overfit by the LM statistic has been observed previously in this model (Chou & Bentler, 1990).

The next column of Table 10.2 shows that the average change in estimates of free parameters, $m(\hat{\delta})$, associated with the "correct" parameter set yielded the largest value among the group with 2 parameters. For this model, the cross-lagged regression weights should be considered substantively important. A substantial change in the original model is, perhaps, more likely to be anticipated. The $m(\hat{\delta})$ statistic is informative in a way that indicates that parameters released in accord with the $T_{LM}$ statistic will have an effect on the existing parameters.

As seen in the next column of Table 10.2, the average change in sampling variability, $m(\hat{\Delta})$, does not provide very discriminating information in this model. That is, the values are quite similar no matter which restriction is considered, and no matter which size of parameter set to be released is considered.

The statistical significance of changes of the first set of free parameters, the first $T_\delta$ column, in fact points to the "right" parameters to consider. That is, the largest $\chi^2$ (28.771) in the fifth column is associated with the correct restrictions to release, while the second largest (28.072) is associated with the correct restrictions plus an additional one. The corresponding result given in the next column of the table yields a similar, but not perfect, result. That is, this $T_\delta$ statistic attains its largest value (30.171) with the correct set, but it also indicates that an extra parameter needs to be considered beyond the true needed changes. However, at set size of 2 or 3, the correct parameters are included in the largest $\chi^2$ statistic.

The statistic $T_\pi$, which was useless in Model 1, performs spectacularly here. As seen in the last column of Table 10.2, at parameter set size 1, only one statistic gives a nonzero value, but it is not a large value. At 2 parameters, the statistic cleanly points to the correct set to release. It does this in a much more unambiguous way than the $T_{LM}$ test itself. At set size 3, it again points to the correct set but would augment this with an added parameter that is in fact not needed in the population model. The same result would be obtained with the $T_{LM}$ statistic.

## Discussion

This study proposes four new statistics that can be considered in the model improvement procedure in covariance structure analysis: the average changes of estimates and standard errors for the maintained free parameters, a significance test on the null hypothesis that some of the free parameter changes are zero, and a test of the significance of estimated changes in a subset of the fixed parameters. The statistics developed here are based on standard definitions of Lagrange multipliers and the associated $\chi^2$ statistic. Generalized definitions of these statistics (e.g., Bentler, 1989, eqs. 10.51, 10.52; Satorra, 1989) can also be used to yield slightly modified definitions of parameter changes, sampling variability changes, and significance tests of the changes. These modifications are obvious. While we have emphasized application to covariance structure models, in fact these statistics are applicable in a much wider range of statistics, since, as noted earlier, the theory is quite abstract.

The significance test on the free parameter changes seems to be generally applicable to the model improvement procedure. This new statistic is the same as the $T_{LM}$ statistic under the typical condition that number of free parameters included in the test is greater than the number of the fixed or restricted parameters. However, the statistic can fruitfully be made different from the LM statistic by forcing the test to concentrate on a smaller set of free parameters. In the illustrative examples, the test performed quite well in both Models 1 and 2. However, a major issue immediately arises. What is the selection criterion for choosing a specific set of free parameters to evaluate for changes? In some applications, we expect that natural choices would arise, for example, factor regression paths might be chosen for emphasis rather than error variances or covariances. In others, the choice might be more arbitrary, leading, perhaps, to behavior of the new statistic that is hard to evaluate. In any case, our small study has demonstrated that, although this new $\chi^2$ statistic has a tendency to overfit a model, as does the LM statistic, it can be a valuable supplementary criterion to model improvement, especially with theoretically guided selection of free parameters in the test.

The test on changes in fixed parameters $T_\pi$, which is new and informative only when a subset of the parameter changes are being studied, proved to be a mixed blessing. In Model 1 it was useless; that is, it could not be computed. In Model 2, it provided an excellent criterion for selection of model changes to make. Certainly, it provided a greater contrast among alternatives than was shown by the $T_{LM}$ test itself.

Nonetheless, it must be emphasized that, at this stage of development, the application of these new statistics is not as straightforward as the LM statistic $T_{LM}$. However, they seem to provide helpful supplemental information to the LM statistic.

The average of absolute change of the free parameters, or $m(\hat{\delta})$, can be expected to be either large or small depending on the completeness of the original model. When a theoretical structure is quite complete, the change of the parameters in the original model would be expected to be small. That is indeed the result that one would like to observe in some situations. On the other hand, when the original model is not thoroughly constructed and theoretically meaningful parameters are left out, the change on the free parameters is then expected to be rather substantial. A large $m(\hat{\delta})$ statistic would be anticipated. Models 1 and 2 demonstrated these two faces of performance in the $m(\hat{\delta})$ statistic under two different situations. Clearly, there will be a subjective element in the application of the $m(\hat{\delta})$ statistic until more definitive research on it is completed. It should be noted that a potential problem in the application of $m(\hat{\delta})$ is the issue of scaling, since $m(\hat{\delta})$ could be sensitive to the identification conditions and variances of constructs and measures. Chou and Bentler (in press) have proposed an extension of Kaplan's (1989) standardization procedure for the estimated parameter change for the fixed parameters. This standardization procedure also can be applied to yield a standardized $m(\hat{\delta})$. Whether such a modification would yield greatly improved performance in this statistic remains to be seen.

The performance of the statistic that summarizes average changes in standard errors or variances of free parameters is not as impressive. In Model 1, the $m(\hat{\Delta})$ statistic did help to locate the "correct" model. In Model 2, however, the $m(\hat{\Delta})$ statistics were all too small. They did not discriminate well among alternatives.

In conclusion, some of the new model modification indexes proposed here seem to be useful adjuncts to the LM statistic in the process of model modification. We believe that these statistics will provide at least as valuable adjunct information as the estimated parameter change recommended by Saris et al. (1987). Nonetheless, as Equations 8 and 14 make clear, the Lagrange multipliers themselves continue to provide the most fundamental information to the process of model modification. This is not surprising, since the Lagrange multipliers measure the sensitivity of the fit function to be minimized with respect to small changes in the constraints (see Bentler, 1990, for a sensitivity theorem on this point). Thus, if one wants to predict changes in the fit function, these statistics, or functions of them, must be the key statistics to evaluate. Whether statistics derived from these multipliers can be more informative in particular contexts than the multipliers themselves remains to be determined.

# References

Aitchison, J., & Silvey, D. S. (1958). Maximum likelihood estimation of parameters subject to restraints. *Annals of Mathematical Statistics, 29,* 813-828.

Bentler, P. M. (1989). *EQS structural equations program manual.* Los Angeles: BMDP Statistical Software.

Bentler, P. M. (1990). Fit indexes, Lagrange multipliers, constraint changes and incomplete data in structural models. *Multivariate Behavioral Research, 25,* 163-172.

Bentler, P. M., & Dijkstra, T. (1985). Efficient estimation via linearization in structural models. In P. R. Krishnaiah (Ed.), *Multivariate analysis VI* (pp. 9-42). Amsterdam: North-Holland.

Bentler, P. M., & Mooijaart, A. (1989). Choice of structural model via parsimony: A rationale based on precision. *Psychological Bulletin, 106,* 315-317.

Browne, M. W. (1984). Asymptotically distribution-free methods in the analysis of covariance structures. *British Journal of Mathematical and Statistical Psychology, 37,* 62-83.

Buse, A. (1982). The likelihood ratio, Wald, and Lagrange multiplier tests: An expository note. *American Statistician, 36,* 153-157.

Chou, C.-P., & Bentler, P. M. (1990). Model modification in covariance structure modeling: A comparison among likelihood ratio, Lagrange multiplier, and Wald tests. *Multivariate Behavioral Research, 25,* 115-136.

Chou, C.-P., & Bentler, P. M. (in press). Invariant standardized estimated parameter change for model modification in covariance structure analysis. *Multivariate Behavioral Research.*

Cox, D. R., & Hinkley, D. V. (1974). *Theoretical statistics.* London: Chapman & Hall.

DeLeeuw, J. (1988). Model selection in multinomial experiments. In T. K. Dijkstra (Ed.), *On model uncertainty and its statistical implications* (pp. 118-138). New York: Springer-Verlag.

Engle, R. F. (1984). Wald, likelihood ratio, and Lagrange multiplier tests in econometrics. In Z. Griliches & M. D. Intrilligator (Eds.), *Handbook of econometrics* (Vol. 2, pp. 775-826). Amsterdam: North-Holland.

Hu, L., Bentler, P. M., & Kano, Y. (in press). Can test statistics in covariance structure analysis be trusted? *Psychological Bulletin.*

Jöreskog, K. G., & Sörbom, D. (1988). *LISREL 7: A guide to the program and applications.* Chicago: SPSS.

Kano, Y., Berkane, M., & Bentler, P. M. (1990). Covariance structure analysis with heterogeneous kurtosis parameters. *Biometrika, 77,* 575-585.

Kaplan, D. (1989). Model modification in covariance structure analysis: Application of the expected parameter change statistic. *Multivariate Behavioral Research, 24,* 285-305.

Lee, S.-Y., & Bentler, P. M. (1980). Some asymptotic properties of constrained generalised least squares estimation in covariance structure models. *South African Statistical Journal, 14,* 121-136.

MacCallum, R. (1986). Specification searches in covariance structure modeling. *Psychological Bulletin, 100,* 107-120.

Rao, C. R. (1947). Large sample tests of statistical hypotheses concerning several parameters with applications to problems in estimation. *Proceedings of the Cambridge Philosophical Society, 44,* 50-57.

Saris, W. E., Satorra, A., & Sörbom, D. (1987). The detection and correction of specification errors in structural equation models. In C. C. Clogg (Ed.), *Sociological methodology 1987* (pp. 105-129). San Francisco: Jossey-Bass.

Satorra, A. (1989). Alternative test criteria in covariance structure analysis: A unified approach. *Psychometrika, 54,* 131-151.

Sörbom, D. (1989). Model modification. *Psychometrika, 54,* 371-384.

# 11

# Nonpositive Definite Matrices in Structural Modeling

WERNER WOTHKE

Students of covariance structure analysis often encounter errors indicating that a matrix is not positive definite. While the mathematical definition of positive definiteness is clear and concise, users of structural equation models can be overwhelmed by the many different conditions that cause violations of positive definiteness and by the consequences such violations can have in the various stages of applied multivariate data analysis. Intended as a relatively simple guideline, this chapter discusses the most frequent cases.

The following section gives examples of the ways in which a covariance or correlation matrix may fail to be positive definite. (The corresponding formal definition of this concept and its relation to the eigenvalues of the matrix are presented in the chapter appendix.) The subsequent section presents methods for diagnosing violations of positive definiteness. This is followed by a discussion of lack of positive definiteness with sample covariance and correlation matrices, and by some guidelines on how to choose start values so that the initial model covariance matrix will be positive definite. These are followed by a review of possible causes of indefinite final estimates of model parameters. Since lack of admissibility precludes the examination of model fit using the $\chi^2$ statistics, I suggest a menu of techniques to obtain *boundary* solutions for which fit can be evaluated. The chapter closes with a concluding discussion.

256

Because much of the material presented here was developed as a direct response to problems encountered by LISREL (Jöreskog & Sörbom, 1989) users, most of the worked examples are LISREL applications. However, indefiniteness problems can be observed equally well with many other structural equation programs, such as CALIS (SAS Institute, 1991a), EzPATH (Steiger, 1989), EQS (Bentler, 1989), and LISCOMP (Muthén, 1988), and the examples in this chapter are easily translated to their particular command syntax. Furthermore, the occurrence of indefinite matrix problems or negative variance estimates is not limited to structural equation models, but is a general matter of concern in several other areas of multivariate statistics, such as exploratory factor analysis (MacCallum, 1983; Thurstone, 1947), hierarchical linear models (Aitkin, 1989), covariance components analysis (Longford, 1989), random regression (Braun, Jones, Rubin, & Thayer, 1983), and analysis of variance (see Winer, 1971, p. 425).

## Examples and Definitions

### Some Properties of Covariance Matrices

It is well known that correlation, covariance, and moment matrices (generically called *covariance* matrices hereafter) must be square and symmetric. Perhaps not so well known is that covariance matrices must also satisfy a number of additional rules that further restrict the patterns of permissible values among their elements. Consider the following examples.

The numbers on the diagonal (the variances) must all be positive. Matrix 1 is not an admissible covariance matrix because its second diagonal value is −2.1.[1]

$$\begin{pmatrix} 1.0 & & \\ 0.3 & -2.1 & \\ 0.5 & 0.3 & 1.0 \end{pmatrix} \quad [1]$$

The values on the diagonal restrict the range of possible off-diagonal values. Variables 1 and 3 in Matrix 2 have a covariance of 1.5, which is larger than the geometric mean of their respective variances. The resulting correlation coefficient would be 1.06—an inadmissible value. Covariance coefficients $\sigma_{ij}$ must not be greater in absolute value than $(\sigma_i^2 \sigma_j^2)^{1/2}$. Or, equivalently: Correlations must fall into the range between −1 and 1.

$$\begin{pmatrix} 2.0 & & \\ 0.3 & 0.5 & \\ 1.5 & 0.2 & 1.0 \end{pmatrix} \qquad [2]$$

The admissible range of a correlation between two variables $i$ and $j$ is codetermined by the correlations of all other variables with $i$ and $j$. Matrix 3 shows variable 2 correlated at 0.90 with both variables 1 and 3, which, in turn, are correlated at −0.5.

$$\begin{pmatrix} 1.0 & & \\ 0.9 & 1.0 & \\ -0.5 & 0.9 & 1.0 \end{pmatrix} \qquad [3]$$

This is a violation of the triangular inequality condition among triplets of correlation coefficients. If the two correlations of pairs (1,2) and (2,3) are taken to be 0.90, then the correlation of (1,3) can range only between the positive values 0.62 and 1.0. In general terms, the triangular inequality condition restricts the range of permissible values for the correlation of variables $i$ and $j$ to fall between the two limiting values

$$\cos[\arccos(\rho_{il}) - \arccos(\rho_{jl})]$$

and

$$\cos[\arccos(\rho_{il}) + \arccos(\rho_{jl})]$$

where the index $l$ stands for any arbitrary third variable in the same correlation matrix. In larger matrices there are additional, higher-order rules for quartuplets, quintuplets, and so on, of covariances and correlations. For instance, the two ranges implied for the correlation between $i$ and $j$ by a third variable $l$ and a fourth variable $k$ must have a common, nonempty intersection.

Matrix 4 is rank deficient, containing variances and covariances of *three* variables, all of which can be represented in *two* dimensions.

$$\begin{pmatrix} 1.00 & & \\ 0.30 & 2.00 & \\ 0.65 & 1.15 & 0.9 \end{pmatrix} \qquad [4]$$

Because the third variable was generated as the arithmetic mean of the first two variables, it does not provide any information on its own. In other words, the third variable is redundant. A rank-deficient matrix does not have the regular inverse required for many multivariate data analysis methods (Graybill, 1983, sec. 1.6; Green & Carroll, 1976, chap. 4; Searle, 1982, chap. 6). While rank deficiency does not, by itself, violate any characteristics of covariance matrices, it often makes applications of structural modeling techniques difficult, if not impossible.

### Eigenvalues and Positive Definiteness

When the question arises whether the values of a symmetric matrix could or could not reflect the variances and covariances of a set of variables, a series of tests can be performed along the lines of the preceding examples. First, there should be a check whether all diagonal entries are positive; second, all implied correlations must range between $-1$ and $1$; then, the triangular inequality can be tested among all triplets of correlation coefficients; and so on. While the simple range checks for variances and correlations are easy and can be performed by hand, tests of triangular inequality conditions and other higher-order restrictions quickly become too tedious. Fortunately, a more automated procedure is available.

The general criterion that distinguishes a covariance matrix from other symmetric matrices is *positive definiteness*. This concept can be advantageously defined as a function of the eigenvalues or characteristic roots of a matrix (the chapter appendix gives the traditional definition). For purposes of this chapter, it is sufficient to keep in mind that $p$ eigenvalues can be computed for any symmetric $p \times p$ matrix. Associated with each unique eigenvalue is an eigenvector (or characteristic vector), and the (normed) eigenvectors are commonly referred to as *principal component coefficients* (Anderson, 1984, chap. 11). The so-called principal components are obtained from the raw data by applying these coefficients as weights in a weighted sum of the variables. Importantly, the variance of a principal component equals the value of the associated eigenvalue. The complete set of $p$ vectors of principal component coefficients and $p$ eigenvalues can be used to reconstruct the original matrix. Procedures for computing eigenvalues and eigenvectors are well known and are incorporated in easily accessible statistical packages, such as GAUSS (Aptech Systems, 1988) or SAS/IML (SAS Institute, 1985); mathematical subroutine packages, such as IMSL (IMSL

Institute, 1980) or NAG (Numerical Algorithms Group, 1990); or specialized programs (Wothke, 1991).

Given its eigenvalues, it is easily determined whether a matrix is positive definite or not: A matrix is *positive definite* if all its $p$ eigenvalues are greater than zero; it is *semidefinite* if one or more eigenvalues are zero and the remaining ones are positive, and *indefinite* if at least one eigenvalue is negative. For instance, Matrix 3 yields the eigenvalues

$$( 2.04711, 1.50000, -0.54711 ). \qquad [5]$$

The matrix is indefinite because one of its eigenvalues is negative. The example Matrices 1 and 2 also have negative eigenvalues. These matrices are therefore indefinite.

Matrix 4 has the eigenvalues

$$( 2.91825, 0.98175, 0.00000 ). \qquad [6]$$

The smallest eigenvalue is zero, so that Matrix 4 is semidefinite. Semidefinite matrices are rank deficient and do not have a regular inverse. While there are several approaches for computing a generalized inverse of a semidefinite matrix (see Green & Carroll, 1976), they do not give unique solutions and have not found much use in structural equation modeling.

Finally, consider the $3 \times 3$ diagonal matrix

$$\begin{pmatrix} 2.0 & & \\ 0.0 & 1.0 & \\ 0.0 & 0.0 & 0.9 \end{pmatrix}. \qquad [7]$$

Its eigenvalues are

$$( 2.0, 1.0, 0.9 ). \qquad [8]$$

This example demonstrates the rule that, in diagonal matrices, the set of eigenvalues is equal to the diagonal entries.

### Smoothing an Indefinite Matrix

For diagnostic purposes, or for heuristic data analyses entertained to generate new ideas for further research, it is possible to smooth the offending indefinite matrix so that at least preliminary model estimates can be obtained. Two smoothing approaches have been proposed: smoothing by adding a ridge and principal component smoothing.

## Smoothing by Adding a Ridge

Adding a ridge involves multiplying the diagonal (the *ridge*) of the matrix with a constant greater than unity. This process may be repeated until the negative eigenvalues disappear. This method has previously been given as the *ridge option* incorporated in LISREL 7 (Jöreskog & Sörbom, 1989). It is also an integral part of ridge regression methods when based on empirical Bayes assumptions (for discussions, see Amemiya, 1985, pp. 60-69; Draper & Smith, 1981, pp. 313-325).

While the ridge method does not, in itself, provide diagnostics about the nature of the indefiniteness in the original matrix, it *fixes up* the data in the sense that needed numerical operations, including matrix inversion, become possible.

## Principal Component Smoothing

Principal component smoothing involves three steps:

(1) Determine the eigenvalues and eigenvectors of the indefinite matrix. Some eigenvalues will be negative.

(2) Using all *positive* eigenvalues and associated eigenvectors, calculate the semidefinite components of the matrix. The resulting matrix will have larger diagonal entries than the original indefinite matrix.

(3) If all variances in the diagonal of the original indefinite matrix were strictly greater than zero, rescale the reproduced matrix to these original variances.

This method is already incorporated in the TESTFACT program (Wilson, Wood, & Gibbons, 1984) to overcome negative eigenvalues that are routinely observed with tetrachoric correlation matrices. An essentially equivalent approach is used in the principal component or latent root regression methods (discussed in Draper & Smith, 1981, pp. 327-337; Spanos, 1986, pp. 432-440).

Smoothing by principal components leads to a semidefinite matrix and may therefore not immediately qualify for further analysis by some existing estimation methods. However, all covariance components associated with the negative eigenvalues of the offending indefinite matrix are contained in the residuals from the smoothed covariance matrix. Valuable insight into the source of the indefiniteness problem can be gained from inspecting the size and patterns of these residuals.

### Application of Smoothing Methods

Because the two smoothing methods transform indefinite matrices in different ways, each presents particular strengths and weaknesses. Principal components smoothing produces a matrix that is only semidefinite. Its strength is as a diagnostic tool to determine the source of an indefiniteness problem, but model estimation by some methods may not be possible. The ridge method, on the other hand, generates a strictly positive definite matrix that can be subjected to standard multivariate estimation techniques, but is not very useful for diagnosing the indefiniteness issue. In practical applications, neither of the two methods may give entirely satisfactory results. In such cases, better results may be achieved by combining the two approaches.

*Example 1.* Principal components smoothing yields the rescaled semidefinite components of Matrix 3 as

$$\begin{pmatrix} 1.0 & & \\ 0.596 & 1.0 & \\ -0.290 & 0.596 & 1.0 \end{pmatrix} \qquad [9]$$

and the residual matrix as

$$\begin{pmatrix} 0.0 & & \\ 0.304 & 0.0 & \\ -0.210 & 0.304 & 0.0 \end{pmatrix}. \qquad [10]$$

The pattern of residuals reflects the generation principle of Matrix 3: The entries in elements $(2,1)$ and $(3,2)$ were deliberately chosen so high, and the value in element $(3,1)$ so small (or so large on the negative side), that the triangular inequality condition could not be satisfied.

### Sample Covariance Matrices

Covariance matrices computed from sample data are normally positive definite. However, there are a few situations in which indefinite

matrix problems tend to occur with some frequency. Since model estimation by normal-theory maximum likelihood (ML) or generalized least
squares (GLS) methods requires the sample covariance matrix to be
positive definite, the researcher has the choice of (a) collecting the data
or formulating the structural model strategy in ways that avoid the
indefiniteness problem, (b) smoothing the offending matrices and set-
tling for heuristic instead of statistically stringent data analysis, or (c)
using a different estimation method. Which of these options applies
depends on the source of indefiniteness. It is convenient to distinguish
between *collinearities* among variables, pairwise deletion of *missing
data,* and non-Pearsonian correlations.

## Collinearities

The sampled data may comprise collinearities (or linear dependencies), in the sense that either one variable is completely determined as
a weighted sum of some of the other variables or two or more different
subsets of variables produce the same weighted sums. In statistical
applications, an extended definition of collinearities is often used that
incorporates *approximate* linear dependencies indicated by small positive eigenvalues and their associated eigenvectors (Draper & Smith,
1981, p. 158; Mason & Gunst, 1985). These approximate collinearities
can arise from a perfect linear dependency, occluded by a very small
variance due to rounding error.

### Causes of Collinearities

A simple example of collinearity would be a correlation matrix that
includes all the items of an educational test plus its total score; the
collinearity would arise from the fact that the test score is calculated as
the sum of the individual item scores. A second type of linear dependency may occur when the items of an assessment battery are selected
according to a completely crossed factorial design. This could, for
instance, involve a dual classification with respect to personality traits
as well as assessment methods. Suppose that each item in such a battery
is scored twice, once into a trait score and once into a method subscore.
The resulting covariance matrix of all trait and method scores will
exhibit a collinearity problem, because the sum of the trait scores will
equal the sum of the method scores. In such cases, the collinearity
problem can often be traced with a conceptual analysis of the measurement

and scoring situation. Frequently, a collinearity problem depends on an unintended flaw in the data coding.

An aspect that is sometimes overlooked is that the covariance matrix must really be based on *at least as many* observed cases as variables. Stated more exactly, there must be at least as many distinct response patterns as variables. If, conversely, the number of variables is larger than the number of response patterns, the covariance matrix will necessarily contain collinearities.

Outliers in the raw data, defined as extreme observations relative to the remainder of the sample, are another, often neglected, source of collinearity. In the multivariate case, outliers are not just very small or very large values that can be detected with a series of univariate histograms or boxplots; rather, multivariate outliers can deviate from the main body of the data in any direction, changing the covariance structure in various ways, and are often obscured in marginal distributions.

## *Diagnosis of Collinearities*

Eigenvalues and eigenvectors are the most general tools for diagnosing the makeup of collinearity structures in the data. If the covariance matrix has a single zero-valued (or approximately zero-valued) eigenvalue, then the associated eigenvector describes the collinearity exactly. In Matrix 3, for example, the zero eigenvalue is associated with the eigenvector

$$( -0.408, -0.408, 0.816) .\qquad\qquad [11]$$

In other words, the principal component

$$-0.408 * \mathrm{var}_1 - 0.408 * \mathrm{var}_2 + 0.816 * \mathrm{var}_3$$

has zero variance, and must therefore equal some constant value $\kappa$. Since

$$\mathrm{var}_3 = \kappa/0.816 + (\mathrm{var}_1 + \mathrm{var}_2)/2 ,$$

variable 3 matches the average of the two variables 1 and 2 plus some constant.

When there are *several* eigenvalues at or near zero, it can still be informative to inspect the associated eigenvectors, even though they are not uniquely determined (the relative orientation of these eigenvectors is not fixed, so they may be rotated without losing any algebraic information). The examination should consider a complete set (or basis) of such eigenvectors at once. Variables with zero weights on all these eigenvectors are not involved in any collinearity. Conversely, variables with nonzero weights are part of at least one collinearity structure and should be checked more closely.

When collinearities are caused by groups of outliers in the data, combining several data screening methods for multivariate outlier detection can be more informative than merely examining the eigenvalues and eigenvectors; among the techniques suggested by Mason and Gunst (1985), for example, are scatterplots of the major principal components of the covariance matrix and scatterplots of specific suspicious variable pairs. Additional methods might involve $\chi^2$-based measures of multivariate deviation or use of one of several three-dimensional data visualization programs that have become available on personal and workstation computers in the past few years, such as AcroSpin (Parker, 1989), JMP (SAS Institute, 1991b), or SAS-Insight (SAS Institute, 1991c).

## Remedies for Collinearities

Appropriate corrections for collinearity problems are self-evident in many cases. Variables recognized as redundant, or data points clearly identified as outliers, may simply be removed from the analysis. When the sample size is too small relative to the number of variables, one can reduce the number of variables and/or collect more cases.

Should these corrections not be acceptable, one can still consider smoothing the matrix by principal components or by adding a ridge, as discussed above. These methods are standard corrective techniques for collinearity problems in multiple regression, but have not found much acceptance in the structural equation modeling field. The only systematic use of matrix smoothing appears to be in Version 7 of the LISREL program, which applies an automatic ridge correction to indefinite or semidefinite sample covariance matrices when maximum likelihood or generalized least squares estimation methods are used. But because these smoothing methods actually change the analyzed covariance matrix and can produce radically different fit-$\chi^2$ statistics, their use should be guarded. While it is often acceptable to smooth pilot data for use in preliminary analyses, more important modeling tasks require other means of dealing with collinearity problems. As an alternative to matrix smoothing, estimation by the unweighted least squares (ULS) method may be considered because it does not require a positive definite sample covariance matrix.

In some modeling problems, especially in the econometric field, collinearity issues arise from identities dictated by the structural equations. Solutions for these kinds of situations involve trade-offs among model specification, choice of estimation method, and exclusion of certain variables in the sample covariance matrix. For example, Jöreskog and Sörbom (1989, pp. 156-162) present an econometric analysis where the sample covariance matrix contains collinearities by virtue of the model. Parameter estimation from this semidefinite matrix can be performed by ULS, but a ridge has to be added for maximum likelihood estimation. Jöreskog and Sörbom show as an alternative that the structural collinearities can be removed from the sample covariance matrix and incorporated directly into the structural model specifications, thereby permitting maximum likelihood estimation without an added ridge.

### Pairwise Deletion of Missing Data

Missing observations due to nonresponse, response sampling design, morbidity, and various other reasons are a standard occurrence in social science data. As the following two subsections indicate, determining how the sample covariances should be computed in the presence of such missing data is not always easy. In applied research, however, covariances are frequently computed based simply on the pairwise deletion of missing data. Yet, under pairwise deletion of missing data the estimated sample covariance matrices may become indefinite. The problem is that pairwise deletion implies strict (and often unreasonable) assumptions about the missing data generating process.

### *How Pairwise Deletion Can Cause Indefiniteness Problems*

When the variables in a data set are not completely observed, the means, variances, and covariances of observations with missing data may be different from those with complete responses. Consider the following example.

There are two groups of equal sample size. In Group 1, three variables were assessed, yielding the covariance matrix

$$\begin{pmatrix} 1.16 & & \\ -0.32 & 1.20 & \\ 0.71 & 0.73 & 1.22 \end{pmatrix}. \qquad [12]$$

In the second group, the last variable is completely missing. The remaining covariance matrix has meaningful entries for only the first two variables:

$$\begin{pmatrix} 1.16 & & \\ -0.42 & 1.20 & \\ n/a & n/a & n/a \end{pmatrix}. \qquad [13]$$

To keep computations easy, the observed means and variances for variables 1 and 2 are chosen to be invariant across groups. Only the covariance between variables 1 and 2 is different. Then the combined covariance matrix, based on pairwise deletion of missing data,

$$\begin{pmatrix} 1.16 & & \\ -0.37 & 1.20 & \\ 0.71 & 0.73 & 1.22 \end{pmatrix}. \qquad [14]$$

is indefinite, as indicated by its eigenvalues

$$( 2.055, 1.549, -0.024 ). \qquad [15]$$

This example uses only two patterns of "missingness"—data being observed either on all three variables or only on the first two. When there are several patterns of missing data, means and covariance structures of the observed data portions must be statistically equivalent across all patterns. Then the process generating the missing observations is said to be ignorable (Little & Rubin, 1987), that is, unrelated to the data themselves, and, with large multinormal samples, pairwise deletion of missing data will generally produce positive definite covariance matrix estimates.

## Alternatives to Pairwise Deletion

When the missing data process is nonignorable, or when there is considerable sampling variation due to small sample size, covariance matrices computed under pairwise deletion of missing data are often indefinite. To avoid this indefinite matrix problem, one could use listwise deletion of missing cases (which can be practical if there are only a few cases with missing data), employ one of the imputation methods discussed by Little and Rubin (1987), which then often converge toward a semidefinite boundary solution or, if random error is added to the imputations, may result in a matrix with similar off-diagonal entries but with a ridge correction of the diagonal values. A different approach involves computing a separate covariance matrix for each missing data pattern and formulating a multiple-group model for incomplete observations (Allison, 1987; Jöreskog and Sörbom, 1989, pp. 284-288). This latter option also provides a powerful method of modeling nonignorable missing data processes as group differences in the structural model itself (Muthén, Kaplan, & Hollis, 1987). However, Allison's approach is currently practical only with relatively few patterns of missing data, each based on a large number of observations.

## Tetrachoric and Biserial, Polychoric and Polyserial Correlations

Analyses based on Pearson correlations or covariances of binary or Likert-type response data often produce artifacts caused by difficulty structures, guessing factors, or other nonnormalities (Mislevy, 1986; Jöreskog & Sörbom, 1988, chap. 1). Several authors have therefore promoted the alternate use of polychoric and polyserial correlations for ordered categorical variables (or tetrachoric and biserial coefficients for strictly dichotomous ones), which are generally much less biased estimators of the population correlations (Christoffersson, 1975; Jöreskog, 1990; Jöreskog & Sörbom, 1988; Muthén, 1984).

### Methods for Analyzing Polychoric and Polyserial Correlations

While the recommendations for using polychoric and polyserial correlations are well taken, it is now becoming common knowledge that matrices of non-Pearsonian correlation coefficients are often indefinite even with large sample sizes, and model estimation with normal-theory maximum likelihood or generalized least squares methods does not apply (Bock, Gibbons, & Muraki, 1988; Mislevy, 1986). For estimating structural equation models of polychoric or polyserial sample correlations, Muthén (1984) and Jöreskog (1990) have therefore developed limited information estimators for categorical variable methodologies (CVM) based on Browne's (1984) asymptotically distribution-free (ADF) estimator. To apply CVM, an estimate of the asymptotic sampling covariance matrix of the polychoric and polyserial sample correlations must be computed from the raw data. Model estimation is by weighted least squares, using the inverse of the asymptotic covariance matrix as a weight. Under the CVM approach, the sample correlation matrix does not have to be positive definite, but the asymptotic covariance matrix must be. CVM can be usefully employed when the number of variables is relatively small and the sample sizes are very large. However, since the storage and computational requirements for the asymptotic covariance matrix are proportional to the fourth power of the number of variables, CVM is practically limited to 25 variables (Mislevy, 1986).

An alternative to CVM and normal-theory maximum likelihood methods is multinomial full-information estimators based on modern item-response theory (IRT) (Bartholomew, 1987; Bock et al., 1988; Wilson et al., 1984). Because solutions generated by these methods are estimated directly from the multivariate response patterns, item correlation matrices are needed only for start value computations, a task for which approximations are usually sufficient. Currently, such an IRT implementation of the exploratory factor analysis model for binary response variables is available in the TESTFACT program (Wilson et al., 1984), which can easily accommodate a four-factor model of 70 items on a fast PC or workstation computer. Limitations of the IRT-based approach lie in the type of data and type of models that can be analyzed with currently available programs. Extensions toward structural equation models and toward Likert-type data should appear in commercially maintained computer programs within the next few years.

If all the above strategies fail, the matrix could still be analyzed by unweighted least squares, as long as correct standard errors for the model estimates are not needed. Provided that the estimates lie inside the admissible parameter space and the model covariance matrix $\Sigma$ remains positive definite, the ULS method provides consistent point estimates of the model parameters.

## Other Options for Analyzing Indefinite Covariance Matrices

While some frequently occurring indefinite matrix problems are easily resolved, it is clear that the preceding suggestions will sometimes not be sufficient or will not be regarded as practical. In these cases, the ULS estimation method may be worth considering. Alternatively, if a heuristic data analysis is sufficient, and the parameter estimates need to be only approximately correct, smoothing options by the ridge and/or principal component methods may be employed to adjust the offending covariance matrix.

## Start Values

Problems with indefinite estimates of model component matrices usually occur at two stages of the model estimation process—the generation of starting values and the evaluation of the final set of estimates. Start values generation is discussed in this section; final model estimates are addressed in the following section.

### Model Estimation and Start Values

The need to supply start values is intrinsic to how maximum likelihood and least squares estimates of structural models are computed. Many structural equation models do not allow a direct algebraic (i.e., closed-form) solution for calculating the parameter estimates. For this reason, structural equation programs such as LISCOMP (Muthén, 1988), LISREL 7 (Jöreskog & Sörbom, 1989), and EQS 3 (Bentler, 1989) generally employ iterative methods to compute the model estimates. Iterative model estimation requires an initial choice of preliminary parameter values. These initial values result in a corresponding model covariance matrix $\hat{\Sigma}_0$ whose fit to the sample covariance matrix is evaluated. Using the fit information, the programs compute a new, improved set of provisional estimates that, in turn, generates a new model covariance matrix $\hat{\Sigma}_1$ to be compared to the sample covariance matrix, and so on. This procedure is repeated until the fit of the model covariance matrix at step $i$, $\hat{\Sigma}_i$, cannot be improved further, given the choice of the current structural model.

Indefinite matrix problems due to a particular choice of starting values occur especially with maximum likelihood estimation. This method requires that the model covariance matrix $\hat{\Sigma}_i$ is of full rank and positive definite at all steps of the iterative estimation process. Structural equation programs generally cannot recover from a situation where the initial values of maximum likelihood estimates produce an indefinite $\hat{\Sigma}_0$. Other iterative estimation methods, such as generalized least squares, also tend to perform more gracefully if $\hat{\Sigma}_0$ is positive definite or semidefinite.

### Automatic Start Values

Some linear structural equation programs, like LISREL 7, have built-in procedures to supply initial estimates automatically by instrumental variables (IV) or two-stage least squares (TSLS) methods (Jöreskog, 1983; Jöreskog & Sörbom, 1989). A vital concept of these methods is that of a *reference variable,* an observed variable (or weighted sum of several observed variables) that is used in place of a latent factor. There must be a distinct reference variable for each latent variable, and, consequently, automatic start values are available only for models with at least as many observed as latent variables.

Factor scores and path coefficients are estimated by weighted (TSLS) or unweighted (IV) regression of the remaining observed variables onto the reference variables, and covariance matrices of latent factors and error terms are estimated in a second stage by unweighted least squares, as outlined in Jöreskog (1983) and Jöreskog and Sörbom (1989). Both IV and TSLS methods yield start values close to the final solution in many standard modeling situations.

Start value generation by these relatively mature methods has certain limits. First of all, model specifications with more latent than observed variables (e.g., MacCallum & Ashby, 1986; Wothke & Browne, 1990) cannot be served. Second, each latent variable in the model must have a separate, independent reference variable. Because this is not the case with second-order factors, automatic start values cannot be produced for higher-order factor analysis. Third, IV or TSLS estimation of the factor and error variances and covariances may yield semidefinite or indefinite matrices, especially when the model is not identified or misspecified (see below).

When automatic start value procedures fail, or when programs provide only rough or no initial values, such as EQS (Bentler, 1989) or LISCOMP (Muthén, 1988), start values have to be explicitly supplied with the model. Two basic strategies for selecting start values may be considered: (a) substituting unweighted least squares estimates[2] or (b) user-supplied start values. While ULS estimation often generates usable start values in a fast and almost automatic fashion, user-supplied start values can be advantageous when results from prior studies permit approximate guesses of parameter values and when ULS estimates are not admissible. Both strategies fulfill specific purposes and are discussed below.

## Start Value Generation by Unweighted Least Squares

The unweighted least squares method determines model parameter estimates so that the mean squared residual between the model covariance matrix $\hat{\Sigma}$ and the sample covariance matrix is minimized. As long as the model is identified, ULS is a very robust estimation technique that imposes few additional requirements on the model and sample covariance matrices. In particular, ULS estimates can be obtained even for semidefinite or indefinite sample covariance matrices. In addition, ULS is quite robust with respect to start value selection. Being itself an iterative technique, ULS estimation requires initial values for its parameter estimates, but values of zero are usually sufficient.

Using ULS to generate start values for maximum likelihood or generalized least squares solutions is not difficult. First, ULS estimates are obtained for the same structural equation model and saved to a disk file. Then the same model is reestimated by ML or GLS, but, instead of using automatically generated start values, the ULS solution is read from the disk file. Note: To turn off the automatic start value generating function in LISREL, the NS keyword must appear on the OUtput_requests command.

### Choosing One's Own Start Values

It is always possible to "hand pick" start values, even though it can sometimes be challenging to keep the resulting model covariance matrix positive definite. The task is generally easy when existing parameter estimates from previous studies or theory-derived parameter values can be used. However, these kinds of prior values are often available for only some of the parameters in the model, and more or less crude initial estimates must suffice for the remaining ones. The rest of this section gives practical, albeit occasionally cumbersome, rules for generating such arbitrary start values for some or all of the model parameters.

Fortunately, the minimization algorithms used by the LISCOMP, LISREL, and EQS programs are robust enough so that start values can be based on fairly cursory guesses of the final value. As a general rule, the minimization algorithms tend to converge better when initial values are somewhat smaller than the expected final estimates (Bock & Bargmann, 1966). Other important factors for user-supplied initial estimates are (a) keep them within the admissible range of the particular parameter, (b) within or slightly below the same order of magnitude as the expected final estimates, so that (c) the resulting model covariance matrix is positive definite.

The strategies for selecting initial parameter estimates differ somewhat according to the type of model used. It is convenient to adapt the LISREL distinction of three major model types: factor analysis, path models for directly observed variables, and path models with latent variables. While the models below are discussed primarily in the parameter matrix notation featured by the LISREL approach, it should be easy to adapt the pertinent rules to equation-oriented programs, such as EQS.

## Start Values in Factor Analysis

The classical factor analysis model has the three component matrices $\Lambda$ (factor loadings), $\Phi$ (factor covariances), and $\Theta$ (covariance matrix of unique components), from which the model covariance matrix $\Sigma$ is computed as

$$\Sigma = \Lambda\Phi\Lambda' + \Theta . \tag{16}$$

In traditional factor analysis, the factor covariance matrix $\Phi$ must be (strictly) positive definite and $\Theta$ diagonal with positive entries. Suppose that the model has $k$ factors, is identified (Bollen, 1989, pp. 238-254), and that the scale of the factors is defined by fixing their variances (the diagonal entries of $\Phi$) at unit values. When a sample correlation matrix is analyzed, it is usually adequate to set initial values for the free entries of $\Lambda$ at or near $1/(2k)^{1/2}$; for instance, set the factor loadings at 0.4 for a three-factor model or 0.35 for a four-factor model. The off-diagonal values of $\Phi$ can be initialized at zero, and the diagonal values of $\Theta$ set to a value in the neighborhood of 0.5. For covariance matrix analysis, the start values for elements of $\Lambda$ should be adjusted proportionally to the observed standard deviations, and start values for elements of $\Theta$ proportionally to the variances. It is important that the initial matrix $\Phi$ is at least semidefinite and $\hat{\Theta}$ (strictly) positive definite, in order to keep the initial model matrix $\hat{\Sigma}_0$ positive definite.

Modern extensions of factor analysis allow for factors with single indicators and for correlations among the unique components. Single-indicator models require that the corresponding row and column elements of $\Theta$ be fixed at zero values.[3] To avoid any indefiniteness problems in $\hat{\Sigma}_0$, the corresponding sections of $\hat{\Phi}$ must be initialized to be strictly positive definite and the corresponding factor loadings fixed at unity or some other suitable nonzero value. Correlated unique components, that is, free off-diagonal elements of $\Theta$, can be initialized at zero.

## Start Values in Path Models With Directly Observed Variables

In path models with directly observed variables, parameters in four matrices have to be initialized. It is common to distinguish between exogenous ("cause") and endogenous ("effect" and intermediate) variables. Then the four matrices are as follows: the covariance matrix of the exogenous variables, $\boldsymbol{\Phi}$; the regression coefficients of endogenous onto exogenous variables, $\boldsymbol{\Gamma}$; the regression coefficients of endogenous onto other endogenous variables, $\boldsymbol{B}$; and the covariance matrix of structural residuals, $\boldsymbol{\Psi}$.[4] The implied model covariance matrix, partitioned into endogenous and exogenous components, is

$$\boldsymbol{\Sigma} = \left( \begin{array}{c|c} (\boldsymbol{I}-\boldsymbol{B})^{-1}(\boldsymbol{\Psi}+\boldsymbol{\Gamma}\boldsymbol{\Phi}\boldsymbol{\Gamma}')(\boldsymbol{I}-\boldsymbol{B}')^{-1} & (\boldsymbol{I}-\boldsymbol{B})^{-1}\boldsymbol{\Gamma}\boldsymbol{\Phi} \\ \hline \boldsymbol{\Phi}\boldsymbol{\Gamma}'(\boldsymbol{I}-\boldsymbol{B}')^{-1} & \boldsymbol{\Phi} \end{array} \right). \qquad [17]$$

Structural equation models come at various levels of complexity, ranging from a traditional regression between two observed variables to systems of reciprocal causation among variables, possibly incorporating correlations among the structural residuals. Rules for model identification cover a similar range from simple to complicated (Bollen, 1989, pp. 88-104, 326-333; Goldberger, 1973) and must be met by the start values. If the model is recursive—that is, does not contain any reciprocal or circular causation chains—and if the structural residuals are generally uncorrelated, then identification of parameters is usually easy to establish.

Start value selection is easiest for recursive models: $\boldsymbol{\Phi}$ should be set to the covariance matrix of the exogenous variables, $\boldsymbol{\Psi}$ should be initialized as a diagonal matrix with entries at or below the expected residual variances of the endogenous variables. Since the values of the free parameters in $\boldsymbol{B}$ and $\boldsymbol{\Gamma}$ depend on the variances and covariances of $\boldsymbol{\Phi}$ and $\boldsymbol{\Psi}$ as well as on the data of the sample covariance matrix, it can already be exceedingly difficult to predict what sign the estimates will have, much more so to arrive at a start value in the same order of magnitude as the final estimate. The most practical strategy in such a case is to initialize the free parameters in $\boldsymbol{B}$ and $\boldsymbol{\Gamma}$ at values of zero or close to zero and delegate further estimation to the program's minimization algorithm.

In nonrecursive models, start values of path coefficients in the $\boldsymbol{B}$ matrix must be chosen so that "rank" and "order" conditions for model identification are satisfied (Bollen, 1989, pp. 88-104, 326-333; Goldberger, 1973). They must also be chosen so that $(\boldsymbol{I}-\boldsymbol{B})$ is a full-rank matrix and can be inverted as required by Equation 17. Therefore, and for conceptual reasons, $\boldsymbol{B}$ must have zeros in the diagonal, and off-diagonal start values of positive or negative unity should generally be avoided, even though they may be admissible. One way to ensure that $(I - B)$ can be inverted is to keep the absolute values of the off-diagonal entries in $B$ less than unity.

### Path Models With Latent Variables

When, in either recursive or nonrecursive models, the exogenous variables are latent rather than observed, the covariance matrix $\Phi$ is generally estimated by the model. If observed indicators of the exogenous constructs are available, a separately estimated factor model can provide the start values for $\Phi$. In other cases, such as second-order factor analysis models, $\Phi$ may have to be initialized with positive values in the diagonal and zeros elsewhere.

If both the endogenous and exogenous variables are latent, the model usually comprises two factor-analytic measurement equations for the two sets of constructs, in addition to a structural equations part connecting the latent variables. Such a model has been termed the "full LISREL model" by Jöreskog and Sörbom (1989). Even though the full model appears to be rather more complex, its start values should be chosen according to the same component rules discussed above for the factor analysis and structural equation submodels. The only conceptual difference is that the covariance matrix of the endogenous factors is completely determined by the structural part of the model, $(I - B)^{-1}(\Psi + \Gamma\Phi\Gamma')(I - B')^{-1}$.

### Model Estimates

The maximum likelihood and least squares fit criteria employed by contemporary structural equations programs are generally unbounded[5] and can therefore converge toward estimates outside the range of admissible parameters, usually diagnosed in LISREL as *nonpositive definite* covariance component matrices. Dealing with such inadmissible parameters is not a new issue. The factor-analytic field, for instance, adopted the term *Heywood case* several decades ago (Thurstone, 1947) to refer to factor solutions with zero or negative estimates of unique variance components. Furthermore, indefinite matrix solutions are not admissible on conceptual grounds with any factor or structural equation model;[6] the model estimates must therefore always be at least semidefinite, even in cases where the sample covariance matrix is indefinite and asymptotically distribution-free estimation (Browne, 1984) is used.

### Causes of Indefinite Model Estimates

This section discusses the several modeling aspects associated with indefinite matrix estimates: too little information provided by the data, the presence of outliers and nonnormalities, too many parameters in the structural model, empirical underidentification, and model misspecification.

### Too Little Information Provided by the Data

Indefinite matrix problems occur frequently when the data provide relatively little information for a particular model. The Monte Carlo studies by Anderson and Gerbing (1984) and by Boomsma (1982, 1985) demonstrate that the chances for negative variance estimates rise with *smaller sample sizes,* as the *number of observed indicator variables* for each factor decreases, and when *indicators* have *smaller factor loadings.* The importance of these conditions cannot be overstated: For small models with four observed variables and two latent factors, with sample sizes between 50 and 150, Anderson and Gerbing report the frequencies of inadmissible solutions between 10% and 86%. For three-indicator models (i.e., six observed variables and two latent factors) with sample sizes of 150 observations or fewer, and data generated from a model with factor loadings as low as 0.4, rates of inadmissible solutions lie between 16% and 53%. Only when the sample size is increased to 300 or beyond, or with population factor loadings of 0.9, could admissible solutions be obtained in virtually all cases. Boomsma (1982, 1985) presents similar findings. In these situations, the best advice is to use larger samples, collect additional indicator variables for the latent constructs, and/or substitute indicator variables with higher validity.

### Outliers and Nonnormalities

Outliers and other deviations from multinormality in the raw data can be a source of indefinite matrix problems. Bollen (1987, 1989) gives exemplary evidence of how outliers in the data can lead to inadmissible estimates. Mason and Gunst (1985) tell a similar story of how outliers can introduce near collinearities to the sample covariance matrix and create subsequent problems in regression estimation. While there appears to be some consensus that outliers and nonnormal data structures can lead to biased and even inadmissible estimates, little or no systematic information has been available on the degree to which nonnormality affects admissibility of the solutions. The current practical advice is that outlier screening (and, if conceptually justified, outlier removal) is an important step in the data preparation phase. If there is no good substantive reason to remove groups of outliers from the data, or if skewness and kurtosis statistics indicate that the data are generally nonnormal, ADF may be a more robust estimator in large samples than ML and GLS methods.

*Too Many Parameters*

The number of parameters that can reasonably be included in a structural model is partly determined by the degree of systematic information contained in the data. That these issues are interdependent is demonstrated by Jöreskog and Sörbom (1989, pp. 239-243) in an example involving an exploratory factor model that produces indefinite matrix estimates. The data in this example had been randomly generated from a more restricted (population) factor model. At the selected sample size of 200, the 95% probability interval for one of the unique variances extends into the range of negative numbers and a negative variance estimate is indeed observed for this parameter. While a larger sample size would also have prevented the Heywood case, Jöreskog and Sörbom show that the apparent overparameterization of the model is an equally likely cause for obtaining offending estimates. By removing some redundant factor loading parameters from the models, the uniqueness estimates can be kept within their admissible range. This example is particularly interesting because it shows that restricting the factor pattern (and not the offending uniqueness parameters) can produce a desired admissible solution.

*Empirical Underidentification*

Empirical underidentification can produce aberrant, and possibly inadmissible, parameter estimates. The following example (based on Rindskopf, 1984a) demonstrates what is meant by *empirically unidentified.*

*Example 2.* Consider a restricted factor analysis of four indicators and two oblique factors, so that one pair of the indicators loads only on the first factor, the other pair only on the second factor. Such a model can be written in terms of the model Equation 16, using the factor loading matrix

$$\begin{pmatrix} \lambda_{1,1} & 0 \\ \lambda_{2,1} & 0 \\ 0 & \lambda_{3,2} \\ 0 & \lambda_{4,2} \end{pmatrix}, \tag{18}$$

the factor correlation matrix

$$\Phi = \begin{pmatrix} 1 & \\ \varphi & 1 \end{pmatrix}, \tag{19}$$

and the unique variance components

$$\Theta = \mathrm{Diag}(\theta_1, \theta_2, \theta_3, \theta_4). \tag{20}$$

This factor model is easily specified with most packaged programs for structural equation models; in LISREL, for instance, using automatic start values, the necessary command lines are as follows:

```
Two-factor model, empirically underidentified.
DAtaparameters NObservations=100 NInputvariables=4
CMatrix FIle=<contains sample covariance matrix>
MOdelparameters NX_variables=4 NKsi_factors=2 Continue
 PHi=STandardized
FRee LX(1,1) LX(2,1) LX(3,2) LX(4,2)
OUtput_requests
```

With EQS, the same model can be formulated as:

```
/TITLE
 Two-factor model, empirically underidentified.
/SPECIFICATIONS
 CASES=100; VARIABLES=4;
/EQUATIONS
 V1 = *F1 + E1;
 V2 = *F1 + E2;
 V3 = *F2 + E3;
 V4 = *F2 + E4;
```

```
/VARIANCES
 F1 TO F2 = 1.0;
/COVARIANCES
 F2,F1 = *;
/MATRIX
  <sample covariance matrix>
/END
```

Usually, this model will be overidentified with one degree of freedom and it is possible to test its fit. However, as Rindskopf (1984a) points out, the model will not be identified when the correlation between the two factors becomes zero. Accordingly, a value of $\hat{\varphi} = 0$ would be obtained from a (hypothetical) sample correlation matrix such as

$$S_1 = \begin{pmatrix} 1.0 & & & \\ 0.6 & 1.0 & & \\ 0.0 & 0.0 & 1.0 & \\ 0.0 & 0.0 & 0.6 & 1.0 \end{pmatrix}, \qquad [21]$$

so that the loading parameters (Equation 18) and the uniqueness coefficients (Equation 20) cannot be uniquely estimated. Some or all of these parameter estimates will depend on what start values were supplied. Using its version of automatic start values, LISREL 7 arrives at the following estimates:

$$\hat{\Lambda} = \begin{pmatrix} 1.000 & 0.000 \\ 0.600 & 0.000 \\ 0.000 & 1.000 \\ 0.000 & 0.600 \end{pmatrix}, \qquad [22]$$

$$\hat{\Phi} = \begin{pmatrix} 1 & \\ 0 & 1 \end{pmatrix}, \qquad [23]$$

and

$$\Theta = \text{Diag}(0.000, 0.640, 0.000, 0.640). \qquad [24]$$

Heywood estimates are obtained for the two uniqueness parameters $\theta_1$ and $\theta_3$, because the entire model is unidentified, as indicated by the LISREL warning message:

```
W_A_R_N_I_N_G : TD 2,2 may not be identified. Standard
                error estimates, T-values, Modification
                Indices and Standardized residuals
                cannot be computed.
```

The EQS solution is identical to the LISREL results above, except that no diagnostics are provided about the underidentification of the model. Instead, the EQS program prints a warning that the estimates for the parameters $\theta_1$ and $\theta_3$ are constrained at their lower bounds. Apparently, the automatic inequality constraints on variance estimates that are incorporated in EQS (see the subsection on inequality constraints on error variances, below) can mask the detection of empirically underidentified solutions.

Note that the nonidentification warning given by LISREL does not have to involve the inadmissible parameter estimates. It merely reflects the situation that one of the four parameters $\lambda_{1,1}$, $\lambda_{2,1}$, $\theta_1$, and $\theta_2$ is not identified for the covariance matrix $S_1$. The issue of empirical under-identification must be resolved before the related indefinite matrix problem is addressed.

## Model Misspecification

When a specified confirmatory model is very different from structures that the data would support, inadmissible covariance component estimates can result. When the factor model in Example 2 is applied, for instance, to the hypothetical sample covariance matrix

$$S_2 = \begin{pmatrix} 1.0 & & & \\ 0.6 & 1.0 & & \\ 0.8 & 0.6 & 1.0 & \\ 0.6 & 0.8 & 0.6 & 1.0 \end{pmatrix}, \qquad [25]$$

correlations between indicators of different factors would be larger than correlations among indicators of the same factor. Because such a correlation pattern is inconsistent with factor-analytic reasoning, the maximum likelihood estimation yields the indefinite factor covariance matrix

$$\hat{\Phi} = \begin{pmatrix} 1 & \\ 1.167 & 1 \end{pmatrix} \qquad [26]$$

with a factor correlation of 1.167. This type of indefiniteness problem should be interpreted as a strong indication that the model is not supported by the data.[7] In contrast, admissible parameter estimates may be obtained from an alternative model with a factor loading pattern for covariance Matrix 25 restricted to

$$\Lambda = \begin{pmatrix} \lambda_{1,1} & 0 \\ 0 & \lambda_{2,2} \\ \lambda_{3,1} & 0 \\ 0 & \lambda_{4,2} \end{pmatrix}. \tag{27}$$

In the previous example of LISREL commands, the next to last line would simply have to be replaced by

```
FRee LX(1,1) LX(3,1) LX(2,2) LX(4,2) \\
```

The modified factor model yields admissible ML estimates for matrix $S_2$.

## Solutions for Indefinite Model Estimates

Some solutions are intrinsic to the causes of indefiniteness, with obvious corrections. For instance, if the data provide too little information for the model, additional data must be obtained or the model must be simplified. The remedies discussed above apply correspondingly. In cases of empirical nonidentification, the underidentified model components must be fixed or removed.

When the indefiniteness problem is less tractable, inequality constraints on individual variances or on entire covariance matrices can provide the instrument for needed close diagnosis and final resolution. Incorporating these inequality constraints into linear structural models involves creative use of some matrix algebra tools. Because somewhat different methods are involved, constraints for variances and for entire covariance matrices are discussed separately below.

### Inequality Constraints on Error Variances

A simple but effective method for incorporating inequality constraints on variance terms has been presented by Rindskopf (1983). It is based on the notion that the *standard deviation* of an error term should be estimated rather than its variance, for independent of whether the estimated standard deviation term is negative or positive, its square, the derived variance estimate, will always be nonnegative.

*Example 3.* To obtain nonnegative uniqueness estimates with the factor model of Example 2, the following reparameterization is advantageous: Extend the factor loading matrix to the partitioned form

$$\Lambda^{(c)} = \begin{pmatrix} \lambda_{1,1} & 0 & \delta_{1,1} & 0 & 0 & 0 \\ \lambda_{2,1} & 0 & 0 & \delta_{2,2} & 0 & 0 \\ 0 & \lambda_{3,2} & 0 & 0 & \delta_{3,3} & 0 \\ 0 & \lambda_{4,2} & 0 & 0 & 0 & \delta_{4,4} \end{pmatrix}, \qquad [28]$$

the factor correlation matrix correspondingly to

$$\Phi^{(c)} = \begin{pmatrix} 1 & \varphi & 0 & 0 & 0 & 0 \\ \varphi & 1 & 0 & 0 & 0 & 0 \\ 0 & 0 & 1 & 0 & 0 & 0 \\ 0 & 0 & 0 & 1 & 0 & 0 \\ 0 & 0 & 0 & 0 & 1 & 0 \\ 0 & 0 & 0 & 0 & 0 & 1 \end{pmatrix}, \qquad [29]$$

and set the previous matrix of unique components, $\Theta$, to zero. The matrix product $\Lambda^{(c)}\Phi^{(c)}\Lambda^{(c)\prime}$ contains all the terms of the factor model. The factor loadings described in Matrix 18 appear in the first two columns of the augmented matrix $\Lambda^{(c)}$, the factor covariance matrix is found in the upper left partition of $\Phi^{(c)}$, and the standard deviations $\delta_{i,i}$ of the unique components are in the rightmost four columns of $\Lambda^{(c)}$. The identity matrix in the lower-right partition of $\Phi^{(c)}$ is needed for computing the unique variances, but does not have a substantive interpretation.

The constrained model is specified with LISREL as:

```
Two-factor model, inequality constraints on error variances.
DAtaparameters NObservations=100 NInputvariables=4
CMatrix FIle=<contains sample covariance matrix>
MOdelparameters NX_variables=4 NKsi_factors=6 Continue
 PHi=SYmmetric,FIxed LX=FUll,FIxed TDelta=ZEro
FRee LX(1,1) LX(2,1) LX(3,2) LX(4,2)
FRee LX(1,3) LX(2,4) LX(3,5) LX(4,6)
```

```
STartvalue 0.5 ALL
VAlue 1.0 PHi(1,1) PHi(2,2) PHi(3,3) PHi(4,4) PHi(5,5) PHi(6,6)
FRee PHi(2,1)
OUtput_requests NS
```

Note that automatic start values cannot be computed in this case, since the model has more latent than observed variables. To prevent any action by the start value routine, initial values are declared explicitly (on the line STartvalue 0.5 ALL) and the automatic start value option should be turned off (the line OUtput_requests NS).

Some structural equation programs, such as EQS (Bentler, 1989), impose these types of inequality constraints on the error variance terms by default. That is, the parameterization of Example 3 is already built into these programs. To undo such a default in order to obtain unbounded estimates, if only to investigate questionable parameter estimates further at or near the imposed limiting value, different "tricks" may be needed.

*Constraints on Covariances*

Any semidefinite symmetric matrix $A$ can be expressed as the product of a square matrix $C$ and its transpose,

$$A = CC'. \qquad [30]$$

In particular, $C$ may be selected to be a lower triangular matrix (Graybill, 1983, p. 208), also known as the Cholesky factor of $A$. If $A$ is indefinite, the decomposition (Equation 30) is not possible with a real-valued matrix $C$. Conversely, if a real-valued lower triangular matrix $C$ can be estimated, its product $CC' = A$ must be at least semidefinite. Applications of triangular matrix decompositions in structural equation models are given, for instance, by Fulker, Baker, and Bock (1983) or Wothke and Browne (1990); see also Jöreskog and Sörbom (1989, p. 244).

*Example 4.* The factor model of Example 2 is reparameterized so that all covariance matrices remain semidefinite.

In LISREL, the constraints require use of the so-called full model. Both the semidefinite covariance matrices of unique terms and of latent factors can be modeled in the structured matrix product

$$\Gamma\Phi\Gamma' = \begin{pmatrix} \Delta & 0 \\ 0 & C \end{pmatrix} \begin{pmatrix} I & 0 \\ 0 & I \end{pmatrix} \begin{pmatrix} \Delta & 0 \\ 0 & C' \end{pmatrix}, \qquad [31]$$

with the standard deviations of the unique terms estimated in the diagonal matrix **Δ** and the lower triangular (Cholesky) factor of the covariance matrix of latent constructs in **C**. The matrix of factor loadings is estimated accordingly in a subsection of the structured matrix

$$B = \left(\frac{0 \mid \Lambda}{0 \mid 0}\right),$$   [32]

with **Λ** identical to Matrix 18.

The scale constraints for the latent factors may be declared either in the factor loading submatrix **Λ** or in the diagonal of the lower triangular submatrix **C**. The model specification for the LISREL program uses the program's component matrices BEta, GAmma, and PHi:

```
Two-factor model, semidefinite covariance matrices.
DAtaparameters NObservations=100 NInputvariables=4
CMatrix FIle=<contains sample covariance matrix>
MOdelparameters NY_variables=4 NEta_factors=6 Continue
 NKsi_factors=6 LY=IZero BEta=FUll,FIxed Continue
 GAmma=FUll,FIxed PHi=SYmmetric,FIxed Continue
 TEpsilon=ZEro PSi=ZEro
MAtrix BEta
0 0 0 0 1 0
0 0 0 0 1 0
0 0 0 0 0 1
0 0 0 0 0 1
0 0 0 0 0 0
0 0 0 0 0 0
FRee BEta(2,5) BEta(4,6)
PAttern GAmma
1 0 0 0 0 0
0 1 0 0 0 0
0 0 1 0 0 0
0 0 0 1 0 0
0 0 0 0 1 0
0 0 0 0 1 1
STartvalue 0.5 GAmma(1,1) - GAmma(6,6)
VAlue 1.0 PHi(1,1) PHi(2,2) PHi(3,3) PHi(4,4) PHi(5,5)
```

```
VAlue 1.0 PHi(6,6)
OUtput_requests NS ADmissibility_check=200 RSiduals
```

Using matrix $S_2$, this model yields the factor loadings

$$\hat{\Lambda}^{(c)} = \begin{pmatrix} 1.000 & 0 \\ 0.999 & 0 \\ 0 & 1.000 \\ 0 & 0.999 \end{pmatrix}, \qquad [33]$$

the factor covariance matrix

$$\hat{\Phi}^{(c)} = \begin{pmatrix} 0.668 & \\ 0.668 & 0.668 \end{pmatrix}, \qquad [34]$$

and the unique variances

$$\hat{\Theta}^{(c)} = \text{Diag}(0.333, 0.333, 0.333, 0.333). \qquad [35]$$

The solution encounters a boundary condition because the covariance matrix $\hat{\Phi}^{(c)}$ is rank deficient. In effect, the solution has collapsed to a one-dimensional exploratory factor model.

Output from boundary solutions often contains warnings that certain parameters are not identified. These warning messages may be disregarded if they concern parameter estimates on the boundary. In some cases, boundary solutions produce benign identification warnings for other parameters in the model that are dependent on the (now semidefinite) covariance matrix. For instance, in a path model with latent variables, some of the regression coefficients may become unidentified when two or more exogenous factors are perfectly correlated. Since perfect correlation implies that the involved factors are empirically equivalent, their respective regression coefficients must also be equal to one another. This type of identification problem is simply resolved by reparameterizing the perfectly correlated factors as a single latent variable.

A major purpose for estimating a model under semidefiniteness constraints is to obtain information about what promotes indefinite estimates in an unconstrained parameterization. One readily available piece of information is the difference of residuals between constrained and unconstrained solutions. Patterns in this matrix can reveal data structures that should be modeled differently. In Example 4, the difference between the two residual matrices is

$$\begin{pmatrix} 0.000 & & & \\ -0.067 & 0.000 & & \\ 0.132 & -0.067 & 0.000 & \\ -0.067 & 0.134 & -0.067 & 0.000 \end{pmatrix} . \qquad [36]$$

Note the two large residual differences for the covariances of variable pairs (3,1) and (4,2). These elements are underestimated by the constrained, but not by the unconstrained, model version. Similarly, the remaining off-diagonal differences are negative, indicating that these elements are overestimated by the constrained factor model. A reformulation of the factor model, such as the version proposed in Example 3, accommodates the residual differences in a new model so that the solution will be admissible.

## Model Testing and Inequality Constraints

As a general, and somewhat counterintuitive, rule, the effect of inequality constraints on the fit of a structural equation model cannot be tested with the familiar difference $\chi^2$ test. There are two reasons: First, imposing inequality constraints does not affect the number of parameters in the model (it only restricts the *range* of the estimated values); that is, the more restricted model has the same degrees of freedom as the unrestricted model. Therefore, a difference $\chi^2$ test would have zero degrees of freedom. However, there does not exist a sampling $\chi^2$ distribution with zero degrees of freedom against which the test statistic could be compared. Second, when inequality constraints are introduced to avoid indefinite matrix problems, the fit-$\chi^2$ statistic of the one offending, inadmissible solution is not meaningful in the first place—and neither would be a derived statistic concerning the difference between the models.

While the fit of the more restricted, admissible solution can be evaluated using $\chi^2$-based statistics, no general method appears to be available to compare the model estimates with and without inequality constraints (see Rindskopf, 1983, for further discussion). To analyze the impact of the inequality constraints, or to gain insight into the nature of the indefiniteness problem, one must inspect the changes in residual structures due to the added inequality constraints.

## Suitability of Semidefiniteness Constraints

Inequality constraints for variances and covariance matrices can be gainfully incorporated when the parameters in these matrices are otherwise either completely unconstrained or composed of simple diagonal or block diagonal matrix patterns. Useful modeling lessons can be learned from examining differences of model residuals brought about by the added constraints. In this sense, triangular and square root decompositions are powerful instruments in the structural modeler's toolbox.

Inequality constraints in structural models often lead to boundary solutions that have the unfortunate property that "standard errors" of the parameter estimates are no longer meaningful. Yet, the fit-$\chi^2$ statistic and the size and pattern of the residuals remain valuable means of heuristically guided model evaluation, and can augment exploratory and conceptual approaches to further analysis of the data set.

The efficiency of inequality constraints has been studied in two independent Monte Carlo studies by Dillon, Kumar, and Mulani (1987) and Gerbing and Anderson (1987). Neither study reports a particular advantage of imposing inequality on unique variance terms in the factor-analytic model. Dillon et al. find it sufficient simply to fix an offending estimate at zero, while Gerbing and Anderson go a step further, reporting that "respecified solutions add little interpretability to that of initial, improper solutions" (p. 110). However, the conclusions from these two studies are of limited practical validity, because only unique terms in factor analysis models were examined, the models themselves were rather small, and all models had been specified correctly. Inequality constraints should remain indispensable tools for the residual analysis of many misspecified models.

## Concluding Remarks

Nonpositive definite matrices can appear at a variety of stages in linear structural model analysis. In this chapter, I have tried to describe the current state of affairs of working with indefinite matrices. A number of cases have been discussed, from calculating sample correlation and covariance matrices and choosing good initial estimates to reparameterizing structural models so that their covariance matrices will be at least semidefinite.

Yet it must also be mentioned that there are perfectly admissible models that by design comprise indefinite covariance matrices and will trigger benign "error" or "warning" messages in standard structural equation programs. For instance, positive semidefinite error covariance matrices are routinely generated when some, but not all, latent variables have single indicators, as would be the case in a regression equation comprising a combination of fixed predictor variables and random predictors measured with error. Then the model covariance matrix of error in predictor components is necessarily indefinite, for, although its diagonal entries for the random predictors should contain positive estimates, the diagonal entries for the fixed variables are structural zeros. In other cases, such as those demonstrated in Example 4 above, semidefinite covariance matrix estimates are obtained because the model is "overfactored." Collapsing perfectly correlated factors will usually remove the immaterial warning messages. In certain other situations, even matrices with negative eigenvalues can be admissible. Rindskopf (1984b), for instance, describes how "imaginary" variables with fixed negative variances may be employed to constrain the variances of model variables to be smaller than certain maximum values.

In many applications, strategies described in this chapter will be helpful in resolving problem solutions, but some modeling attempts will nevertheless be left stranded outside the real-valued space. There is a definite need for the development and teaching of a more general statistical solution to the estimation problems discussed here. A Bayesian approach incorporating moderately informative prior distributions of the parameter estimates would appear to be a promising alternative to the "frequentist" maximum likelihood and least squares estimators currently in use. For categorical variable analysis, which should be a standard methodology in the empirical social sciences, some of the multivariate developments in the IRT field have shown excellent performance for exploratory item factor analysis (Mislevy, 1986); an adaptation of these estimation methods to restricted factor analysis and structural equation models seems imminent.

# APPENDIX
## Traditional Definition of Positive Definiteness

Let us assume that the reader has at least a working familiarity with the basic vector and matrix algebra used in structural linear models. At a minimum, this would include the concepts of vector and matrix addition, multiplication, and transposition; the rank of a matrix; the matrix inverse; and its eigenvalues and eigenvectors.

This section makes use of the concept of linear combinations of variables and the resulting derived variances.

*Linear combination.* Suppose that

$$x = (x_1, \ldots, x_p)' \qquad [A1]$$

is a $p$-variate vector of observed variables and

$$w = (w_1, \ldots, w_p)' \qquad [A2]$$

is a series of $p$ linear weight coefficients. Then the vector product

$$y = w'x \qquad [A3]$$

$$= \sum_{i=1}^{p} w_i x_i \qquad [A4]$$

is a weighted sum or *linear combination* of $x$ with weights $w$.

*Zero vector.* A vector $v$ is zero, expressed as

$$v = 0 \qquad [A5]$$

if all its elements $v_i$ are equal to zero. Conversely, if at least one of the elements $v_i$ is different from zero, then the entire vector $v$ is also said to be different from zero.

*Variance of a linear combination.* Suppose the $p$ variables $x$ have the common $p \times p$ variance-covariance matrix $\Sigma_x$. Then the variance of the derived variable $y = w'x$ is

$$\sigma_y^2 = w'\Sigma_x w . \qquad [A6]$$

*Positive definiteness of a matrix.* A covariance matrix $\Sigma_x$ is *strictly positive definite* if all possible weighted sums have a variance greater than zero, except for the one "trivial" case when all weight coefficients are themselves equal to zero.

The same is expressed in matrix notation as follows (Graybill, 1983, p.396; Searle, 1982, p.77): The symmetric matrix $\Sigma_x$ is (strictly) positive definite if for every $w \neq 0$

$$w'\Sigma_x w > 0 \ . \qquad\qquad [A7]$$

If the inequality does not hold strictly, such that

$$w'\Sigma_x w \geq 0 \qquad\qquad [A8]$$

for each and every vector $w$, and the equality holds for at least one nonnull vector $w$, then $\Sigma_x$ is said to be *positive semidefinite*. If

$$w'\Sigma_x w < 0 \qquad\qquad [A9]$$

for at least one vector $w$, then $\Sigma_x$ is called *indefinite*.

In practice, a covariance matrix cannot be allowed to be indefinite, because this would imply that a certain weighted sum of its variables has a negative variance. Since the variance is computed as the mean squared deviation from the mean, all real-valued variables must have nonnegative variances.

*Eigenvalues and positive definiteness.* Searle (1982, pp. 309-310) shows that a symmetric matrix is positive definite if and only if all its eigenvalues are strictly positive. The matrix is semidefinite if and only if all eigenvalues are nonnegative. For practical purposes, *positive definiteness* of a symmetric matrix may therefore be defined as a function of the eigenvalues of that matrix.

## Notes

1. When matrices are symmetric, only their lower triangular section is reproduced.

2. I would like to thank Scott Long for suggesting the use of ULS estimates as initial values. This important technique had been overlooked in the original version of the manuscript.

3. Note that, when the diagonal elements of a covariance matrix are fixed at zero, LISREL 7 produces a message such as the following for both the initial and final sets of estimates:

W_A_R_N_I_N_G : THETA DELTA is not positive definite.

This message, triggered by diagonal zeros, has been the source of considerable confusion among students, probably because it does not reflect on the admissibility of the remaining estimated parameters of the same matrix. Whether the estimated sections of the matrix are positive definite should be tested by other means.

4. All structural equation models, as well as factor analysis models, can be expressed in terms of the two matrices $B$ and $\Psi$ alone. The distinctions between exogenous and endogenous components, and between factor analysis and structural equation models, are conceptually convenient.

5. Some programs, like EQS, force all variance estimates to be nonnegative, but covariance parameters are not usually restricted to any particular range. Consequently, these programs may still produce indefinite covariance matrix estimates.

6. There is one exception: A model may contain fixed indefinite matrices as a trick to impose inequality constraints on some parameters (see Rindskopf, 1983, 1984b).

7. Note that EQS 3, although producing the same set of inadmissible estimates, issues the following messages:

PARAMETER ESTIMATES APPEAR IN ORDER.

NO SPECIAL PROBLEMS WERE ENCOUNTERED DURING OPTIMIZATION.

These statements are obviously incorrect. Apparently, EQS does not evaluate the eigenvalues of the estimated component covariance matrices.

## References

Aitkin, M. (1989). Profile predictive likelihood for random effects in the two-level model. In R. D. Bock (Ed.), *Multilevel analysis of educational data.* New York: Academic Press.

Allison, P. D. (1987). Estimation of linear models with incomplete data. In C. C. Clogg (Ed.), *Sociological methodology 1987* (pp. 71-103). San Francisco: Jossey-Bass.

Amemiya, T. (1985). *Advanced econometrics.* Cambridge, MA: Harvard University Press.

Anderson, J. C., & Gerbing, D. W. (1984). The effect of sampling error on convergence, improper solutions, and goodness-of-fit indices for maximum likelihood confirmatory factor analysis. *Psychometrika, 49,* 155-173.

Anderson, T. W. (1984). *An introduction to multivariate statistical analysis.* New York: John Wiley.

Aptech Systems, Inc. (1988). *GAUSS, Version 2.0: System and graphics manual.* Kent, WA: Author.

Bartholomew, D. J. (1987). *Latent variable models and factor analysis.* New York: Oxford University Press.

Bentler, P. M. (1989). *EQS structural equations program manual.* Los Angeles: BMDP Statistical Software.

Bock, R. D., & Bargmann, R. E. (1966). Analysis of covariance structures. *Psychometrika, 31,* 507-534.

Bock, R. D., Gibbons, R., & Muraki, E. (1988). Full-information item factor analysis. *Applied Psychological Measurement, 12,* 261-280.

Bollen, K. A. (1987). Outliers and improper solutions: A confirmatory factor analysis example. *Sociological Methods & Research, 15,* 375-384.

Bollen, K. A. (1989). *Structural equations with latent variables.* New York: John Wiley.

Boomsma, A. (1982). The robustness of LISREL against small sample sizes in factor analysis models. In K. G. Jöreskog & H. Wold (Eds.), *Systems under indirect observation: Causality, structure, prediction* (Part 1). Amsterdam: North-Holland.

Boomsma, A. (1985). Nonconvergence, improper solutions, and starting values in LISREL maximum likelihood estimation. *Psychometrika, 50,* 229-242.

Braun, H. I., Jones, D. H., Rubin, D. B., & Thayer, D. T. (1983). Empirical Bayes estimation of coefficients in the general linear model from data of deficient rank. *Psychometrika, 48,* 171-181.

Browne, M. W. (1984). Asymptotically distribution-free methods in the analysis of covariance structures. *British Journal of Mathematical and Statistical Psychology, 37,* 62-83.

Christoffersson, A. (1975). Factor analysis of dichotomized variables. *Psychometrika, 10,* 1-19.

Dillon, W. R., Kumar, A., & Mulani, N. (1987). Offending estimates in covariance structure analysis: Comments on the causes of and solutions to Heywood cases. *Psychological Bulletin, 101,* 126-135.

Draper, N. R., & Smith, H. (1981). *Applied regression analysis.* New York: John Wiley.

Fulker, D. W., Baker, L. A., & Bock, R. D. (1983). Estimating components of covariance using LISREL. *Data Analyst, 1,* 5-8.

Gerbing, D. W., & Anderson, J. C. (1987). Improper solutions in the analysis of covariance structures: Their interpretability, and a comparison of alternate respecifications. *Psychometrika, 52,* 99-111.

Goldberger, A. S. (1973). Structural equation models: An overview. In A. S. Goldberger & O. D. Duncan (Eds.), *Structural equation models in the social sciences.* New York: Seminar.

Graybill, F. A. (1983). *Matrices with applications in statistics* (2nd ed.). Belmont, CA: Wadsworth.

Green, P. E., & Carroll, J. D. (1976). *Mathematical tools for applied multivariate analysis.* New York: Academic Press.

IMSL Institute, Inc. (1980). *IMSL Library, Edition 8: Reference manual.* Houston, TX: Author.

Jöreskog, K. G. (1983). Factor analysis as an errors-in-variables model. In H. Wainer & S. Messick (Eds.), *Principals of modern psychological measurement.* Hillsdale, NJ: Lawrence Erlbaum.

Jöreskog, K. G. (1990). New developments in LISREL: Analysis of ordinal variables using polychoric correlations and weighted least squares. *Quality and Quantity, 24,* 387-404.

Jöreskog, K. G., & Sörbom, D. (1988). *PRELIS: A program for multivariate data screening and data summarization. User's guide* (2nd ed.). Chicago: Scientific Software.

Jöreskog, K. G., & Sörbom, D. (1989). *LISREL 7 user's reference guide.* Chicago: Scientific Software.

Little, R. J. A., & Rubin, D. R. (1987). *Statistical analysis with missing data.* New York: John Wiley.

Longford, N. T. (1989). Fisher scoring algorithm for variance component analysis of data with multilevel structure. In R. D. Bock (Ed.), *Multilevel analysis of educational data.* New York: Academic Press.

MacCallum, R. (1983). A comparison of factor analysis programs in SPSS, BMDP, and SAS. *Psychometrika, 48,* 223-231.

MacCallum, R., & Ashby, F. G. (1986). Relationships between linear systems theory and covariance structure modeling. *Journal of Mathematical Psychology, 30,* 1-27.

Mason, R. L., & Gunst, R. F. (1985). Outlier-induced collinearities. *Technometrics, 27,* 401-407.

Mislevy, R. J. (1986). Recent developments in the factor analysis of categorical variables. *Journal of Educational Statistics, 11,* 3-31.

Muthén, B. (1984). A general structural equation model with dichotomous, ordered categorical, and continuous latent variable indicators. *Psychometrika, 49,* 115-132.

Muthén, B. (1988). *LISCOMP: Analysis of linear structural equations with a comprehensive measurement model.* Chicago: Scientific Software.

Muthén, B., Kaplan, D., & Hollis, M. (1987). On structural equation modeling with data that are not missing completely at random. *Psychometrika, 52,* 431-462.

Numerical Algorithms Group, Inc. (1990). *NAG FORTRAN Library, Mark 14: User's guide.* Downers Grove, IL: Author.

Parker, D. (1989). *AcroSpin.* Evanston, IL: SYSTAT.

Rindskopf, D. (1983). Parameterizing inequality constraints on unique variances in linear structural models. *Psychometrika, 48,* 73-83.

Rindskopf, D. (1984a). Structural equation models: Empirical identification, Heywood cases, and related problems. *Sociological Methods & Research, 13,* 109-119.

Rindskopf, D. (1984b). Using phantom and imaginary latent variables to parameterize constraints in linear structural models. *Psychometrika, 49,* 37-47.

SAS Institute Inc. (1985). *SAS/IML: User's guide for personal computers, Version 6.* Cary, NC: Author.

SAS Institute Inc. (1991a). *The CALIS procedure: Analysis of covariance structures.* Cary, NC: Author.

SAS Institute Inc. (1991b). *JMP: Statistical visualization software for the Apple Macintosh.* Cary, NC: Author.

SAS Institute Inc. (1991c). *SAS-Insight: Statistical visualization software for workstations.* Cary, NC: Author.

Searle, S. R. (1982). *Matrix algebra useful for statistics.* New York: John Wiley.

Spanos, A. (1986). *Statistical foundations of econometric modeling.* Cambridge: Cambridge University Press.

Steiger, J. H. (1989). *EzPATH: A supplementary module for SYSTAT and SYGRAPH.* Evanston, IL: SYSTAT.

Thurstone, L. L. (1947). *Multiple factor analysis.* Chicago: University of Chicago Press.

Wilson, D. T., Wood, R., & Gibbons, R. T. (1984). *TESTFACT: Test scoring, item statistics, and item factor analysis.* Chicago: Scientific Software.

Winer, B. J. (1971). *Statistical principles in experimental design* (2nd ed.). New York: McGraw-Hill.

Wothke, W. (1991). *SMOOTH: Program for eigenvalue smoothing of indefinite symmetric matrices.* Chicago: Scientific Software.

Wothke, W., & Browne, M. W. (1990). The direct product model for the MTMM matrix reparameterized as a second order factor analysis model. *Psychometrika, 55,* 255-262.

*12*

# Testing Structural Equation Models

## KARL G. JÖRESKOG

Testing structural equation models is viewed as a way of testing a specified theory about relationships between theoretical constructs. The main point of this chapter is that this is not just a matter of reading the data into a structural equations program, obtaining a chi-square, and accepting or rejecting the model. Rather, as Tukey (1977) so elegantly puts it, "It is important to understand what you CAN DO before you learn to measure how WELL you seem to have DONE it" (p. v).

There are many issues to be considered before an attempt of a statistical test should even be made. Although the formal statistical theory for testing structural equation models is well developed, this is based on many assumptions that should be checked. Failure to meet some of these assumptions may in fact invalidate the formal test. There are many sources of errors that are bound to have a major effect on inferences. The point is that we cannot afford to ignore errors that are brought about by a variety of decisions that precede the actual fitting of the model to the data.

The main issues in the translation of a theory to a statistical model are outlined in the following section. This is followed by a discussion of the nature of inference and a review of the statistical goodness-of-fit test as an asymptotic chi-square test for testing the covariance structure implied by the statistical model. There are many hidden assumptions in

AUTHOR'S NOTE: The research reported here has been supported by the Swedish Council for Research in the Humanities and Social Sciences under the program Multivariate Statistical Analysis.

this test. These assumptions and how to check them are also discussed. The presentation is mostly nontechnical.

In this chapter, I distinguish among three situations:

- *Strictly confirmatory* (SC): In a strictly confirmatory situation the researcher has formulated one single model and has obtained empirical data to test it. The model should be accepted or rejected.

- *Alternative models* (AM): The researcher has specified several alternative models (or competing models) and, on the basis of an analysis of a single set of empirical data, one of the models should be selected.

- *Model generating* (MG): The researcher has specified a tentative initial model. If the initial model does not fit the given data, the model should be modified and tested again using the same data. Several models may be tested in this process. The goal may be to find a model that not only fits the data well from a statistical point of view but also has the property that every parameter of the model can be given a substantively meaningful interpretation. The respecification of each model may be theory driven or data driven. Although a model may be tested in each round, the whole approach is model generating rather than model testing.

In practice, the MG situation is by far the most common. The SC situation is very rare because few researchers are contented with just rejecting a given model without suggesting an alternative model. The AM situation is also rare because researchers seldom specify the alternative models a priori. The AM and MG situations are discussed in the final two sections of this chapter.

## From Theory to Statistical Model

Most theories in the social and behavioral sciences are formulated in terms of hypothetical constructs, which are theoretical creations that cannot be observed or measured directly. Examples of hypothetical constructs are prejudice, radicalism, alienation, conservatism, trust, self-esteem, discrimination, motivation, ability, and anomia. The measurement of a hypothetical construct is done indirectly through one or more observable indicators, such as responses to questionnaire items that are *assumed* to represent the construct adequately.

In theory, the researcher defines the hypothetical constructs by specifying the dimensions of each construct (see, e.g., Bollen, 1989, pp. 179-184).

The theory specifies further how the various constructs are postulated to be interrelated. This includes first of all the classification of the constructs into dependent (caused, criterion, endogenous) and independent (causal, explanatory, exogenous) constructs. Second, for each dependent construct, the theory specifies which of the other constructs it is postulated to depend on. The theory may also include a statement about the sign and/or relative size of the direct effect of one construct on another.

Since the theoretical constructs are not observable, the theory cannot be tested directly. All the researcher can do is examine the *theoretical validity* of the postulated relationships in a given context. Before the theory can be tested empirically, a set of empirically operationable indicators must be defined for each dimension of each construct. There must be clear rules of correspondence between the indicators and the constructs such that each construct and dimension is distinct (Costner, 1969).

The theoretical relationships between the constructs constitute the structural equation part of the model, and the relationships between the observable indicators and the theoretical constructs constitute the measurement part of the model. In order to test the model, each of these parts must first be formulated as a statistical model.

The statistical model involves the specification of the form of the relationship, linear or nonlinear. The structural relationships are usually assumed to be linear, but nonlinear models have also been proposed (see, e.g., Kenny & Judd, 1984). If the observed indicators are continuous, that is, measured on interval or ratio scales, the measurement equations are also assumed to be linear, but this may require a logarithmic, exponential, or other type of transformation of the observable indicators. If the observed indicators are ordinal, one usually assumes that there is a continuous variable underlying each ordinal variable and formulates the measurement model in terms of the underlying variables (see, e.g., Jöreskog & Sörbom, 1988; Muthén, 1984; Olsson, 1979).

It is not expected that the relationships in the model are exact deterministic relationships. Most often, the independent constructs in the model account for only a fraction of the variation and covariation in the dependent constructs, because there may be many other variables that are associated with the dependent constructs and that are not included in the model for various reasons. The aggregation of all such omitted variables is represented in the model by a set of stochastic error terms, one for each dependent construct. By definition, therefore, these error terms represent the variation and covariation in the dependent constructs left unaccounted for by the independent constructs. The fundamental assumption in structural equation models is that the error term in each relationship is uncorrelated with all the independent constructs. Studies should be planned and designed and variables should be chosen so that this is the case. Failure to do so will lead to biased and inconsistent estimates (omitted variables bias) of the structural coefficients in the linear equations and will invalidate the testing of the theory. This is one of the most difficult specification errors to test (see the section below on obstacles to clean inference).

The relationships in the measurement model also contain stochastic error terms that are usually interpreted to be the sum of specific factors and random measurement errors in the observable indicators. It is only in specially designed studies such as panel models or multitrait-multi-method designs that one can separate these two components of error terms. In cross-sectional studies, the error terms should be uncorrelated from one indicator to another. This is part of the definition of being indicators of a construct. If the error terms for two or more indicators correlate, this means that these indicators measure *something else* or *something in addition* to the construct they are supposed to measure. If this is the case, the meaning of the construct and its dimensions may be different from what is intended. It is a widespread misuse of structural equation modeling to include correlated error terms[1] in the model for the sole purpose of obtaining a better fit to the data. Every correlation between error terms must be justified and interpreted substantively.

The testing of the structural model—that is, testing of the initially specified theory—may be meaningless unless it is first established that the measurement model holds. If the chosen indicators for a construct do not measure that construct, the specified theory must be modified before it can be tested. Therefore, the measurement model should be tested first. It may be useful to do this for each construct separately, then for the constructs taken two and two, and then for all constructs simultaneously. In doing so, one should let the constructs themselves be freely correlated; that is, the covariance matrix of the constructs should be unconstrained.

## Nature of Inference

Once a model has been carefully formulated, it can be confronted with empirical data and, if all assumptions hold, various techniques for covariance structure analysis (briefly reviewed in the next section) can be used to test whether or not the model is consistent with the data.

The inference problem is of the following general form. Given assumptions A, B, C, . . . , test model $M$ against a more general model $M_a$. Most researchers will take assumptions A, B, C, . . . for granted and proceed to test $M$ formally. But what if one or more of the assumptions does not hold? This may be a robustness question, but the assumptions should be checked before the test is made, whenever this is possible. This is considered in detail in a later section.

If the model is rejected by the data, the problem is to determine what is wrong with the model and how the model should be modified to fit the data better. This situation is considered in the final section of this chapter.

If the model fits the data, it does not mean that it is the "correct" model or even the "best" model. In fact, there can be many *equivalent* models all of which will fit the data equally well as judged by any goodness-of-fit measure. This holds not just for a particular data set but for any data set. The direction of causation and the causal ordering of the constructs cannot be determined by the data.[2] To conclude that the fitted model is the "best," one must be able to exclude all models equivalent to it on logical or substantive grounds. For a good discussion of causal models, see Bollen (1989, chap. 3). Further discussion of equivalent models is found in Stelzl (1986), Jöreskog and Sörbom (1989, 1990), and Lee and Hershberger (1990).

Even outside the class of models equivalent to the given model, there may be many models that fit the data almost as well as the given model. Covariance structure techniques can be used to distinguish sharply between models that fit the data *very badly* and those that fit the data *reasonably well*. To discriminate further between models that fit the data almost equally well requires a careful power study (see Jöreskog & Sörbom, 1989, pp. 217-221; Matsueda & Bielby, 1986; Satorra & Saris, 1985; see also Saris & Satorra, Chapter 8, this volume).

To be really testable in a strict sense, the theory should be overidentified in the sense that the structural equation part of the model should be overidentified. If the covariance matrix of the construct variables is unconstrained by the model, any test of the model is essentially just a test of the measurement models of the indicators of the constructs. Given that the measurement models hold, the only way to test a saturated structural equation model is to examine whether estimated parameters agree with a priori specified signs and sizes and whether the strengths of the relationships are sufficiently large.

## Testing a Covariance Structure

Once the relationships in the theoretical model have been translated into a statistical model for a set of linear stochastic equations among random observable (the indicators) and latent (the theoretical constructs) variables, the model can be estimated and tested on the basis of empirical data using statistical methods. The statistical model and its assumptions imply a covariance structure $\Sigma(\theta)$ for the observable random variables, where $\theta = (\theta_1, \theta_2, \ldots, \theta_t)$ is a vector of parameters in the statistical model. The testing problem is now conceived of as testing the model $\Sigma(\theta)$. It is assumed that the empirical data are a random sample of size $N$ of cases (individuals) on which the observable variables $z_1, z_2, \ldots, z_k$ have been actually observed or measured. From these data a sample covariance matrix $S$ is computed, and it is this matrix that is used to fit the model to the data and to test the model.

The model is fitted by minimizing a fit function $F[S, \Sigma(\theta)]$ of $S$ and $\Sigma(\theta)$, which is nonnegative and zero only if there is a perfect fit in which case $S$ equals $\Sigma(\theta)$. The family of fit functions $F$ includes all the fit functions that are used in practice (see, e.g., Jöreskog & Sörbom, 1989).

Suppose that $S$ converges in probability to $\Sigma_0$ as the sample size increases, and let $\theta_0$ be the value of $\theta$ that minimizes $F[\Sigma_0, \Sigma(\theta)]$. We say that the model holds if $\Sigma_0 = \Sigma(\theta_0)$. Furthermore, let $\hat{\theta}$ be the value of $\theta$ that minimizes $F[S, \Sigma(\theta)]$ for the given sample covariance matrix $S$, and let $n = N - 1$.

To test the model, one can use

$$c = nF[S, \Sigma(\hat{\theta})] . \tag{1}$$

If the model holds and is identified, this is approximately distributed in large samples as $\chi^2$ with $d = s - t$ degrees of freedom, where $s = k(k + 1)/2$. To use this test formally, one chooses a significance level $\alpha$, draws a random sample of observations on $z_1, z_2, \ldots, z_k$, computes $S$, estimates the model, and rejects the model if $c$ exceeds the $(1 - \alpha)$ percentile of the $\chi^2$ distribution with $d$ degrees of freedom. As will be argued in the next section, this is a highly limited view of the testing problem.

If the model does not hold, $\Sigma_0 \neq \Sigma(\theta_0)$ and $c$ in Equation 1 is distributed as noncentral $\chi^2$ with $s - t$ degrees of freedom and noncentrality parameter (Browne, 1984)

$$\lambda = nF[\Sigma_0, \Sigma(\theta_0)] , \tag{2}$$

an unknown population quantity that may be estimated as

$$\hat{\lambda} = \text{Max}\{(c - d), 0\} \qquad [3]$$

(see Browne & Cudeck, Chapter 6, this volume). One can also set up a confidence interval for $\lambda$.

Once the validity of the model has been established, one can test structural hypotheses about the parameters $\theta$ in the model. Typically these hypotheses are of one of the following forms:

- that certain $\theta$s have particular values (fixed parameters)
- that certain $\theta$s are equal (equality constraints)
- that certain $\theta$s are specified linear or nonlinear functions of other parameters

Each of these types of hypotheses leads to a model with fewer parameters, $u$, say, $u < t$, and with a parameter vector $v$ of order $(u \times 1)$ containing a subset of the parameters in $\theta$. In conventional statistical terminology, the model with parameters $v$ is called the *null hypothesis* $H_0$ and the model with parameters $\theta$ is called the *alternative hypothesis* $H_1$. Let $c_0$ and $c_1$ be the value of $c$ for models $H_0$ or $H_1$, respectively. The *likelihood ratio test statistic* for testing $H_0$ against $H_1$ is then

$$D^2 = c_0 - c_1, \qquad [4]$$

which is used as $\chi^2$ with $d = t - u$ degrees of freedom. The degrees of freedom can also be computed as the difference between the degrees of freedom associated with $c_0$ and $c_1$. The *Lagrangian multiplier test* (LM) or the *Wald test* (W) (see, e.g., Chou & Bentler, 1990; see also Bentler & Chou, Chapter 10, this volume) may also be used to test the hypothesis. These have the advantages that the minimum of the fit function need be evaluated only under one of the models, $H_0$ or $H_1$. The three tests are asymptotically equivalent.

To use these tests formally, one chooses a significance level $\alpha$ (probability of Type I error) and rejects $H_0$ if $D^2$ (or the equivalent LM or W statistic) exceeds the $(1 - \alpha)$ percentile of the $\chi^2$ distribution with $d$ degrees of freedom.

## Obstacles to Clean Inference

The statistical theory outlined in the previous section, as well as other statistical theories for covariance structures such as the pseudo-maximum likelihood theory of Arminger and Schoenberg (1989) (see also Long & Trivedi, Chapter 4, this volume), assumes that the data used to fit the statistical model represent a random sample of individuals from a population of individuals on which the $k$ observable variables $z_1$, $z_2, \ldots, z_k$ in the model could be observed and measured. A population might be all people of ages 16-65 living in a particular country, state, or region, or all schoolchildren in Grade 8 at a particular time and in a particular country, state, or region.

As in most other statistical analyses, this is a highly idealized assumption seldom met in practice. Most empirical research employing structural equation models does not even report what the population is and how the sample was selected. In practice, one analyzes the data at hand and argues that the inference is to a hypothetical population from which the data might have been drawn or that the assumed relationships in the model have an inherent stochastic component.

However, the statistical theory for covariance structures accounts only for *sampling error* that occurs under a specified sampling scheme for a given population. That is, the standard error of a parameter estimate is a measure of uncertainty in the parameter that would arise under repeated random sampling in this highly idealized situation. Similarly, the chi-square goodness-of-fit test is valid only as a statistical test under this situation. Without a clear definition of population and sampling scheme, it is difficult to attach a meaning to such often-used terms as *significance level,* p *value, power,* t *value,* and *standard error.*

In practice, there may be many other sources of error than just sampling error that affect the results of analysis. Groves (1989) gives a rather complete account of the many types of errors that can occur in surveys and their effects on inferences drawn. It is useful to distinguish among the following:

(1) *coverage error,* arising because some persons in the population are not given any chance of being included in the sample
(2) *nonresponse error,* caused by the failure to collect data on all persons in the sample

(3) *measurement error*, that is, errors in recorded responses arising from
   (a) effects of *interviewers* on respondents' answers to survey questions
   (b) *respondents'* inability to answer questions, lack of requisite effort to obtain correct answers, or other psychological factors
   (c) weaknesses of the wording of survey *questionnaires*
   (d) the *mode of data collection,* such as written questionnaires, test administration, use of face-to-face or telephone communication
(4) *specification errors* in the model, such as incorrect distributional assumptions, correlations between error terms and independent variables due to omitted variables, incorrect functional form, or otherwise incorrectly specified structural or measurement relations
(5) *technical errors,* such as incorrect procedures in the analysis of the data

Most of the statistical literature on structural equation modeling deals with problems of sampling and specification error in the case of independently and identically distributed observations. Many papers in the social science literature deal with the problem of designing studies so as to identify and estimate various sources of measurement errors. Clogg and Dajani (1991) discuss and illustrate various effects on modeling that other types of errors can have.

Ideally, there is a *universe* $U^*$ to which inferences should be made. There may also be an idealized sampling scheme for collecting a *target sample* $S^*$ (see Kish, 1987). On this target sample, many measurements $Z_1, Z_2, \ldots, Z_K$ would be taken. $K$ is often much larger than $k$, the number of observable variables in the structural equation model. It is not unusual for social surveys to contain 300 or more variables. Of the $K$ variables in the target sample, some are included and others are excluded in the model for various reasons and purposes. Other variables in the model may be combinations (indices or other summarizations) formed from some of $Z_1, Z_2, \ldots, Z_K$.

The actual sample $S$ analyzed may differ from $S^*$ for various reasons. Nonresponse as well as incomplete lists in the sampling frame are serious obstacles to valid inferences. Missing data on some of the variables, attrition and mortality in panel studies, budget constraints, and other contingencies are other reasons for $S$ being different from $S^*$. The characteristics of the individuals who end up in the analyzed sample may be very different from those of the target sample. A parameter estimate $\hat{\theta}$ obtained from $S$ may differ substantially from the same parameter estimate $\hat{\theta}^*$ that would have been obtained from $S^*$.

The ideal of a simple random sample or even a correctly stratified sample is seldom met in social surveys. Commonly, the sampling involves stratification and clustering and even quota sampling. Clustering destroys the independence among sample units, which complicates the inference problem further. Typical examples are when households are sampled and several individuals in the household are interviewed or when schools or classes are sampled and all students in the school or class are measured. Weights might be assigned to cases in order to adjust for stratification features of the sampling design. These weights may be taken into account when the covariance or correlation matrix is computed (see, e.g., Jöreskog & Sörbom, 1988), but this is seldom done in studies employing structural equation models. Other violations of random sampling arise because of attrition or other sample selection mechanisms and when subsamples of individuals are selected for analysis on the basis of certain characteristics in the data.

Although there is no statistical supermodel that deals with *all* the issues of complex causal relations along with the likely consequences of nonresponse, missing values, and other sample selection procedures, variable inclusion and exclusion, and possible misspecification of functional form, there are a number of papers dealing with missing values, sample selection, heterogeneity, and other specification errors. These approaches are more complicated to apply than the simple approach described in the previous section and are therefore often ignored by most empirical researchers using structural equation models.

When data are missing, it is important to distinguish between missing completely at random (MCAR) and missing at random (MAR) (see Little & Rubin, 1987; Rubin, 1987). Classical approaches such as listwise deletion or substitutions of a single value give biased estimates under MAR, the most common situation. Using the MAR specification, a number of authors interpret missing-data patterns as multiple groups (independent samples) with parameter restrictions across groups (Allison, 1987; Bound, Griliches, & Hall, 1986; Hauser & Sewell, 1986; Muthén, Kaplan, & Hollis, 1987; Werts, Rock, & Grandy, 1979). Lee (1986) views the missing data as latent variables and estimates the covariance structure under MCAR by direct maximization of the likelihood function under normality. A more general approach that is valid also under MAR is given by Arminger and Sobel (1990), who use pseudo-maximum likelihood estimation. Using procedures for multiple imputation developed by Rubin (1987), it is in principle possible, although in practice very computer-demanding, to create many complete-data data sets and use these to obtain consistent and efficient estimates of parameters under fairly general assumptions about missing values and distributions. Mislevy (1991) outlines the application of such procedures to latent variable modeling, and Rubin (1991) discusses the use of the EM algorithm and simulation variations of it to solve the incomplete data problem. For the simulation approach, Rubin (1991) argues that "several hundred random draws often may yield better practical inferences than traditional analytic solutions based on asymptotic approximations" (p. 245).

The issue of testing for specification errors in the statistical model has been addressed by several authors (see, e.g., Kaplan, 1990). Testing for fixed or free structural parameters or other constraints can be done by likelihood ratio tests, Lagrangian multiplier tests, or Wald tests, as stated in the previous section. Arminger and Schoenberg (1989) discuss the more difficult problem of testing for misspecification caused by error terms that are correlated with the independent variables in the model. Kenny and Judd (1984) discuss a model involving a nonlinear relation for a latent variable. Muthén (1989) reviews and illustrates methods for dealing with heterogeneity arising from the fact that several groups of people may have different parameters.

Other sources of error have to do with how the data are handled after they have been arranged as a rectangular data matrix to be read by a structural equation program. This concerns the scale type of the variables (continuous, censored, truncated, or ordinal), the distribution of the variables, the type of matrix (covariance, correlation, or other type of moment matrix) to be analyzed, and the type of weight matrix to be used. This may also include special considerations for handling outliers in the data. Typically, covariance matrices are computed for continuous variables, but special techniques must be used to handle censored and truncated variables.

A particular case is when the observed variables are ordinal, a common situation in the social sciences. Observations on an ordinal variable are assumed to represent responses to a set of ordered categories, such as a five-category Likert scale. It is only assumed that a person who responds in one category has more of a characteristic than a person who responds in a lower category. Ordinal variables are not continuous variables and should not be treated as if they are. It is common practice to treat scores such as 1, 2, 3, . . . , assigned to categories as if these have interval scale properties. Ordinal variables do not have origins or units of measurement. As soon as one starts talking about means, variances, and covariances of ordinal variables, one is already committed to ignoring the ordinality problem. There are no scores $z_{ai}$ that can be used to compute these quantities. The only information we have are counts of cases in each cell of the $k$-way contingency table. To use ordinal variables in structural equation models requires techniques other than those that are employed when the variables are continuous. Typically, this involves using polychoric correlations and weighted least squares (Jöreskog, 1990). Special care must be taken to obtain a correct weight matrix, which must be a consistent estimate of the asymptotic covariance matrix of the polychoric correlations based on a large sample. These problems are often ignored in practice, which may seriously bias results and conclusions. Typical examples are when product-moment correlations based on raw scores are analyzed or when a matrix of polychoric correlations is analyzed by the maximum likelihood method. A very general model for variables of different scale types has been developed by Muthén (1984) (see also Lee, Poon, & Bentler, 1986).

Another source of error occurs when a correlation matrix is analyzed although the model is not scale invariant (Cudeck, 1989; Shapiro & Browne, 1990). This can affect standard errors and chi-square.

Still another kind of error occurs when the asymptotic normality approximation has not been achieved for the parameter estimates because of small sample size or specification errors in the model. Then standard errors and chi-square values may be highly inaccurate. It is possible to check the asymptotic normality of a parameter estimate by plotting the concentrated fit function against values of the parameter around the parameter estimate (see Jöreskog & Sörbom, 1989, pp. 101-103). The plotted curve should be approximately quadratic around the minimum.

The main point of this section is that there are many sources of error that are likely to have major effects on inferences drawn from the application of structural equation models. Researchers should be aware of potential errors and test for them whenever possible.

## Selection of One of Several A Priori Specified Models

The previous sections have focused on the testing of a single specified model, including the checking of the assumptions on which the test is based. This section considers the alternative models situation, in which the researcher has specified a priori a number of alternative or competing models $M_1, M_2, \ldots, M_k$, say, and wants to select one of these. Here it is assumed that all models are identified and can be tested with a valid chi-square test, as above. It is also assumed that all models give reasonable results apart from fit considerations. Any model that gives unreasonable results can be discarded from further consideration.

We begin with the case when the models are nested so they can be ordered in decreasing number of parameters (increasing degrees of freedom). $M_1$ is the most flexible model, that is, the one with most parameters (fewest degrees of freedom). $M_k$ is the most restrictive model, that is, the one with fewest parameters (most degrees of freedom). If the models are nested, each model is a special case of the preceding model; that is, $M_i$ is obtained from $M_{i-1}$ by putting restrictions on the parameters of $M_{i-1}$.

We assume that model $M_1$ has been tested by a valid chi-square test (as discussed in previous sections) and found to fit the data and to be interpretable in a meaningful way. We can then test sequentially $M_2$ against $M_1$, $M_3$ against $M_2$, $M_4$ against $M_3$, and so on. Each test can be a likelihood ratio test of the form found in Equation 4, a Lagrangian multiplier test, or a Wald test. If $M_i$ is the first model rejected, one takes $M_{i-1}$ to be the "best" model. Steiger, Shapiro, and Browne (1985) prove that likelihood ratio tests are mutually asymptotically independent (under regularity conditions) even if none of the models holds. Kaplan and Wenger (1992) discuss the role of asymptotically independent tests and separable hypotheses as they pertain to specification error, power, and model modification. They suggest that the asymptotic covariance matrix of the estimated parameters under each model can give useful information about whether hypotheses are separable and transitive.

Another approach is to compare the models on the basis of some criteria that take parsimony (in the sense of number of parameters) as well as fit into account. This approach can be used regardless of whether the models can be ordered in a nested sequence or not. Three strongly related criteria have been proposed: the AIC measure of Akaike (1974, 1987), the CAIC of Bozdogan (1987), and the single sample cross-validation index ECVI by Browne and Cudeck (1989). These are all simple functions of chi-square and the degrees of freedom:

$$\text{AIC} = c - 2d = c + 2t - 2s$$

$$\text{CAIC} = c - (1 + \ln N)d = c + (\ln N + 1)t - (1 + \ln N)s$$

$$\text{ECVI} = (c/n) + 2(t/n) \, ,$$

where $c$ is the chi-square measure of overall fit of the model given by Equation 1 and $n$, $s$, and $t$ are defined as above. Although ECVI is quite similar to AIC, the rationale for ECVI is quite different from AIC and CAIC. Whereas AIC and CAIC are derived from statistical information theory, the ECVI is a measure of the discrepancy between the fitted covariance matrix in the analyzed sample and the expected covariance matrix that would be obtained in another sample of the same size.

To apply these measures to the decision problem, one estimates all models, ranks them according to one of these criteria, and chooses the model with the smallest value. Browne and Cudeck (Chapter 6, this volume) point out that one can also take the precision of the estimated value of ECVI into account.

For a given data set, $n$ and $s$ are the same for all models. Therefore, AIC and ECVI will give the same rank order of the models, whereas the rank ordering of AIC and CAIC can differ. To see how much they can differ, consider the case of two nested models $M_1$ and $M_2$ differing by one degree of freedom. Let $D^2 = c_2 - c_1$. The conventional testing procedure will reject $M_2$ in favor of $M_1$ if $D^2$ exceeds the $(1 - \alpha)$ percentage point of the chi-square distribution with one degree of freedom. If $\alpha = 0.05$ this will lead to accepting $M_1$ if $D^2$ exceeds 3.84. AIC will select $M_1$ if $D^2$ exceeds 2, whereas CAIC will select $M_1$ if $D^2$ exceeds $1 + \ln N$.

## Model Assessment and Modification

We now consider the model generating case. The problem is not just to accept or reject a specified model or to select one out of a set of specified models. Rather, the researcher has specified an initial model that is not assumed to hold exactly in the population and may only be tentative. Its fit to the data is to be evaluated and assessed in relation to what is known about the substantive area, the quality of the data, and the extent to which various assumptions are satisfied. The evaluation of the model and the assessment of fit are not entirely statistical matters. If the model is judged not to be good on substantive or statistical grounds, it should be modified within a class of models suitable for the substantive problem. The goal is to find a model within this class of models that not only fits the data well from a statistical point of view, taking all aspects of error into account, but also has the property that every parameter of the model can be given a substantively meaningful interpretation.

The output from a structural equations program provides a lot of information useful for model evaluation and assessment of fit. It may be useful to classify this information into three groups:

- examination of the solution
- measures of overall fit
- detailed assessment of fit

(1) Examine the parameter estimates to see if there are any unreasonable values or other anomalies. Parameter estimates should have the right sign and size according to theory or a priori specifications. Examine the squared multiple correlation (SMC) for each relationship in the model. An SMC is a measure of the strength of linear relationship. A small SMC indicates a weak relationship and suggests that the model is not good.

(2) Examine the measures of overall fit of the model, particularly the chi-square (see below). A number of other measures of overall fit, all of which are functions of chi-square, may also be used. If any of these quantities indicate a poor fit of the data, proceed with the detailed assessment of fit in the next step.

(3) The tools for examining the fit in detail are the residuals, relative residuals, and standardized residuals; the modification indices; and the expected change (see below). Each of these quantities may be used to locate the source of misspecification in the model and to suggest how the model should be modified to fit the data better.

## Chi-Square

Earlier, we regarded $c$ in Equation 1 as a chi-square test for testing the model against the alternative that the covariance matrix of the observed variables is unconstrained. This is valid if all assumptions are satisfied, if the model holds and the sample size is sufficiently large. In practice it is more useful to regard chi-square as a *measure* of fit rather than as a *test statistic*. In this view, chi-square is a measure of overall fit of the model to the data. It measures the distance (difference, discrepancy, deviance) between the sample covariance (correlation) matrix and the fitted covariance (correlation) matrix. Chi-square is a badness-of-fit measure in the sense that a small chi-square corresponds to good fit and a large chi-square to bad fit. Zero chi-square corresponds to a perfect fit. Chi-square is calculated as $N - 1$ times the minimum value of the fit function, where $N$ is the sample size.

Even if all the assumptions of the chi-square test hold, it may not be realistic to assume that the model holds exactly in the population. In this case, chi-square should have a noncentral rather than a central chi-square distribution (see Browne, 1984).

## Other Goodness-of-Fit Measures

A number of other goodness-of-fit measures have been proposed and studied in the literature. For a summary of these and the rationales behind them, see Bollen (1989). All of these measures are functions of chi-square.

### Goodness-of-Fit Indices

Since chi-square is $N - 1$ times the minimum value of the fit function, chi-square tends to be large in large samples if the model does not hold. A number of goodness-of-fit measures have been proposed to eliminate or reduce its dependence on sample size. This is a hopeless task, however, because even though a measure does not depend on sample size explicitly in its calculation, its sampling distribution will depend on $N$. The goodness-of-fit measures GFI and AGFI of Jöreskog and Sörbom (1989) (see Tanaka & Huba, 1985) do not depend on sample size explicitly and measure how much *better* the model fits compared with no model at all. For a specific class of models, Maiti and Mukherjee (1990) demonstrate that there is an exact monotonic relationship between GFI and chi-square.

Another class of fit indices measures how much *better* the model fits compared with a baseline model, usually the independence model. The first indices of this kind were developed by Tucker and Lewis (1973) and Bentler and Bonett (1980). Other variations of these have been proposed and discussed by Bollen (1986, 1989) and Bentler (1990).

### Fit Measures Based on Population Error of Approximation

The use of chi-square as a central $\chi^2$-statistic is based on the assumption that the model holds exactly in the population. As already pointed out, this may be an unreasonable assumption in most empirical research. A consequence of this assumption is that models that hold approximately in the population will be rejected in large samples. Browne and Cudeck (Chapter 6, this volume) propose a number of fit measures that take particular account of the error of approximation in the population and the precision of the fit measure itself. They define an estimate of the population discrepancy function (see McDonald, 1989) as

$$\hat{F}_0 = \text{Max}\{\hat{F} - (d/n), 0\},$$

where $\hat{F}$ is the minimum value of the fit function, $n = N - 1$, and $d$ is the degrees of freedom, and suggest the use of a 90% confidence interval to assess the error of approximation in the population.

Since $\hat{F}_0$ generally decreases when parameters are added in the model, Browne and Cudeck suggest using Steiger's (1990) root mean square error of approximation (RMSEA)

$$\epsilon = \sqrt{\hat{F}_0/d}$$

as a measure of *discrepancy per degree of freedom*. These authors suggest that a value of 0.05 of RMSEA indicates a close fit and that values up to 0.08 represent reasonable errors of approximation in the population. A 90% confidence interval of RMSEA and a test of RMSEA < 0.05 give quite useful information for assessing the degree of approximation in the population.

*Information Measures of Fit*

One disadvantage with chi-square in comparative model fitting is that it always decreases when parameters are added to the model. Therefore, there is a tendency to add parameters to the model so as to make chi-square small, thereby capitalizing on chance and ending with a model containing nonsense parameters. A number of measures of fit have been proposed that take parsimony (in the sense of as few parameters as possible) as well as fit into account. These approaches try to deal with this problem by constructing a measure that ideally first decreases as parameters are added and then has a turning point such that it takes its smallest value for the "best" model and then increases when further parameters are added. The AIC and CAIC measures as well as the ECVI discussed previously belong in this category.

These measures for the estimated model may be compared with the same measures for the "independence" model, that is, the model in which all observed variables are uncorrelated (if the variables are normally distributed they are independent and their covariance matrix is diagonal; this model has $k$ parameters and $k(k - 1)/2$ degrees of freedom, where $k$ is the number of observed variables). It will also be useful to compare these measures for the model estimated with those of the saturated model with $k(k + 1)/2$ parameters and zero degrees of freedom. The chi-square for the independence model should also be considered. This provides a test of the hypothesis that the observed variables are uncorrelated. If this hypothesis is not rejected, it is pointless to model the data.

### Detailed Assessment of Fit

If, on the basis of overall measures of fit or other considerations, it is concluded that the model does not fit sufficiently well, one can examine the fit more closely to determine possible sources of the lack of fit. For this purpose, fitted and standardized residuals and modification indices are useful.

### Fitted and Standardized Residuals

A residual is an observed minus a fitted covariance (variance). A relative residual is a residual divided by the fitted covariance (variance). A standardized residual is a residual divided by its estimated standard error. There are such residuals for every pair of observed variables. Fitted residuals depend on the unit of measurement of the observed variables. If the variances of the variables vary considerably from one variable to the other, it is rather difficult to know whether a fitted residual should be considered large or small. Relative and standardized residuals, on the other hand, are independent of the units of measurement of the variables. In particular, standardized residuals provide a "statistical" metric for judging the size of a residual.

A large positive residual indicates that the model underestimates the covariance between the two variables. On the other hand, a large negative residual indicates that the model overestimates the covariance between the variables. In the first case, one should modify the model by adding paths that could account for the covariance between the two variables better. In the second case, one should modify the model by eliminating paths that are associated with the particular covariance.

All the standardized residuals may be examined collectively in two plots: a stem-leaf plot and a Q-plot. A good model is characterized by a stem-leaf plot in which the residuals are symmetrical around zero and with most residuals in the middle and fewer in the tails. An excess of residuals on the positive or negative side indicates that residuals may be systematically under- or overestimated in the sense above. In the Q-plot, a good model is characterized by points falling approximately on a 45° line. Deviations from this pattern are indicative of specification errors in the model, nonnormality in the variables, or nonlinear relationships among the variables. In particular, standardized residuals that appear as outliers in the Q-plot are indicative of a specification error in the model.

*Modification Index*

A modification index (Sörbom, 1989) may be computed for each fixed and constrained parameter in the model. Each such modification index measures how much chi-square is expected to decrease if a particular constrained parameter is set free and the model is reestimated. Thus the modification index is approximately equal to the difference in chi-square between two models in which one parameter is fixed or constrained in one model and free in the other model, and all other parameters estimated in both models. The largest modification index tells us which parameter to set free to improve the fit maximally.

Associated with each modification index is an expected parameter change (EPC) value (Jöreskog & Sörbom, 1989; Saris, Satorra, & Sörbom, 1987). This measures how much the parameter is expected to change, in the positive or negative direction, if it is set free. If the units of measurement in observed and/or latent variables are of no particular interest, Kaplan (1989) suggests using a scale-free variant SEPC of EPC.

Modification indices are used in the process of model evaluation and modification in the following way. If chi-square is large relative to the standard, one examines the modification indices and relaxes the parameter with the largest modification index *if this parameter can be interpreted substantively*. If it does not make sense to relax the parameter with the largest modification index, consider that with the second largest modification index, and so on. If the sign of certain parameters are specified a priori, positive or negative, the expected parameter change associated with the modification index can be used to exclude models with parameters having the wrong sign.

## Strategy of Analysis

A suitable strategy for data analysis in the MG situation may be the following:

(1) Specify an initial model on the basis of substantive theory, stated hypotheses, or at least some tentative ideas of what a suitable model should be.

(2) Estimate the measurement model for each construct separately, then for each pair of constructs, combining them two and two. Then estimate the measurement model for all the constructs without constraining the covariance matrix of the constructs. Finally, estimate the structural equation model for the constructs jointly with the measurement models.

(3) For each model estimated in Step 2, evaluate the fit as described in the previous subsections. In particular, pay attention to chi-square, standard errors, $t$ values, standardized residuals, and modification indices. If chi-square is large relative to its standard, the model must be modified to fit the data better. For model modification, follow the hints given above. If chi-square is small relative to the standard, the model is overfitted, and parameters with very large standard errors (very small $t$ values) could possibly be eliminated. If chi-square is in the vicinity of the standard, the model may be acceptable, but examine the estimated solution to see if there are any unreasonable values or other anomalies. For each model estimated, if this step leads to a modified model, repeat this step on each modified model.

(4) The last model estimated in the previous step should be one that fits the data of the sample reasonably well and in which all parameters are meaningful and substantively interpretable. However, this does not necessarily mean that it is the "best" model, because its results may have been obtained to some extent by "capitalizing on chance." The model modification process may have generated several "reasonable models" that should be cross-validated on independent data. If no independent sample is available, but the initial sample is large, one may consider splitting the sample into two subsamples and using one (the calibration sample) for exploration as described previously and the other (the validation sample) for cross-validation. The cross-validation is done by computing a validation index (Cudeck & Browne, 1983) for each model. The validation index is a measure of the distance (difference, discrepancy, deviance) between the fitted covariance matrix in the calibration sample and the sample covariance matrix of the validation sample. The model with the smallest validation index is the one that is expected to be most stable in repeated samples. If the smallest validation index occurs for the best fitted model in the calibration sample, it is good. If the smallest validation index occurs for some of the other models that have been fitted, one must decide, on substantive grounds, which of the two models to retain.

## Notes

1. I do not mean here the situation when error terms correlate for the same variable over time or other designed conditions due to specific factors or method factors (see Aish & Jöreskog, 1990).
2. Different equivalent models will give different parameter estimates, and some may give estimates that are not meaningful. This fact may be used to distinguish some equivalent models from others.

## References

Aish, A. M., & Jöreskog, K. G. (1990). A panel model for political efficacy and responsiveness: An application of LISREL 7 with weighted least squares. *Quality and Quantity, 24,* 405-426.

Akaike, H. (1974). A new look at the statistical model identification. *IEEE Transactions on Automatic Control, 19,* 716-723.

Akaike, H. (1987). Factor analysis and AIC. *Psychometrika, 52,* 317-332.

Allison, P. D. (1987). Estimation of linear models with incomplete data. In C. C. Clogg (Ed.), *Sociological methodology 1987* (pp. 71-103). San Francisco: Jossey-Bass. ·

Arminger G., & Schoenberg, R. J. (1989). Pseudo maximum likelihood estimation and a test for misspecification in mean and covariance structure models. *Psychometrika, 54,* 409-425.

Arminger G., & Sobel, M. E. (1990). Pseudo-maximum likelihood estimation of mean and covariance structures with missing data. *Journal of the American Statistical Association, 85,* 195-203.

Bentler, P. M. (1990). Comparative fit indexes in structural models. *Psychological Bulletin, 107,* 238-246.

Bentler, P. M., & Bonett, D. G. (1980). Significance tests and goodness of fit in the analysis of covariance structures. *Psychological Bulletin, 88,* 588-606.

Bollen, K. A. (1986). Sample size and Bentler and Bonett's nonnormed fit index. *Psychometrika, 51,* 375-377.

Bollen, K. A. (1989). *Structural equations with latent variables.* New York: John Wiley.

Bound, J., Griliches, Z., & Hall, B. W. (1986). Wages, schooling and IQ of brothers and sisters: Do the family factors differ? *International Economic Review, 27,* 77-105.

Bozdogan, H. (1987). Model selection and Akaike's information criteria (AIC): The general theory and its analytical extensions. *Psychometrika, 52,* 345-370.

Browne, M. W. (1984). Asymptotically distribution-free methods in the analysis of covariance structures. *British Journal of Mathematical and Statistical Psychology, 37,* 62-83.

Browne, M. W., & Cudeck, R. (1989). Single sample cross-validation indices for covariance structures. *Multivariate Behavioral Research, 24,* 445-455.

Chou, C.-P., & Bentler, P. M. (1990). Model modification in covariance structure modeling: A comparison among likelihood ratio, Lagrange multiplier, and Wald tests. *Multivariate Behavioral Research, 25,* 115-136.

Clogg, C. C., & Dajani, A. N. (1991). Sources of uncertainty in modeling social statistics: An inventory. *Journal of Official Statistics, 7,* 7-24.

Costner, H. L. (1969). Theory, deduction, and rules of correspondence. *American Journal of Sociology, 75*, 245-263.

Cudeck, R. (1989). Analysis of correlation matrices using covariance structure models. *Psychological Bulletin, 105*, 317-327.

Cudeck, R., & Browne, M. W. (1983). Cross-validation of covariance structures. *Multivariate Behavioral Research, 18*, 147-167.

Groves, R. M. (1989). *Survey errors and survey costs.* New York: John Wiley.

Hauser, R. M., & Sewell, W. H. (1986). Family effects in simple models of education, occupational status, and earnings: Findings from the Wisconsin and Kalamazoo studies. *Journal of Labor Economics, 4*, 834-115.

Jöreskog, K. G. (1990). New developments in LISREL: Analysis of ordinal variables using polychoric correlations and weighted least squares. *Quality and Quantity, 24*, 387-404.

Jöreskog, K. G., & Sörbom, D. (1988). *PRELIS: A program for multivariate data screening and data summarization. A preprocessor for LISREL* (2nd ed.). Chicago: Scientific Software.

Jöreskog, K. G., & Sörbom, D. (1989). *LISREL 7: A guide to the program and applications* (2nd ed.). Chicago: SPSS.

Jöreskog, K. G., & Sörbom, D. (1990). Model search with TETRAD II and LISREL. *Sociological Methods & Research, 19*, 93-106.

Kaplan, D. (1989). Model modification in covariance structure analysis: Application of the expected parameter change statistic. *Multivariate Behavioral Research, 24*, 285-305.

Kaplan, D. (1990). Evaluating and modifying covariance structure models: A review and recommendation. *Multivariate Behavioral Research, 25*, 285-305.

Kaplan, D., & Wenger, R. N. (1992). *Asymptotic independence and separability in covariance structure models.* Manuscript submitted for publication.

Kenny, D. A., & Judd, C. M. (1984). Estimating the nonlinear and interactive effects of latent variables. *Psychological Bulletin, 96*, 201-210.

Kish, L. (1987). *Statistical design for research.* New York: John Wiley.

Lee, S., & Hershberger, S. (1990). A simple rule for generating equivalent models in covariance structure modeling. *Multivariate Behavioral Research, 25*, 313-334.

Lee, S.-Y. (1986). Estimation for structural equation models with missing data. *Psychometrika, 51*, 93-99.

Lee, S.-Y., Poon, W.-Y., & Bentler, P. M. (1990). A three-stage estimation procedure for structural equation models with polytomous variables. *Psychometrika, 55*, 45-51.

Little, R. J. A., & Rubin, D. B. (1987). *Statistical analysis with missing data.* New York: John Wiley.

Maiti, S. S., & Mukherjee, B. N. (1990). A note on the distributional properties of the Jöreskog-Sörbom fit indices. *Psychometrika, 55*, 721-726.

Matsueda, R. L., & Bielby, W. T. (1986). Statistical power in covariance structure models. In N. B. Tuma (Ed.), *Sociological methodology 1986* (pp. 120-158). San Francisco: Jossey-Bass.

McDonald, R. P. (1989). An index of goodness-of-fit based on noncentrality. *Journal of Classification, 6*, 97-103.

Mislevy, R. J. (1991). Randomization-based inference about latent variables from complex samples. *Psychometrika, 56*, 177-196.

Muthén, B. (1984). A general structural equation model with dichotomous, ordered categorical, and continuous latent variable indicators. *Psychometrika, 49*, 115-132.

Muthén, B. (1989). Latent variable modeling in heterogeneous populations: Presidential address to the Psychometric Society, July 1989. *Psychometrika, 54,* 557-585.

Muthén, B., Kaplan, D., & Hollis, M. (1987). On structural equation modeling with data that are not missing completely at random. *Psychometrika, 52,* 431-462.

Olsson, U. (1979). Maximum likelihood estimation of the polychoric correlation coefficient. *Psychometrika, 44,* 443-460.

Rubin, D. B. (1987). *Multiple imputation for nonresponse in surveys.* New York: John Wiley.

Rubin, D. B. (1991). EM and beyond. *Psychometrika, 56,* 241-254.

Saris, W. E., Satorra, A., & Sörbom, D. (1987). The detection and correction of specification errors in structural equation models. In C. C. Clogg (Ed.), *Sociological methodology 1987.* San Francisco: Jossey-Bass.

Satorra, A., & Saris, W. E. (1985). The power of the likelihood ratio test in covariance structure analysis. *Psychometrika, 50,* 83-90.

Shapiro, A., & Browne, M. W. (1990). On the treatment of correlation structures as covariance structures. *Linear Algebra and Its Applications, 127,* 567-587.

Sörbom, D. (1989). Model modification. *Psychometrika, 54,* 371-384.

Steiger, J. H. (1990). Structural model evaluation and modification: An interval estimation approach. *Multivariate Behavioral Research, 25,* 173-180.

Steiger, J. H., Shapiro, A., & Browne, M. W. (1985). On the multivariate asymptotic distribution of sequential chi-square statistics. *Psychometrika, 50,* 253-263.

Stelzl, I. (1986). Changing causal relationships without changing the fit: Some rules for generating equivalent LISREL models. *Multivariate Behavioral Research, 21,* 309-331.

Tanaka, J. S., & Huba, G. J. (1985). A fit index for covariance structure models under arbitrary GLS estimation. *British Journal of Mathematical and Statistical Psychology, 38,* 197-201.

Tucker, L. R., & Lewis, C. (1973). A reliability coefficient for maximum likelihood factor analysis. *Psychometrika, 38,* 1-10.

Tukey, J. W. (1977). *Exploratory data analysis.* Reading, MA: Addison-Wesley.

Werts, C. E., Rock, D. A., & Grandy, J. (1979). Confirmatory factor analysis applications: Missing data problems and comparison of path models between populations. *Multivariate Behavioral Research, 14,* 199-213.

# About the Contributors

**James C. Anderson** is the William L. Ford Distinguished Professor of Marketing and Wholesale Distribution and a Professor of Behavioral Science in Management at the J. L. Kellogg Graduate School of Management, Northwestern University. His research interests are in the areas of measurement and structural equation modeling, and working relationships between firms in business markets.

**P. M. Bentler** is Professor of Psychology at the University of California, Los Angeles. His research deals with theoretical and statistical problems in psychometrics, especially structural equation models, as well as with personality and applied social psychology, especially drug use and abuse.

**Kenneth A. Bollen** is a Professor of Sociology at the University of North Carolina at Chapel Hill. His major research interests are in international development and statistics. He is the author of *Structural Equations With Latent Variables* (1989).

**Michael W. Browne** is Professor in the Departments of Psychology and Statistics at The Ohio State University. His research interests are in the areas of psychometrics and multivariate statistical analysis.

**Chih-Ping Chou** is Assistant Professor of Research in the Department of Preventive Medicine at the University of Southern California. His research interests include statistical and computational problems in covariance structure modeling, multivariate statistical analysis, and measurement.

**Robert Cudeck** is Associate Professor in the Department of Psychology at the University of Minnesota. He is interested in applications of quantitative psychology and psychometric methods.

**David W. Gerbing** is an Associate Professor in the School of Business Administration at Portland State University. His research interests are in the areas of measurement and structural equation modeling, factor analysis, and personality and attitude scale development.

**Karl G. Jöreskog** is Research Professor of Multivariate Statistical Analysis at the Swedish Council for Research in the Humanities and Social Sciences, with an office in the Statistics Department of Uppsala University, Sweden. His main interest is in the theory and applications of structural equation models and other types of multivariate analysis, particularly their applications in the social and behavioral sciences. He is coauthor of *LISREL 7: A Guide to the Program and Applications,* published by SPSS.

**J. Scott Long** is Professor of Sociology at Indiana University. His current research concerns sex differences in the scientific career.

**Bengt O. Muthén** obtained his Ph.D. in statistics at the University of Uppsala, Sweden, and is currently Professor at the Graduate School of Education at the University of California, Los Angeles. His research interests include structural equation modeling, especially in the area of categorical and other nonnormal data. He developed the LISCOMP computer program, which implements many of his statistical procedures. He was the 1988-1989 President of the Psychometric Society.

**Adrian E. Raftery** is Professor of Statistics and Sociology at the University of Washington. He received his doctorate in mathematical statistics from the University of Paris VI in 1980 and then taught for 5 years at Trinity College Dublin before coming to the University of Washington in 1985. His research interests in statistics include time-series analysis, spatial statistics, population estimation, applied Bayesian statistics, and applications to sociology, biology, and environmental issues. His substantive research in sociology involves social mobility, educational stratification, and fertility analysis. He is a past or present Associate Editor of the *Journal of the American Statistical Association, Journal of the Royal Statistical Society, Series B,* and *Sociological Methodology.*

**Willem E. Saris** is Professor of Social Science Methods and Techniques at the University of Amsterdam. He also is the director of the Netherlands' Institute of Market and Opinion Research at the same university. He received his master's degree in sociology at the University of Utrecht and his Ph.D. in social science at the University of Amsterdam. He has published numerous professional articles and books.

**Albert Satorra** is Professor of Statistics in the Department of Economics of the Universitat Pompeu Fabra in Barcelona. His area of interest is statistical methodology in social sciences, especially structural equation modeling, a topic on which he has published numerous articles in leading journals.

**Robert A. Stine** is Associate Professor of Statistics in the Wharton School of the University of Pennsylvania. His current research areas include resampling methods, time-series analysis, and statistical computing.

**J. S. Tanaka** was an Associate Professor of Educational Psychology and Psychology at the University of Illinois, Champaign-Urbana, until the time of his death in November 1992. He received his Ph.D. in quantitative psychology from UCLA in 1984 and was previously in the Department of Psychology at New York University. His areas of research interest included multivariate statistics and structural equation modeling with latent variables.

**Pravin K. Trivedi** is Professor of Economics at Indiana University. His recent work is in specification tests in parametric models.

**Werner Wothke** is Vice President of Technical Operations at Scientific Software, Inc., and is primarily involved in designing and producing statistical software. He holds a Ph.D. in research methodology of behavioral science from the University of Chicago, has extensive consulting experience in structural equation modeling and test theory applications, and has taught applied statistics at several universities. His work presented in this volume was motivated by frequent calls to Scientific Software's technical support hot line.